W9-DCJ-678

THE BOOKS OF CONTEMPLATION

SUNY Series in Judaica:
Hermeneutics, Mysticism, and Religion

Michael Fishbane, Robert Goldenberg, and Arthur Green

THE BOOKS OF CONTEMPLATION

Medieval Jewish Mystical Sources

Mark Verman

STATE UNIVERSITY OF NEW YORK PRESS

Production by Ruth Fisher
Marketing by Bernadette LaManna

Published by
State University of New York Press, Albany

For information, address the State University of New York Press,
State University Plaza, Albany, NY 12246

Library of Congress Cataloging-in-Publication Data

Verman, Mark, 1949-
    The books of contemplation: medieval Jewish mystical sources/
Mark Verman.
        p. cm.–(SUNY studies in Judaica)
    Includes bibliographical references and index.
    ISBN 0-7914-0719-5 (alk. paper).–ISBN 0-7914-0720-9 (pbk.:
alk. paper)
    1. Cabala–History. 2. Mysticism–Judaism–History.   I. Title.
II. Series
BM526.V47 1992
296. 1'6–dc20   90-44905
                                                                            CIP

10   9   8   7   6   5   4   3   2   1

for Shully, with love

CONTENTS

PREFACE

The Jewish mystical tradition constitutes a vast repository of texts. There has never been a comprehensive attempt to enumerate all of them. Undoubtedly, such an undertaking would yield thousands upon thousands of entries. Only a small fraction of these has ever been published. The majority of these treatises are extant in manuscripts, preserved in libraries and private collections, scattered throughout the world. To be sure, countless works have been lost owing to the vicissitudes of Jewish history.

Even smaller is the number of Jewish mystical writings that have been made accessible to an English-speaking audience. Accordingly, it is with great pleasure that I am able to present the core treatises of one of the pioneering groups of medieval Jewish mystical theologians, the "Circle of Contemplation."

Chapter One offers a historical overview of the Jewish mystical tradition, as well as a basic introduction to the key writings of the "Circle." Chapter Two contains critical editions and annotated translations of these significant works, based upon extensive manuscript research. Chapters Three through Five delve into the theological, philological, and historical dimensions of these texts.

Frequently, biblical passages are cited in these works. The translation is essentially my own and is based upon the Masoretic edition of the Hebrew Scriptures, in consultation with standard translations.

ACKNOWLEDGMENTS

Profound thanks to the Compassionate One.

This research project began many years ago, as a Harvard University dissertation. I am grateful to Professor Isadore Twersky, my dissertation adviser, for his encouragement and wide-ranging support, as well as the critical insights of Professors Bernard Septimus and Moshe Idel. Thanks also to Professor Joseph Dan, who stimulated my interest in this particular topic. In many respects my work is but an extended footnote to Gershom Scholem's trailblazing.

I am indebted to William D. Eastman, Ruth Fisher and the rest of the production staff at SUNY Press for undertaking the publication of this technically challenging work. I am especially grateful to Dr. Arthur Green, the series editor, who provided invaluable guidance in transforming an esoteric thesis into a more accessible monograph.

The Jay Phillips Foundation of Minneapolis has been most generous in its support of my teaching and continued research these past five years. A mere word of gratitude to colleagues at St. John's University and elsewhere must suffice. I would be remiss, however, if I did not thank Ken Arbit for his critique of Chapter One and Mrs. Idella Moberg for typing much of the text onto diskettes and preparing the index, as well as Harry Silver for his editorial assistance.

Without the cooperation of numerous libraries and institutions–including Widener, Jewish Theological Seminary, Jew's College, and Hebrew Union College–this work could not have been written. I am particularly indebted to Benjamin Richler and the rest of the staff of the Institute of Microfilmed Hebrew Manuscripts at the National Library in Jerusalem.

Throughout the years, friends and family have been a welcomed source of support. No one has borne the burden of this undertaking as patiently as my beloved wife, Dr. Shulamit Adler. She also has an uncanny ability to decipher illegible words in manuscripts, a skill that aided me on innumerable occasions.

1

INTRODUCTION TO *THE BOOK OF CONTEMPLATION, THE FOUNTAIN OF WISDOM,* AND *THE BOOK OF UNITY*

In western Europe, around the year 1230,[1] an obscure Jewish luminary writing under the nom de plume, Rabbi Hammai, composed a short yet profound theosophical treatise, probing the recondite nature of the Divine realm. *Hammai*, it should be noted, is an Aramaic epithet signifying "seer" or "visionary."[2] He entitled his trenchant essay *Sefer ha-'Iyyun, The Book of Contemplation* (hereafter, *Contemplation*). As it circulated throughout Spain and Provence it influenced other Jewish mystics. Within a few decades, dozens of texts were composed reflecting the idiosyncratic doctrines and terminology of *Contemplation*. Accordingly, it has become scholarly convention to refer to all of these works under the rubric of the writings of the "Circle of Contemplation" (hereafter "Circle").[3]

Contemplation is undoubtedly one of the seminal texts of the Jewish mystical tradition. Not only did it have a marked impact on contemporaneous works, but it continued to be studied and cited in

---

1. On the contentious issue of dating, see below pp. 179-185.

2. The Aramaic *hamma'/hammy* connotes seeing or observing. Thanks are due to Marc Brettler for this insight. Moreover, as Bernard Septimus has suggested, the rabbinic ending *'alef, yud* would signify one who engages in visionary or contemplative activity.

3. This construct was first formulated by Scholem and stems from the earliest period of his career, *"Zur Frage der Entstehung der Kabbala," Korrespondenzblatt des Vereins zur Grundung und Erhaltung einer Akademie für die Wissenschaft des Judentums,* 9 (1928), 18-21. Subsequently, he mapped out the boundaries of the "Circle" by compiling a bibliographical catalogue of thirty-two distinct texts, *Reshit ha-Kabbalah* (Jerusalem 1948) 255-262. His most extensive discussion of these writings is found in *Origins of the Kabbalah* (Princeton 1987), 309-364.

subsequent centuries.[4] This in itself would justify serious research, and it was for this reason that I began my investigation of this text a number of years ago. What started out as a straightforward project became something much more fascinating with the startling discovery that there were in fact a whole series of interrelated texts, preserved only in manuscripts, bearing the name *Contemplation* and attributed to the mysterious Rabbi Hammai. Moreover, the only version of this work that was generally known and cited by scholars, such as Gershom Scholem, proved to be the last in the series, and therefore the farthest removed from the original composition and its doctrines.

During the thirteenth century the different recensions of *Contemplation* were readily accessible, as is evidenced by contemporary citations. After that time only the last version remained in the public domain–the others became sequestered in unstudied manuscripts. A comparative analysis reveals that the various recensions underwent substantive changes. As we shall eventually see, the theological doctrines of the earliest version differ radically from the last. Presumably, this is indicative of a succession of authors that felt compelled to revise and reformulate the book's original teachings.

Insofar as there is more than one text bearing the name *The Book of Contemplation*, it is appropriate to refer to these works collectively as *The Books of Contemplation*. The bulk of this monograph will be devoted to a presentation and analysis of these texts. We shall offer critical editions of the surviving Hebrew manuscripts, basing our results on some fifty different witnesses, currently preserved in libraries throughout the world. In addition, these treatises will be

---

4. Throughout this study numerous references will be made to the connections between *Contemplation* and other Spanish mystical writings from the early thirteenth century. Its influence on somewhat later authors is discernible in the late thirteenth-century German theologian R. Moses b. Eliezer ha-Darshan and the following late thirteenth- and early fourteenth-century figures: R. David b. Abraham ha-Lavan, R. Isaac of Acco, R. Menahem Recanati, and R. Joseph of Hamadan. In the subsequent centuries many of the pivotal kabbalists likewise referred to this text, including: R. Shem Tov ibn Shem Tov, R. Meir ibn Gabbai, R. Moses Cordovero, and R. Hayyim Vital.

Nor was interest in *Contemplation* confined to Jewish authors. Beginning with Johannes Reuchlin, who cites *Contemplation* a number of times in his *De Arte Cabbalistica*, other Christian Renaissance theosophists followed suit, including Agrippa and Kircher. For bibliographical references to these and other sources, cf. M. Verman, *Sifrei ha-Iyyun* (Harvard U. diss. 1984), 155-163.

translated and annotated, with a focus on significant theological and philological issues.

There is a second pivotal treatise that will also be considered. It is entitled *Ma'yan ha-Ḥokhmah, The Fountain of Wisdom* (hereafter, *Fountain*), and is dramatically claimed by its anonymous author to represent the mystical secrets transmitted by the mysterious angel, Pe'eli, to Moses! Undeniably, it represents one of the most creative and penetrating attempts at formulating a systematic theory of cosmogony found in Judaism–second only, in the estimation of this writer, to the preeminent classical work, *Sefer Yeẓirah, The Book of Creation* (hereafter, *Creation*).

Like *Contemplation, Fountain* was composed in western Europe in the early 1200s. Together, these two books formed the cornerstones of the extensive literary corpus of the "Circle." Each of the several dozen other texts that constitutes the "Circle" refers directly or indirectly to one and usually both of these works. What is all the more interesting is that this pattern of cross-referencing even occurs in the second and subsequent recensions of *Contemplation* itself.

Although the actual relationship between *Contemplation's* proto-version and *Fountain* is unclear and problematic, in the next chapter it will be suggested that *Fountain* was written as a critical response to proto-*Contemplation* and hence postdates it. Whatever their origins, these two distinct and markedly different treatises soon became intertwined. The corpus of writings that they inspired was vast and many faceted. As such, it represents one of the most intriguing examples of medieval Jewish theological cross-fertilization.

Among the reasons why this relationship proved so fruitful was that these writings exquisitely complement each other. *Contemplation* is concerned with theosophy and cosmology, namely how the intra-Divine and extra-Divine realms are constituted. *Fountain*, on the other hand, deals with cosmogony, i.e. how the cosmos was generated. Together they offered a potent combination of radical theology and speculative science, which profoundly influenced those mystics active in Spain in the latter half of the thirteenth century.[5]

There is a third, fragmentary text entitled *The Book of Unity*, which completes this cycle of the quintessential writings from the "Circle." Like *Contemplation*, it too is attributed to R. Hammai. Although undeniably an outgrowth of *Contemplation*, it nonetheless

---

5. In rabbinic parlance these two texts would be referred to as *ma'aseh merkavah* (the account of the Chariot, i.e., Ezekiel ch. 1) and *ma'aseh bere'-shit* (the account of creation, i.e., Genesis ch.1).

exhibits some of the distinctive terminology of *Fountain*. What makes this brief work truly fascinating is its focus on three supernal lights within the Godhead, said to correspond to three aspects that represent one essence. The superficial similarity between this formulation and Christian theology of the Trinity is quite apparent, yet nonetheless surprising.[6]

To be sure, the writings of the "Circle" did not appear in a vacuum. They are clearly part of the Jewish mystical tradition and exhibit identifiable literary and historical connections with earlier texts. Many of the concepts and terms that are used in these treatises stem from the classical writings of *merkavah* (chariot) theosophy, so called owing to their dependence upon Ezekiel's description of the Divine chariot. A major branch of *merkavah* mysticism is preserved in the *hekhalot* (palaces) literature–a collection of writings offering graphic descriptions of celestial domains.[7] These texts, stemming from the rabbinic period, are variously dated from the second to eighth centuries. Not only is there evidence of the influence of these works on the "Circle," but the standard recension of the *Contemplation* even mimics *hekhalot* texts, composed nearly a millenium earlier. Moreover, in chapter 5 we shall present evidence that the writers of *The Books of Contemplation* were directly influenced by other mystical groups, including the *ḥasidei 'ashkenaz*, German pietists. The *ḥasidei 'ashkenaz* traced their esoteric tradition back many centuries, to geonic times, and were the primary preservers and transmitters of these *hekhalot* writings.

Accordingly, in order to appreciate the origins and background of the "Circle," an understanding of the basic contours of the Jewish mystical tradition is essential. What follows is a brief overview of its development. Initially, we shall focus on the symbiotic relationship between prophecy and mysticism and the reasons for their partial bifurcation. In addition, historical, sociopolitical and literary factors will be examined. The themes and issues that will be analyzed are directly pertinent to our primary concern insofar as they resurface in

---

6. See Scholem's comments on this issue, *Origins*, 353; for a related discussion see Y. Liebes, "Christian Influences on the Zohar" [Hebrew] *Meḥkerei Yerushalayim be-Maḥshevet Yisra'el* 2:1 (1982-83), 43-74.

7. The most comprehensive edition of these texts is found in P. Schafer, *Synopse zur Hekhalot-Literatur* (Tubingen 1981); I. Gruenwald's *Apocalyptic and Merkavah Mysticism* (Leiden 1980) offers a systematic survey of the corpus; see also the recent study by D. Halperin, *The Faces of the Chariot* (Tubingen 1988).

the Middle Ages and are clearly reflected in the writings of the "Circle."

JEWISH PROPHECY AND MYSTICISM

It is generally agreed that prophecy and mysticism represent distinct phenomena. Prophecy is dependent upon Divine communication and was situated at the core of biblical Judaism. By affirming the covenantal relationship, it sought to promote the religious and moral integrity of Israelite society. Not surprisingly, most of the pivotal figures of the Hebrew Scriptures were depicted as being prophets.

Mysticism, on the other hand, has different concerns. Definitions of mysticism abound. Gershom Scholem, in his classic study *Major Trends in Jewish Mysticism*, favored Aquinas's formulation that mysticism entails knowledge of God through experience, *cognitio dei experimentalis*.[8] Hence, mysticism pertains to individuals and their personal spirituality, whereas prophecy is bound up with national destiny.[9]

Biblical mysticism, however, was not isolated from prophecy. Both were predicated on Divine encounter. This interplay of prophecy and mysticism is underscored in the scriptural portrayal of Moses. On the one hand, Moses is depicted as the prophet par excellence. "There has never again arisen in Israel, a prophet like Moses" (Deut. 34:10). The Rabbis expressed this as follows: "All the prophets looked through an opaque glass, but Moses looked through a translucent glass."[10] At the same time, Moses was the most sublime mystic. He encountered God "face to face"[11] and longed to experience God as no one ever had.[12]

---

8. See Scholem's discussion, *Major Trends in Jewish Mysticism* (New York 1972), 4.

9. See the discussion in A.J. Heschel, *The Prophets* (New York 1962), 2:141f.

10. *B. Yevamot*, 49b; cf. Paul's statement 1 Cor. 13:12 "For now we see in a mirror darkly, but then face to face." On Paul's concluding phrase, which is likewise related to Moses, see the next note.

11. Exod. 33:11, Num. 12:8, and Deut. 34:10.

12. Compare the discussion of Exod. 33:18 in *Fountain*, p. 57 below.

It is noteworthy that in addition to this personal, experiential component, Jewish mysticism is also characterized by an intense literary enterprise. It is not simply that the most significant testimonies of mystical activity have been preserved in writing. Rather, it is these literary expositions themselves that are the cornerstones of Jewish mysticism. Jewish mystics read and responded to the earlier writings. Presumably, these later figures had their own experiences; nevertheless, they were conditioned and influenced by the literary heritage. Accordingly, significant themes and motifs continually reappear.

This literary cross-referencing is not only apparent in later periods, it is even evident in biblical times.[13] For example, if one were to compare the descriptions of the celestial kingdom and the enthroned Deity, as found in various passages in the Hebrew Scriptures, many common features would emerge. As these accounts are pivotal for postbiblical mysticism and offer an interesting counterpoint to works that we shall be studying, it is worthwhile to quote the essential elements of the following five biblical texts and then reflect on their interrelationships.

After the revelation at Mount Sinai, Moses and the elders ascended the mountain. "And they saw the God of Israel and there was under His feet as it were a pavement of sapphire stone, like the very heaven for [its] clearness" (Exod. 24:10). A second, brief account was conveyed by the prophet Micaiah, son of Imlah. "I saw the Lord sitting on his throne and all the host of heaven standing beside him on his right hand and on his left" (1 Kings 22:19).

Turning now to Isaiah's description of his visionary experience, which constitutes the cornerstone of the doxology in the Jewish and Christian liturgies, we read:

> I saw the Lord sitting upon a throne, high and lifted up; and
> His hem filled the temple. Above Him stood the seraphim;
> each had six wings. And one called to another and said:
> "Holy, holy, holy is the Lord of hosts; the whole earth is full
> of His glory" (Isa. 6:1-3).

---

13. On the phenomenon of biblical cross-referencing, see M. Fishbane's comprehensive study *Biblical Interpretation in Ancient Israel* (Oxford 1985), as well as R. Alter's insightful discussion, "Language as Theme in the Book of Judges," *The Eleventh Annual Rabbi Louis Feinberg Memorial Lecture* (University of Cincinnati 1988).

Within the mystical tradition, Ezekiel's vision plays an especially prominent role. Most of the first chapter of this book describes the Divine chariot and its four celestial creatures. It is concluded by a graphic depiction of the Lord.

> Above the firmament over their [i.e. the holy creatures'] heads
> there was the likeness of a throne, in appearance like
> sapphire; seated above the likeness of a throne was a likeness
> as it were of a human form. Upward from what had the
> appearance of his loins I saw as it were gleaming bronze, like
> the appearance of fire enclosed round about. Downward from
> what had the appearance of his loins I saw as it were the
> appearance of fire, and there was brightness round about him.
> Like the appearance of the rainbow that is in the cloud on the
> day of rain, so was the appearance of the brightness round
> about (Ezek. 1:26-28).

The final account that we shall consider is the most explicit depiction of the Deity in the Hebrew Scriptures and is found in the *Book of Daniel.*

> As I looked, thrones were placed and one that was ancient of
> days took his seat; his raiment was white as snow, and the
> hair of his head like pure wool; his throne was fiery flames,
> its wheels were burning fire. A stream of fire issued and came
> forth from before him; a thousand thousands served him, and
> ten thousand times ten thousand stood before him; the court
> sat in judgment, and the books were opened (Dan. 7:9-10).

All of these descriptions depict God, enthroned in Heaven. This image conveys not only Divine sovereignty but also judgment, as stated explicitly in *Daniel.* Moreover, the Lord is surrounded by the angelic hosts; however, only in *Daniel* is there an attempt to enumerate them. The image of sapphire appears in several of the passages, as does fire. It should also be noted that the earlier accounts are the briefest, and that it was only in the exilic and post-exilic period that the luminaries provided extensive descriptions of their visions.

Accordingly, there is a cumulative effect in that subsequent generations studied and were influenced by the combined legacy of the past. Thus, all those engaged in Jewish mysticism did so by consciously grappling with its literary heritage. It is quite significant and by no means coincidental that the standard medieval term for Jewish mysticism was *kabbalah*, literally, "reception" of the traditional teaching.[14] So pervasive is this interfacing of motifs that it is virtually impossible to read a single page of any Jewish mystical text without coming upon a citation or allusion to a previous work, be it biblical or postbiblical.[15]

HISTORICAL OVERVIEW

In considering the development of Jewish mysticism, it is evident that it is concentrated into periods of intensity. It has not been the case that in any given century or era, one is as likely to find widespread activity as another; rather the pace quickens, then slows. This is indicative of an organic and vibrant tradition periodically flowering. For this reason it is imperative to consider the general historical contours of Jewish mysticism with its recurring patterns and concerns, in order to better appreciate specific developments, such as the "Circle."

Were one to chart this activity one could point to an early period, corresponding to the visionary experiences of Isaiah, Ezekiel, and Zechariah, namely, eighth to sixth century B.C.E., followed by a hiatus until the third and second centuries B.C.E. with the composition of works such as *1 Enoch* and *Daniel*. Another hiatus ensued until the mid-first century C.E., which witnessed visionary Jewish-Christians, such as Paul and *Revelation*'s John, the apocalyptic writers of *4 Ezra, 2 Baruch*, and other texts, as well as the rabbinic sage R. Yohanan b. Zakkai and his disciples. This was followed by the period of *hekhalot* (celestial temples or palaces) literature, whose provenance has been the subject of much scholarly debate and is still unresolved, though presumably this literary corpus falls somewhere between the second and eighth centuries C.E.

Afterwards there is a lengthy gap with only sporadic activity until the beginning of the thirteenth century, at which time there was a veritable explosion. It lasted approximately 100 years and was the most productive and creative epoch in the entire history of Jewish mysticism. Scores of individuals composed hundreds of treatises,

---

14. On the etymological history of this term, see G. Scholem, *Origins*, 38f.

15. This raises the significant yet complex issue of determining which accounts represent an authentic experience as opposed to an echoing of a literary convention. Instructive in this regard are Michael Fishbane's previously mentioned study of biblical texts and Carol Newsom's application of this methodology in "Merkabah Exegesis in the Qumran Sabbath Shirot," *Journal of Jewish Studies* 38:1 (1987), 11-30.

including the writings of the "Circle" and the undisputed jewel of the mystical tradition, the *Zohar, The Book of Splendor.* This multivolumed commentary on the *Pentateuch* emerged at the end of the thirteenth century, although pseudepigraphically attributed to rabbinic sages of classical Judaism. Moreover, it is clear that R. Moses de Leon, assumed by scholars to be the author of the *Zohar,* was familiar with the writings of the "Circle." In both the *Zohar* and R. Moses' Hebrew writings, one finds evidence of key concepts from the "Circle."[16]

While every one of these periods that we have identified warrants its own study in order to fully assess contributing factors and underlying forces that promoted it; nevertheless, some general observations can be made. Each can be characterized as a time of historical crisis and turbulence. Therefore, the exigencies of history can be viewed as catalysts promoting theological rethinking and reformulation.[17] Accordingly, an appreciation for the historical context is a prerequisite for any informed study of mysticism.

The era of the biblical prophets witnessed the disintegration of the Israelite monarchy and the loss of self-rule, coupled with the destruction of the first Temple. Eventually the exiles were allowed to return, and Jerusalem and the Temple were restored. It is understandable that this prolonged period of national trauma promoted radically new perspectives on the historical process, as well as an intense reconsideration of the significance of the Temple and the function of prophetic vision. The traditional role of prophets, like Elijah, had been the advocacy of renewing the Mosaic covenant, thereby restoring the religious integrity of the nation. It was a task that focused entirely on responding to the current situation. Unlike their predecessors, prophets such as Amos and Isaiah began contem-

---

16. For a recent discussion of this issue, as well as numerous bibliographical references, see E. Wolfson *The Book of the Pomegranate* (Atlanta 1988), 39f., as well as *Sefer ha-Rimmon* (Brandeis U. diss. 1986), 34, n. 34.

17. An important case study pertaining to events of this century that illustrates this point is N. Polen's "Divine Weeping: Rabbi Kalonymous Shapiro's Theology of Catastrophe in the Warsaw Ghetto," *Modern Judaism* 7:3 (1987), 253-269; see also the references on p. 269, n. 66. Another interesting example is found in a recent study by an Israeli psychologist, Benjamin Beit-Hallahmi, who has gauged a dramatic increase in the pursuit of personal salvation following the traumatic Yom Kippur War of 1973; see *Lehigh Valley Center for Jewish Studies Newsletter* 3:1 (1987), 3.

plating the eschaton, the final act in the historical drama. For Isaiah this entailed the advent of a messianic redeemer.[18] Eventually, messianism took on a realized aspect. In the prophecies of Haggai and Zechariah, the Messiah, or more accurately Messiahs, were identified as the contemporary leaders of the Jerusalem community, who were divinely charged with the rebuilding of the Temple.[19]

According to the Jewish tradition, classical biblical prophecy ended with Malachi in the fifth century.[20] This assumption was widely accepted and is evidenced by the fact that according to both the Jewish and Christian scriptural canon, *Malachi* is positioned as the last of the prophetic books. An ancient acknowledgment of the postprophetic period is the assertion in one of the later psalms, "We have not seen any signs for us. There is no longer any prophet. None amongst us knows for how long" (Ps. 74:9).

In order to understand the impetus for the theory that biblical prophecy ceased with Malachi, it is necessary to consider the circumstances of this prophet. His prophecy reflects the disillusionment of the postrestoration period, in which the messianic expectations articulated by his predecessors, Haggai and Zechariah, did not come to fruition. Malachi chastises the nation for their faithlessness; nevertheless, he concludes his prophecy by offering some consolation– the Day of the Lord will eventually transpire and Elijah will return to usher in the eschaton.

It is significant that Malachi specifically identifies the messianic herald as Elijah and not an unnamed, future prophet. To be sure, there is propriety in having Elijah, the great defender of the Lord, return from Heaven for one final mission. Nevertheless, this underscores that prophecy would never be fully reinstituted, only that it would achieve ultimate closure. In reflecting on Israelite history and the dramatic events of the sixth and fifth centuries B.C.E., the prophets realized that history had run its course. There was cataclysm and exile, followed by renewal and restoration. All that was lacking was for the messianic age to begin; hence, there was no need for further prophecy.

After Malachi, it was assumed that God no longer communicated to the Israelites in the same direct manner. According to the

---

18. See esp. Isa. 11:1-10.

19. See esp. Hag. 2:20-23 and Zech. 2:14; 6:11-13.

20. See *B. Yoma*, 9b and the next note.

Talmudic sages, lesser forms of prophecy were instituted. "After the last prophets Haggai, Zechariah, and Malachi had died, the prophetic spirit (*ruaḥ ha-kodesh*) departed from Israel, but they still availed themselves of the *bat kol*."[21] The expression, *bat kol*, is frequently mentioned in rabbinic literature and connotes a heavenly echo. It can be translated literally as "daughter of the voice." This reflects the notion that it is not the actual voice of God, but rather an offspring or secondary form of communication.

Presumably, this mediated form of Divine communication was not totally satisfying for some, indicative as it was of partial estrangement from God and a diminishing of Divine revelation. Not surprisingly, within Jewish sectarian conventicles the prophetic tradition continued, accompanied by intense mystical activity. What emerged was a radically different type of spirituality, which combined apocalyptic symbolism and the visionary theosophy of *merkavah* mysticism. To be sure, both of these elements were based on the biblical tradition. Its innovation stemmed from its distinctive concerns, as well as its pseudonymous packaging. All of these writings claimed to represent ancient and not contemporary prophecy. The earliest evidence of this activity is found in apocalyptic works stemming from the second century B.C.E., principally: *1 Enoch*, which may in fact date back to the third century, *The Testament of Levi*, and *Daniel*.

The composition of these apocalyptic classics coincided with the power struggle between the Ptolemies and Seleucids over control of Israel, culminating in the ascendancy of Antiochus Epiphanes IV in the second century B.C.E. He attempted to assert control by outlawing Jewish religious practice. The successful Macabbean revolt ensued. Not only did this turbulent period serve as the historical catalyst for *Daniel*, wherein Antiochus is depicted as the little horn,[22] but it also fostered Jewish sectarianism. This is evident by the earliest references to the pietist group, the Hasideans, who were active in the revolt. The Essenes also originated around this time.[23]

A startling characteristic of many of these apocalyptic writings is the description of individuals, frequently aided by an angelic guide,

---

21. *B. Yoma*, 9b; a parallel source is found in *B. Sotah*, 48b.

22. See Dan. 7:8 and 8:9f. On the image of the horn as a conquering king/ kingdom, cf. Zech. 1:18f. and Ps. 75.

23. For an accessible collection of primary sources on the Hasideans and the Essenes, see G. Nickelsburg and M. Stone, *Faith and Piety in Early Judaism* (Philadelphia 1983).

ascending to heaven. The highlight of their celestial tour is a vision
of the Divine throne. This underscores the theme of Divine tran-
scendence, as opposed to immanence. God no longer descends into
the mundane world to converse with humans via prophets. Instead,
it was necessary for individuals to enter the celestial realm.

Although it is beyond the scope of this work to trace the development of this phenonmenon,[24] it is worth noting that Ezekiel's
experiences are usually neglected in such discussions. To be sure,
Ezekiel never actually ascended to heaven; nevertheless, he often
claims to have been transported by the Divine Spirit from his Babylonian domicile. For example, we read "and the Spirit lifted me up
between earth and heaven and brought me to Jerusalem in visions of
God" (Ezek. 8:3).

It is significant that all of the early texts and most of the later
ones are pseudepigraphic and in general attributed to ancient biblical
figures. This indicates that the real authors were sensitive to the issue
of legitimization in a society that did not recognize contemporary
prophecy. Nowhere is this condemnation more evident than in rabbinic circles. Of the numerous apocalyptic texts that are known, only
one, *Daniel*, is cited in classical rabbinic literature.[25] Rabbinic dis-
dain for these works is evident by their classification as *sifrei
genuzim*, "sequestered books" (= *apocrypha*). So effective was this
suppression of postbiblical prophetic writings that almost none of
these works have even been preserved in their original language of
Hebrew or Aramaic. Had it not been for the fact that in the early
Christian period they had been translated into Greek and other
regional languages, such as Ethiopic, these intensely religious, Jewish
writings would have been entirely lost.[26]

---

24. A multifaceted study of this topic is A. Segal, "Heavenly Ascent in Hel-
lenistic Judaism, Early Christianity and their Environment," *Aufsteig und
Niedergang der Romischen Welt* 2, H. Temporini and W. Hasse eds. (Berlin
1980), 1333-1394; see also, M. Himmelfarb, "From Prophecy to Apocalypse," in *Jewish Spirituality*, Vol. 1, A. Green ed. (New York 1987),
145-165. For a recent monograph that investigates the Mesopotamian background of *Enoch*, see H. Kvanvig, *Roots of Apocalyptic* (Neukirchener 1988).

25. Such is the assertion by H. L. Ginsberg, *Studies in Daniel* (New York
1948), 119f.

26. The use of Jewish sectarian writings, now referred to as pseudepigrapha,
by early Christians is well known. For example, *Jude* verse 14 directly quotes
1 Enoch. Paul was likewise influenced by *Enoch*, as will be discussed below.

1 Enoch, Levi and *Daniel*, mentioned above, were preserved by the Qumran community, and it is therefore not surprising that the next echoes of *merkavah* theosophy are found in Essene writings presumably composed in the first century B.C.E. The most significant of these are Sabbath hymns, referred to as the "Angelic Liturgy." Although these are not apocalyptic narratives; nevertheless, important themes such as the multiplicity of heavens and the centrality of the Divine throne are depicted herein.[27]

The Romans succeeded the Hellenists, and the situation for the Jews in Israel steadily deteriorated throughout the first century C.E., as successive uprisings were quashed. Eventually, the suppression of Jewish nationalism culminated in the destruction of the second Temple in 70 C.E. Throughout this period there was an intensification in eschatological speculation as evident in the activities of John the Baptist, the early Christians and the sectarian apocalypticists, like *4 Ezra*. Nevertheless, it is significant that in the first century C.E. prior to the destruction of the Temple, virtually all the *merkavah* material is located within the Jewish-Christian milieu.[28] Only in the post-Temple period was there *merkavah* activity in rabbinic circles.

Ostensibly, early Christianity adhered to the notion that biblical prophecy ended with Malachi. As previously noted, even in the Christian canon *Malachi* is the last book of the Old Testament. Moreover, the extensive usage of the prophetic writings of the Hebrew Scriptures by the New Testament writers is significant. It was not simply that the early Christians were seeking support for their views and that they interpreted these texts typologically by assuming that Jesus is the hidden referent of biblical prophecy. Rather, the New Testament writers implicitly subscribed to the theory that the Hebrew Scriptures represent the reservoir of Divine prophecy. Accordingly, it was necessary to relate all essential elements of Jesus' life to ancient biblical prooftexts.

An instructive example of this phenomenon is the career of John the Baptist as recorded in the New Testament. Clearly, John is depicted as being a great prophetic figure. Nevertheless, he is consciously portrayed as emulating the prophets of old, not only in his dress and lifestyle, but also in his message. It is significant that John's

---

27. See especially Newsom's previously cited article, "Merkabah Exegesis."

28. There are a few other texts to consider, such as *The Apocalypse of Zephaniah* and *2 Enoch* that may also have originated from this period; however, their connection to *merkavah* theosophy is somewhat tenuous.

vision and charge to the nation is simply a recapitulation of Isaiah 40:3-5.[29] Whether this portrayal is an accurate depiction of John's activities, or a product of the literary imagination of the authors of the Gospels, its implications are the same regarding the overarching significance of classical biblical prophecy for the postbiblical epoch.

Despite this tendency, which considered prophecy as having become obsolete, there is an authoritative statement that runs counter to this trend. In *Deuteronomy* there is an explicit promise of a future prophet.

> I will raise up for them a prophet like you (i.e., Moses) from among their brethren; and I will put My words in his mouth, and he shall speak to them all that I command him (Deut. 18:18).

This was seized upon by those circles anxious to promote prophetic activity. One such example, is found in John 16:12-15 and his discussion of the Paraclete, who will complete the program initiated by Jesus. It is also conceivable that Paul saw himself in this role, for he frequently mentions that he was privy to celestial revelations, and he describes his birth in terms that are modelled after biblical prophets.[30]

It is also worth noting that Paul's description in 2 Cor. 12:1-4 is the first autobiographical *merkavah* account, insofar as all earlier texts are pseudepigraphic. He acknowledges that he had been taken up to the third heaven and Paradise, wherein he was granted revelations, too mysterious to convey.[31] One can speculate that the strength

---

29.   See, for example, Mark 1:3 and Matt. 3:3. The utilization of this verse in Qumran documents is also significant; see the conclusion of the *Manual of Discipline* in T. Gaster, *The Dead Sea Scriptures* (New York 1976), 65. On the probable connection between John and the Qumran community, see J. Robinson "The Baptism of John and the Qumran Community," *Harvard Theological Review* 50 (1957), 175-191.

30.   Paul's audacious statement, "Then God, who had specially chosen me while I was still in my mother's womb" (Gal. 1:15), parallels Jer. 1:5 and Isa. 49:1. The return of the "prophet" was also awaited by the Essenes, cf. Gaster, *Dead Sea*, 63. On the "prophetic" mission of the Q community, cf. I. Havener, *Q: The Sayings of Jesus* (Wilmington 1987).

31.   A lucid study of this material is found in J. Tabor, *Things Unutterable: Paul's Ascent* (New York 1986), see also A. Segal, "Paul and Ecstasy," *1986 SBL Seminar Papers* (Atlanta 1986), 555-580.

of his conviction and his willingness to suffer martyrdom overcame the social pressures that forced previous visionaries to write pseudonymously. It seems that only the Jewish-Christian milieu was supportive of such acknowledgments, another example being John, the author of *Revelation*.

To be sure, Paul was clearly functioning within the framework of apocalypticism. This is most evident in his earliest writings, which were in closest proximity to his ascension experience. In both *1* and *2 Thessalonians* one can perceive the strong influence of *1 Enoch's* eschatology, especially in Paul's discussions of the polarity of good and evil. Hence, he was familiar with at least some of the earlier sectarian literature.

Toward the end of the first century c.e. there was a resurgence of Jewish sectarian *merkavah* writings, including such works as: *4 Ezra, 2* and *3 Baruch*, and both *The Apocalypse* and *The Testament of Abraham*.[32] It should be noted that they all were responding to the destruction of the Temple, an event that naturally triggered the apocalyptic imagination. The concomitant evolution of *merkavah* activity within rabbinic circles had a profound impact on subsequent developments in the Jewish mystical tradition. Owing to its direct influence on the theology of the "Circle," it is necessary to explore this phase more fully.

Merkavah mysticism occupies an exalted status in rabbinic thought. According to the *Mishnah* (i.e., rabbinic law codification),[33] it is the most esoteric topic and is elsewhere characterized as exceedingly great–in contrast to standard rabbinic disputation, referred to as a small matter.[34] Therefore, it is not surprising that some of the most significant rabbinic figures, such as Rabban Yohanan b. Zakkai and R. Akiva, engaged in it.

Moreover, the dating of Paul's ascension is problematic, cf. Segal's comments, p. 557. Perhaps "14 years ago" is not to be taken literally; it may simply have been a literary convention, as it appears to be in Gal. 2:2. An interesting, Gnostic reworking of the Pauline testimony is found in the *Apocalypse of Paul*, in *The Nag Hammadi Library*, J. Robinson ed. (San Francisco 1988), 256-259.

32. These writings are found in *The Old Testament Pseudepigrapha*, Vols. 1 and 2, J. Charlesworth ed. (Garden City 1983).

33. *M. Ḥagigah*, 2:1.

34. *B. Sukkah*, 28a, and *B. Baba' Batra'*, 134a.

When one surveys rabbinic accounts of *merkavah* speculation, two basic conclusions emerge. The first is that since no pharisaic or rabbinic figure prior to Rabban Yohanan is accredited with having been involved in it, this activity postdates 70 c.e. Secondly, Rabban Yohanan and his disciples concentrated on the esoteric exegesis of *The Book of Ezekiel*, whereas R. Akiva and his colleagues are depicted as having undergone profound visionary experiences.

To be sure, rabbinic Judaism, as it evolved under the direction of Rabban Yohanan and his students, must also be seen as a response to the destruction of the Temple. In this time of persecution and national catastrophe, the newly constituted class of rabbis were attempting to preserve and redefine Judaism. Their enemies were not only the occupying Roman legions, but also the *minim*: a general term for heretics, used in reference to Jewish sectarians of all persuasions, including Jewish-Christians.

Instead of individual visionaries ascending to Heaven, the early rabbis, headed by Rabban Yohanan b. Zakkai, advocated the controlled study of the initial chapter of *Ezekiel*, which they referred to as *ma'aseh merkavah*, the account of the Chariot.[35] They insisted upon restricting access to this material, by asserting their role as the only authoritative exegetes of Scripture. Presumably, in so doing they were attempting to counter the widespread sectarian involvement in *merkavah* mysticism.[36] Their ominous assertion that such activity was potentially dangerous was underscored by an anecdote about a child who was killed when he inadvertently conjured up a destructive spirit. Such warnings likewise illustrated the rabbinical intention to control this material.[37]

---

35. This material has been analyzed by numerous scholars. Halperin's intriguing monograph, *Faces*, offers an extensive bibliography; however, the particular thesis that I am advocating concerning the polemical motivations of the rabbis differs from previous discussions. A similar position, though focusing on different material and issues, was advocated by Herbert Basser, "The Rabbinic Attempt to Democratize Salvation and Revelation," *Studies in Religion* 12:1 (1983), 27-33. Basser asserted that "in the Talmudic period a degree of mystic ritual and belief was tolerated by the rabbis, but in subtle ways they tried to discourage public teachings of a mystic nature which they may have viewed as a threat to rabbinic religion," p. 27.

36. See above for our discussion of Paul and *merkavah* mysticism. The visionary experience at the core of *The Revelation of John* is another example of the impact of this particular form of theosophy upon early Christianity.

37. *B. Ḥagigah*, 13a.

A further indication of the essentially polemical thrust of the rabbinic *ma'aseh merkavah* enterprise is the fact that there are no records whatsoever of the actual content of their mystical contemplation. Although there are numerous accounts of Rabban Yohanan and his students having engaged in it, none of these narratives preserve even the briefest allusion to what they actually thought and experienced. Instead, these narratives simply emphasize the fact that if one is worthy to pursue this discipline, he will be praised by Heaven and his teachers; if unworthy, the consequences will be extreme.

It was only later that rabbis, like Akiva and Elisha b. Abuyah, were portrayed as having undertaken a visionary ascension.[38] In rabbinic literature, and especially in *hekhalot* texts, extensive depictions of their experiences are found. Moreover, it is likely that this change was precipitated by the surfacing of original Jewish sectarian writings within a particular rabbinic circle. According to *Ḥagigah* 15b, Elisha b. Abuyah used to bring heretical books into the rabbinical seminary. Furthermore, it is conceivable that these unnamed heretical works were in fact apocalyptic texts since Elisha is credited with having seen the Divine angel Metatron seated on the Throne of Judgment. This represents the development of an apocalyptic motif. Significantly, Elisha is named in a rabbinic listing of key members of the Jewish-Christian sect.[39]

It is also conceivable that Akiva's teacher, R. Eliezer, played a role in fostering Akiva's radical orientation. There is a famous incident, recorded in the *Talmud*, pertaining to a debate, in which R. Eliezer appealed directly to Heaven for support and was answered. Nevertheless, his opponent, R. Joshua, retorted that the Torah is not in Heaven. Afterwards R. Eliezer was excommunicated by his colleagues, and it was relegated to Akiva to inform him of this.[40] Elsewhere we are told that R. Eliezer was actually arrested on the charges

---

38. For a recent discussion of the seminal *pardes* (celestial orchard) account, involving R. Akiva and Elisha b. Abuyah, see Halperin's *Faces*, 31-37 and 194-206.

39. *Kohelet Rabbah*, 7:26:3 cited and discussed by R. Kimelman, "*Birkat Ha-Minim* and the Lack of Evidence for an Anti-Christian Jewish Prayer in Late Antiquity," in *Jewish and Christian Self-Definition*, Vol. 2, E.P. Sanders ed. (Philadelphia 1980), 232.

40. *B. Baba' Meẓi'a*, 59b.

of being a Jewish-Christian heretic! Although he easily defended himself, afterwards he admitted to Akiva that one day he was conversing
with a Jewish-Christian who transmitted a teaching in the name of
Jesus which "gave me pleasure."[41]

Although the link between apocalyptic mysticism and prophecy
persisted until the early Christian period, it appears to have been bro-
ken with the rabbinic involvement in *ma'aseh merkavah*. With the
resumption of visionary ascent by R. Akiva and his colleagues, the
apocalyptic impulse was only partially revitalized. One can mention
in this regard Akiva's support for the messianic claims of the revolu-
tionary Bar Kokhba and the apocalyptic subtheme evident in
Hekhalot Rabbati, one of the centerpieces of *hekhalot* literature.[42]

Ostensibly normative Judaism asserts that prophecy has long
since ceased; nonetheless, it has remained a significant issue for Jewish luminaries throughout the ages. During every period of intense
mystical activity, individuals have attempted to reforge the channel
of Divine communication. Prominent mystics involved in prophecy
include R. Abraham Abulafia from the thirteenth century,[43] R.
Hayyim Vital in the sixteenth century[44] and the twentieth-century
savant, R. David Cohen, the Nazirite.[45]

During the late twelfth and thirteenth centuries there was a
remarkable resurgence of prophetic activity in Jewish circles. One of
the more intriguing halakhic works of the period was a collection
entitled *Responsa from Heaven*. Its author, R. Jacob of Marvege,

---

41.   *T. Ḥullin* 2:24; this text was discussed by L. Schiffman, *Who Was a Jew?*
(Hoboken 1985), 71f.

42.   On the latter issue, see Gruenwald *Apocalyptic*, 157ff. See *M. Sanhedrin*
10:1 for Akiva's condemnation of heretical books.

43.   See the recent series of books by M. Idel: *The Mystical Experience in
Abraham Abulafia* (Albany 1988); *Studies in Ecstatic Kabbalah* (Albany
1988); and *Language, Torah, and Hermeneutics in Abraham Abulafia*
(Albany 1989).

44.   The actual techniques for achieving prophecy constitute the climax of
Vital's *Gates of Holiness*. For nearly 400 years this material was suppressed
and has only recently been published in *Ketavim Ḥadashim me-Rabbenu
Ḥayyim Vital*, J. Hillel ed. (Jerusalem 1988).

45.   R. David was the leading disciple of R. Abraham Isaac Kook, the for-
mer Chief Rabbi of Israel. R. David's magnum opus was entitled, *The Voice
of Prophecy* (Jerusalem 1970).

would formulate an inquiry pertaining to religious law, prior to retiring at night, and while asleep he would receive a reply, presumed to have come from heaven.[46]

Moreover, at this time a number of individuals, including R. Ezra of Moncontour, are even referred to by the term *navi'*, "prophet."[47] Several brief accounts have been preserved which portray R. Ezra as ascending to heaven in order to receive instruction concerning celestial secrets. The most interesting of these is found in a text emanating from the circle of the *ḥasidei 'ashkenaz* concerning the anticipated advent of the messianic age.

> The prophet from Montcontour ascended to heaven and inquired of Haggai, Zechariah and Malachi when the eschaton would transpire. Each of them composed three verses [in response].[48]

It is interesting and significant that R. Ezra is depicted as questioning the last of the biblical prophets about the messianic age. This implies that R. Ezra functioned as a continuation of the prophetic lineage.

Even in the kabbalistic treatises from the early thirteenth century, the issue of prophecy receives special treatment. R. Azriel of Gerona's letter to the mystics of Burgos offers a veritable primer on achieving prophecy. This text played a significant role in the development of the "Circle," as will be discussed in chapter 5. Prophecy is also an important concern of a text entitled *The Gate of Concentration by the Early Kabbalists*. This work was published by Scholem,

---

46. On R. Jacob of Marvege, see G. Scholem, *Origins*, 240 and n. 88, as well as the recent textual studies by I. Ta-Shema, "*She'eilot u-Teshuvot min ha-Shamayim*," *Tarbiz* 57:1 (1987), 51-66 and N. Danzig, "*Teshuvot ha-Ge'onim Sha'arei Teshuvah u-She'eilot u-Teshuvot min ha-Shamayim*," *Tarbiz* 58:1 (1989), 21-48.

47. For Scholem's analysis of this material, see *Origins*, 239f.; see also M. Idel, *Kabbalah: New Perspectives* (New Haven 1987), 91ff., for a discussion of a comparable figure from mid-thirteenth-century France, R. Michael the Angel. Another important study is A. J. Heschel's survey article, "Prophecy in the Middle Ages," [Hebrew] in the *Alexander Marx Jubilee Volume* (New York 1950), 175-208.

48. Cited by Scholem in *Tarbiz* 2 (1931), 514.

who assumed that it was likewise written by R. Azriel. It too exhibits numerous affinities in terminology with the "Circle."[49]

At the outset it should be emphasized that in the Middle Ages, Jewish mystical activity was not confined to any one locale, rather it was diffused. In the thirteenth century Jewish mysticism flourished throughout western Europe, in Germany, France, Spain, and elsewhere. Owing to the fact that this efflorescence occurred in so many diverse areas, one would be hard-pressed to isolate one decisive factor that applies universally. Nonetheless, the fact that the first generation of full-fledged mystical writers in all the countries mentioned above were virtually contemporaneous is a strong indication of some commonality and cross-fertilization.

Jewish life in western Europe at that time was quite precarious. Commencing at the nadir of the eleventh century and periodically thereafter, Jewish communities in western Europe were ravaged by each new wave of Crusaders as they marched off to fight the infidels. These harsh persecutions, occurring primarily in Germany but of concern to all of the Jews, compelled many to reflect on basic theological issues such as theodicy. Working within the traditional Jewish understanding of history as being divinely controlled, many were puzzled by the course of events and sought rationales to justify what had happened. One finds evidence of this kind of soul-searching in the Crusade chronicles that have been preserved.[50] Accordingly, this was a traumatic period in which theological reflection was stimulated.

The connection between the Crusade massacres and the nascence of medieval Jewish mysticism is best exemplified by the literary career of R. Eleazar b. Judah of Worms. R. Eleazar was the major literary figure of the aforementioned *hasidei 'ashkenaz*. This group of

---

49. Scholem originally published *Sha'ar ha-Kavvanah le-Mekubbalim ha-Rishonim* in *Monatsschrift für Geschichte und Wissenschaft des Judentums* (1934) 78:511. He subsequently translated and discussed it in *Origins*, 416-419; see also A. Kaplan, *Meditation and Kabbalah* (York Beach 1985), 117-122. Kaplan's presentation is particularly useful in that he incorporates R. Hayyim Vital's insightful kabbalistic commentary.

50. A useful collection of the major Jewish chronicles is S. Eidelberg, *The Jews and the Crusaders* (Madison 1977).

German pietists was one of the most influential medieval Jewish sects. During the late twelfth and thirteenth centuries it had members throughout the Rhineland. Moreover, its ideological formulations greatly influenced all subsequent Jewish religious ethics, following the dissemination of R. Eleazar's religious handbook, *The Book of the Apothecary*, and the movement's constitutional anthology, *The Book of the Pietists.*[51] R. Eleazar also composed dozens of treatises, including a mammoth five-volume work entitled *Secrets of the Mysteries*. Although some theological originality is evident, what is of greatest significance is that this constitutes a major repository of classical rabbinic and geonic theosophical speculation.

According to R. Eleazar's own account, this esoteric material had been transmitted to him by his uncle, R. Judah Hasid, who was the leader of the sect and the principal author of *The Book of the Pietists*. He, in turn, had been instructed by his ancestors going back many generations and centuries to the enigmatic figure, Abu Aaron.[52] Moreover, R. Eleazar felt compelled to compose his treatises, thereby making public these secret doctrines, only after the death of his teacher. He lamented that his son had died, having been killed in a Crusader pogrom, and that therefore there was no one to receive these teachings. Accordingly, R. Eleazar decided to undertake a very ambitious literary enterprise, consisting of seventy-three distinct treatises on the entire spectrum of esoterica. Eventually, he was able to accomplish much of what he had intended.[53]

R. Eleazar's work had widespread influence and was one of the primary catalysts for the literary outpouring of mystical writings. According to popular legend, R. Eleazar was revered as the introducer of *kabbalah* into Spain.[54] It is noteworthy that all of the writings of the "Circle" are either anonymous or pseudonymous. Although most of these works are attributed to classical rabbis, R. Eleazar is the only contemporary figure to be so honored. He is also

---

51. Ivan Marcus's monograph, *Piety and Society: The Jewish Pietists of Medieval Germany* (Leiden 1981), constitutes an important study of the movement's social ideology. Their mystical theology was the subject of J. Dan's *Torat ha-Sod shel Ḥasidut 'Ashkenaz* (Jerusalem 1968).

52. The text of this tradition is found in Marcus, *Piety*, 67. On Abu Aaron and the historiography of the *kabbalah*, see ch. 4.

53. J. Dan, *'Iyyunim be-Sifrut Ḥasidei 'Ashkenaz* (Ramat Gan 1975), 44-57.

54. On this and other issues related to R. Eleazar and the spread of *kabbalah*, see below, p. 199.

portrayed as the principal conduit of esoteric transmission in the fan-
tastical lineages that are found in the "Circle's" treatises, which surfaced in Castile and are ascribed to R. Yehushiel and R. Kashisha.
(These texts are discussed in chapter 4.)

The centerpiece of the theology of R. Eleazar, and the *hasidei
'ashkenaz* as a whole, was the doctrine of the twofold *kavod*, "Divine
Glory." This was an extension of a biblical concept rooted in Moses'
petition to God, "Please show me Your glory (*kevodekha*)" (Exod.
33:18). God responded, "You cannot see My face" (v.20); "And you
shall see My back, but My face will not be seen" (v. 23). This differentiation between those Divine qualities that are perceptible and an
imperceptible essence had been previously developed by early medieval Jewish philosophers, such as Saadia.[55]

A classic and influential formulation of the twofold Glory theory is found in R. Nathan of Rome's Talmudic lexicon, *'Arukh*, com-
piled around 1100.

> There is a Glory, which is above the Glory. The Glory that is
> the great splendor and closely connected with the *shekhinah*
> (Divine Presence), man cannot see it. Concerning this it is
> stated, "For man shall not see Me and live" (Exod. 33:20).[56]

One can readily see the impact of this doctrine of an exalted
Divine Glory in *The Book of Contemplation* and subsequent texts
from the "Circle." All recensions begin by referring to the most recondite aspect of the Godhead which is termed "the Innermost." The
self-assigned goal of the book is to reveal "the root of the entire existence of the Glory, which is hidden from sight."[57] Hence, these writings are an attempt to penetrate the superperceptible reality of the
Godhead.

As mentioned above, the connection between historical events
and the spread of esoteric teachings is clear in the case of R. Eleazar
of Worms. Moreover, the other two principal areas of Jewish mystical activity, southern France and Spain, were equally turbulent. During the initial decades of the thirteenth century, Christendom was

---

55.   On the theory of the Glory and the *hasidei 'ashkenaz*, see G. Scholem,
Trends, 110-116 and J. Dan, *Torat ha-Sod*, 104-170. See also the extended
discussion below, p.38, n. 9.

56.   R. Nathan of Rome, *'Arukh ha-Shalem* 6 (Jerusalem 1969), 110.

57.   See below, p. 37.

bellicose. The ecclesiastical authorities in France were engaged in a two-pronged attack against the spread of Aristotelean philosophy, which they combatted with a series of bans, and the Catharist heretics, resulting in the Albigensian Crusade and the establishment of the Inquisition.[58]

Jews were also caught up in these events. Paralleling the adverse ecclesiastical reaction to the philosophical enterprise, there was a comparable attempt on the part of a group of rabbis in southern France to suppress the study of Maimonides' writings. In 1233 these books were denounced to inquisitors in Montpellier and were subsequently burned.[59] Another example of the religious intensification of the period was the immigration to Israel of scores, perhaps even hundreds, of rabbis in 1211.[60]

Having noted that the early thirteenth century witnessed the spread of philosophy and in particular Maimonides' writings, it is appropriate at this juncture to briefly consider the relationship between philosophy and medieval Jewish mysticism. It was the theory of Heinrich Graetz, the foremost Jewish historian of the nineteenth century, that the *kabbalah* was essentially a polemical response to medieval Jewish philosophy. Although Scholem was highly critical

---

58.   See W. Wakefield, *Heresy, Crusade and Inquisition in Southern France: 1100-1250* (Berkeley 1974). On the possible connections between the Cathars and early *kabbalah*, see S. Shahar's article, "Catharism and the Beginnings of the Kabbalah in Languedoc," [Hebrew] *Tarbiẓ* 40 (1971), 483-507, which was recast as "The Relationship between Kabbalism and Catharism in the South of France" in *Les Juïfs dans l'histoire de France*, M. Yardeni ed. (Leiden 1980), 55-62. Her contention that medieval rabbinic condemnation of heresy as "dualism" is proof of an acquaintance with Cathar doctrines is unconvincing, as this simply represents the classical rabbinic term for heresy; on this latter issue, see A. Segal, *Two Powers in Heaven* (Leiden 1977). An early work that contains interesting material is L. J. Newman's *Jewish Influences on Early Christian Reform Movements* (New York 1925), regardless of Scholem's disparagement of this monograph in *Origins*, 16, n. 14.

59.   For a balanced presentation of the pertinent primary sources and scholarly interpretation of this early incident in the Maimonidean controversy, see J. Cohen, *The Friars and the Jews* (Ithaca 1982), 52-60.

60.   The historicity of this event, as well as the spiritual and pietistic motivations of those involved, has been methodically analyzed by E.Kanarfogel, "The 'Aliya of 300 Rabbis in 1211," *Jewish Quarterly Review* 76:3 (1986), 191-215.

of this hypothesis,[61] the impact of philosophy on the *kabbalah* should not be diminished.

All of the early kabbalistic works exhibit significant influence from philosophy. This is even the case with respect to the *Bahir*, which was considered by Scholem to be the earliest kabbalistic text. It also pertains to the earliest identifiable circle of kabbalists, namely the Provençal group. It is unlikely to be a mere coincidence that it was in this same family circle, which included R. Abraham b. David of Posquières, that translations of the key Judeo-Arabic philosophical works were initially commissioned and disseminated. Moreover, one has only to read the letters of R. Ezra of Gerona, the first full-fledged literary figure among the kabbalists, to appreciate that the starting point for his discourse is a critical response to Maimonides' theories on creation.[62] It is therefore fitting that in our subsequent analysis of the principal writings of the "Circle" the widespread influence of the philosophical tradition will be examined.

TRADITION, ESOTERICISM, AND PSEUDEPIGRAPHY

As we noted, in the early thirteenth century Jewish mystical activity was evident in a variety of locales throughout western Europe: the Rhineland, northern France, Provence, Catalonia, and Castile. Each of these areas fostered distinct groups that developed their own particular doctrines, though there were contacts between some of the groups. It is worth noting, however, that Castilian mysticism, of which the "Circle" is an important element, is exceptional for several reasons. First of all, it had the longest period of productivity. By the middle of the thirteenth century, the German Pietists had virtually disbanded and the Unique Cherub theosophists had disappeared as mysteriously as they had appeared; there were no important kabbalists in Provence, and their major Catalonian counterpart, Nachmanides, emigrated to Israel in 1267 and died soon after. To be sure, Nachmanides' disciples preserved his basic, kabbalistic teachings, but in general, they refrained from breaking new ground. More will be said about this later.

---

61. G. Scholem, *Origins*, 7ff.

62. R. Ezra's letters were published by Scholem, "*Teʻudah Ḥadashah le-Toldot Reshit ha-Kabbalah*," in *Sefer Bialik* (Tel Aviv 1934), 155-162.

In thirteenth-century Castile, on the other hand, new schools of thought emerged, and many of the most highly valued works from the vast treasury of the Jewish mystical tradition were composed there, including the undisputed jewel, the *Zohar, The Book of Splendor*. So great was Castile's fame that at the end of the century a certain R. Isaac, from Acco in northern Israel, heard rumors of its marvellous teachings, and journeyed far and long to corroborate their veracity.

The question that confronts us is why did intense mystical activity last but a few decades elsewhere in western Europe, whereas in Castile it continued to flourish for at least a century? When one compares the various groups, certain social patterns emerge. The German Pietists were founded by a prominent scholar, R. Samuel the Pious. He was succeeded by his son, R. Judah, who was the first important literary figure of the movement. R. Judah was in turn succeeded by his disciple and nephew, R. Eleazar of Worms. R. Eleazar was the most prolific and creative of the Pietists. Following the death of his teacher and the murder of his only son at the hands of Crusaders, R. Eleazar launched an ambitious literary campaign in an effort to preserve the hitherto esoteric tradition of the Pietists.[63]

Turning now to the kabbalists' tradition of their origins, we see that their founder was likewise a prominent scholar, R. Abraham of Posquières. He was succeeded by his son, R. Isaac the Blind, who was the first important literary figure of the movement. Isaac was in turn succeeded by his disciple and nephew, R. Asher b. David. This dynastic chain is thus the exact counterpart of the German Pietists. R. Asher appears to have been the last of the Provençal kabbalists. Contemporaneous with R. Isaac the Blind, kabbalists in Catalonia were also active. These included Rabbis Ezra, Azriel, and Nachmanides–all from Gerona.

One can speculate that the reason that these movements lost their strength after only two generations was that they revolved around a very small number of individuals that were either directly related, or shared a teacher-disciple bond. Moreover, there was a strong elitist quality to all of these groups. The German Pietists advocated a polarized view of society, in which the masses where depicted as wicked sinners, constantly posing a challenge to the righteous. Their religious manual, *The Book of the Pietists*, even acknowledges

---

63. J. Dan, *'Iyyunim*, 44-57.

that they tried, apparently unsuccessfully, to establish their own self-contained communities.[64]

Although the early kabbalists were not separatists, nevertheless, they asserted that their mystical theology was based on an esoteric tradition which was not to be publicized. This was stated explicitly by R. Isaac in his well-known letter to Nachmanides and the latter's cousin, R. Jonah. R. Isaac vehemently responded to reports that the *kabbalah* was being publicly disseminated. He wrote:

> For I was filled with great concern when I saw scholars, men
> of understanding and pietists, engaging in long discourses and
> presuming in their books and letters to write about the great
> and sublime matters [of the *kabbalah*]. But what is written
> cannot be kept in the closet; these things are lost or the
> owners die and the writings fall into the hands of fools or
> scoffers, and the name of heaven is thus profaned. . . . I often
> warned them against this tendency, but since I separated
> myself from them, they have been the cause of much harm. I
> am of an entirely different habit, since my forefathers were
> indeed the most distinguished in the land and public masters
> of the Torah but never did a word [relating to the mystical
> lore] escape their lips.[65]

Nachmanides and his disciples likewise operated in this fashion. As Moshe Idel has observed, "Nahmanides intended to keep his kabbalistic tradition limited to his intimate students, and he succeeded."[66] Idel continues by contending that Nachmanides' successors imposed even more restrictions. They consciously wrote commentaries on Nachmanides' teachings that "disclosed only a part of the meanings of these secrets, and this was often done in a veiled and obscure jargon."[67] An interesting support for this assessment is reflected in a statement by the fourteenth-century scholar, R. Nissim of Gerona. He refrained from discussing Nachmanides' doctrines,

---

64. Marcus associates the Pietists' radical sectarianism with the leadership of R. Judah Ḥasid; cf. *Piety*, ch. 4, "The Radical Mode of Sectarian Pietism," 55-74.

65. G. Scholem, *Origins*, 394.

66. M. Idel, "We Have No Kabbalistic Tradition On This," in *Rabbi Moses Nahmanides: Explorations*, I. Twersky ed. (Cambridge 1983), 66.

67. *Ibid.*

because I did not receive it from a learned kabbalist and even though I have seen the commentaries on Nahmanides' secrets, nevertheless they do not reveal the principles of that science, but they reveal a span and obscure several spans more.[68]

Returning to R. Isaac the Blind's letter to Nachmanides, we find that his denigration of what was happening in Castile provides us with our first clue as to why the fate of theosophy was different there. "I have also heard from the regions where you dwell and concerning the inhabitants of Burgos that they openly hold forth on these matters, in marketplaces and in the streets."[69]

Thus, in Castile, the kabbalistic enterprise had become exoteric. Unlike the other areas, wherein these pursuits were confined to a small tight-knit group, in Castile they were widespread. For example, the "Circle" generated a corpus of more than forty treatises, apparently representing the fruit of almost as many authors. Although these texts reflect common terms, they do not conform to any specific doctrinal system. It is apparent that the heterogeneous nature of Castilian mysticism was a product of this public campaign: numerous texts were being circulated, studied, and responded to.

Another peculiarity of the "Circle" is that none of its dozens of treatises are attributed to their original authors. All of these writings are either anonymous or pseudonymous–and, reflecting the idiosyncracies of the texts themselves, there is no overriding pattern to the pseudepigraphy. Some texts make fantastic claims like *Fountain*, which was supposedly revealed to Moses by a mysterious angel. In addition, a number of the writings are attributed to Talmudic sages, such as R. Nehuniah and Rabban Gamliel.

Although pseudepigraphy was the norm for the "Circle," the vast majority of the mystical works written in Germany, France, and Gerona were claimed by their rightful authors. Moreover, this proclivity toward pseudepigraphic attributions continued to pervade Castilian theosophy in the latter half of the thirteenth century. As we shall see in Chapter 4, R. Isaac Cohen's writings offer innumerable examples, as does the *Zohar* itself. Not insignificantly, this too is the pattern in the *Bahir*, perhaps the earliest of the kabbalistic treatises.

Insofar as these authors generally did not reveal their motives for adopting this form of expression, we can usually only surmise why

---

68. *Ibid.*

69. G. Scholem, *Origins*, 394.

they chose to do so. A possible exception is the case of R. Moses de Leon, if remarks attributed to his wife are to be believed. The supposed comments of de Leon's wife were transmitted by the aforementioned R. Isaac of Acco. As de Leon was responsible for disseminating the *Zohar*, even this unsubstantiated testimony is important and is worth considering at some length.

As noted above, R. Isaac journeyed to Spain in order to search for the source of the *Zohar*. He eventually located R. Moses de Leon in Valladolid. De Leon suggested that R. Isaac meet him in his hometown of Avila, where he promised to show him the original text. Unfortunately, de Leon died en route and R. Isaac had to rely on other witnesses. He eventually encountered R. Joseph, one of the patricians from Avila. Together, they encouraged the latter's wife to contact R. Moses de Leon's widow. She reportedly told R. Joseph's wife the following:

> From his head, heart, mind and intellect he composed everything that he wrote down. And I said to him when I saw him writing without anything before him–why do you say that you are copying from a book when you have no such book and from your head you are composing it? Isn't it better for you to acknowledge that it is from your intellect that you are writing? Wouldn't this engender more honor for you? And he answered me and said, 'If I were to make known to them my secret that I am writing from my intellect, they would not pay attention to my words, nor would they give me a penny for them, for they would say that from his heart he is inventing them. But now that they hear that I am copying from the *Zohar* that Rabbi Shimon bar Yohai composed by means of the Holy Spirit, they purchase it for much money, as you have seen.'[70]

As intriguing as this evidence is, it is nevertheless only thirdhand and is, therefore suspect. Although this account is often referred to in scholarly literature, one of its more interesting elements is infrequently stressed. Upon learning of the apparent fraud, R. Isaac of Acco was utterly dismayed. He responded as follows:

---

70.   Compare A. Neubauer, "The Bahir and the Zohar," *Jewish Quarterly Review* 4 (1892), 361-365 and I. Tishby, *Mishnat ha-Zohar* (Jerusalem 1949), 1:30.

When I heard these words of his (i.e., R. Joseph of Avila), I was crushed and utterly bewildered. I believed then that there was no [original] book, rather he wrote by means of a Writing Name.[71]

R. Isaac's conclusion that R. Moses de Leon did not simply fabricate the *Zohar*, but instead composed it by means of magical conjuration appears to have been widely held. Immediately after the sudden passing of R. Moses, R. Isaac had met a certain R. David from Pancorbo who likewise asserted,

Know in truth that it is clear to me, without doubt, that never did it (i.e., the *Zohar*) come into the possession of R. Moses, nor does the *Zohar* exist. However, R. Moses was a conjuror of the Writing Name, and through its power did he write everything connected with this book.[72]

Therefore, according to both R. Isaac and R. David, de Leon practised a magical form of automatic writing, involving the conjuration of spirit powers. If this were the case, it might indicate that de Leon's use of pseudepigraphy was not simply a ruse, but may have entailed the author entering into a paranormal state, in an effort to commune psychically with the deceased sages that he quoted. Be that as it may, it is undeniable that the pseudepigraphic writings that emanated from Castile were generally accepted as authentic. Although there were some sceptics, many believed in the ancient Palestinian origins of the *Zohar* and the other texts. This would help to explain their popularity and why they were able to become rapidly entrenched in the society.

In summary, we have seen that the fate of medieval Jewish theosophy differed geographically, as well as in duration. In most of Europe it was relatively short-lived, while in Castile it flourished for over a century, before finding a new home. Its unparalleled growth in Castile can be traced to three interrelated factors. Elsewhere theosophy was esoteric and highly controlled, but in Castile it was widely publicized and exoteric. This resulted in a plethora of writings that did not conform to any fixed doctrinal system. As a result, Castilian *kabbalah* became the most vibrant, creative, and eclectic form of

---

71. *Ibid.*

72. *Ibid.*

medieval Jewish mysticism. It engendered quite radical theological
doctrines, particularly in respect to cosmic dualism and the mythic
roots of evil. This was highlighted in R. Isaac Cohen's writings and
is central to the *Zohar*. Finally, in Germany, Provence, and Catalonia, great stress was placed on authoritative family tradition and
teaching, as the term *kabbalah* suggests. In Castile, however, there
was no comparable heritage. In its stead, fictitious geneologies were
concocted by individuals like R. Isaac Cohen. Pseudepigraphy, whatever its motivations, afforded these radical works instant legitimization and allowed them to tenaciously take root. Eventually, this
would have an impact upon most aspects of medieval Jewish life and
thought.

2

THE BOOKS OF CONTEMPLATION AND THE FOUNTAIN OF WISDOM

The following texts represent the corpus of writings referred to in the previous chapter as *The Books of Contemplation*. Most of these works have never been published, and none have been treated critically. Some have been preserved in unique manuscripts, whereas others have a rich scribal heritage. Where feasible, both a Hebrew edition as well as an English translation will be offered. The Hebrew edition will present variant readings found in the different manuscripts. Explanatory notes accompany the translations. In order to facilitate subsequent discussion, a translation of *The Fountain of Wisdom* is also provided.

The versions of *Contemplation* can be arranged in four major groups, under the rubric of four discrete recensions. The so-called *Contemplation-Short* (text no. 1) represents the proto-text of *Contemplation*. It is followed by a translation of *Fountain*, the other seminal treatise of the "Circle." Afterwards, there is *Contemplation-Long*, the second recension. *Contemplation-Thirteen Powers*, represents the third major recension. It is followed by the fourth recension, *Contemplation-Standard*, which is a composite of the earlier recensions and offers new material. Two short texts complete the corpus of material. The first concludes, "I am R. Hammai" and is an interesting abridgment of the introduction to *Contemplation-Short*. Finally, there is R. Hammai's *Book of Unity*, which offers a radical synthesis of *Contemplation* and *Fountain*.

In Appendix I, ten subtexts of the third and fourth recensions will be presented. The actual relationship between the recensions and their subtexts will be discussed in Appendix II. In general, however, the arrangement of these works follows their conjectural, chronological order. Accordingly, it is assumed that *Contemplation-Short* is the progenitor of *The Books of Contemplation*, whereas *Contemplation-Standard*, so named because it is the most common version, represents the final redaction. The relationship between *The Books of Contemplation* and *Fountain* is also crucial. In Appendix II, evidence will be presented to support the contention that *Contemplation–Short* preceded and influenced *Fountain*. Furthermore, the impact of *Fountain* upon the subsequent recensions of *The Books of Contemplation* is readily discernible.

Many of the following Hebrew editions are diplomatic presentations of the treatises; namely, the manuscript deemed to be the single best witness of a given text was chosen to represent that work. In the apparatus, variants from the other manuscripts are presented. The advantage of such a procedure is that it is based on a textual reality. It thereby offers a version of a work that is extant and not simply the product of scholarly intuition–no matter how alluring it is to attempt textual re-creations.[1] Occasionally, it was necessary to deviate from this procedure, when no single manuscript of a work was judged to be adequate on its own. Also, a diplomatic edition of *Contemplation–Standard* has already been published. Accordingly, an eclectic edition seemed a desirable contribution in this case. The translations, however, are eclectic and based on the best readings, whatever their source.

SYMBOLS USED IN THE APPARATUS

( ) = an omission
< > = an addition
: = read instead

CONTEMPLATION–SHORT

This treatise has been preserved in five manuscripts: Bodleian 1947, ff. 8b-10a, designated in the apparatus by ב; Guenzburg 283, ff. 63b-64a, designated by ג; Mousayeff 63, f. 13a-13b, designated by מ; Jewish Theological Seminary of America 1805, ff. 49-50b, designated by י; and Florence 44:14, ff. 171-172, designated by פ. These five manuscripts are quite consistent, thereby indicating that the text is

---

1. I am indebted to Moshe Bar-Asher for this basic approach to textual editing.

in a relatively good state of preservation. The manuscripts can be divided into two major families. Mousayeff and J.T.S. form one group, with J.T.S. being a later derivative copy. Bodleian and Guenzburg constitute another family, with Guenzburg occasionally exhibiting unusual and unique readings. Florence vacillates between the two families and was evidently derived from both.

The transcription that follows is based on Mousayeff 63, which was deemed to be the single best witness.[2] Although it has suffered some damage, its lacunae were readily emended through comparison with the other manuscripts, especially J.T.S. 1805. It should also be noted that J.T.S. 1805 is especially important in that it is the only codex that presents more than one recension of *The Book of Contemplation*.

The earliest citations from *Contemplation–Short* are found in other writings of the "Circle of Contemplation." For example, text 6, which represents an intriguing reworking of *Contemplation–Short*'s introduction, constitutes the preface of the *Commentary on the Tetragrammaton*. It was composed in the latter half of the thirteenth century and has been preserved in an early fourteenth-century manuscript.[3] Interestingly, when *The Book of Contemplation* was originally published in 1798 in *Sefer Likkutei me-R. Hai Ga'on*, the opening lines of this edition were drawn from *Contemplation–Short*; however, the rest of the text published therein was derived from *Contemplation-Standard*. Since no manuscript exhibits this composite pattern, one must assume that the editor possessed manuscripts of both of these recensions, and shifted from one to the other.

---

2. Only a poorly filmed copy of this codex is available at the Microfilm Institute in Jerusalem's National Library. Fortunately, I was able to work directly from the manuscript, which though damaged is for the most part legible. I am grateful to Allon Mousayeff for his assistance in this regard.

3. See G. Scholem, *Origins*, 323, n. 255.

CONTEMPLATION-SHORT

1 זה ספר העיון שחיבר רב חמאי ראש המדברים על ענין הפנימיות וגילה
בו עיקר כל מציאות הכבוד הנסתר מן העין אשר אין כל בריה יכולה
לעמוד על עיקר מציאותו ומהותו על דרך האמתית כמות שהוא באחדות
השוה שבהשלמתו מתאחדים עליונים ותחתונים והוא יסוד כל נעלם
5 וגלוי וממנו יוצאים כל הנאצלים מפליאת האחדות וכל הכחות המתגלגים
מסתר עליון הנקרא אמן פי׳ שממנו נמשך כח קיום הנקרא אב האמונה
שמכחו האמונה נאצלת והוא המאציל הקדמון שהוא קודם לכל הקדומים
הנאצלים מפליאת אחדותו שכלם מתגלים בדרך אצילות כריח מריח ונר
מנר שזה מתאצל מזה וזה מזה וכח המאציל בנאצל ואין המאציל חסר
10 כלום. כך הקב״ה המשיך כל כחותיו אלו מאלו בדרך אצילות והוא
מתאחד בהם כלהב האש המתאחד בגווניו והוא מתעלה למעלה באחדותו
ומתרומם עד שאין סוף לרוממותו. וכשעלה בדעת לבראת כל פעולותיו
ולהאמיץ כחו ולהמציא כל יצוריו ברא כח אחד וזה הכח הוא הנקרא
החכמה הקדומה הנקראת תעלומה וקודם שברא זה הכח לא היה כחו ניכר
15 עד שנראה זיוו ונגלה כבודו בזו החכמה. על זה נקראת אותה חכמה
אמונה מפני שהקב״ה הוא חיי אותה חכמה ועצמה. וזה שנקרא הקב״ה
אל אמונה. והמהות שאנו יכולין להשיג מאמתתו ית׳ הוא ענין אור
החיים זך כתם טוב נכתב ונחתם בזיו שפרירו כלול מזיו זוהר בהיר
כדמות צורת נשמה שאין בה שום השגה כלל צחצוח שאינו מושג כלל
20 והוא מתאחד בחכמה הקדומה. ומאותה החכמה הנקראת תעלומה המשיך
הקב״ה כל הכחות הרוחניים בשעה אחת והיו כלם מתנועעים ומתצלצלים
בצחצוחם ומתרוממים למעלה עד שחבשם הקב״ה כלם בבת אחת. וזהו שכתוב
ויגד לך תעלומות חכמה וכתיב מבכי נהרות חבש ר״ל מבכי מלהתיך אלו
הכחות שהם אספקלריאות המאירות וצחצוחם באור נוגה וזהו משמע
25 נהרות כדכתיב ונהורא עמיה שרי. חבשם ונעשו כלם אגד אחד והיו

---

1 (זה) ג נ/חמאי: חמא ג/חמאי (גאון) נ   3 כמות: כמו ג   4 שבהשלמתו:
שבאחדותו ג פ/יסוד: יסודם ב/(כל) ב/(נעלם: עולם פ   5 מפליאת: מפליאות ג נ/
(האחדות) ג/המתגלים: המתגלגלים פ   6 מסתר עליון: מכתר עליון הנעלם ב מכתר
עליון פ/אמן: אומן ג קיום: קדוש ג/אב: אם ג   7 (שמכחו האמונה) ב נ
8 מפליאת: מפליאות ב/(בדרך: בדרך ג/אצילות: האצילות ב   9 (וזה מזה) ג/וזה
(מתאצל) נ   10 (כך הקב״ה המשיך כל כחותיו אלו מאלו בדרך אצילות) ג
11 האש: אש נ/מתעלה: מתאחד פ   12 בדעת: בדעתו ב ג/לבראת: לברוא ג
(לבראת) ב/פעולותיו: פעליו ב ג   13 (הוא) ג   15 ונגלה: ונראה ב/בזו: בזה נ/
(אותה) ב/חכמה: החכמה פ   16 חיי אותה: הייאזת ב היה אותה נ/ועצמה: עצמה
פ   18 כתם: כתב ג/נכתב: נכתם פ/שפרירו: שפרידו פ   19 כלל: כלול ב
20 הקדומה: קדומה ג/החכמה: חכמה ג   21 הרוחניים: הרוחניות נ/מתנועעים:
מתרועעים ב   22 בצחצוחם: בצחצוחים ב   23 חכמה (כי כפלים לתושיה) ב ג/
(מבכי) ג (מבכי מלהתיך) נ/מלהתיך: מלהתוך פ   24 הכחות (שום) פ/וצחצוחם:
וצחצוחים ב/באור: כאור ב   25 ונעשו: נעשו ג/אגד אחד: אגודה אחת ג/והיו
(כלם) נ

מתאחדים בצד העליון הדבוק באחדות החכמה. באותה שעה המשיך הקב"ה
כל כח וכח בפני עצמו לאחד אחד. הראשון אור מופלא וזהו שנ'
ותעלומה יוציא אור. וזהו דכתיב ה' אלהי גדלת מאד הוד והדר לבשת.
גדלת שהיית אפשר לעמוד מבלי חקר ובלי גבול לבד. הוד זיו החכמה
הקדומה. הדר זהו האור המופלא. אחר כך ברא הקב"ה מהאור המופלא (30)
החשמל שהוא תחלה למעשה העליונים והוא כמין פלס משפיע בכל צד
כחותיו. מאמצע לראש ומראש לאמצע. ומאמצע לשמאל ומשמאל לאמצע.
ומימין לשמאל ובכל צד. ונעשה עליו מלאך עומד שיש בו פרצוף פנים
כאדם ויש בו כח לדבר כאדם ולשמוע כאדם וזהו כמראה אדם עליו
מלמעלה. ולא אדם ממש. והוא כח מושכל והוא סבה ראשונה לכל הסבות. (35)
ועליו נאמר עוטה אור כשלמה. ואחר נוטה שמים כיריעה. והחשמל הוא
כנגד י' של ארבע אותיות מפני שיש בו עשרה כחות ואלו הן ת' שהוא
תמונה ועל זה נאמר יעמוד ולא אכיר מראהו תמונה לנגד עיני. השני
ג' גדולה. ה' הגבורה על מה שנא' לך ה' הגדולה והגבורה והתפארת
והנצח וההוד... והממלכה... והעושר והכבוד. ודממה דקה. (40)
ועוד חשמל הוא כנגד מיכאל והוא נקרא אורפניאל הרי הענין שקבלתי
מן החשמל ומה שאני יודע בו באמת. מן החשמל נמשך ערפל. הע' הוא
רמז לשבעים שמות של הקב"ה. הר"פ מערפל כשתוציא מהם רל"ו שהזכיר
ר' ישמעאל בספר השיעור ישארו מ"ד כשתוציא ב' שתשים עם הלמד של
ערפל ישארו מ"ב כנגד ארבעים ושתים אותיות. ועוד ערפל הוא כנגד (45)
גבריאל וכנגד תגריאל וכנגד ה' של ארבע אותיות מפני שיש בו חמשה
כחות ואלו הן קדושה טהרה צדקה חסד ומשפט הרי ענין ערפל וכשאמרו
לשון נוגה ר"ל בצורת כתיבת הקדש כי מיכאל מימין וגבריאל משמאל.
ור' אלעזר בן ערך רמז בתפלתו מימינך חיים ומשמאלך מות. העין השלם
שבו נאמר כי לה' עין אדם. כל זה פירשו לי בענין ערפל. מערפל נמשך (50)
כסא הנוגה. ומכסא הנוגה האופן הגדולה הנקראת חזמית שבה מסתכלין
החוזים ואמרו לי כי אלו הארבע כחות חשמל וערפל וכסא הנוגה והאופן
הגדולה הם עומדים למעלה כמו יסודות והקב"ה מתאחד בהם כמו נשמה
בגוף ומתעלה מהם עד שאין סוף לרוממותו. ואלו הארבע כחות הם כנגד
ארבע אותיות של שם ר"ל ציון הגבול להכיר גודל תפארתו ועז גבורתו (55)
של הקב"ה מפני שזה הענין כמות שהוא נקרא היכל הקדש הפנימי והוא

---

27 מופלא: המופלא נ   29 שהיית: שהיה ג/ובלי: ומבלי ג/(זיו) מ   31 והוא:
וזהו ג/בכל: לכל ב ג   33 ובכל: ולכל ג   36 ואחר: ואחריו ג (ואחר) ב/הוא:
היא ב   37 י': ה"א ב/של (שם) ג/(ת') ג/שהוא: שהן ג   38 (תמונה לנגד עיני) ג
(לנגד עיני) ב   39 ג' גדולה ה' הגבורה: גדולה ג' גבורה ג (ה' הגבורה) ב
41 (הוא) ג/הרי: הרי זה ג הם מ הוא נ   42 הוא: היא ב   43 (מערפל) ב/
כשתוציא: לכשתוציא נ/רל"ו: כ"ל ב כולן ג   44 כשתוציא (מהמ"ד) נ/עם: על ב
45 (כנגד ארבעים ושתים אותיות) ב   46 תגריאל: תגראל ב הגואל ג/בו: לו ג
47 וכשאמרו: ונאמ' ג ובאמת פ   48 לשון: בלשון ב (לשון נוגה ר"ל) ג   49 העין:
הענין ב   50 (לי) נ/(לי) ג/בענין ערפל: בערפל פ   51 (הנקראת) ב/חזמית: חזאזית ג/
שבה (אין) ב פ (היו) ג   53 יסודות (בגוף) ב /יסודות והקב"ה מתאחד בהם כמו)
ג   55 שם (וזה ענין של שם) ב (וזהו ענין שם) ג פ

כל העיקר המצוי בשרשי המחשבה ועל זה אמרו שרשי המחשבה הם שרשי
הנפש. ואחר האופן הגדולה נמשך הכרוב והוא ככפורת מתגלגל לפני כל
הכחות שהזכרנו למעלה בגלגל צחצחו ואחר כך גלגלי המרכבה שהם סבות
השמים. ואחר כך האויר הסובב והפרגוד שהוא כמין פתח פתוח לפני כל
הכחות של מעלה והוא עומד בכח המנהיג ופעמים הוא סגור ופעמים הוא
פתוח והכל נקרא היכל ה'. ומטטרון שר הפנים עומד לפני הפרגוד
וזהו שהזכיר ר' עקיבא באלפא ביתא שלו שאמר הקב"ה בשביל מטטרון
שמתיו משרת לפתח היכלי מבחוץ. וכל זה הענין מורה שהוא סוף למעשה
העליונים ותחלה ליסוד התחתונים שנא' והוא מהשנא עידנייא
וזימנייא. ולחכימא ברמיזא.

60

65

---

57 (ועל זה אמרו שרשי המחשבה) ג/הם שרשי: הם הגיוני ב הגווני ג   58 הנפש:
הנפשי ג/והוא ככפורת: והיא כפרדת ג   59 שהזכרנו: שזכרנו ג/ואחר כך: ואחרי
ב   61 (עומד) ג/(הוא) נ   65 ליסוד: למעשה   66 וזימנייא (מהעדא מלכין
ומקים מלכין יהב חכמתא לחכימין ומנדעא לידעי בינה) ב (ולחכימא ברמיזא) ב/
ברמיזא (ועל דרכיך נגה אור. ההוויות היו. והמדות נתפשטו תם ש"ל.) ג (ועל דרכיך נגה
אור) פ

This[4] is *The Book of Contemplation*[5] that Rabbi Hammai,[6] the principal spokesman,[7] composed on the topic of the Innermost.[8] In it he revealed the essence of the entire existence of the Glory, which

---

4. The opening lines of this treatise are virtually identical in the later recensions, *Contemplation–Long* and *Contemplation–Standard*.

5. *Sefer ha-'Iyyun.* *'Iyyun* (contemplation) is a postbiblical term, found in such rabbinic expressions as *'iyyun tefillah,* concentration during prayers, in *B. Shabbat,* 127a; cf. L. Ginzberg's discussion cited in I. Efros, *Philosophical Terms in the Moreh Nebukim* (New York 1924), 140; and *'iyyun kisei ha-kavod,* contemplation of the Throne of Glory, *Midrash Mishlei,* S. Buber ed., (Vilna 1893) ch. 10, p. 67. In the medieval period, resulting from the classic translations of Jewish philosophical treatises by the Ibn Tibbonide family, *'iyyun* became synonymous with philosophical inquiry. For example, in the opening lines of Bahya ibn Pakuda's *Hovot ha-Levavot* 1:1 we read, "His existence and the truth of His unity, by means of contemplation (*me-derekh ha- 'iyyun*)." In addition to the similar usage of *'iyyun,* it is apparent that the author of *Contemplation–Short* adopted this style of discourse and rhetoric. Other than in the title of the three recensions, *'iyyun* is not used or alluded to in the body of these treatises; however, in *Contemplation–Long* the related term *me'ayen,* one who contemplates, is found, see lines 76, 83 and 85. Interestingly, in the *Pseudo-R. Hai Responsa* the term *me'ayenim* is used disparagingly to refer to philosophers. For a discussion of a group of Jewish philosophers, active in mid-fourteenth-century Provence, and referred to as *me'ayenim,* see A. Berman, *K.S.* 53:2 (1978), 368-372.

6. On the significance of the name *Hammai,* i.e., "visionary," see above p. 1. Beginning with writers in the late fifteenth century, R. Hammai is referred to as a *ga'on,* namely, the head of a Babylonian rabbinical seminary; see R. Isaac Mar Hayyim's letter, written in Naples in 1491 and published by Y. Nadav, *Tarbiz* 26 (1956-57), 453. Of the five manuscripts of *Contemplation–Short,* only in J.T.S. 1805, which is the latest and stems from the eighteenth century, is this geonic ascription found.

7. *rosh ha-medabrim.* The term *medabrim,* "spokesmen," is biblical, see Exod. 6:27; for *rosh ha-medabrim,* cf. *B. Berakhot,* 63b and *B. Shabbat,* 33b, especially Rashi there. Ibn Ezra associated this expression with Saadia; see H. Malter, *Saadia Gaon* (Philadelphia 1942), 52, n. 85. It is interesting that in Maimonides' *Guide for the Perplexed,* both of the expressions, *ba'alei ha-'iyyun* and *medabrim,* refer specifically to the Mutakallimun; cf. I. Efros, *Philosophical Terms,* 15.

8. *penimiyyut.* This term indicates the innermost, or most recondite aspect of the Divinity. See R. Isaac the Blind's *Perush le-Sefer Yezirah,* p. 3, l. 57, "for the created being is powerless to discern the Innermost

is hidden from sight.[9] No creature can truly comprehend the essence
of His existence and His nature, since He is in the state of balanced

---

(*penimiyyut*)–this alludes to Thought [trying] to conceive the Infinite."
Already in a responsum of R. Hai Gaon this designation is used in reference
to mystical visions, *Teshuvot ha-Ge'onim*, Y. Musafia ed. (Lyck 1864), 32,
#99. See also *Sha'arei 'Orah*, 1:62, wherein R. Joseph Gikatilla refers to
hakhmei ha-penimiyyut, "the savants of the Innermost." See also the discussion of the evolution of the term *penimi* in I. Twersky, *Rabad of Posquieres*
(Cambridge 1962), 243, n. 16.

9. *ha-kavod ha-nistar min ha-'ayin*. This expression is very similar to that
which is found in *Hekhalot Zutarti*, Elior ed., 25 *kevodo she-nistar
me-panenu*, (His Glory, which is hidden from us). In the *Pseudo-R. Hai
Responsa*, this concept is related to the verse, "the Glory of God hides a
thing" (Prov. 25:2), which most likely is its ultimate source.
Scholars such as Scholem and Dan have focused on the parallel passage in
Contemplation–Standard; unfortunately, they only used those two mss. of
this text (i.e., Mousayeff 64 and Munich 408) which have an abbreviated
reading, namely, *ha-kavod ha-nistar*, ("The Hidden Glory"). Based on this
deficient reading, they developed the theory that *The Book of Contemplation*
espoused a doctrine of two Divine Glories, one hidden and one revealed; see
most recently J. Dan, "*Kavod ha- Nistar*," in *Dat ve-Safah*, M. Hallamish ed.,
71-77. Nevertheless, all of the other mss. of *Contemplation–Standard* have
the same phrasing of *Contemplation–Short*–"The Glory, which is hidden
from sight." Furthermore, it must be stressed that in none of *The Books of
Contemplation* is there any allusion to the theory of two Glories. Moreover,
in tracing the development of the concept of the Divine Glory, these same
scholars focused on Saadia's theory of the *kavod nivra'*, the Created Glory,
see especially Dan, *Torat ha-Sod*, 104-111. However, it is clear that the
author of *Contemplation–Short* does not use the term *kavod* to indicate a
form of Divine hypostasis, as Saadia propounded. Just the opposite is the
case, for the Glory is subsequently equated with *seter 'elyon*, Supreme Hiddenness, the most recondite aspect of the Divinity. *Contemplation–Short's*
use of *kavod* is similar to R. Bahya ibn Pakuda's statement in the introduction to his *Hovot ha-Levavot*, wherein he speaks of *kavod* in terms of the
incomprehensible Divine quiddity, "it is impossible for us to conceive of
Him from the perspective of the essence of His Glory, may He be blessed."
In addition, one finds among Jewish mystics of the period a tendency to criti-
cize Saadia's concept of the created Glory; see R. Judah Hasid's commentary
on the *'alenu* prayer, cited in J. Dan, *'Iyyunim be-Sifrut Hasidei 'Ashkenaz*
(Ramat Gan 1975), 82 "if, as R. Saadiah contends that He is a created Glory,
we would not be able to proclaim about a created Glory, that it is our God."
See also the interesting comments in *Bahir* #133, A. Kaplan ed., 49, and
Nachmanides, *Perush ha-Torah*, on Gen. 46:1, criticizing Maimonides' *Guide*
1:64; cf. 1:19, as well.

unity;[10] for in His completeness the higher and lower beings are united. He is the foundation of everything that is hidden and revealed. From Him issues forth all that is emanated from the wondrousness of the Unity and all the powers[11] that are revealed from the Supreme Hiddenness,[12] which is called *'aman.*[13] The explanation

---

10. *'aḥdut ha-shaveh.* In this term we can see the influence of R. Azriel of Gerona, for the concept of *hashva'ah,* equanimity, is central to his writings; cf. Scholem, *Origins,* 439, n. 174. Tishby has noted that R. Azriel "usually employs this concept in connection with the conjunction of opposites within the Supernal Root, *shoresh ha-'elyon,*" "*Kitvei ha-Mekubbalim R. Ezra ve-R. Azriel me- Gerona,*" *Sinai,* 16 (1945), 166. These specific lines in *Contemplation–Short* bear a strong resemblance to a statement in R. Azriel's *Sha'ar ha-Sho'el:* "He is [in a state of] complete balance when in perfect unity.... He is the essence of all that is hidden and revealed," in *Derekh 'Emunah* (Jerusalem 1967), 3.
Although it is generally assumed that *shaveh* implies equivalence or balance, H. Yalon demonstrated that *shaveh* is synonymous with *ḥibbur,* conjoined, *Pirkei Lashon* (Jerusalem 1971), 212f. For a recent study of the possible Islamic philosophical sources of *'aḥdut ha-shaveh,* see A. Goldreich, "*Me-Mishnat Ḥug ha-'Iyyun,*" *Meḥkerei Yerushalayim be-Maḥsevet Yisra'el* 6:3 (1987), 141-156.

11. *koḥot* pl., *koaḥ* sing. powers, or celestial forces.

12. *seter 'elyon,* a borrowing from Ps. 91:1. In R. Azriel's letter to Burgos there is a statement whose impact on this and the subsequent recensions is evident, "all the actions, things and objects that are revealed from the Supreme Hiddenness that is hidden, for from that which is hidden does the revealed come into being"; see Scholem, *Kabbalot,* 72.

13. *'Aman* is a problematic term. According to the way it is written in *Contemplation–Long* and the later recensions, it can either be vocalized *'omen* (nurturer) or *'uman* (artisan). Since this Divine state is described as having generated *'emunah* (faith), *Contemplation–Thirteen Powers* refers to the passage in Isa. 25:1 "*'emunah 'omen,*" faithfulness and truth. While it is possible that *Contemplation–Short* likewise intended the term to be read *'omen,* it is more likely that either *'amen,* or *'aman,* artisan, as in Cant. 7:2, was intended. Wolfson (*Philo,* I, p. 167) has pointed out that the seminal verse Prov. 8:30, which according to the masoretic tradition reads, "And I was to Him an *'amon,*" i.e., one who has been raised, is rendered in the Septuagint *harmouza,* i.e., an artisan, thereby implying the reading *'aman.* Moreover, this verse from *Proverbs* was discussed at length in the opening section of *Bere'shit Rabbah,* and was variously interpreted there. One of the explanations offered for the word *'amon* was "hidden." In the midrashic commentary attributed to Rashi, there is the explanation, "that is to say, something which is hidden from the world, but it is known that it exists."

is that from Him the sustaining power[14] emanated, which is called Father of Faith,[15] since faith was emanated from its power.

He is the primal emanator, for He preceded all the primordial elements that were emanated from the wondrousness of His Unity. Furthermore, all of them are revealed by the process of emanation,

---

Furthermore, R. Azriel's writings are replete with references to these and related terms; however, as Tishby has noted, R. Azriel's intent is often obscured; cf. *Perush ha-'Aggadot*, 24, n. 3. At one point R. Azriel asserts that "*'amen* constitutes the juncture of the ten *sefirot* and the unity of all" *Perush*, 20.

One of the fragments from the "Circle," the *Responsa of R. Yekutiel*, expounds upon the mystical significance of *'amen*; see R. Shem Tov ibn Gaon, *Baddei 'Aron*, 229. Scholem discussed the connection between R. Yekutiel's writings and R. Azriel, *Origins*, 327, n. 263. See also R. Joseph Gikatilla, *Sha'arei 'Orah*, 1:121-24 and *Zohar*, 3:285b.

14.   *koah kiyyum*. This term seems to have been coined by R. Azriel. In his *Sod ha-Korbanot*, Vatican ms. 211, f. 9a, it appears several times in conjunction with *koah ha-ribbui*. Therein it is identified with the central *sefirot: teferet, hesed* and *pahad* (i.e., *gevurah*); see also f. 10b. In his *Perush Kedushah* it is specifically associated with *gevurah*; Scholem, "Seridim," 220.

15.   An extended analysis of this key passage is found below, pp. 132-133. *Av ha-'emunah* (Father of Faith) is modeled after *'el 'emunah* (God of faith) in Deut. 32:4. A possible source for *'av ha-'emunah* is the epithet "father of pious faith" (*'av hasid 'emunah*), ascribed to R. Judah Hasid and others from the *hasidei 'ashkenaz*; see *Merkavah Shelemah*, 30. The specific association of father and the Holy One, blessed be He, is rabbinic; cf. *B. Berakhot*, 35b. In Philo, *De Ebrietate* 30, 3, (Cambridge 1954), 333, "Father" is identified as the demiurge and "Mother" as *sophia*. Furthermore, the equation of faith and wisdom is significant. It is also found in R. Azriel's *Perush ha-'Aggadot*, 106.

Although faith (*'emunah*) is usually associated with human beliefs, in these sources it is clearly related to the Divine realm. Similarly, in an early thirteenth-century poem on Divine unity by the Spanish rabbinic authority, R. Meir Abulafia, one finds faith used to refer to God's thought processes, "and the hearts tired of trying to grasp His faith, except He, the force of whose schemes are infinite," *Yedi'ot Makhon*, Vol. 2, 81; cf. Broyde's discussion there of this verse. See below, R. Meshullam's *Kabbalah*, p. 208. Accordingly, in thirteenth-century Spanish writings the word "faith" underwent an interesting transformation. Perhaps the most striking example of this phenomenon is the usage of the Aramaic equivalent *mehemnuta'*, which is one of the key terms in the *Zohar* and is associated with the configuration of the *sefirot*; cf. Y. Leibes, *Perakim be-Millon Sefer ha-Zohar* (Jerusalem 1977), 398.

like a scent from a scent or a candle-flame from a candle-flame;[16] since this emanates from that and that from something else and the power of the emanator is within that which was emanated. The emanator, however, does not lack anything. Thus, the Holy One, blessed be He, generated all of His powers–these from those, by the process of emanation. Moreover, He is united with them like the flame of fire, which is united with its colors,[17] and He ascends above in His Unity and is exalted, such that there is no end to His exaltedness.

When it arose in His mind to create all His actions and display His power and produce all of His creations, He created one power. This power is called Primordial Wisdom,[18] which is called mystery.[19]

---

16. This phrasing occurs in R. Azriel of Gerona's writings; see below, p. 196.

17. This also is found in R. Azriel, see below, p. 196.

18. *ha-ḥokhmah ha-kedumah.* This is one of the central concepts of *The Book of Contemplation* and the "Circle," in general. This term is already found in R. Moses Kimhi's commentary on *Proverbs*, "he acknowledged that He possesses the state of the primordial wisdom (*ha-ḥokhmah ha-kedumah*), for the universe was created ex nihilo" Paris ms. 107, f. 108a; cf. G. Scholem, *Origins*, 317, n. 244. A somewhat earlier source is R. Abraham bar Hiyya, who refers in passing to "the wisdom that is wondrous, mighty and primordial," *Megillat ha-Megalleh*, 13. In the writings of the *ḥasidei 'ashkenaz*, we find mention of "wisdom from antiquity (*ḥokhmah kadmoniyyot*) that preceded the Torah," (Bodleian 1566, f. 14a) and in R. Elhanan's *Sod ha-Sodot*, there is reference to "ancient wisdom" (*ḥokhmah kadmonit*), J. Dan ed., *Tekstim*, 12. *Ḥokhmah kedumah* also appears in a commentary on *Midrash Konen*, which Scholem attributed to R. Isaac the Blind, *Origins*, 287, and J. Dan, *The Early Kabbalah*, (Mahwah 1986) 79, n.18. It appears to both Moshe Idel and myself that this is a later source–late thirteenth or early fourteenth century–and that the R. Isaac referred therein is not R. Isaac the Blind. Possibly the referent is R. Isaac Cohen. The concept of wisdom as the starting point of creation was expressed in the Palestinian Targum on Genesis, which in its standard form commences "With wisdom God created ... " and in the Neophyti manuscript, "From the beginning, with wisdom God created ... " This notion finds biblical support in Prov. 3:19 and 8:23, as well as the *Wisdom of Solomon*, 7:21ff. This latter text was apparently accessible in Spain during this period, as evidenced by Nachmanides' quotations of a Syriac translation in the introduction of his Torah commentary as well as his sermons; cf. *Kitvei Rabbenu Moshe ben Naḥman*, vol. 1, H. Chavel ed. (Jerusalem 1963), 163 and 182.

19. *ta'alumah.* The association between *ta'alumah* and *ḥokhmah* is based on Job 11:6, "the mysteries of wisdom" (*ta'alumot ḥokhmah*).

Before He created this power, His power was not discernible, until His radiance was seen, and His glory was revealed in this wisdom.[20] Accordingly, this wisdom was called faith, for the Holy One, blessed be He, animated this wisdom itself. Therefore, the Holy One, blessed be He, is called "God of faith" (Deut. 32:4). The quality of His truth, may He be blessed, that we are able to perceive, entails the pure light of life. It is pure gold, written and sealed[21] in the radiance of His beauteous canopy.[22] It consists of a brightly shining radiance, like the image of the form of the soul[23] that is entirely imperceptible–an entirely imperceptible brightness.

He is united with the Primordial Wisdom. From this wisdom that is called mystery, the Holy One, blessed be He, generated all the spiritual powers simultaneously. All of them vibrated and whirred in their brightness and were exalted above, until the Holy One, blessed be He, bound all of them together. So it is written, "And He shall tell you the mysteries of wisdom" (Job 11:6). It is also written, "He bound the streams (*neharot*) from flowing (*me-bekhi*)" (Job 28:11).[24] *Me-bekhi* means "from flowing." These powers are the shining speculums,[25] and their brightness is like the light of Venus. This is the meaning of *neharot*,[26] as is written, "And the light (*u-nehora*) dwells with Him" (Dan. 2:22). He bound them together and they became

---

20.   The two terms, *ziv*, "radiance," and *kavod*, "glory," are probably synonymous. Scholem (*Gnosticism*, 68) noted that *ziva rabba* is the Aramaic equivalent of *ha-kavod ha- gadol*. Interestingly, in Mandean texts the primal syzygy was described as follows, "Radiance (*ziwa*) is the Father and light (*nhura*) the Mother," E. Drower, *The Secret Adam*, (Oxford 1960), 6. See below p. 60, n. 85.

21.   The concept of gold which is signed and sealed is reminiscent of the priestly crown, Exod. 39:30.

22.   *shaprir*. cf. Jer. 43:10. See G. Vajda, "*Perush*," *Kovez 'al Yad*, 16:1 (1966), 187 on lines 32f.

23.   Compare with *Hekhalot Zutarti*, Elior ed., 26 "and like the form of the soul, which no creature can distinguish."

24.   See Moshe Idel's analysis of this verse, as interpreted in midrashic literature, *Kabbalah*, 78.

25.   *'ispaklarya'ot*, cf. B. *Yevamot*, 49b and I. Gruenwald, *Re'uyyot Yehezke'l*, *Temirin* 1 (1972), 133f.

26.   Compare Ezra of Gerona's, *Perush le-Shir ha-Shirim*, 482f. Therein he likewise interprets *neharot* from Job 28:11, in light of Job 3:4.

a single bundle. They were united in the exalted realm,[27] which is attached[28] to the unity of wisdom.

At that moment the Holy One, blessed be He, emanated each power individually–one at a time. The first was Marvellous Light.[29] Thus it is stated, "And from the mystery He produced light" (Job 28:11). In addition it is written, "Lord, my God, You are exceedingly great; You are clothed in majesty and beauty" (Ps. 104:1). "You are great" for You were able to exist alone,[30] without scrutiny or limit. "Majesty" refers to the splendor of the Primordial Wisdom. "Beauty" is the Marvellous Light.

Afterwards the Holy One, blessed be He, created the *ḥashmal* [31] (electrum) from the Marvellous Light. It is the beginning of the hierarchy of exalted beings,[32] and is like a scale whose powers have an

---

27. *ẓad ha-'elyon*. It can also be rendered supreme aspect (or side) and is derived from the Aramaic *ẓad 'ila'a* in Dan. 7:25. This term is also found in R. Azriel's commentary on *Sefer Yeẓirah*, 455, wherein he associates *ẓad ha-'elyon* with *rom ma'alah*, (the exalted level), i.e., the highest of the *sefirot*, namely *keter*.

28. *ha-davuk*. Dan (*Ḥugei*, 93) has pointed out that Ibn Ezra in his *Yesod Mora'*, ch. 12, uses the term *devekut* in the specialized meaning of emanation, which may also be appropriate for our passage. A similar usage is also evident in Judah ha-Levi's *Kuzari* 1:1, Zefaroni ed., 6.

29. *'or mufla'*. This expression, though not in technical sense, is found in *Hekhalot Rabbati, Battei Midrashot*, 1:84. R. Abraham bar Hiyya propounds a theory of five successive worlds, the first of which is called *ha-'or ha-nifla'*, *Megillat ha-Megalleh*, 22. In *The Fountain of Wisdom*, *'or mufla'* appears as the first of a series of ten lights, which emanated from the primordial darkness, see below p. 59; see also, R. Jacob Cohen, *Perush ha-'Otiyyot*, in Scholem's *Kabbalot*, 42.

30. Dan (*Ḥugei*, 40) interprets the parallel statement in *Contemplation–Standard*, as God did not need to create, for such a need would have diminished His perfection.

31. *Ḥashmal* is usually translated as electrum or amber. M. Greenberg in *Ezekiel 1-20* (Garden City 1983), 43, suggests that the Akkadian *elmesu*, indicating an undefinded precious stone, may be a cognate. In the Bible it is only found in Ezekiel's visions. It assumed a special significance in Jewish esoteric literature, stemming from the Talmudic discussion found in *B. Ḥagigah*, 13af., which was oft-cited in *The Books of Contemplation*.

32. These are angelic entities. The implication is that the higher elements, namely Primordial Wisdom and Marvellous Light, belong somehow to the Divine realm; see below, p. 125.

effect on every direction–from the middle to the top and the top to the middle; from the middle to the left and the left to the middle; from right to left and every direction. Standing upon it, an angel was fashioned,[33] with a face like a man. It possesses the power to speak like a man and to listen like a man. Thus it is written, "like the appearance of a man, up above it" (Ezek. 1:26)–but not a real man. It is the intellectual power and the primal cause of causes. Concerning it, it is said, "He covers Himself with light like a garment," and subsequently, "He stretches out heaven like a curtain" (Ps. 104:2).

Moreover, the *hashmal* corresponds to the *yod* of the Tetragrammaton,[34] since it possesses ten powers.[35] They are [as follows]. [The first is] *tav*, which is *temunah* (image). Concerning this it says, "And it stood but I could not discern its appearance, an image was before my eyes" (Job 4:16). The second is *gimel–gedullah* (greatness); then *heh–ha-gevurah* (the valor). This is based on what is stated, "For You, Lord, are the greatness and the valor and the beauty and the endurance and the majesty . . . and the dominion . . . and the wealth and the glory" (1 Chron. 29:11-12). "And the impalpable whisper" (1 Kings 19:12). Furthermore, *hashmal* corresponds to Michael,[36] and is

---

33. In *Contemplation–Long* this angel is identified as *'Arafi'el/'Anafi'el*; see below, p. 75.

34. This basic construct, namely that there are four central powers: *hashmal, 'arafel, kisei ha-nogah* and *'ofan ha-gedullah*, corresponding to the letters of the Tetragrammation, is derived from the *kabbalah* of R. Meshullam the Zadokite; see below p. 209. This theory parallels the kabbalists who related various *sefirot* to the Tetragrammaton; cf. R. Ezra's comments in J.T.S. ms. 1878, f. 12a-b, and the *Perush ha-Yihud*, presumably by R. Azriel, J.T.S. ms. 2194, f. 29a-b.

35. Most of these powers that are enumerated are derived from the verses 1 Chron. 29:11f, which were cited at the start of Ibn Gabirol's poem *Keter Malkhut* that authors of the "Circle" read and utilized; cf. G. Scholem, "*'Ikvotav shel Gavirol ba-Kabbalah*," *Me'asef Sofrei 'Erez Yisra'el* (1940), 160-178. These verses also provided the kabbalists with the names for most of the *sefirot*. On the parallel kabbalistic notion of two sets of ten powers, see M. Idel, "*Sefirot she-me-'Al ha-Sefirot*," *Tarbiz*, 51 (1982), 239-280.

36. Each of the four powers is linked with a specific archangel. This series of four archangels is derived from *hekhalot* literature; cf. *Ma'aseh Merkavah, Battei Midrashot*, 1:59. This text, which is also known as *Mesekhet Hekhalot*, was also utilized by the authors of *Contemplation–Long* and *Contemplation–Standard*. It was R. Meshullam the Zadokite, who connected these powers with the archangels; see below p. 209.

(also) called 'Orpani'el[37] (Light of God's Countenance). Behold this comprises what I have received concerning *ḥashmal*, and what I truly know about it.[38]

'Arafel (darkness) was generated from the *ḥashmal*. The *'ayin*[39] alludes to the seventy names of the Holy One, blessed be He.[40] Concerning the *resh* and *peh*[41] from *'arafel*, when you subtract 236 from them that R. Ishmael mentioned in his *Book of the Measure*,[42] there remains forty-four. When you subtract two, which you place with the *lamed* of *'arafel*,[43] there remains forty-two, corresponding to the

---

37. A secondary pattern was also developed, related to a sequence of seven angels. Again, the source is *hekhalot* literature; cf. *Sefer ha-Razim*, 67, and *Ma'aseh Bere'shit, Battei Midrashot*, 1:62; see also Tobit 12:15. On this motif of seven archangels in the Qumran liturgy, cf. T. Gaster, *The Dead Sea Scriptures* (Garden City 1976), 285-295. This material also was utilized by R. Meshullam; see below, p. 209 and *Contemplation–Standard*, p. 104.

38. This form of self-disclosure is unique to *Contemplation–Short*, in comparison with the other recensions of *The Books of Contemplation*, and is a good indication that this version represents the proto-text. Moreover, it indicates that the author was, at least partly, dependent upon traditions that he received orally.

39. This is the initial letter of *'arafel*, and it has the numerical value of seventy.

40. This doctrine is found in numerous *hekhalot* texts, such as *Hekhalot Zutarti*, 68, *Shi'ur Komah*, (see M. Cohen, *The Shiur Qomah*, (Lanham 1983), 197 and also 207f.), *3 Enoch* 5 (Hebrew), as well as the *'Otiyyot de-R. Akiva, Battei Midrashot*, 2:350. This latter text is explicitly referred to below.

41. The numerical value of these two letters is 280.

42. The enigmatic treatise, *Shi'ur Komah* was also known as *Book of the Measure* (*Sefer ha-Shi'ur*); cf. M. Cohen, *The Shiur Qomah*, 46f. Therein 236,000 parsangs was considered the basic measure of the limbs of the Divine Being; cf. Cohen, 107 and 155f., n. 80. Medieval writers contended that this figure was derived from the description in Ps. 147:5, *rav koah* (full of power), which equals 236; cf. J. Dan, *Torat ha-Sod*, 121, 138, and 256, and R. Isaac of Acco, *Me'irat 'Ainayim* (Jerusalem 1955), 55a.; see also G. Scholem, *Gnosticism*, 129.

43. *Lamed*, which is the last letter of *'arafel*, equals thirty. Combining it with the extra two yields thirty-two, which corresponds to the numerical value of the first and last letters of the Pentateuch, as well as the doctrine of the thirty-two paths of wisdom, through which God created the cosmos, mentioned at the start of *Sefer Yeẓirah*.

forty-two letters.[44] In addition, *'arafel* corresponds to Gabriel and Tagri'el,[45] as well as the *heh* of the Tetragrammaton, since it possesses five powers. They are: holiness, purity, justice, mercy, and judgment. This comprises the topic of *'arafel*. And thus they referred to *nogah* (light), that is to say as it is written in Hebrew characters[46]–for Michael is on the right, and Gabriel on the left.[47] R. Eleazar b. Arakh alluded to this in his prayer, "On Your right is life and on Your left death."[48] This is the perfect *'ayin*,[49] concerning which it is stated, "For the eye (*'ayn*) of man is the Lord's" (Zech. 9:11). All of this they explained to me concerning *'arafel*.[50]

Throne of Light (*kisei ha-nogah*) was generated from *'arafel*. From the Throne of Light [emanated] the Wheel of Greatness (*'ofan-gedullah*), which is called *ḥazḥazit* (looking-glass),[51] within which the seers would gaze. They told me that these four powers: *ḥashmal*, *'arafel*, Throne of Light, and Wheel of Greatness, stand

---

44. Namely, the forty-two-letter name of God; see *B. Kiddushin*, 71a; R. Jacob of Marvege, *She'elot u-Teshuvot min ha-Shamayim* (#9); R. Eleazar b. Judah, *Sefer ha-Ḥokhmah*, who refers to R. Hai Gaon, and J. Trachtenberg, *Jewish Magic and Superstition*, 91ff. and 289, n. 22 and n. 30.

45. This follows the two sequences noted above, nn. 36 and 37.

46. For an analysis of this passage, see below pp. 189-190.

47. Compare *Pirkei de-R. Eliezer*, ch. 4; see also *Hekhalot Zutarti*, 30, and *Sefer ha-Bahir* (#11).

48. The identification of this text is unclear. To be sure, within the "Circle" there is a text entitled *Tefillat ha-Yiḥud de-R. Eliezer [sic!] b. Arakh*, Warsaw ms. 9, ff. 169a-170b, but this is actually the *Tefillat ha-Yiḥud le-R. Nehuniah b. ha-Kanah*. Perhaps the *Pirkei de-R. Eliezer*, ch. 4, is intended; another possibility is R. Eleazar b. Judah's *Perush ha-Merkavah*, Paris ms. 850, f. 59b; cf. R. Elior, *Hekhalot Zutarti*, 71.

49. This is an allusion to the opening of this discussion of the *'ayin* of *'arafel*.

50. See above, n. 38.

51. This term seems to have been coined by the author. It is derived from *maḥazit*, a looking-glass, see *Mekhilta, Yitro*, 2:21; see also R. Moses Cordovero, *Pardes Rimmonim*, 23:8, f. 16a. In medieval Jewish philosophical writings *ḥezyon* refers to astronomy and *ḥozim* are astronomers; cf. I. Efros, *Studies*, 189.

above like foundations.[52] Moreover, the Holy One, blessed be He, is united with them like a soul in a body,[53] and transcends them until there is no limit to His exaltedness. These four powers correspond to the four letters of the Tetragrammaton, that is to say, the marking of the border[54]–in order to indicate the magnitude of His beauty and the mighty valor of the Holy One, blessed be He. This self-same topic is called the Inner Holy Palace.[55] It is the entire essence of that which exists in the roots of conceptualizing. Concerning this they have said, "The roots of conceptualizing are the roots of the soul."[56]

After the Wheel of Greatness, the Cherub was generated. It is like a curtain revolving in the revolution of its brilliance, before all the above-mentioned powers.[57] Then there are the Wheels of the Chariot (*galgalei ha-merkavah*), which are the catalysts of the heavens. Next is the Encompassing Ether (*'avir ha-sovev*), and [then] the

---

52. *yesodot*; also fundamental elements; see below, R. Meshullam's *Kabbalah*, p. 210; on the four fundamental elements see the sources mentioned by L. Ginzberg in I. Efros, *Philosophical Terms*, 135, and I. Efros, *Studies*, 243.

53. This analogy of the soul in the body is found in R. Ezra's *Perush le-Shir ha-Shirim*, 507.

54. This passage was cited by Nachmanides' correspondent; see below, pp.182-183.

55. *hekhal ha-kodesh ha-penimi*. This concept seems to be rooted in a discussion by Ibn Ezra, in his commentary on Dan. 10:21. According to Ibn Ezra there was a threefold emanational sequence: the first world, the middle world, and the lower world. He designated the middle realm as *hekhal ha-kodesh*. Note the discussion in *Contemplation–Burgos*, lines 45-47, which refers to *hekhal ha-kodesh ha-penimi*, *hekhal ha-kodesh ha-tikhon*, and *hekhal ha-kodesh ha-'aharon*; see below, p. 229. See also R. Asher b. David, who refers to "the inner Glory which is called the Holy Palace," Parma ms. 1420 109bf., which seems to be an allusion to *tif'eret*, or an even higher *sefirah*.

56. This statement also reflects the oral tradition that underlies the treatise; see above, n. 38. The source of this comment appears to be R. Azriel of Gerona's *Perush*, 82; see the extended discussion below, p. 194.

57. R. Elhanan b. Yakar, in his *Sod ha-Sodot*, describes the final stage of the Celestial Chariot in similar terms, "in a circle, and it became like a curtain surrounding all of the Chariot (*ma'aseh merkavah*)," in *Tekstim*, J. Dan ed., 20.

Celestial Curtain (*pargod*) that is like an open door before the higher powers.[58] It stands under the power of the Director.[59] Sometimes it is closed, and sometimes it is open. Furthermore, everything is called the Palace of the Lord.[60]

Metatron, the Prince of the Countenance, stands before the Celestial Curtain. So it was mentioned by R. Akiva in his *'Alpha' Beta'*: "For the Holy One, blessed be He, said concerning Metatron, 'I have positioned Metatron outside, as an attendant at the door of My palace.'"[61] This entire discussion indicates that he comprises both the end of the supernal realm and the beginning of the lower world, as is said, "And He changes times and seasons" (Dan. 2:21). For the wise a hint (is sufficient).[62]

---

58. On the development of the concept of the *pargod*, "celestial curtain" or "cosmic veil," in the biblical and postbiblical period, see F. Fallon, *The Enthronement of Sabaoth* (Leiden 1978), 55.

59. *ha-manhig.* It is unclear to whom this epithet applies. From the concluding lines of the treatise, it is likely that this refers to Metatron, who is described as guarding the door. In *Contemplation–Short*'s acknowledged source, *'Otiyyot de-R. Akiva,* (*Battei Midrashot* 2:352), Metatron even opens the celestial doors. In *Contemplation–Long,* p. 76, this task is assigned to 'Arafi'el, and in R. Azriel's *Sha'ar ha-Sho'el* 3, the term *ha-manhig* is associated with the *'ayn sof* (Divine Infinitude).

60. See above, n. 55. An interesting comparative parallel is found in the seminal Sufi theosophist Suhrawardi Maqtul, who expressed his theory of *ishraq,* Divine illumination, in terms of the image of the celestial "Temples of Light," *Le Livre des Temples de la Lumière,* in *Quinze Traités de Sohravardi,* H. Corbin trans., 50f.

61. *'Otiyyot de-R. Akiva, Battei Midrashot,* 2:351f.; cf. *Bere'shit Rabbati,* f. 28.

62. This is a standard statement, found in Jewish esoteric writings, when sensitive material is being discussed. Owing to the placement of the verse from Daniel, it is evident that the author of *Contemplation–Short* considered Metatron to be the subject of this statement, thereby indicating his role as the one who controls events in the earthly realm. See above, n. 59, where the author seems to be obfuscating Metatron's role as the Director. In a similar esoteric vein, one reads in R. Meshullam's *Kabbalah* (in a passage not transcribed below on p. 210): "YHVH Metatron, the wise will understand, for they did not give me permission to publicize this matter, but the wise will understand."

For other discussions of Metatron in the "Circle," see below (4:2, p. 232), as well as *Secret of the Seventy-Two-Letter Name,* which explicates how

THE FOUNTAIN OF WISDOM

The Fountain of Wisdom (*Ma'yan ha-Ḥokhmah*) has long been recognized as one of the jewels of the Jewish mystical tradition. R. Moses Cordovero, the sixteenth-century sage and one of the foremost proponents of the *kabbalah,* included *The Fountain of Wisdom* in his list of the most highly recommended texts.[63] There is also the significant testimony of R. Dov Baer of Mezritch, the eighteenth-century Hasidic leader and successor to the movement's founder, the Ba'al Shem Tov. R. Dov Baer acknowledged that when he became a disciple of the Ba'al Shem Tov, the latter taught him *The Fountain of Wisdom* and explained each and every word to him. This was the only text to which they devoted such attention.[64] Surprisingly, it has received only passing attention by modern scholars.[65]

The Fountain of Wisdom is an extremely challenging work. It is one of the most ingenious attempts to characterize the process of cosmogony, namely, how the universe came into being. Undoubtedly, anyone interested in modern theories of cosmological astronomy will find the discussions of droplets of vapor quite intriguing.

Although this text has been printed in several editions, Scholem is essentially correct in his observation that "the printed editions are extremely corrupt, such that this significant book has become totally unintelligible in them."[66] To be sure, it has also been preserved in some thirty manuscripts. Of those that I have examined, none can stand on its own–all exhibit terminological inconsistencies. Accordingly, a systematic study of all of the witnesses is a desideratum, and only after a critical edition has been prepared could any definitive

---

Metatron acquired an additional letter (i.e., *yod*) in his name, and *R. Nehuniah b. ha-Kanah's Prayer of Unity,* wherein Metatron is equated with *malkhut* (Sovereignty). An interesting discourse from this period, although not from the "Circle" per se, on the creation of Metatron is found in Florence 2:41, f. 196a and 196b.

63. Moses Cordovero, *'Or Ne'erav,* 3:3, 24.

64. Dov Baer of Mezritch, *Maggid Devarav le-Ya'akov* R. Schatz-Uffenheimer ed. (Jerusalem 1976), 2.

65. See G. Scholem, "Name of God," *Diogenes* 80 (1972), 170f, and *Origins,* 321; J. Dan, *Ḥugei,* 43ff.

66. G. Scholem, *Reshit,* 256.

analysis emerge. For the time being, the following eclectic translation, based upon printed editions and a number of manuscripts, must suffice.[67]

This book is *The Fountain of Wisdom* that Michael gave to Pe'eli[68] and Pe'eli to Moses. Moses revealed it for the enlightenment of [subsequent] generations. When David understood the nature of its knowledge he exclaimed, "I shall acknowledge my gratitude to You, Lord, with all my heart. I shall honor Your Name forever" (Ps. 86:12).

These are the *tikkun*,[69] combination, utterance, sum, and computation of the explication of the Ineffable Name–unique in the branches of the root of vocalization[70] that is magnified in the thirteen types of transformation.[71]

---

67. The printed editions of *Ma'yan ha-Hokhmah* that were consulted include Warsaw (1863) and Israel (1968), which is a reprint of Warsaw (1886); the mss. include: Florence 2:15, f. 1a-5b; Florence 2:18/5 f. 83a-85b; Parma 86/13; Zurich 177/11; Jerusalem 8° 330 f. 204-207; Leghorn 3; J.T.S. 1822/1. A recent translation of the middle third of the text, based upon Jerusalem 8° 330, is found in *Early Kabbalah*, J. Dan ed., 49-53.

68. The vocalization of this angelic name is unclear; nevertheless, it is obvious that it echoes the biblical narrative concerning the birth of Samson. "And the angel of the Lord said to him, 'Why do you ask about my name for it is wondrous (*pel'i*),'" (Judges 13:18). The motif of an angel transmitting Divine secrets to Moses is ancient. For example, in the intertestamental *Book of Jubilees*, the Angel of the Divine Presence dictated the Pentateuch to Moses, *The Old Testament Pseudepigrapha*, J. Charlesworth ed. (Garden City 1985), 2:54.

69. The term *tikkun* is pivotal in this text. Although this word usually indicates "restoration" or "embellishment," in *Fountain* it refers to an analytical process: uncovering the fundamental elements of the object of the inquiry. Perhaps it should be rendered as "analysis" or "code." Tom Sibley, a colleague in mathematics, has suggested "algorithm." Its connection with the rabbinic term *takkanah*, "regulation" is germane; see also the extended discussion below, p. 160-162.

70. *Tenu'ah* connotes any kind of movement. While occasionally herein this term is used in this broad sense, most often the specific connotation of vocalization is implied.

71. Although the thirteen transformations (*temurot*) are not explicitly identified, it is possible that what is intended is simply the interplay between the terms: *tikkun*, combination, utterance, sum, and computation, for when one

How is the *tikkun* [accomplished]? It derives the word through the utterance and the utterance through the word; the *tikkun* through the combination and the combination through the *tikkun*; the sum through the computation and the computation through the sum–until all the words are positioned in the font of the flame and the flame in the font–until there is no measuring or quantifying the light that is hidden in the superabundance of the secret darkness. Then everything is brought forth through the concluding operation, by means of the thirteen types of transformation. The transformations are attributes and the attributes are transformations. All are grasping one another, one on top of the other, and spreading outwards through the vocalizations–and the vocalizations through the additions and the additions through the deficiencies and the deficiencies through the extremities and the extremities through the excesses and the excesses through the abundances and the abundances are upon the *'alef*, (i.e., the first letter of the Hebrew alphabet).

Now we shall investigate those secret matters that are revealed and hidden like *'aDoNaY* (Lord). The *'alef* is divided into five heads. How so? When you open your mouth to say "ah," behold two vocalizations [result]. These two vocalizations are two letters *'a, 'a*. And if you pronounce *'a, 'a*, they divide into four: *'a 'a 'a 'a*. If you place two at the start and two at the end, you will discover that there is some ether between them. You are unable to assert that this ether is not an *'alef*, nor is it less than this. Accordingly, there are five: *'a 'a 'a 'a 'a*. Since an *'alef* is never less than two, when you calculate them, (i.e., the five *'alefim*), you will discover that they are ten, corresponding to *yod*, (i.e., the tenth letter). The computation of *yod* is twenty,[72] which becomes forty, and the forty are eighty, and the eighty are 160–by means of the doubling property.

Let us now return it back to the root of the *yod* (i.e., ten). How so? When you calculate this 160 by decades, you will discover that

---

adds up the number of times that these terms appear in this passage, the sum is thirteen. These processes resemble and may have been modeled after the five operations performed on letters, which are listed in *Sefer Yeẓirah*, 2:2.

72. This reflects the binary nature of vocalized letters. Interestingly, the numerical value of the constituent Hebrew letters of *yod* is also 20, (10 + 6 + 4). It should also be pointed out that the sequence of doubling decades, i.e., 10, 20, 40, 80, and 160, has five elements, thereby paralleling the five *'alefim*.

there are sixteen decades. Remove two from each decade[73] and you discover them to total thirty-two. If you double these, you will discover them to be sixty-four. Adding the four *'alefim*, with their doubles yields seventy-two, which corresponds to the seventy-two Names[74] of the Holy One, blessed be He. These are the essence of everything. They are positioned on the crown. By them He opens and closes, sends and confines, whatever is pleasing in the eyes of the Creator. When you remove them, there will remain an *'alef*, which is the *'alef* that is pivotal amongst them.

Now I shall return to the first principle, which is prior to its vocalization. From it the individual flames spread out. They are distant from the vocalizations in order to clarify the matter. [Be careful] if you must approach the flames, which are seven times stronger than strong, hotter than hot, and fierier than fire. They all grasp the wings of the *yod*. The *yod* is the transformation. The transformation is the vocalization. The vocalization is the combination. The combination is the fashioning. The fashioning is the utterance.

[Continue] until you investigate, consider, seek out, reconcile, and establish the four Names dependent upon the *yod*. This constitutes the explanation of the four Names dependent upon the *yod*. These are the four letters that are like a coal connected to a flame, and the flame divides into four heads. All refer to one subject. Accordingly, this *yod* is a gushing fountain and its waters spread out into twenty-four parts. Each part has four roots. Each of the roots has four branches. Each branch has four vocalizations. The vocalizations split into an indeterminate [number], until they return again to the fountain from whence they ushered forth. Similarly, [this applies to] these four Names of which we spoke. There are four of these Names. The first is *'eHYeH*; the second is *YHVH*; the third is *'aDoNaY*; the fourth is *YeYa'eY*.

Know, understand, investigate, consider, comprehend, and juxtapose one thing against another and consider the analogies, until you fathom the explanation of these matters. For all wisdom and understanding, all comprehension and thought, inquiry, knowledge, vocalization, reflection, speech, whispering, voice, action, guarding, and undertaking–all are found in this Name. When you want to compre-

---

73. Perhaps this is intended to correspond to the two ethers, present in each decade.

74. Some manuscripts state seventy Names. While this corresponds to the ancient tradition as noted above, p. 45, its mathematics is nonetheless problematic.

hend and become enlightened about these four letters, calculate them using the 231 gates.[75] From them you will ascend to activity, from activity to experience, from experience to visualization, from visualization to inquiry, from inquiry to knowledge, from knowledge to ascension and from ascension to certainty–until you fathom the explanation of each and every thing and are enlightened in the seventy languages. Then you will understand the words of man, the speech of domesticated animals, the chirping of birds, the utterances of wild animals, and the barking of dogs; [all of] which are accessible for the wise to know.[76.] From thence you will become enlightened in the highest of the levels: namely, comprehending the conversations of palm trees, the vocalizations of the seas, and the perfection of hearts and innermost thoughts. Finally, you will attain complete clarity and tranquility, in order to consider the thought of the Supreme One, who dwells in the Ether; there is no level higher than this.

Not all can contemplate this entity. This inquiry is limitless. Concerning it Job remarked wisely, "You shall discover God through inquiry" (Job 11:7). This refers to the examination of the vocalization, which is fundamental to a thing and which is derived from the source of the utterance. It expands into the fourfold division. Concerning this we were compelled to state that it is fourfold. We derived a measure from a weight, a weight from a square, a square from a handbreadth, a handbreadth from a span, a span from a palm–all from the circle. Moreover, the circle we derived from the *'alef* and the *'alef* from the *yod*.

The *yod* is the fountain. Its roots are rooted and its streams are connected and the droplets are based in the *tikkun* of the circle. The circle surrounds that which encompasses, thereby encircling that which stands, causing it to stand, thence to inquire, to be still, and finally to shout. As the shout issues forth, it gives birth, springs forth, and expands. This expansion strengthens and radiates. This is the Primal Ether. In it all the general principles return to details and the details to principles. All are included within the *yod*. They all ring out and return and shout. In their return they become a circle. In their circle they are heated and flow like molten silver that is heated by fire–until all are joined, one with the other, like a piece of silver

---

75. Other manuscripts read "236 gates." Presumably, this is an allusion to the 231 pairs of letter combinations that are referred to in *Sefer Yeẓirah*, 2:4.

76. The knowledge of the language of animals and so on was traditionally attributed to classical rabbinic sages, such as Hillel in *Masekhet Sofrim*, 16:9, and his successor, R. Yohanan b. Zakkai, in *B. Sukkah*, 28a.

that is refined and soldered, this to that, through being heated by fire. The pieces are joined, piece to piece, until they return as one.

This is what we have said concerning the vocalization. When a man opens his mouth to say '*a*, it becomes two parts: Voice and Breath. The vocalization is the Voice, since it is produced by means of the pronunciation. It corresponds to the [first] '*a*. Moreover, the Breath is the Ether, corresponding to the second '*a*. Hence, there are two: '*a*, '*a* (i.e., '*alefim*). The two together are called Speech due to the ether that comes from both of them. This is [the meaning of the expression] "Voice, Breath, and Speech."[77] Similarly, the second '*alef* is also "Voice, Breath, and Speech." The third '*alef* is likewise "Voice, Breath, and Speech." The fourth '*alef* is likewise "Voice, Breath, and Speech." For we have already noted that two vocalizations produce four '*alefim*, four times; you will discover four words: word, word, word, word. Take these four words that correspond to the ether between the '*alefim*, which divides into four, and return them to twos–in order to include two words in one. This results in the extra '*alef*.

These are the five '*alefim*. The four are the powers that strengthen and intensify and are transformed in the building of the body. The remaining '*alef* is the master of them all. It is the unique master. From it issues forth the sparks, which radiate in the green flames. They divide into several colors. Each color is indicative of its nature and informs anyone who gazes upon them, how he should gaze and in what way he should inquire and comprehend it; in what manner he should comprehend the visual representation, in order to investigate, analyze, and become enlightened.

How does each and every vocalization become equated, divided, adhering, dispersed, collected, whitened, and mixed[78]–emanating in numerous hidden crowns that are crowned and adorned? They are indicative of allotted matters: all are successive, hidden, obscure, and revealed. All return to one source and one matter, until all branches of the flame return–two as one. The one corresponds to thirteen and the thirteen to one. This is like the calculation of ten. How so? The '*a* is two, as we said. The five '*a*, '*a*, '*a*, '*a*, '*a* all double, yielding ten. If you divide these ten into three groups, one will remain. This one is the '*alef*. Moreover, the numeri-

---

77. *Sefer Yeẓirah*, 1:9.

78. There are numerous variant readings for this particular word–none of them satisfactory.

cal value of [the word] *'ehad* (one) is thirteen.[79] This is the *'a.*

Now I will explain fully how the *'alef* totals four. When you multiply four by four, this yields sixteen. Subtract the *'alef,* which actually represents two, and fourteen are left. Subtract from them the ether that emanates from both of them and is considered [in conjunction] with this one *'alef*–hence, three are being subtracted from sixteen. When you subtract three from sixteen, thirteen remain, corresponding to the thirteen attributes.[80] Each of these thirteen attributes refers to its own particular aspect. Each one is according to the properties of its place, enumeration, number, principle, utterance, and counting, as well as the conduits of the fountains and the scepters of the well-springs.

Now observe and focus your heart on the first attribute, which is long, firmly established and straight–just like a scepter. Concerning these matters, all of these attributes are called flames, and the flames are scepters, and the scepters are well-springs. Each wellspring divides into seven aspects. Each aspect becomes a source; each source becomes a structure. The structure freezes and the congealing becomes a coal. Within this coal all the well-springs grasp. Concerning this, it is stated, "flames attached to a coal."[81] From the flames emanate the ether. The ether is the essence, which is indicative of the structure, deed, *tikkun,* weight, calculation, utterance, and composition. The root-principle is the essence of everything.

Now we must reconcile, understand, contemplate, and consider the investigations of our hearts, thoughts and meditations, with the sight of our eyes, the movement of our spirit, the whispering of our tongue, and the utterance of our lips–until we can comprehend with absolute certainty the knowledge of all of these matters. We shall begin with the first subject, since it is the head of all beginnings, and the goal of all *tikkun.* It will instruct us about the good path.

Know that the Holy One, blessed be He, was the first existent being. Only that which generates itself is called an existent being.

---

79. ' = 1, ḥ = 8, and d = 4; hence, 13.

80. The rabbinic expression "thirteen attributes" refers to the thirteen attributes of Divine mercy, derived from Exod. 34:6 and 7; cf. *B. Rosh ha-Shanah*, 17b.

81. *Sefer Yezirah,* 1:7.

Since He generated Himself, we can comprehend and conduct an investigation into His existence. How did it (i.e., God's manifestation) begin? By what way did it proceed or stand? By which path was it? Was it one lane or many lanes or numerous divisions, or by which modes did it proceed? What was it? That is to say, [was it] either a road, lane, or path?–for the paths are narrow and short, the lanes are bigger, and the roads are wider still. The paths are like children, the lanes are like mothers, and the roads are engraved in the [primal] image of male and female. Accordingly, they dispersed and became whitened through marvellous marvels and the marvels from wonders, and from the wonders were flames and from the flames threads were drawn out and issued forth. Then the threads became thick and their thickening continued until they became scepters.

This is the root-principle that everything turns backwards and proceeds to dissolve until it returns to ether, as it once was. The Ether is the root-principle. Prior to the creation of the supernal heavens, which are called the 370 quarters[82] that constitute the dwelling-place of the Holy One, blessed be He; prior to the fashioning of 'arafel, ḥashmal, Curtain, Throne, Angel, Seraph, 'ofan, Living Creature, Star,[83] Constellation, Quadrangle that is squared, and from which issued forth the waters; prior to the creation of the waters, lakes, fountains, reservoirs, rivers, streams; prior to the creation of the wild and domesticated animals, birds, fish, reptiles, insects, Adam, shades, demons, night spirits, ghosts, and types of ether; prior [to all of the above] there was the Ether, which is the root-principle. From it emerged a light, more refined than a thousand thousands thousands and ten thousand myriads of varieties of light. This is the Primal Ether. It is the root-principle. Accordingly, it is called the Holy Spirit.

---

82. Some manuscripts read 377, whereas the printed editions read 390. Joseph Dan offers the reading 377. He notes that 390 corresponds to the numerical value of *shamayim* (Heavens) and that 377 can be derived by subtracting the thirteen attributes from 390, *Early Kabbalah*, 53, n. 2. If, in fact, 370 is correct, perhaps this alludes to the constellation *'ash*, referred to in Job 9:9, whose letters correspond to 370; see below, p. 78, for a discussion of *ḥashmal* = 378 in *Contemplation-Long*.

83. Some manuscripts read instead "cherub." This list is significant owing to its similarity to the hierarchy of powers that are characteristic of *The Book of Contemplation*. Assuming that the author of *Fountain* had in fact read *Contemplation*, this would obviously provide a *terminus a quo* for the dating of *Fountain*.

Know and comprehend that prior to all of these things that we have mentioned above there was only this Ether, as we have already stated. It was obscured by two things, pertaining to two sources. From the first flowed an undefinable light, infinite and immeasurable. The flow was rapid like sparks that are produced simultaneously and disperse into many directions when the blacksmith wields his hammer. Afterwards one spring was emanated from which emanated darkness. This darkness was mixed with three colors. The first was dark like the morning star that is greenish. The second was a mixture of green and blue, and the third was darkened white mixed with green, blue, and red.

This corresponds to the Primal Darkness that ushered forth from the Ether. Do not hasten to investigate or contemplate it, for even Moses, our Rabbi, of blessed memory, was not allowed to ask questions about it. Thus even a question, and how much more so an investigation [is prohibited]. All that [Moses] said, he only said in order not to distort the knowledge of the image of the Holy One, blessed be He, in his heart. When this knowledge was properly secure [in his mind], that is to say, when this matter was clarified in his heart and he knew with proper knowledge, and it was focused in his mind–even though he was not allowed to investigate and gaze on such a supernal state or to inquire about it–when he perceived its foundation with complete concentration and the image of the knowledge of the Holy One, blessed be He, did not distort in his heart, he was happy.

Then he asked his pointed question, as is stated, "Please, inform me of Your ways" (Exod. 33:18). The Holy One, blessed be He, responded to him concerning this matter, "You cannot see My Face" (Exod. 33:20): that is to say, the knowledge of this Darkness that you are requesting, for it was all of Me and My source. You are unable to clearly fathom an examination of it. Concerning this it is stated, "And You will see My Back, but My Face will not be seen" (Exod. 33:23). This has been translated [into Aramaic] "You shall see my end, but my beginning shall not be seen."[84] That is to say, what preceded Me, you will be unable to perceive–lest you might say about Me that I am like the other unique entities; [for] you might say that so-and-so derived from this source, and this source derived from this other source. Accordingly, you will not possess knowledge of this Darkness that is the focal point of My existence. However, from here on you shall know everything. That is to say, from this Darkness and

---

84. Onkelos, ad loc.; cf. Maimonides, *Guide* 1:21.

what is below it you shall know [all], even the creation of My essence
and the essence of My Name and My Glory.

At that time, Moses began to gaze upon the Primal Ether, which
is the root-principle, as we have already stated, and discovered that
it is obscured by two things, pertaining to two sources. From the first
flows light and from the second, darkness. These outpourings are
drawn by channels and streams. The stream is transformed into
something resembling a pipe and the pipe is transformed into something exceedingly thin, like a thread. Through this thinness it is
directed and pulled until it ejects very small droplets. These droplets
then intensify and become conglomerates. The conglomerates con-
tinue to enlarge until they are drawn and emerge with great strength.
They draw close and mix with each other. They spread out and join
together, until moisture emerges from them. This moisture pours out
and is drawn and then solidifies. The solidification radiates, becomes
whitened and clarified, until the original conglomerates that we mentioned have been disseminated. From them emerges a kind of foam,
floating on the surface of the water. All of this becomes moisture.

From this moisture emerges wind/spirit. It is the Holy Spirit.
Concerning this there is the allusion, "And the spirit of God hovered
upon the surface of the water" (Gen. 1:2). That is to say, the spirit
strengthens in holiness and becomes numerous sharp points. Each
sharp point becomes a branch. Each branch becomes a root unto
itself. From each of them emerges several powers, matters, and
things. Behold the explanation and analogy in order that you will
understand and know that the Holy Spirit is the wind/spirit that
emerges from the moisture which has been drawn out of the outpourings. From one of them flows light and from the second, darkness.
And the foam that remains is white, colored with red, for the red is
fixed in the white and white in the red. Thus these things collect and
adhere immeasurably one to the other, until they become exceedingly
thin.

These two sources from whence flowed the outpourings are one
thing that stems from the Primal Darkness. This teaches about form,
creation and differentiation of form. The created entity, which is separate and different from the image of her counterparts, is in the shape
of something straight that has been bent. She is in the middle and
encompasses and is positioned at the head. She suckles power for all
of them and is sustained with all of them. All are drawn out and
emerge from her. She has no image or difference except the appearance of white and red. Therefore, she became two parts and from the
parts stemmed the sources. From one source flows light which is
divided into two colors. They are those that we have already men-

tioned, the color of white and red. From the second source flows the darkness. It is a mixture of three colors: green, blue, and white. Behold there are five colors for the two sources that are transformed and change their colors as they are emanated. For when they existed potentially within the Primal Darkness there were only two colors, like the rest of the darkness, but when their colors were emanated, they were transformed into many colors that are included in the five colors that we mentioned above.

These five colors constitute the flame that emerges from the Ether. They divide in their movement. For we have previously stated that the two outpourings are one thing which stems from the Primal Darkness. It teaches about form and creation. This form, when it is transformed, is portrayed in numerous hues and colors. There are ten hues. There are also ten individual colors. This results in one hundred. The one hundred turn backwards in the utterance and computation, and sum of the word in the word, and the computation in the computation, and the utterance in the utterance, until it returns to the computation of the *'a* (=1). The *'a* is the root-principle.

These ten colors flow from the darkness. They are the following: light from light, radiance from radiance, lustre from lustre, radiance from light, light from radiance, lustre from light, light from lustre, lustre from radiance, radiance from lustre, and flaming fire from flaming fire. Behold, there are ten. The first is Marvellous Light; this is light from light. The second is Hidden Light; this is radiance from radiance. The third is Sparkling Light; this is lustre from lustre. The fourth is Bright Light; this is radiance from light. The fifth is Brightened Light; this is light from radiance. The sixth is Illuminating Light; this is lustre from light. The seventh is Refined Light; this is light from lustre. The eighth is Bright and Brightened Light; this is lustre from radiance. The ninth is Clear Light; this is radiance from lustre. The tenth is Splendorous Light; this is flaming fire from flaming fire.

Now we shall return to explain each light, lustre, and radiance that is in them–according to this pattern, in order that you should know and understand that the Primal Darkness is not included in their enumeration. From it everything emerges and from it emerged the spring[s] that gushed forth from it. It is [also] called the Light That Is Darkened From Illuminating, for it is hidden and impossible to know the essence of the existence of this darkness. Accordingly, it is called Darkening Darkness, not because it resembles murk, but because no creature can look at it. Even the angels seated in the front row of the Kingdom of Heaven lack the power to look at it. It is like a human who lacks the power to look at the eye of the harsh sun.

Moreover, all of the lights emerge from it, and therefore, it is only called Darkening Darkness because it is exalted, hidden, and concealed from all perception by the prophets.

These are their paths according to their origins. This is the explication of the well-springs, which have already been mentioned—each and every one according to its nature. The first is the Marvellous Light, which has no color unto itself; nonetheless, it manifests the power of every color. It is like a mirror in which everything is seen, yet it possesses no color [of its own]. For the Marvellous Light receives the exchange from the Light That Is Darkened From Illuminating. It is the head of all the colors, even though it does not possess a fixed color. It is similar to sky-blue.

All are equal within it, for the Darkness That Is Darkened From Illuminating is the 'a, of which we have spoken. It is the Voice of vocalization that is called movement—for movement is the second 'a, which is called Breath. It is the Holy Spirit, that is to say, that which was prior. It was one source and it was the Voice. When it turned into two sources, the second source emerged. From it emerged the Breath. This is called the Holy Spirit. That is to say, prior it was one and afterwards it became two. The first [stage] resembled a fountain which has little water. This source continued to gush forth and increase until there flowed from this fountain a single, small[er] fountain. From these two spread forth numerous fountains—fountain after fountain—until there is an infinite number [of them]. This is what David, of blessed memory, alluded to "I was a youth and I have grown old" (Ps. 37:25). That is to say, the primal fountain, which is the Light That Is Darkened From Illuminating, was like a green fire containing all of the well-springs. When it existed in its ether, and they did not yet have any movement, it was little and unnoticed, like a child that is small and [gradually] grows up from its smallness. However, when all the well-springs flowed from it, its radiance was seen and its glory was revealed.[85] One thing emerged from another, until there emerged ten well-springs from it. These well-springs are called flames, for they are like a coil that possesses many threads. These threads grasp the flame, and the flame [grasps] the coal.

Know and comprehend! Concerning the Light That Is Darkened From Illuminating about which we speak, it is a fire that surely burns.

---

85. This phrasing is also found in *Contemplation-Short* and is of vital significance for determining the relationship between these two texts; cf. above, p. 42, and below, p. 248.

From it split and spread out and continued to increase all of the movements and vocalizations, until they return to four. These four are the four letters that constitute a fire that consumes fire. Everything is included in them. They are *'eHYeH*. Concerning the *'alef*, we have already stated that it constitutes two movements and each of these movements is transformed into two and divides into two. Furthermore, the ether which encircles that which stands is [also] counted as one. Behold there are five–*'a, 'a, 'a, 'a, 'a*. When you calculate two movements for each of them, behold there are ten, corresponding to the *yod*. This *yod* that is alluded to in the calculation of the *'alef* is the power of the *yod* of the four-letter [Name], (i.e., *'eHYeH*), and of [the Name] *'aDo[NaY]* and of the fourth Name that we mentioned above.[86] You should know that these letters constitute the head of the four Names. All of them are included in the letter *'alef*, which corresponds to ten. When you make from these ten tens, you will discover 100.

This is the *tikkun* that we began to speak about. It is necessary for the act to be regulated (*tikkun*) in order to comprehend something fully and its existence within the unity of the Holy One, blessed be He. The riddle is [contained] within the analogy; the analogy is within the goal; the goal is within the act; the act is within the *tikkun*. This is the *tikkun*, by directing your heart upon these four letters that constitute the Ineffable Name. In them is hidden a flowing stream and an overflowing fountain. They divide into several parts and run like lightning. Their light continues to increase and grow stronger.

The root-principle of all of them is *YHVH*. It has the numerical value twenty-six, corresponding to the twenty-six movements which emerged from the Primal Ether that divided into two parts–each part separate unto itself. Each part has the numerical value thirteen, corresponding to the thirteen sources that separated from *'a*. For we have already stated that the *'a* has the numerical value four insofar as the two movements within it are divided into four. When you calculate their square value in order to empower it, you will discover sixteen. Subtract from them three, which are the Voice, Breath, and Speech[87]–representing their root-principle–and the thirteen attributes remain.[88]

---

86. That is *YeYa'eY*.

87. *Sefer Yezirah*, 1:9.

88. See above, n. 80.

Direct your heart to know how the Voice emerged from the Primal Light and how the vocalization emerged from the Voice, until it became a movement. From the movement, how the Breath was drawn from it because movement itself is called Breath, and from the power of their connected fusion, how the ether emerged, which is the third power. From the combination of these three emanated the thirteen sources, which are called attributes. Each and every source is divided into two. These are twenty-six attributes having the numerical value of the four letters of the Ineffable Name, which is written in order, and this is its order *YHVH*, blessed is the name of glory of His eternal kingdom.

Now it is incumbent upon us to explain what is the Primal Ether and how the Voice emerged from it and how Breath emerged from the Voice and how the Speech emerged from both of them; moreover, how the thirteen sources emerged from them. In addition, how many sources there were before they reached the sum thirteen–whether [emerging] by themselves or by means of another power. And how each of the thirteen sources was divided into two sources, eventually yielding twenty-six attributes. And these attributes, how they were drawn out and transformed from two into one–until they returned to thirteen, and the thirteen into five and the five into three and the three into two and the two into one.

This matter will be elucidated and clarified by means of its *tikkun*. The *tikkun* about which we have spoken is the start of everything. It is the direction of the heart, intention of the thought, calculation of the viscera, purification of the heart, until the mind is settled and logic and language are formed. From language [stems] clarification, and from clarification the word is formed. From the word is the utterance and from the utterance is the deed. This is its beginning.

Know that the Primal Ether is from the Ether about which we have spoken. It is the first source. It is the fire that consumes fire. This fire possesses twenty-six well-springs, and all these well-springs are included within it. No creature can adequately know the beginning in its entirety. These well-springs vibrated and were drawn out together until they all became one well-spring. When they were joined together it became clear that there was a green well-spring. Of the two well-springs: one was green and the second was sky-blue. Then the green well-spring increased and this Ether sparkled and continued to revolve and shine until there was formed in it the image of a fissure. From this fissure there gushed forth and increased and sparkled the sky-blue well-spring. Within this sky-blue well-spring from the fissure there emerged two sources. One [emerged] from the first source which is the Primal Ether and it is the green well-spring, and the second was from the sky-blue well-spring.

The first [source] which emerged from the Light That Is Darkened From Illuminating, which is the Primal Ether, the source that emerged from it is called *ḥashmal*. When it emerged, the Ether ruptured, and from this rupture Voice issued forth. This Voice spread out and increased until it became twenty-six thousand, thousand, thousands and myriad of myriads kinds of light. From the light emerged a radiance and from the radiance a lustre and from the lustre a light and from the light a flaming fire. That is to say that the lights were giving off sparks, flashing, spreading out, and increasing in the power of the strength of their size. There was no base for them to stand and rest upon, until there issued forth a shout. This shout was the Breath that was the least of all of them, and all were included in it, and it was in the Voice. This is the Holy Spirit. Eventually twenty-six parts were formed. Two of these correspond to the lights that gushed forth from them. The name of the first source is *'aHVY*[89] and the name of the second is *HVY*. There remain twenty-four parts. These twenty-four were formed into four sections. From the first were formed ten sources, five from the second, six sources from the third, and five from the fourth.[90] From these were formed the sign which is called the Ineffable Name. It is *YHVH*. These four were divided into seventy-two letters. It is for this reason that these four letters, *YHVH*, are the Ineffable Name for they represent the root-principle of the seventy-two letters, and the root-principle of the seventy-two letters is thoroughly intertwined with them.

Know that when the seventy-two letters were created, *ḥashmal* was formed as a garment for them. It is cloaked in them and they are cloaked in it. They are all included in *ḥashmal*, and *ḥashmal* is included in all of them. *Ḥashmal* and the lights are cloaked in the letters and the letters fly within the *ḥashmal*. The lustre and the radiance are strengthening; the sparks are glittering; the Holy Spirit is superimposed; light is glittering; the radiance is shining; the brightness is radiating; the lustre is pure and the pure is sanctification.

---

89. The source of this term is the twelfth-century treatise by R. Judah ha-Levi *Kuzari*, ch. 3:3, p. 221, and 4:25, p. 266, wherein ha-Levi contends that these four letters were the basis for the Tetragrammaton. This Name was utilized by other writings of the "Circle"; see below p. 102, n. 202.

90. This division into ten, five, six, and five corresponds to the numerical value of the letters of the Tetragrammaton *YHVH*.

From the sanctification there is holiness. From the holiness there is Breath. The Breath is cloaked in holiness and the holiness in Breath. Therefore, it is called the Holy Spirit.

CONTEMPLATION–LONG

This treatise has been preserved in its entirety in a unique, seventeenth- or eighteenth-century manuscript, J.T.S. 1805, f. 52-54, which forms the basis of the ensuing transcription. The opening lines of this text, 1 through 10, are also found in a fragment of the treatise, Hebrew University 8° 266, designated in the apparatus by י. Some of the readings from this latter manuscript seem superior to our text, and it is unfortunate that the rest of this version is missing. The middle section of the treatise, lines 88 through 105, was quoted in the mid-thirteenth century kabbalistic prayer commentary, which Scholem dates as being written prior to 1260.[91] This text has been preserved in a number of manuscripts. Variants designated by א, indicate a consensual reading. ב refers to Berlin Qu. 942; פ to Florence 2:32, and ל to British Museum 751.

It is also worth noting that the "Circle's" popular *Commentary on the Book of Contemplation* constitutes an intriguing exposition on the introduction of this recension of *Contemplation*–for therein one finds phrases that are only present in this particular version.

---

91. G. Scholem, *Origins*, 345, n. 291.

CONTEMPLATION–LONG

ספר העיון זהו ספר העיון שחיבר ר׳ חמאי ראש המדברים על ענין 1
הפנימיות וגילה בו עיקר כל מציאות הכבוד אשר אין כל בריה יכולה
לעמוד על עיקר מציאותו ומהותו על דרך האמיתי כמו שהוא באחדות
השוה שבשלימותו מתאחדים עליונים ותחתונים והוא יסוד כל נעלם
וגלוי ממנו יוצאים כל הנבראים בדרך האצילות כריח מריח וכנר מנר 5
שזה מתאצל מזה וזה מזה וכח המאציל בנאצל ואין המאציל חסר כלום.
והוא כח קיום שכל הנמצאים בהשגחת המחשבה נאצלים מפליאת אחדותו
והוא מתאחד באחדות שאינו משתנה אלא ע״י הכרחתו שהוא משפיע בכל
צד כחותיו ומשפיל ומכריע בלי שינטה מאמצעות עילייו והוא יכול
להטות ולעמוד בכל בכיוון וביושר באמצע כל הכחות המסותרים 10
בפנימיותו בלי הטייה והוא כולל כל הצדדים בסתר ובגלוי מתחיל
מלמעלה ומסיים מלמטה וגומר פנים ואחור וימין ושמאל ויש לו כח
דמות וכח תמונה וכח צורה אינה ניכרת והוא מיוחד ויחודו מגולה
ומכוסה נסתר ונעלם וביאר ר׳ חמאי ז״ל ענין הפנימיות בחיבורי זה
הספר על דרך מעשה מרכבה ופי׳ נבואת יחזקאל וזהו תחלת הספר 15
ותחלת דיבורו. יתברך ויתעלה שם הנאדר בגבורה אשר הוא אחד מתאחד
באחדות השוה הקדמון מבלי תחלה והוא תחלת כל חקר הבא מאין חקר
וראש כל גבול והוא מבלי גבול אפשרי לעמוד בעצמו. אחד שהוא קודם
לכל הנבראים ולכל הקדומים הנאצלים מכחו שלא היה קדמון בלי תחלה
חוץ ממנו ית׳ וכל הכחות הנמצאים משתתים ביחודו בהשואה אחת והוא 20
מתעלה ומתעלם בסתרי הפעולות והמעשים הנעשים מכח הנעלם ומתאחד
כלהב אש מתאחד בגווניו. ואלו הפעולות המתגלים מכחו ממש הם עשרה.
א׳ אור המופלא. ב׳ חשמל. ג׳ ערפל. ד׳ כסא הנוגה. ה׳ אופן
הגדולה. ונק׳ חזחזית. ו׳ הכרוב. ז׳ גלגלי המרכבה. ח׳ האויר
הסובב. ט׳ הכח הנק׳ מטטרון. י׳ הפרגוד. שכלם נקראים כתרי כבוד 25
מגולגלין בתארי חופה שנא׳ כי על כל כבוד חופה והם פרדס אוצר
הקדושה מורות על תכונת מציאות האחד שהכל היה מאחדותו והוא מתאחד
כאחד והכל שלם כאחד והכל שכל אחד וכל יצור כאחד וכל דיבור כאחד
וכל שם כאחד וכל חק כאחד וכל מקום כאחד ויסוד הכל רצון אחד שהוא
אור המופלא אשר שם לו דרך אחד אחד להשוות בינינו בכל אחד ואחד ואם 30
ישתנה אחד מאחד הכל הולך אל מקום א׳ שהוא מקום האחדות השוה
שקודם שברא הקב״ה שום כח מאלו הכחות לא היה כחו ניכר עד שנראה
אינו ישנו. ובממשות החכמה הקדומה הנקראת אמונה ותעלומה שנמצאת
מאין חקר בכח היחוד השוה דכתיב והחכמה מאין תמצא מעל על כל נעלם 35
תמצא שהוא הנעלם בתעלומות חכמה דכתי׳ ויגד לך תעלומות חכמה מאין
תמצא ממיעוט תמצא שהוא מניעות הצד העליון שבאחדות השוה וזה הצד

---

1 זהו: זה י   3 דרך: הדרך י / כמו: כמות י   5 ממנו: וממנו י / האצילות: אצילות י
/ כריח: בריח י   7 בהשגחת: בהשגת י   8 שאינו: שאינה י / הכרחתו: הכרעתו י
שהוא: כי הוא י   9 ומשפיל: למשפיע י   10 להטות (עצמו) י

נקרא אומן פי' אב האמונה שמכחו האמונה נאצלת וזו האמונה הוא
תחלת האחדות שהיחוד מתפשט בו בכח מופלא שהוא שוה מכל צדדיו סופו
בתחלתו ותחלתו בסופו ואמצעיתו בראשו ובסופו להודיע כחו שמעמיד
בו את כל הנבראים בכח קיום ובשרשי אמונה וסובל כל יסודי עולם   40
ומדותי' כמנהג דרכי אמונה ונושא את כל הנמצאים ומנהיגם בכח
מושכל כגבור שנושא קמיע בזרועו והוא רחוק מהשגת שכל ומתנשא בסתר
הקדושה העליונה שהיא החכמה הנקראת אמונה ומתנהג באמת וביושר ועל
זה נקרא אל אמונה ומהותו הוא אור מזוקק חיים באור כתר טוב ומוחתם
בזיו שפרירו כלול מזיו זוהר ומצוחצח שאינו מושג כלום בהיר כדמות   45
צורת נשמה שאין בה שום השגה כלל והוא סיבה ופלא מפליא פליאות
שהם בסתרי הפעולות הנסתרות הנקראות עצות שמהם תצא סיבה לסבב כל
סיבה בסתר ובגלוי והם עשרה כחות הנסתרים שהם הנאצלים מצד העליון
הנעלם עד מאד ואינו גלוי ולכך נאמר אי"ן שזה האחדות אינו נמצא
ואינו גלוי כי מאין תמצא ר"ל מפליאת האחדות הדבוק בצד העליון   50
שאם תרצה להשיגו לא תשיגנו אם כן תשלול ממנו כל המושג וכל הגלוי
שאם ישאלך אדם כיצד הוא דבר זה שתאמר לו כן מאחדות אם כן יש לנו
לומר שזו החכמה הנמצאת מן האחדות הנסתר והנמנע מהשגה ולא בדרך
המציאות המושג לפי שהקב"ה ית' הוא חיי זו החכמה ועצמה וממנה
האציל כל העשרה כחות בדרך אצילות כיצד בתחלת ברא הקב"ה אור   55
המופלא ובשעה שנבראו עמו כמה מיני זוהר מן הכחות האחדות
והיו מתגברים ומתנועעים והאור המופלא היה דבוק בצד החכמה הנקראת
תעלומה ולא היה רשאי להיות מזהיר עד שחידש הקב"ה כל המאורות
הנמשכים מפני חוזק הכחות ומהם היה אור המופלא מתגבר בצחצוח
ומאיר זהו שנאמר מבכי נהרות חבש ותעלומה יוציא אור נהרות   60
נקראים שרשי המאורות החזקים הנקראים זוהרי ההוד ותעלומה היא
החכמה הקדומה יוציא אור שבשעה שבראו הקב"ה פרשו כסוכה שנא' אף
אם יבין מפרשי עב תשואות סוכתו מפרשי הוא האור המתנוצץ מהאור
המופלא שהוא פרוש בכח היחוד כבגד וצחצוח מתגבר ומאיר על היחוד
הנסתר בכח מופלא ע"כ הוא האור המופלא ממש שמרוב זהרו שהוא מזהיר   65
ומצתחצח נחשך מהאיר מפני מראית העין כעין השמש החזק שאין אדם
יכול להסתכל בממשות צחצוחו ואם יסתכל אדם בו נחשכו גלגלי עינו
ואינו רשאי לפותחם מרוב הצחצוח שמתגבר ומאיר כך הקב"ה החשיך זה
אור מופלא מהשגת כל נברא ולא נתן רשות לשום נברא בעולם להשיג
אמיתתו כמות שהוא ומיד כשבראו קראו אורפניאל מפני שמורה על   70
הקב"ה שהוא יחיד שנא' נוטה שמים לבדו ומתיחד בעצם האור המופלא
שהוא כח הנסתר ועל זה נאמר ותמונת ה' יביט פי' אמיתת מציאותו
שהוא משיג בעין שכלו ועוד מורה על הקב"ה שהוא מיוחד בכח דמיון
ואינו שוה לאחד שנא' ואל מי תדמיוני ואשוה יאמר קדוש שהוא קדוש
בכל מיני קדושות ומתקדש בכח קיום ועוד מורה על עשר ספירות בלימה   75
שכלם נאצלים מכח אור המופלא וצריך למעיין שימנה יסוד התולדות
שהוא באחדות השוה הנסתר ולא יאמר הואיל שאין למנות יסוד התולדות
לא אמנה יסודו שהכל אחד ואמנה עשר ספירות לפי שהם סוף למעשה
העליונים ותחלה ליסוד התחתונים ומקום התולדות הוא הצד העליון

הדבוק באחדות השוה והם דבר אחד ולכך אין למנותו באחד עשר שאין 80
אחד עשר סוף אלא תחלה למעשה התחתונים ולכך נאמר עשר ולא תשע עשר
ספירות מלשון מספר ומלשון ספיר כלומר גזרת מספר זה והם שהנביא
רואה מתוכם שהוא צופה לכך אמר עשר ולא תשעה ולא יאמר המעיין
לא אמנה עשרה לפי שאין מראה זו אלא כדי להראות דבר מוגבל ולכך

אמנה תשע שלא העמיד דבר לעולם מעשרה שמא יאמר המעיין הואיל ואמנה 85
עשרה אמנה אותה הגדולה הנראית מתוך היוד והם אחד עשר אין למנות
כן. ואלו הן עשר ספירות בלימה הנאצלים מהאור המופלא האי ת הבי תש
הגי תפ הדי כה ההי חפת הוי דת הזי אש החי ע הטי חמ הי פח התי
היא הספירה העליונה שאין אדם יכול לחקור עליה מפני שאין לה גבול

והיא כח מושכל שנעשית מלאך עומד על החשמל והוא המלאך הנקרא 90
ערפיאל שהוא מיוחד מכל זה האור המופלא והוא תמונה מסותרת מדה
שיש בה פרצוף פנים ופתיחת פה ולשון לדבר וללמד כאדם והוא רצון
שוה ממציא כל הנבראים נקרא תאוה וזהו ונפשו אותה וזהו ויעש ופי' נפשו
רצונו כמו אם יש את נפשכם וזהו הרצון נתרצה שיתברר מן החשמל

רוח וזהו אל אשר יהיה שמה הרוח ללכת ילכו וזהו שנא' בס' יצירה 95
אחת רוח אלהים חיים וזהו הרוח שנחלק לשני חלקים קול ורוח הכל
היה מתגבר מצחצוח המאורות הנמשכים מהשחשמל והרוח היה מתגבר בכח
המנהיג שהוא ערפיאל ומפני שאינו ניכר תמונתו נקרא תי וזהו שנא'
יעמוד ולא אכיר מראהו תמונה לנגד עיני יעמוד ולא אכיר מראהו נאמר

על ערפיאל העומד למעלה מחשמל כנגד האור המופלא שאינו ניכר ממשותו 100
תמונה לנגד עיני שהוא מדה שדומה בה פרצוף פנים כאדם ועליו
נאמר כמראה אדם עליו מלמעלה דממה וקול אשמע שבשעה שערפיאל מתיחד
למעלה כנגד האור המופלא כל כחות החשמל מתגלגלים ומתנועעים בצווה
גדול וזהו הדיבור שנברא מעצמו ועל זה אמרו רז"ל פעמים חשות

פעמים ממללות בחוזק המתצחצחים מן החשמל בכח אורפניאל ועל האור 105
המופלא שהוא נסתר נאמר ועתה לא ראו אור זה האור המופלא שהוא
נסתר מהשגת ראיית העין בהיר הוא בשחקים שהוא מתפשט בכל כחות
הרוחניים ורוח עברה ותטהרם זהו הכרוב הנקרא רוח מטהר הכחות כמו
שאנו עתיד לפרש ועל זה אור מופלא עב מאי תשואות סוכתו הם זהרי

אור המופלא שהם מתצחצחים בכח האור הבהיר הנסתר בפנימיותו. ובשעה 110
שעלה בדעתו של הקב"ה להמציא הנאצלים מכחו נתעטף באור המופלא
שנא' עוטה אור כשלמה מיד נוטה שמים כיריעה וכל זה כדי לגלות
השואתו שהוא שוה בכל צד ומעלה ומטה ופנים ואחור שהם בסתר ובגלוי

---

89 העליונה: הראשונה א/עליה: בממשותה ב פ   90 עומד: ועומד א
91 ערפיאל: ענפיאל ב פ/זה: זהורי א   93 נקרא: ונקרא א/ופי': פי' א
94 נתרצה: ותרצה א   95 רוח (ו)אברא) א/ילכו (ותרגם יונתן רעוה) א
96 הכל: הקול א   98 ערפיאל: ענפיאל א   100 ערפיאל: ענפיאל א/למעלה
מחשמל: ממעל לחשמל א   102 ערפיאל: ענפיאל א   103 החשמל (חשות
ומתנועעים בלי קול ובשפה שהוא מתיחד בחשמל עצמו כל כחות) א   104 בצווח
(קול) ב ל/(הדיבור) א   105 בחוזק (המאורות) א

והוא מודיע כל הנסתר וכל הגלוי והוא מורה על יחודו שהוא ראש

115 וסיבה לשאר הסיבות בין סיבות שיש בהן ממשות בין סבות שאין בהם
ממשות ובשעה שעלה בדעתו של הקב"ה להכין חניית דגלי מעלה פרש עלי
יחודו האור המופלא וזהו שנא' פרשו עליו עננו ומיד המציא כל
הנבראים הנאצלים מכחו של האור המופלא אור צח בגוון ירוק מצוחצח
שהוא מתצחצח בכל מיני זיו וזוהר וזיו חזק והבהיק הקב"ה אותו אור

120 בזיו צחצח טהור שהוא מתגבר ונודע בטוהר האורה המופלא והיה נמשך
אותו האור מפנימיותו כמו אור העין היוצא מתוך שחרות העין שממנו
האור מתנוצץ וזהו האור הנודע בגוון ירוק מצוחצח הוא הנקרא חשמל
ובשעה שנברא היה מתגבר באור צח וזך ומבהיר בדחיפת האור המופלא
שהוא קבוע ביחוד והיה חוזר חופה בהקדמה וביחוד בכל צדי האור

125 המופלא בשינוי ותמורה והוא מצוי בדבר והפכו כמפתח שהוא פותח
וסוגר וממשות החשמל הוא כמין פלס צורה בלא פרצוף פנים שיש בו כח
לבנות ולסתור להרבות ולהמעיט ויש בו שינוי עצם ושינוי מקום בכל
מיני תמורה מימין לאמצע ומאמצע לשמאל ומאמצע לימין בכל מיני
חילוף והוא מתגבר בכל הכחות הרוחניות ונקרא זיו שכינה ומאורותיו

130 מתרבים ונמשכים כפי חשבונותיו והם שלש מאות ושבעים ושמנה והם
מתנועעים ויוצאים ממנו בצחצוח זיו זוהר גדול מתצחצח בכמה מיני
מאורות ובכל אור מתגבר הצחצוח בחוזק והם כניצוצים היוצאים מן
הגחלת שממנה מתרבה השלהבת והפחות שבכל המאורות כזיו גלגל חמה
מתפשט בכל ימות השנה ועולה ויורדת בשש מאות ושש מעלות למעלה

135 מהכפה מהמזרח למערב וכלפי רום כאשר הוא מפורש בספר המדה והכל
מתגלגל ומתפשט מכחו של חשמל וסימנו חית החכמה הקדומה שין שלום
רמז לעושה שלום במרומיו מם ממשלה רמז להמשיל למד לבוש הדר וזהו
שנא' ה' אלהי גדלת מאד הוד והדר לבשת. תם.

The Book of Contemplation. This is *The Book of Contemplation* that Rabbi Hammai, the principal spokesman, composed on the topic of the Innermost. In it he revealed the essence of the entire existence of the Glory. No creature can truly comprehend the essence of His existence and His nature, since He is in a state of balanced unity, for in His completeness the higher and lower beings are united. He is the foundation of everything that is hidden and revealed. From Him issue forth all created beings,[92] by the process of emanation, like a scent from a scent, or a candle-flame from a candle-flame, since this emanates from that and that from something else, and the power of the emanator is within that which was emanated. The emanator, however, does not lack anything.[93]

He is the sustaining power; for all that is extant, under the providence of thought, is emanated from the wondrousness of His Unity. He is unified in the Unity, which does not change, except through His determination. He influences his powers on every side[94] and brings down and balances without deviating from the middle of His supremacy. He is able to incline and stand upon all of them precisely and exactly in the middle of all the hidden powers in His Innerness, without deviating. He comprises all sides, hidden and revealed. He begins above and ends below, and concludes before and behind, and right and left. He possesses the power of shape and the power of image and the power of form, which is not perceived. He is unique and His Unity is revealed and covered, hidden and secret.

R. Hammai, of blessed memory, explicated the topic of the Innermost in the composition of this treatise, according to the account of the Chariot[95] and the explanation of Ezekiel's prophecy. This is the beginning of the treatise and the start of his pronouncement.

Blessed and exalted is the Name which is majestic in valor, for He is One, being unified in the balanced unity. He is primordial, without any beginning, and He is the beginning of all that can be scrutinized, stemming from inscrutability. He is the start of all boundaries and He is without boundary. He is able to exist by Him-

---

92. Until this point the treatise is the same as *Contemplation–Short.*

93. See *Contemplation–Short*, p. 41.

94. In *Contemplation–Short*, p. 43f., this description is revealed to a lower power, *ḥashmal.*

95. *Ma'aseh merkavah*, referring to Ezekiel, ch. 1, cf. *B. Ḥagigah*, 13a, and Scholem, *Kabbalah*, 11f.

self.[96] He is One, for He precedes all created beings and all the primal entities, which were emanated from His power. There is no primordial being without a beginning, except for Him, may He be blessed. All the powers that are extant are equivalent in His Unity, in one equality. He ascends and is hidden in the secrets of the actions and activities undertaken by the hidden power. He is united like a flame that is united with its colors. These actions which are revealed by His very power are ten in number:[97] (1) Marvellous Light, (2) *hashmal*, (3) *'arafel*, (4) Throne of Light, (5) Wheel of Greatness, which is called *hazhazit* (looking-glass), (6) the Cherub, (7) Wheels of the Chariot, (8) the Encompassing Ether, (9) the power that is called Metatron, (10) the Celestial Curtain.

All of them are called crowns of Glory, revolving around the borders of the bridal canopy, as is said, "For over the entire Glory is a bridal canopy" (Isa. 4:5). They are the Celestial Orchard,[98] the treasurehouse of holiness, indicating the quality of the existence of the One, for everything stemmed from His Unity. He is united as one, and everything is perfected as one, and everything is one intelligence, and every creature is as one, and every utterance is as one, and each name is as one, and each law is as one, and each place is

---

96. See *Contemplation–Short*, p. 43.

97. In *Contemplation–Long* there is an explicit statement that there are ten powers, whereas in *Contemplation–Short* it is merely implicit. Although in general *Contemplation–Long* follows the doctrines of *Contemplation–Short*, one can notice certain innovations. Foremost is the general neglect of the concept of Primordial Wisdom, the supreme power in *Contemplation–Short*, and the treatise's focus. It is conspicuously absent from *Contemplation–Long*'s listing of the powers and is only mentioned in passing later on in the treatise, based on material borrowed directly from *Contemplation–Short*. Instead, *Contemplation–Long* focuses its attention on Marvellous Light. One can only speculate as to what motivated the author of *Contemplation–Long* to minimize the importance of Primordial Wisdom. It is clear that he was heavily influenced by contemporary philosophical inquiry, as evidenced by his discussion of Divine providence. Perhaps he was also reacting to a trend among contemporary Jewish philosophers who attacked the concept of the hypostatization of Wisdom; cf. the sources listed by A. Ravitzky, "*Ha-Hypostezah shel ha-Hokhmah ha-'Elyonah*," *Italia* 3 (1982), 22, n. 73.

98. *pardes*, also connected with "paradise"; cf. B. *Hagigah*, 14b, G. Scholem, *Gnosticism*, 16f, and I. Gruenwald, *Apocalyptic and Merkavah Mysticism*, 86ff.

as one. And the basis of everything is one will[99] that is the Marvellous Light, for which He placed one path to be equal amongst us, for the sake of each individual thing. If one thing shall change from the other, everything will go to one place, which is the place of the balanced unity.

Before the Holy One, blessed be He, created any power from amongst these powers, His power was indiscernible–until something appeared from nothing, in the actuality of the Primordial Wisdom, called faith and mystery.[100] It came into being from inscrutability through the power of the balanced unicity,[101] as is written, "And wisdom, from nothingness it shall come into being" (Job 28:12).[102] Elevated above all that is hidden, "it shall come into being." It is hidden in the mysteries of wisdom, as is written, "And He told you the mysteries of wisdom" (Job 11:6). "From nothingness it shall come into being"–from diminution[103] "it shall come into being," since it constitutes the barriers of the exalted realm, within the balanced unity. This side is called *'omen,* meaning the Father of Faith, since faith was

---

99. *razon.* This is subsequently discussed in more detail. The equation of will with the highest of the powers appears to reflect the influence of R. Azriel; see his *Perush ha-'Aggadot,* 81, 84, 107f. and 116. See also R. Asher b. David, who writes, "the will, which is the end point of Thought, namely the Supreme Crown," see *Kabbalat,* J. Dan ed., 53.

100. These two aspects of Primordial Wisdom are likewise discussed in *Contemplation–Short.*

101. *Yiḥud ha-shaveh,* identical to *'aḥdut ha-shaveh* (balanced unity). This exemplifies a tendency of the author of *Contemplation–Long* to rework standard terms; see below, n. 106 and n. 114.

102. It is worth noting that of the two dozen citations in *Contemplation–Long,* from both biblical and postbiblical literature, more than half are from the book of *Job.* On *Job* as a focus for cosmological exegesis, cf. R. Ezra, *Perush le-Shir ha-Shirim,* Third Introduction, 481f., as well as Nachmanides' commentary on *Job.*

103. *me-mi'ut.* The initial stage in the process of creation, called *'ayin* (Nothingness), following Job 28:12, seems to be interpreted herein as representing a diminution of the infinite nature of the Divinity. If this is a correct reading of the passage, then it represents one of the earliest formulations of the seminal, mystical doctrine of *zimzum,* "contraction." Scholem asserted that "the oldest source of this idea" is to be found in another of the treatises of the "Circle," *32 Paths,* Florence ms. 2:18, f. 101a; see *Origins,* 450, n. 202. It seems, however, that this particular passage is actually from a different and later work and that the "Circle's" text does not begin until f. 103a; cf.

emanated from its power.[104] This faith is the start of the Unity, for Oneness is diffused within it through a marvellous power which is equal from all aspects: its end is in its beginning, and its beginning is in its end, and its middle is at its top and its bottom–in order to make known His power through which He maintains all created beings by the sustaining power and the roots of faith.

Moreover, He bears all the foundations of the cosmos and His attributes are in the manner of the ways of faith. He carries all the created beings and directs them with intellectual power, like a hero who carries an amulet on his arm.[105] He is far removed from intellectual perception, and He is elevated within the Supremely Holy Hiddenness,[106] which is the wisdom that is called faith. He functions by truth and integrity, and accordingly, He is called the "God of faith" (Deut. 32:4). His nature is a purified living light within the light of the good crown and is sealed in the radiance of his beauteous canopy, comprised of the shining radiance and brightness that none can perceive. It is a brightness like the image of the form of the soul that is entirely imperceptible.[107]

He is the cause and the marvel, marvellously causing marvels, that are in the secrets of the hidden actions called counsels.[108] From them a cause shall issue forth that causes all causes, hidden and revealed. These are the ten hidden powers that are emanated from the Supreme Realm, that is exceedingly hidden and not revealed.

---

other mss. of this treatise: Vatican 291, f. 11b, J.T.S. 1990:27, and Hebrew U. 8° 488, f. 15b. An indication of the relative lateness of the material to which Scholem referred is a citation of Nachmanides' commentary on *Sefer Yezirah*, Florence 2:18, f. 102b.
It is conceivable that *Contemplation–Long* was influenced by the doctrine of the diminution of the moon, discussed in *B. Ḥullin*, 60b.

104. See *Contemplation–Short*, p. 40.

105. *P. Ḥagigah* 2:1. For various kabbalistic sources that used this image, see G. Scholem, *Kabbalot*, 39, n. 3.

106. *seter ha-kedoshah ha-'elyonah* is a variant of *seter 'elyon ha-ne'elam*; see below p. 153.

107. These two sentences are based on *Contemplation–Short*, p.42.

108. This is based on a statement in R. Azriel's letter to Burgos, "and to give thanks for the marvels of marvels that are in the secrets of the hidden actions, which are called distant counsels" *Kabbalot*, 72.

Therefore, it is stated "nothingness,"[109] for this Unity is not found nor revealed. "From nothingness it shall come into being" (Job 28:12), that is to say, from the marvellousness of the Unity attached to the Supreme Realm. Accordingly, if you want to perceive Him, you will not perceive Him; therefore, you will deny that there is any perceiving or revealing of Him. If someone would ask you how is this thing? You would respond to him, truly from the Unity. Hence, we must say, that this wisdom that came into being from the Unity is hidden and impossible to perceive and not by way of the reality of perception. The Holy One, blessed be He, animated this wisdom itself,[110] and from it He emanated all of the ten powers, through the process of emanation.

How? In the beginning the Holy One, blessed be He, created the Marvellous Light. At the time that is was created, several types of shining light were generated with it, from the powers of Unity. They grew strong and vibrated. Moreover, the Marvellous Light was attached to the side of wisdom called mystery. It was not allowed to shine until the Holy One, blessed be He, innovated all the lights that were generated on account of the strength of the powers. From them the Marvellous Light increases in brilliance and shines. This is as it is stated, "He bound the *neharot* from flowing and the mystery shall produce light" (Job 28:11). The *neharot*[111] are called the roots of strong lights, which are called the shining lights of the splendor. Mystery is the Primordial Wisdom, which produces light.

At the time that the Holy One, blessed be He, created it, He extended it like a pavilion as is stated, "For can any understand the extensions of the clouds, the tumults of His pavilion" (Job 36:29). "The extensions," this is the light that sparkles from the Marvellous Light, extended by the power of the Unity like a garment. Its brilliance strengthens and shines on the hidden Unity by the marvellous power. Therefore, it is the Marvellous Light itself, for from the magnitude of its shining light that shines brilliantly, it is darkened from

---

109. *'ayin.* On the usage of this term by the kabbalists, as a designation for *keter* (Crown), the highest of the *sefirot*, see R. Ezra, *Perush le-Shir ha-Shirim*, 483, and R. Asher, *Kabbalat*, J. Dan ed., 17 and 58; see also the recent article by D. Matt, "Ayin: The Concept of Nothingness in Jewish Mysticism," *Tikkun* 3:3 (1988), 43-47.

110. See *Contemplation–Short*, p. 42.

111. Although the usual translation of *neharot* would be "streams," the author of *Contemplation–Long* is interpreting it as the Aramaic *nehora'*, "light."

illuminating[112] in relation to human perception. It is like the strong sun, since no one can gaze on the essence of its brilliance; for if one would gaze on it, the pupils of his eyes would darken, and he could not open them owing to the magnitude of the brilliant light, which grows stronger and shines. Thus did the Holy One, blessed be He, darken this Marvellous Light from the perception of every creature. Nor did He allow any creature in the universe to perceive its truth, as it really is.

Immediately upon creating it He called it 'Orpani'el,[113] since it refers to the Holy One, blessed be He, who is unique, as is stated, "He alone stretched out the Heavens" (Job 9:8). He united with the essence of the Marvellous Light, that is the hidden power. Concerning this it is stated, "And the image of God he shall see" (Num. 12:8). This means the truth of His existence, which he can see with the eye of his intellect. This also refers to the Holy One, blessed be He, who is unique in the power of imagination and is not comparable to any one thing, as is said, "And to whom shall you compare Me and I shall be equated?" (Isa. 40:25). One should respond "holy," for He is holy in all types of holiness, and is sanctified by the sustaining power. This also refers to the ten *sefirot*, without substance, which were emanated from the power of the Marvellous Light.[114]

It is encumbent upon the contemplator[115] that he also count the foundation of the generations, in that He exists in the hidden balanced unity. He should not say, since one should not count the foundation of the generations, I shall not count its foundation; for everything is one and I shall only count the ten *sefirot*, since they are the end of the supernal realm and the start of the lower world.[116] Moreover, the domain of the generations is the supreme realm, which is attached to the balanced unity, and they are one entity. Therefore,

---

112. This expression was borrowed from *Fountain*; see above p. 59. Other influences of this work on *Contemplation–Long* are noted below, nn. 134 & 136.

113. On *'Orpani'el*, see above, p. 45; see also *Zohar*, 2:247a.

114. The doctrine of a secondary set of ten powers is derived from *Contemplation–Short*, p. 44. There it is associated with *ḥashmal*, a lower power, whereas herein it is connected with Marvellous Light. See also, n. 101 above for *Contemplation–Long*'s pattern of reworking material.

115. See above, p. 37, n. 5.

116. This expression is found in *Contemplation–Short*, p. 48, though in a different context.

one cannot count it as eleven, since eleven is not the conclusion but rather the start of the lower realm. Accordingly, it is stated, "Ten and not nine."[117] Ten *sefirot* is derived from *mispar* (number) and from *sappir* (sapphire),[118] that is to say that it is rooted in the word *mispar*. They are what the prophet looked into when he prophesied.[119] Accordingly, he said, "Ten and not nine." Nor should the inquirer say, I shall not count ten since this figure only indicates something limited, and therefore, I shall only count nine, in order not to concretely establish something from ten–lest the inquirer say, since I have counted ten, I shall also count that greater thing, which is visible within the ten, yielding eleven. One should not count thus.

These are the ten *sefirot*, without substance, which were emanated from the Marvellous Light. The first is *tav*.[120] The second is *tav shin*. The third is *tav peh*. The fourth is *kav heh*. The fifth is *ḥet peh tav*. The sixth is *dalet tav*. The seventh is *'alef shin*. The eighth is *'ayin*. The ninth is *ḥet mem*. The tenth is *peh ḥet*.

The *tav* is the highest *sefirah* that no one can scrutinize because it is boundless. It is the intellectual power, which was made into an angel, standing over the *ḥashmal*.[121] This angel is called 'Arafi'el.[122]

---

117. *Sefer Yeẓirah*, 1:4.

118. This same etymological analysis is found in the 14th-century kabbalistic classic, *Ma'arekhet ha-'Elokut* (Jerusalem 1963), 8a.

119. On the connection between sapphire and prophetic visions, cf. Exod. 24:10 and Ezek. 1:26; see above, p. 6f.

120. Of the letter designations that follow, only this first one, *tav*, is elucidated–being derived from the word *temunah*, image; cf. *Contemplation-Short*, p. 44. The significance of the subsequent letter combinations is unclear. The author of the kabbalistic prayer commentary, which quotes this section, introduces this sequence as simply being a reversal of the Hebrew alphabet; see British Museum 751, f. 39b.

121. Cf. *Contemplation-Short*, p. 44.

122. In *Contemplation-Short* this angel is unnamed; in the J.T.S. ms. of *Contemplation-Long* it is called 'Arafi'el, in the prayer commentary it is rendered 'Anafi'el. Other texts from the "Circle" make reference to 'Anafi'el; see *Thirty-two Paths* and especially the *Book of True Unity*, wherein 'Anafi'el is depicted as the primordial angel, from whom emanated seven *'anafim*: the seven seraphs, listed in *Contemplation-Standard* and headed by 'Orpani'el. 'Anafi'el played an important role in *hekhalot* literature; cf. *3 Enoch*, 11 (Hebrew) and 28 (Hebrew); see also J. Dan's recent analysis, "*'Anafi'el Metatron ve-Yoẓer Bere'shit*," *Tarbiẓ* 52 (1983), 447-457.

It is unique amongst all the radiant lights of the Marvellous Light. It is a hidden image (*temunah*): a quality which possesses a face and a mouth and a tongue to teach, just like a man.[123] It is a balanced will that brings into being all of the creatures. It is called desire,[124] and thus it is stated, "And His soul desired and He did it" (Job 23:13). The explanation of "His soul" is His will, as in "if you truly desire" (Gen. 23:8). This was the will. Moreover, it was desired that the Spirit would be extracted from the *hashmal.* So it is written, "wherever the Spirit shall go, they shall go" (Ezek. 1:12). Jonathan translated it *ra'ava* (will).[125] Hence, it is stated in the *Book of Creation*, "First is the Spirit of the Living God."[126] This is the Spirit that was divided into two sections: voice and breath.[127] The voice[128] would strengthen from the brilliance of the lights, which were generated from the *hashmal* and the breath would strengthen through the power of the director, who is 'Arafi'el. Since his image is not discernible, he is called *tav.* Thus it is stated, "He stood and I did not recognize the appearance of his image before my eyes" (Job 4:16).[129] "He stood and I did not recognize his appearance" refers to 'Arafi'el, who stands above *hashmal* opposite the Marvellous Light, whose essence is not discernible. "An image before my eyes" for he is a quality that seems to possess a face like a man. About whom it is said, "Like the appearance of a man up above Him" (Ezek. 1:26). "I heard the silence and voice" (Job 4:16)–at the time when 'Arafi'el unites above, opposite the Marvellous Light, all the powers of *hashmal* revolve and vibrate in a great shout. This is the speech that is self- generated. Concerning this our sages, of blessed memory, have said, "sometimes they are silent and sometimes they talk,"[130] in the strength of the brilliantly shining lights from *hashmal*, through the power of 'Orpani'el.

---

123. See *Contemplation–Short*, p. 44.

124. *ta'avah. Contemplation–Long* now connects the theme of Divine will, (see above, n. 99), with the angel 'Arafi'el, via *ta'avah* (desire), which commences with the letter *tav*, as does *temunah* (image).

125. *Targum Pseudo-Jonathan*, ad loc.

126. *Sefer Yezirah*, 1:9.

127. Based on the latter part of *Sefer Yezirah*, 1:9.

128. Although J.T.S. ms. reads *ha-kol* (everything), this is obviously a scribal error that is correctly rendered in the prayer commentary.

129. Cf. *Contemplation–Short*, p. 44.

130. *B. Hagigah*, 13b.

Concerning the Marvellous Light that is hidden, it is stated, "And now they have not seen the light" (Job 37:21). This is the Marvellous Light that is hidden from the visual perception of the eye. It is bright in the heavens, for it spreads out amongst all the spiritual powers. "And the breath passed and purified them" (Job 37:21). This is the Cherub[131] that is called breath and purifies the powers, as we shall explain in the future.[132] On top of this Marvellous Light is a cloud. What is the meaning of "the tumults of His pavilion" (Job 36:29)?[133] They are the flashes of the Marvellous Light that shine brightly by the power of the hidden Bright Light,[134] in His Innermost.

When it arose in the mind of the Holy One, blessed be He, to bring into being those that were to be emanated from His power, He wrapped Himself in the Marvellous Light,[135] as is said, "He stretched out the light like a garment" (Ps. 104:2) and immediately afterwards "He stretched out the heavens like a curtain" (Ps. 104:2). All of this was in order to reveal His equanimity, for He is balanced from every side: above and below, before and behind, both hidden and revealed. He made known everything that was hidden and revealed. This refers to His Unity, for it is the start and the cause of the other causes; whether it be causes that possess substance or causes that do not have substance.

When it arose in the mind of the Holy One, blessed be He, to prepare the planting of the supernal flags, the Marvellous Light spread out over His Unity. Thus it is stated, "He spread His cloud above Him" (Job 26:9). Immediately He brought into being all the creatures that were emanated from the power of the Marvellous

---

131. Presumably, this is a reference to the sixth power.

132. No such explanation is forthcoming, and in fact the treatise ends shortly hereafter. It is, however, an indication that the author had intended to write a lengthy treatise on all of the powers, but terminated this project after a discussion of the initial two powers.

133. See above, p. 73.

134. *'or bahir*. This was the term that Saadia employed to denote the Glory; cf. R. Judah Barzeloni, *Perush le-Sefer Yezirah*, 20f.; see also above in *Fountain*, p. 59.

135. Cf. *Bere'shit Rabbah*, 3:4 and *Pirkei de-R. Eliezer*, ch. 3; see also R. Jacob Cohen, *Kabbalot*, 40 and the material presented by A. Altmann, "A Note on the Rabbinic Doctrine of Creation," *Journal of Jewish Studies* 7 (1956), 203-206.

Light–a bright light shining with a green color,[136] which shines with all types of radiance and shininess and strong radiance. Then the Holy One, blessed be He, shone this light in a pure, brilliant radiance which gained strength and became known through the purity of the Marvellous Light. This light was generated from His Innermost, like the light of the eye which issues forth from the pupil of the eye,[137] from which the light sparkles. This light, which is known by the color iridescent green, is called *ḥashmal*. When it was created, it grew stronger in the brilliant and pure light and shone brightly from the pressure of the Marvellous Light that is fixed in the Unity. It again covered the beginning and the Unity on all sides of the Marvellous Light, through change and permutation. It is present in something and its opposite, like a key that opens and closes. The essence of the *ḥashmal* is like a scale,[138] a form without a face. It possesses the power to build and destroy, to increase and decrease. It exhibits change of nature and change of position, in all types of permutations, from right to the middle and from the middle to the left and the middle to the right, in all types of change.[139] It grows stronger through all the spiritual powers.

It is called the radiance of the Divine Presence. Its lights increase and are generated according to its numerical value, which is 378.[140] They vibrate and issue forth from it in the brilliant radiance of a great, shining light–radiating in all types of light. In each light the brilliance grows stronger in intensity. They are like sparks issuing forth from the coal, from which the flame increases. The smallest of these lights is like the radiance of the solar sphere that spreads throughout all the days of the year and ascends and descends through 606 levels above the celestial dome, from the east to the west and

---

136.　Here also we see the influence of *Fountain*, cf. p. 59.

137.　See S. Pines, in *Tarbiẓ* 50 (1981), 345, n. 24, who notes that Arabic philosophers attributed this theory to Plato; cf. I. Efros, *Studies*, 239.

138.　See *Contemplation–Short*, p. 43.

139.　*Ibid.*, p. 44.

140.　The numerical value of *ḥashmal*, which will be shortly discussed is 378. In *Contemplation–Standard* this material is presented as being found in the tractate *Ḥagigah*, which is unfounded. Its source is in the *hekhalot* literature; cf. *Battei Midrashot*, 1:56. Later kabbalists also referred to this passage; compare the material cited by Hasidah, *Ha-Segullah* 28 (1935), 4, n. 28a, also R. Joseph from Hamadan, *Ta‘amei Miẓvot*, Oxford ms. 2446, f. 6b.

upward, as is explained in the *Book of the Measure*.[141] Everything revolves and is diffused by the power of *ḥashmal*. Moreover, it (i.e., *ḥashmal*) is an acronym for: *ḥet–ḥokhmah kedumah* (Primordial Wisdom), *shin–shalom* (peace), which is an allusion to "He makes peace in His exalted region" (Job 25:2), *mem–memshalah* (dominion), alluding to My rule, *lamed–levush hadar* (the garment of splendour), and thus it is stated, "God, my Lord, You are exceedingly great; glory and splendour have You worn" (Ps. 104:1). The end.

CONTEMPLATION–THIRTEEN POWERS

As an independent text, *Contemplation-Thirteen Powers* has been preserved in a unique, sixteenth-century manuscript, British Museum 753, ff. 44b-45a. What follows is a transcription of this manuscript. This text has also been incorporated into several other treatises, thus forming a cohesive group of writings. These works are to be found in Appendix I, numbers 3:1 through 3:5. The oldest of these treatises, which also happens to cite our text in toto, is *Midrash of R. Simon the Righteous*, one of the pivotal writings of the "Circle of Contemplation." Accordingly, *Contemplation–Thirteen Powers* must be considered to be a seminal component of the "Circle."

In general, the version that is found in British Museum 753 is adequate; however, there is evidence of scribal lapses, as in lines 10 and 11 where the wording is jumbled.[142] In order to facilitate the study of this treatise, an apparatus has been added. The variants are drawn from the later texts, numbers 3:1 through 3:3 in the appendix, designated by ד, ה and ו. Only those variants considered to be significant are offered. It is likely that when all three of these works concur on a reading, then that reading is accurate, since these texts have been independently transmitted.

---

141. *Sefer ha-Middah*. The identification of this work is unclear. Perhaps Joseph ibn Aknin's *Ma'amar al ha-Middot*, ch. 5, published in *Ginzei Nistarot* 3 (1872), 193f., is intended.

142. That this is the case is evident when one compares this passage with its counterpart in the other versions of this text, such as the *Midrash* or the other recensions of *Contemplation*. It is noteworthy that a similar wording is found in no. 3:2, *Commentary on the Thirteen Attributes*, a text written in the latter half of the thirteenth century. This would seem to indicate that the error occurred in a very early copy.

CONTEMPLATION–THIRTEEN POWERS

לך ה׳ הגדולה והגבורה והתפא׳ וגומ׳ בענין הזה פירש המפרש וביאר   1
עיקר כל ההויות הנכללות בספר מעשה בראשית וכל זה הענין הוא רמז
לשלש עשרה כחות רוחניות שמזכיר בעל ספר יצירה והם ספר וספר
וספור ויס״ב וכל אלו הי״א כחות יש להם לכל אחד מהם שם חלוק בפני
עצמו ומעלתם זו למעלה מזו. הראשון נק׳ חכמה הקדומה והשני אור   5
המופלא והג׳ החשמל והד׳ ערפל והה׳ כסא הנוגה והו׳ אופן הגדולה
הנק׳ חזחזית פיר׳ מוצא׳ חזיון החוזים והז׳ הכרוב והח׳ גלגל
המרכבה והט׳ האויר הסובב והי׳ הפרגוד הי״א כסא הכבוד הי״ב מקום
הנשמות הנק׳ חדרי גדולה הי״ג סוד המערכה העליונה הנק׳ היכל הקדש
העליון. ואלו הי״ג כחות המתגלגלים מכתר [נ״א מסתר] עליון הנעלם   10
אומן הוא הנק׳ פירושו אב האמונה שמכחו האמונה נאצלת והוא יתׄ
קודם שברא שום דבר היה יחיד מיוחד באין חקר ובלי גבול אפשרי
לעמד בעצמו בכח קיום לכך נק׳ שמו אל ר״ל חזק חזק ולא היה כחו
ניכר ועלה בדעתו להמציא כל פעליו ובָרָא כח אחד ראשון וקראו חכמה
הקדומה ממנה תוצאות תעלומה ותוצאות האמונה נק׳ קדומה שממנה נאצלו   15
שנים עשר כחות הנזכרים. ושקולה היא כנגד העשרה בהשואת האחדות הם
עשר ספירו׳ בלי מה וז״א והחכמה תעוז לחכם מעשרה שליטים החכם הוא
יתׄ כד״א מי כהחכם וממשות כח זה הנק׳ חכמ׳ הקדומה הוא אור חיים
זך ומזוקק כתם טוב נכתב ונחתם בזיו שפריר הצד העליון הנק׳ אין
הנשלל מכל המושג וזהו סוד והחכמ׳ מאין תמצא זה אין הצד העליון הוא   20
רצון באין גבול ולמה נק׳ רצון מפני שבמאמרו נמצא היש מאין גם
הוא אור מזהיר ונק׳ כבוד ה׳ על זה נאמ׳ עוטה אור כשלמה ושהוא
מתאחד באורו וזיוו כלהב אש המתאחד בגווניו ומתעלה עד לאין סוף
ונק׳ אחד על שהיה קודם לכל הקדומים הנאצלים מפליאת אחדותו וזאת
החכמ׳ היא עליונית לעשר ספי׳ ומתחלקת לשש קצוות ימין ושמאל   25
פנים ואחור מעלה ומטה. ימין הוא כח הקיום בלי ממשות פועל פעולות
בכל וזהו ימין ה׳ עושה תוספת רוח הקדש. שמאל כח מושכל בלי ממשות
ויש בו מהות והוא צד אמצעי משפיע כחותיו לכל צד ולא ינטה
מאמצעותיו ומעלויו ר״ל שלא יאצל ממנו רוח הקדש לצד אחד מצדדים

---

3 שמזכיר: שהזכיר ד ה ו /ויס״ב (שהם סוד אחד) ד   4 אחד (ואחד) ד   /חלוק:
ידוע ד ידוע וחלוק ו   5 חכמה קדומה: האויר הקדמון ד   6 אופן הגדולה: אופן
היא אופן הגדולה ה   7 פיר׳ (מקום) ד /גלגל: גלגלי ד   10 המתגלגלים... עליון:
הם מתגלים כאחד מסתר עליון ד המתגלגלין מסתר עליון ה מתגלים מסתר עליון ו
11 אומן הוא הנק׳: הנקרא אומן ד הנקרא אמן ו   12 מיוחד: ומיוחד ד ה /אפשרי:
איפשר ד ה ו   13 לעמד: לעמוד ולהתקיים ה ו /חזק (נ״א חזק תקיף) ה
14 ניכר (אלא לעצמו) ה ו /פעליו (יש מאין) ה   15 נק׳: נק׳ ה ו   17 וז״א: וזה
שכתוׄ ד ה ו   18 הוא: היא ה   21 שבמאמרו (וברצונו) ה ו   22 זה: כן ה /
ושהוא: שהוא ד ה לומר שהוא ו   23 וזיוו: ובזיו ד   27 בכל (יום) ד ו /עושה
(חיל) ד ו   29 יאצל: נאצל ה ו /מצדדים: מצדדיו ד ה ו

וזהו יד ה' כי מכה סוף רוח הקדש. פנים שני כחות שהם הכנה לכל 30
הכחות המתגלים מכתר [נ"א מסתר] עליון שאמרנו ונק' חן וחסד שהם
פנים של רחמים. אחור עצם החכמ' שפע הבינה תכלית השגת החקר
והוא כח בעצמו ומתפשט לכח מוטבע לצייר צורה ולהבדיל כח מכח. מעלה
כח הנק' כתר עליון והוא לשון המתנה והוא צד עליון מתרבה עד אין
סוף ממציא כל הנמצאי' והוא לשון הדר כמו כרב עם הדרת מלך ועוד 35
מורה לשון כתר שכל המשיג משיג שום דבר בידיעה זו מתוך חקירתו ומעלים
ומכסה הודו מעלין עליו כאלו עטרו הקב"ה ועליו נאמ' אשגבהו כי
ידע שמי והאמת כי לא ישיג שום נברא ידיעת דבר זה על אמתת ידיעה
אבל ישלל ממנה כל הגלוי וכל המושג ועל זה נק' המוצא הראשון ר"ל
חכמ' הקדומה תעלומה שהיא נעלמת מלהשיגה על אמתתה ועל השואת 40
אחדותה /

ועול' כתר בחשבונו שש מאות ועשרים עמודי אור שהם יקד יקוד
ונקראים שרשי החכמה הקדומה. מטה הוא הכח הנק' אמונה והוא מדת
הדין והיא סבת השמש והירח והמשכת תנועותיה בלילה וזהו שאומרין
אמן ואמונה בלילה וז"א כי עשית פלא עצו' מר' אמו' אומן. פלא ממשות
הכח עצות מרחוק הם העניני' הרוחניי' המתגלגלים לעין וכל זה מאמונה 45
אומן ענין החכמה הקדומה מבואר מקצתו בזה. פי' חשמל חיות אש ממללות
פ"א חש מל החיש בענין מל הם שבעים שמות וזהו סוד ה' ליריאיו.

---

30 כי מכה סוף: פירוש מכת סילוק ד כי הוא כח חלוף ה כי הוא מכח חלוף ו
31 מכתר: מסתר ד ה ו 32 הבינה (הוא) ה (היא) ו 33 צורה: צורות ד
37 עטרו (של) ה (ל) הקב"ה ו 40 מלהשיגה: מכל השגה ה 41 כתר: סתר / שש
מאות ועשרים: שש מאות וששים ה 42 והוא: והיא ה 44 אמן: אמת ד ה ו /
וז"א: וזהו שכתו' ד ה ו 45 הם העניינים: הדברים והעניינים ה / המתגלגלים:
המתגלים ד ה 46 בזה (תם) ה

"For You, God, are the greatness and the valor and the majesty" (1 Chron. 29:11), etc. Concerning this matter, the interpreter has explained and elucidated the root of all the essences,[143] contained in the *Book of the Account of Creation*.[144] This entire topic is an allusion to the thirteen spiritual powers,[145] to which the author of the *Book of Creation* refers, and they are "*sefer* and *sefar* and *sippur* and the ten *sefirot* without substance."[146] Each one of these thirteen powers has

---

143. *havayot*. This term is found in the writings of many early thirteenth-century mystical theologians. R. Eleazar b. Judah uses this designation to denote the ten infinite qualities of God, based on *Sefer Yezirah* 1:5; see *Yihud shel R. Eleazar*, Casanatense 179, f. 98, and J. Dan, *Torat ha-Sod*, 94-103. For its use by kabbalists such as R. Isaac the Blind, cf. G. Scholem *Reshit*, 118, and *Origins*, 281f. See also R. Azriel, *Perush ha-'Aggadot*, 89ff. R. Ezra coined the expression "the essences were [preexistent], but the emanations (= *sefirot*) materialized," e.g. R. Ezra, *Perush le-Shir ha-Shirim*, H. Chavel ed., 2:494; cf. M. Idel, "*Sefirot*," 241, n. 13. This specific expression was paraphrased by one of the transmitters of *Contemplation–Short*, Guenzburg ms. 283, which ends "the essences were [preexistent], but the attributes were disseminated."

144. *Sefer Ma'aseh Bere'shit*. The identity of this work is unclear. Joseph Dan, commenting on the parallel statement from *Contemplation–Standard*, assumes that *Sefer Yezirah* is hereby intended, *Hugei*, 16. This seems unlikely as *Sefer Yezirah* is specifically mentioned shortly hereafter. R. Eleazar b. Judah mentions a book by this title in *Sefer ha-Rokeah ha-Gadol* (Jerusalem 1960), 23. Also, in *Shi'ur Komah*, (cited in *Sefer Razi'el* 51a), one finds a reference to "*sefer bere'-shit u-va-seder ma'aseh bere'shit*." Another possibility is the commentary on the opening lines of Genesis, presumably composed by R. Isaac the Blind, which commences, "Now I shall briefly explain the topic of the account of creation" J.T.S. 1187, f. 29a and J.T.S. 2194, f. 69a; cf. G. Scholem, *Reshit*, 123. This text discusses the *havayot* and would also account for the peculiar opening line of our text which refers to the *mefaresh*, the interpreter. See also the references in J. Ben-Jacob, *'Ozar ha-Sefarim* (Vilna 1880), 554, n. 1817 (the reference to the Munich ms. should read 22:7 and not 21:5), and M. Zlotkin, *'Ozar ha-Sefarim* (Jerusalem 1965), 175, n. 1817.

145. The major doctrinal innovation of this text is the shift from ten powers, as found in the earlier recensions, to thirteen. This new doctrine was subsequently adopted by *Contemplation–Standard*. The initial ten powers are the same as in *Contemplation–Short*. On the significance of this shift, see below, ch. 3.

146. *Sefer Yezirah*, ch. 1:1 and 2. The precise meaning of the terms: *sefer*, *sefar*, and *sippur* is problematic, though clearly all are connected with the notion of counting. The doctrine that there are thirteen and not ten *sefirot* is mentioned in passing by R. Elhanan b. Yakar; cf. J. Dan, *Tekstim*, 38.

a well-known, distinctive name, and their position is one atop the other. The first is called Primordial Wisdom. The second is Marvellous Light. The third is the *ḥashmal*. The fourth is *'arafel*. The fifth is Throne of Light. The sixth is Wheel of Greatness, which is called *ḥazḥazit* (looking-glass), meaning the source of the seers' vision.[147] The seventh is the Cherub. The eighth is Wheel of the Chariot. The ninth is the Encompassing Ether. The tenth is the Celestial Curtain. The eleventh is the Throne of Glory.[148] The twelfth is the Domain of the Souls,[149] which is called Chambers of Greatness.[150] The thirteenth is the Secret of the Supreme Configuration,[151] which is called the Supreme Holy Palace.[152]

These thirteen powers are revealed together from the Supreme Hiddenness that is concealed,[153] which is called *'omen*, meaning the Father of Faith, from whose power faith was emanated.[154] And He, may He be blessed, before He created anything He was singular and unique, inscrutable and limitless, and able to exist by Himself,[155] through the sustaining power. Accordingly, He is called *'el*, that

---

147. This represents a slight modification of the statement from *Contemplation–Short*, p. 46.

148. *kisei' ha-kavod*; cf. Jer. 17:12.

149. *makom ha-neshamot*. This parallels the kabbalistic concept of *yesod*, (Foundation) which is the second to last of the *sefirot* and the abode of the souls; cf. *Bahir*, #97f., and the commentary *'Or ha-Ganuz*, ad loc.

150. *ḥedrei gedullah*. This expression is found in *hekhalot* literature; cf. *Ma'aseh Merkavah*, ed. G. Scholem, in *Gnosticism*, 107 and *Origins*, 317, n. 243.

151. *sod ha-ma'arakhah ha-'elyonah*. The term *ma'arekhet ha-'elyonah* (supreme configuration) appears in Ibn Ezra's Torah commentary, for example Exod. 6:3, and is related to astrological constellations.

152. On the significance of the image of the celestial palace, see above nn. 55 & 60.

153. *seter 'elyon ha-ne'elam*. This is an expansion of *Contemplation–Short*'s phrasing, "Supreme Hiddenness" (*seter 'elyon*); see above, p. 39, n. 12.

154. Compare *Contemplation–Short*, p. 40, and *Contemplation–Long*, p. 71.

155. See *Contemplation–Short*, p. 43, and *Contemplation–Long*, p. 69.

is to say, very strong.[156] When His power was not yet discernible, except to Himself, it arose in His mind to manifest all of His actions, ex nihilo, and He created one power at first. He called it Primordial Wisdom.[157] From it stem the products of mystery and faith.[158]

It is called primordial, for from it the twelve aforementioned powers were emanated. Moreover, it is equivalent to the ten in the balanced unity. These are the ten *sefirot* without substance. Thus it is written, "And wisdom shall strengthen the wise man more than ten rulers" (Eccles. 7:19). "The wise man," He is the Blessed One, as is said, "Who is like the wise man?" (Eccles. 8:1). The substance of this power that is called Primordial Wisdom is the light of life, pure and refined, good gold written and sealed in the radiance of the splendorous canopy of the exalted realm,[159] which is called *'ayin* (nothingness) for it is devoid of any conceptualization. [160] This is the secret meaning of "And wisdom shall be brought into being from nought" (Job 28:12). This exalted realm is will, without limitation. And why is it called will?[161] For by His word and His will something was produced from nothing. It is also a shining light and is called "the Glory of God." Concerning this it is stated, "He covers Himself with light like a garment" (Ps. 104:2). For He united with His light and splendor like a flame of fire that unites with its colors, ascending to infinity.[162] Moreover, it is called One for it was prior to all the primordial elements that were emanated from the wonderousness of His Unity.[163] This Wisdom is exalted above the ten *sefirot* and is divided into six directions: right and left, before and behind, above and below.[164]

---

156. The linkage of the Divine Name *'el* with "strength" is expressed in several commentaries on *Sefer Yeẓirah* by the ḥasidei *'ashkenaz*; cf. *Perush R. Elḥanan*, G. Vajda ed., in *Koveẓ 'al Yad* 16:1 (1966), 156 and 186, l. 28. R. Meir b. Shimon, in his polemic *Milḥemet Miẓvah*, (Parma 155, f. 249), makes the same association; cf. *Zohar*, 3:132a.

157. *Contemplation–Short*, p. 41.

158. Cf. *Contemplation–Long*, p. 71.

159. *Contemplation–Short*, p. 42.

160. Cf. *Contemplation–Long*, p. 72f.

161. On the theme of Divine will, see above n. 99.

162. *Contemplation–Short*, p. 41.

163. *Contemplation–Short*, p. 40.

164. This is based on *Sefer Yeẓirah*, 1:13.

Right. This is the sustaining power, without substance. It performs actions every day. This is "the right hand of God acts valiantly" (Ps. 118:15)–the increase in the Holy Spirit.

Left. [This is] the intellectual power without substance; nevertheless, it possesses essence. It is the middle aspect whose powers influence each side. It does not deviate from its middleness or superiority.[165] That is to say, the Holy Spirit was not emanated from it to one of its sides. Thus it is "the hand of God,"[166] since it is the power of the adversary of the Holy Spirit.[167]

Before. Two powers which are a preparation for the powers that were revealed from the Supreme Hiddenness, which we previously mentioned. They are called grace and mercy, for they are the faces of compassion.

Behind. Essence of wisdom, the profusion of understanding:[168] it is the limit of the comprehension of inquiry. It is a power in itself and extends to the natural power in order to form images and to separate one power from the other.

Above. The power that is called Supreme Crown.[169] This indicates waiting.[170] It is the exalted realm that increases infinitely, producing all that exists. It also connotes glory as in, "In the multitude

---

165. *Contemplation–Long*, p. 69.

166. This is a common biblical expression, for example, Exod. 9:3.

167. Each manuscript version of this text has its own reading. This indicates that there was a breakdown in the transmission of this passage. Nevertheless, the basic theme is consistent in all of them; namely, that the right side is involved in the transmission of the Holy Spirit, and the left side is the medium for its withdrawal. Similar terms are found in R. Ezra's *Perush le-Shir ha-Shirim*, 494. Significantly, R. Azriel in his *Sod ha-Korbanot* (Vatican 211, f. 8bf.) uses the expression "increase in the Holy Spirit" to indicate the supernal effulgence that results from appropriate intentions concomitant with spiritual activities.

168. This use of *hokhmah* and *binah* (wisdom and understanding) in junction with *keter 'elyon* (see the next note), is indicative of the influence of standard kabbalistic terminology on the author.

169. *keter 'elyon*: highest of the *sefirot*. This term is already found in *Sefer ha-Bahir*, for example, #141. Undoubtedly, the author of *Contemplation–Thirteen Powers* incorporated this term, owing to its similarity to *seter 'elyon*, a key term in the vocabulary of the writers of the "Circle."

170. Cf. Job 36:2, *katar li*, "wait for me," hence the association of *katar* and *keter* (crown).

of the people is the glory of the king" (Prov. 14:28). The term "crown" also refers to anyone who perceives anything about this knowledge, based on their inquiry. It hides and covers His glory. They refer to it as if it were the crown of the Holy One, may He be blessed. Concerning it, it is stated, "I shall upraise him for he knows My name" (Ps. 91:14). The truth is that no creature can perceive the knowledge of this thing through true knowledge, for it is devoid of any revelation of conceptualization.[171] Accordingly, the primal source,[172] that is to say, Primordial Wisdom, is called mystery, for it is hidden from any perception, while in its true state and in its balanced unity. Furthermore "crown" yields the sum of 620[173]pillars of light that are "a burning fire" (Isa. 10:16). They are called the roots of the Primordial Wisdom.

Below. This is the power called faith. It is the attribute of judgment, as well as the cause of the sun and the moon and the pull of its movements at night. This is why they recite "truth and faith" at night.[174] Thus it is said, "For You have done a wonder, counsels from distant times, true faith" (Isa. 25:1). "Wonder" is the substance of the power. "Counsels from distant times," these are the spiritual matters which are revealed to the eye. All of this stems from "true faith."

Through this discussion, the topic of the Primordial Wisdom is partially explicated. *Ḥashmal* means the fiery creatures that talk.[175] Another explanation: *hash mal*. Quickness[176] related to *mal*,[177] which

---

171. Cf. *Contemplation–Long*, p. 73.

172. This seems to be based on *Contemplation–Short*, p. 40f, wherein the expression "the Primordial Emanator" appears in juxtaposition to Primordial Wisdom; however, there the antecedent of the expression is Father of Faith. The expression here, *ha-moẓei' ha-rishon*, "primal source," was probably formulated under the influence of the term *maẓui rishon*, "first existent being," that is found in *Fountain*, see above, p. 55.

173. The numerical value of *keter* (crown) is 620. This doctrine was subsequently incorporated into *Contemplation–Standard*, p. 106 and later writings from the "Circle," such as *The Book of True Unity* and *R. Nehuniah b. ha-Kanah's Prayer of Unity*.

174. From the evening prayer service; cf. *B. Berakhot*, 12a.

175. See *B. Ḥagigah*, 13b.

176. Herein *hash* is interpreted as *hish*, "quick," ; cf. Ps. 90:10.

177. *Mal* has the numerical value of seventy, as does *sod* (secret).

corresponds to the seventy names.[178] This is, "God's secret is for those who fear Him" (Ps. 25:14).

CONTEMPLATION–STANDARD

Of all the versions of *The Book of Contemplation, Contemplation–Standard* is the most common. It has been preserved in some eighteen manuscripts, most written between the fifteenth and seventeenth centuries. Fifteen of these were available to me and utilized. British Museum 752 is the earliest complete copy, dating from the fourteenth century. Unfortunately, its value is mitigated because, as Margoliouth noted in his catalogue, the scribe was not proficient and this codex was "very badly copied throughout."[179]

These manuscripts fall into three major families, readily discernible through a comparison of varied readings of key passages. The only complete version of the first group is Bodleian 1610, designated in the apparatus as א. It is a relatively late manuscript, from the eighteenth century, and replete with scribal errors. A generally superior text from this family is J.T.S. 899a, designated by ב. Unfortunately, it is lacking the initial seven lines, as well as the conclusion of the treatise, from line 120 to the end. There is also J.T.S. 1884, designated by ג. It is a fourteenth-century anthology of kabbalistic sources, which offers approximately two-thirds of the treatise. Other manuscripts related to this family include the subtext no. 4:3, *Contemplation–Standard/Inner Attributes*, as well as the version of *Contemplation–Standard*, which served as the basis for no. 4:1, *Contemplation–Burgos*.

A second family has been preserved in only two manuscripts: Mousayeff 46, designated as ד, and Munich 408, designated as ה. The first of these is the manuscript that Hasidah used, when he published an edition of *Contemplation–Standard* in 1935.[180] Moreover, the Munich ms. was the one that Scholem preferred. As can be readily seen in the apparatus, Munich 408 offers numerous idiosyncratic variants, and Mousayeff 64 is clearly superior (though, to be sure, there are a few errors in the published version of this manuscript).

---

178. See above, p. 45, n. 40.

179. G. Margoliouth, *Catalogue of the Hebrew and Samaritan Manuscripts in the British Museum* (London 1965), 3:31.

180. In *Ha-Segullah*, Vols. 27 and 28, (1935).

Most of the manuscripts belong to the third grouping. These are represented herein by Guenzburg 333, designated by), and J.T.S. 1805, designated by). Also part of this family are Bodleian 2240 and British Museum 752. In addition, there are numerous partial mss., such as Bodleian 1960 and Warsaw 9,[181] which break off at line 96 and are descendants of Guenzburg 333; and J.T.S. 1547 and Vatican 236, which are missing the initial section of the treatise and are off-shoots of Guenzburg 333 and Bodleian 2240. Other mss. related to this family are Bodleian 2296, Bodleian 1833, and Bodleian 1822, all written in the seventeenth century.

J.T.S. 1805 is the most interesting member of this third family. Occasionally, it differs from the rest of this grouping and instead offers readings that reflect the first family. While this may simply be an indication that the copyist had two different manuscripts at hand, almost always are these readings to be judged optimal. Consequently, it seems that this manuscript actually reflects an intermediary stage, between families one and three, and is accordingly an extremely valuable source.

When Hasidah published a transcription of Mousayeff 64 some fifty years ago, he undoubtedly utilized the only manuscript of *The Book of Contemplation* that was then available in Jerusalem. It is ironical that of all the manuscripts extant, and known to me, this is the single best version of the treatise.[182] (The only other manuscript that stands well on its own is J.T.S. 1805.)

Although Hasidah's was the first complete edition of *Contemplation–Standard*, it was not the first such publishing enterprise. In 1798 an anthology of kabbalistic material was published under the title, *Collected Writings from R. Hai Gaon*. Near the beginning of this work approximately one-fifth of *Contemplation–Standard* appears, followed immediately by part of *The Prayer of Unity of Rabban Gamliel*. The remainder of *Contemplation–Standard* appears toward the end of the anthology, under the title, *The Gate of Heaven*.[183] This same corrupt version of the start of

---

181. These two mss. are interesting in that the treatise is prefaced with the enigmatic statement: "Rabbi Jose said, I will begin to write *The Book of Contemplation*."

182. For Scholem's differing assessment of these texts, see *Origins*, 312, n. 231.

183. *Likkutim me-R. Hai Gaon* (1913), 17 and 78f.

Contemplation–Standard was also published in the mid-nineteenth century by Adolf Jellinek.[184]

The following transcription is an eclectic text, based on the best readings from the major representatives of all three families. Owing to the relative accessibility of Hasidah's diplomatic edition, it was felt that the textual reconstruction of an eclectic version would likewise contribute to our understanding of this treatise.

---

184. A. Jellinek, *Ginzei Ḥokhmat ha-Kabbalah (Leipzig 1853), 10-12.*

CONTEMPLATION–STANDARD

1 זה ספר העיון שחיבר רב חמאי ז״ל ראש המדברים על עניין הפנימיות וגילה
בו עיקר כל מציאות הכבוד הנסתר מן העין אשר אין כל בריה יכולה
לעמוד על עיקר מציאותו ומהותו על דרך האמיתי כמות שהוא
באחדות השוה שבהשלמתו מתאחדים עליונים ותחתונים. והוא יסוד כל

5 נעלם וגלוי וממנו יוצאים כל הנאצלים מפליאת האחדות. וביאר רב חמאי
כל אלו העניינים על דרך מעשה מרכבה ופי׳ נבואת יחזקאל ע״ה. וזהו
תחלת הספר על הסדר. יתברך ויתרומם שם הנאדר בגבורה אשר הוא אחד
מתאחד בכחותיו כלהב אש המתאחד בגוונין וכחותיו מתאצלים מאחדותו
כאור העין היוצא מתוך שחרות שבעין ונאצלים אלו מאלו כריח מריח

10 וכנר מנר שזה מתאצל מזה וזה מזה וכח המאציל בנאצל ואין המאציל
חסר כלום. כך הקב״ה קודם שברא שום דבר היה דבר יחיד קדמון מבלי חקר
ובלי גבול בלא חיבור ובלא פירוד בלא שינוי ובלא נענוע והיה נסתר
בכח קיום ובשעה שהיה קדמותו מושכל קודם לכל הקדומים היוצאים
באצילות המתמצע והיה נעלם אפשרי לעמוד בעצמו ולא היה כחו ניכר.

15 וכשעלה בדעתו להמציא נראה כבודו ונגלה כבודו וזיוו
ביחד ופי׳ ידיעתו הוא בחמשה עניינים ואלו הן תקון צרוף ומאמר
ומכלל וחשבון. וידיעת אלו החמשה עניינים הוא מיוחד בענפי שורש
התנועה המתגברת בשורש שלשה עשר מיני תמורה. כיצד הוא התקון
להוציא דבר במאמר ומאמר בדבר ומכלל בחשבון וחשבון במכלל עד

20 להעמיד כל הדברים במעיין השלהבת והשלהבת במעיין עד אין חקר ואין

---

1 (זה) ב ד ה ז /(שחיבר) ד ה /חמאי (גאון) ב ד /(ז״ל) ו ז /ז״ל (גאון) ה /ענין
(הספירות) ה /הפנימיות: פנימיות א   50-1 (זה... זהו) ג   7-1 (ראש... הסדר)
ב   2 בו: כי ו /עיקר כל: כל עיקר א /מציאות: מוצאות ב /הכבוד: כבוד ד ה /(מן
העין) ד ה /העין: ו /יכולה (להשיג ו) ו   3 דרך: הדרך ז /האמיתי: האמת ו /
כמות: כמו ו   4 שבהשלמתו: שבהשלמותו ד ז שבשלמותו ה   5 וגלוי: וגילוי א /
יוצאין א /הנאצלים: נאצלים א /מפליאת: מפליאות א מפליאה ו /וביאר: פי׳ ו
/חמאי (ז״ל) א ו   6 כל אלו: כי אלה א /ופי׳ נבואת: ונבואת ו ז   7 תחלת:
התחלת א /הספר: השם ו /שם: השם ו ז /הנאדר: הנהדר ה הנאור ו   8 בכחותיו:
בכל כחותיו א /כלהב: כלהבת ו /בגוונין: בגוונותיו ד ה בגאותיו ו /מאחדותו:
מאחדותיו ו   9-8 (כלהב... ונאצלים) א   9 העין: עין ו   10 וכנר: ונר ה /(וכח
המאציל בנאצל) א   11 חסר: מחסר ה /הקב״ה (ית׳ שמו) ה /(ית׳ ויתי׳ ז /שברא:
שנברא ו /קדמון: וקדמון ו   12 ובלי: ומבלי ו /בלא: בלי ה מבלא ו /(פירוד בלא) ו /
בלא שינוי ובלא נענוע: בלי שינוי נענוע א   13 קיום: קימם ד קיים ה הקיום ו ז /
הקדומים: הקודמים ב ו הקדמונים ז   14 והיה: והוא ה /(אפשרי) ו /לעמוד: עומד ו /
ולא: לא ו   15 להמציא: להוציא א /(כל) ב /פעליו: פעוליו ו /נראה: ונראה א /
כבודו: כבוד א (כבודו) ב /ונגלה: ונעלה ז   16-15 ונגלה... ביחד: היא א כח ו /ומאמר:
ומאמרות א   17 ומכלל: מכלל א /וחשבון: וחשבון (הוא) ה /החמשה: חמשה ז /בענפי:
בכנפו א   18 המתגברת: המתגבר ב ד ה   19 (עד) ו   20 (להעמיד... עד) ז /
הדברים: דבריהם ו /במעיין: כמעיין א /(השלהבת והשלהבת במעיין) א

מספר לאורה המתעלמת בתוספת החשך המסותרת וידיעת האחדות ועיקרו
הוא זה החשך ופירושו הוא מבואר בכאן כמו שפירש אותו ר' ישמעאל
בן אלישע כהן גדול בלשכת הגזית דתנן אמר ר' ישמעאל אותו היום
היינו מצויין אני ור' עקיבא בן יוסף לפני ר' נחוניא בן הקנה
25 והיה שם ר' חנינא בן תרדיון ושאלתי לר' נחוניא בן הקנה ואמרתי לו
רבי הראני כבוד מלכו של עולם כדי שיתבאר ידיעתו בלבי כשאר פעליו.
אמר לי בן גאים תא ונעסוק בעזקתא רבתא דחתמין בה שמיא וארריתא
שמיה ובעזקתא דארעא דהיא אה"ו ואראה לך הכל נכנסתי לפני לפנים
בהיכל הקדש החיצון והוצאתי משם ספרו של ר' נחוניא בן הקנה הנקרא
30 ספר היכלות ומצאתי כתוב בתחלת הספר כך. אדיר בחדרי גדולה היושב על
גלגלי מרכבתו בחתימת אהיה אשר אהיה ובעזקתא רבתא דחתמין בה שמיא
ארריתא שמיה סימן אחד ראש אחדותו ראש יחודו תמורתו אחד יחיד
ומיוחד /
יחיד מיוחד אחד ובעזקתא דארעא דאה"ו שמיה סימן אחד היה היה ויהיה.
והמתמצע בין שניהם הוה דבר דבור על אופניו. היה קודם שברא העולם
35 הוה בעולם הזה ויהיה בעולם הבא וסימנו פעל יפעול ובזה הסדר
הם מפורשים עיקר כל ההויות הנכללות בספר מעשה בראשית שהם עצות
המתגלים מסתר עליון הנעלם הנקרא אומן פירוש אב האמונה שמכחו
האמונה נאצלת והוא יתברך מתאחד בכחותיו ומתעלה ומתרומם מהם עד
שאין סוף לרוממותו והוא מיוחד באלו השלשה עשר כחות ויש לכל אחד
40 ואחד שם ידוע בפני עצמו וכלם מעלתם זו למעלה מזו. הראשון נקרא
חכמה קדומה והשני אור מופלא והשלישי חשמל והרביעי ערפל והחמשי
כסא הנוגה אופן הגדולה הנקראת חזחזית פירוש מקום מוצא

21 בתוספת: בתוספות א /המסותרת: המוסותרת א   22 (הוא זה) ב (הוא) ז /שפירש:
שפירשתי א /(אותו) ה   23 (בלשכת הגזית) ו ז   24 היינו: אנו א (היינו) ב /
מצויין: מצואים א מצואין ב מצויים ו ז /לפני ר': ור' ו ז /הקנה: הקנא ה (רבי) ז
25 (והיה... הקנה) ו ז /חנינא: חנניה ד ה /נחוניא: נחוניה ה /בן בן ה /הקנה: הקנא ה
רבי ב   26 (רבי) ב /הראני: הראנו ד ה נא א /מלכו: מלכותו ב /פעליו: פועליו ס"א
פועליו ו   27 רבתא: רבא ז /דחתמין: דחתומים ו /בה: ביה ד ה /וארריתא:
וארקתא ה   28 שמיה: דשמיא ה /ובעזקתא: בעזקתא א /דהיא: דא א דהו ו /אה"ו:
אהוי ד אהני ד שמיה א /ואראה: אראה ז /הכל (באותה שעה) א /נכנסתי: ונכנסתי ו ז
/לפנים: הלפנים א ולפנים ז   29 החיצון: והחיצון ה   30 ספר: ספרי ב /כתוב
(כך) ב /(כך) ב /אדיר... אדיר: אדיר היושב בחדרי גדולה היושב ב /היושב: יושב ו
31 גלגלי: גלגל א /בחתימת: בחתימתו ז /רבתא: רבא ו /דחתמין: ביה א (בה) ו
32 שמיה: שמי ה /(והוא) א /אחדותו: אחדות ז /יחודו: יחוד ו /תמורת: תמורת ו /(נ"א
תפארתו) א   33 מיוחד: ומיוחד א ו /אחד: יחיד ו (אחד) ז /אה"ו: דאהו"י ד ה דהו
אה"ו ו אה"ז ז   34 והמתמצע (והמתמצע) ה /הוה: היה (נ"א הוה) א /דבור: דבר א /
שברא: שנברא ב ו ז (את) א   35 בעולם: לעולם ז /וסימנו: והסימן א וסימן ו /
יפעול: יפעל א ויפעל ו ז   36 הם מפורשים: הוא מפורש ו /מפורשים: מפרשים א /
עצות: עדות ו   37 המתגלים: המתגלות ד ה /עליון: העליון ו /אומן (נ"א אין) א
(שמכחו האמונה) א ה   39 שאין: אין א   40 בפני: לפני ו /וכלם: וכולן ז /
מעלתם: מעלותם ו   41 והשני (נק) ב /אור: הוד ו   42 הנקראת: הנקרא ז /
(מקום) א /מוצא: מוציא א ו (מוצא) ב

חזיון החוזים והשביעי נקרא כרוב והשמיני נקרא גלגלי המרכבה
והתשיעי אויר הסובב והעשירי פרגוד והאחד עשר כסא הכבוד והשנים
עשר מקום הנשמות הנקרא חדרי גדולה והשלשה עשר סוד המערכה העליונה   **45**
הנקרא היכל הקדש החיצון ואלו הי״ג כחות הם מתגלים כאחד מסתר
עליון הנעלם הנקרא אומן פי׳ אב האמונה שמכחו האמונה נאצלת והוא
ית׳ קודם שברא שום דבר נק׳ אל ר״ל חיזוק חזק שלא היה כחו ניכר
וכשהתחיל להמציא פעליו המציא שתי תוצאות תעלומה ותוצאות האמונה
השואת האחדות והמהות שאנו רשאים להשיג מחקר בורא עולם זהו. דע   **50**
שאדון כל העולם ית׳ שמו הוא אור חיים זך מזוקק כלול מזיו זוהר
אור צחצוח שאינו מושג כלום בהיר כדמות צורת נשמה שאין בה שום
השגה כלל והוא ית׳ שמו אע״פ שאינו מושג הוד יקרו בשביל כבוד
בריותיו עושה לו לעצמו דומיה כאילו היה גוף ממש ובשביל כבודם של
ישראל יש מלאך ממונה לפני הקב״ה שמברך בכל יום בשמם של ישראל   **55**
כדי שיקדש שמו של הקב״ה בכבוד קדושתם של דרי מטה והקב״ה מיוחד
בשבעה מלאכים היושבים ראשונה במלכות שמים העליונים ואלו הן
אורפניאל תיגראל דנראל פלמיאל אסימון פסכאל בואל ועליהם נאמר
שרפים עומדים ממעל לו שש כנפים שש כנפים לאחד והוא לשון מחנות
שמסובבות פנים ואחור והם נקראים נשמות כדתנן בספר עצם לבנת הספיר   **60**
הקב״ה הוא נשמה לנשמה שכל אלו הז׳ מחנות הם נקראים נשמה ואדון הכל
נשמה לזו הנשמה והוא מתעלה במדת החסד ומתרומם עד שאין סוף

43 חזיון: חזון ו / (נקרא) ב / (נקרא) ב / (גלגלי) ב / גלגלי א ב / המרכבה: מרכבה א
44 אויר: אור ד (גלגל) א ב / הסובב: הסוע ו   45 הנשמות: הנפשות א ב / (הנקרא
חדרי גדולה) ו / והשלשה עשר: שלש עשרה א   46 הנקרא: הנקראת ו / כחות הם:
כחותיהם א / (הם) ב ו / מתגלים כאחד: מתגדלים באחד א   47 עליון: העליון ב ו /
(הנעלם) ה   48 שברא: שנברא ו / ר״ל: כלומ׳ ה פי׳ ו / (חיזוק) א ה / חזק (מפני)
א   49 להמציא: למצא ו / פעליו: פעליו ו / שתי: שני ד ה ו / פר״ר שנים עשר) ה /
(ותוצאות האמונה) ו / האמונה: תעלומה ז   50 והמהות: וההוהות ו / שאנו: שאינן א
שאין ה שאינו ז   51 העולם: העולמים א / שמו [אעפ״י שאינו מושג] א / מזוקק:
ומזוקק ו / (זוהר) ב / (אור) ג / צחצוח: צחצוחי א / (כדמות) ג / (שום)   52 (אור) ג
א   53 הוד: סוד ו ז   54 (לו) ה / והוא: הוא ו ז / דומיה: דומיא א ג דמות ו / כבודם:
כבודן א ב ז כבודו ג ו / (של ישראל) ג   55 מלאך (אחד) ו / (ממונה) ג / שמברך:
שמתברך א / בכל יום: בכבודן א / יום: ויום ג / בשמם: בשמן ג בשמן ז (בשמם) א
55-56 (שמברך... הקב״ה) ה   56 שיקדש: שיתקדש א / בכבוד: בשביל ג / קדושתם:
קדושתן א קדושתנו ו / מטה (שמברך בכל יום בשמם של ישר׳ כדי שיקדש שמו של הקב״ה
ית׳ בכבוד קדושתם של דרי מטה) ה   57 (שמים העליונים) ג / העליונים: עליונים ה /
הן: הם ב ג   58 אורפניאל: פניאל ו (סוד ופני לא יראו) ג / תיגראל: תיגדאל ב
תגראל ה / דנראל: דנדאל ב ד ו דנאל ג / פלמיאל א / כלמיאל: פסכאל א / פסראל א
פסראל ג מסכאל ו / בואל: ביאל ו (שש כנפים לאחד) ב ג ז   60 נקראים:
נקראין ג / נשמות: בשמות ז / כדתנן: כדתני ו / בספר: בסיפרי ג (בספר) ו
61 הקב״ה: והק׳ ו / הוא: שהוא ב / לנשמה: לנשמות ו / והז׳: ז׳ ו שבעה ז / (הם) ג ו /
נקראים: נקראות א / הכל (הוא) א ה   62 לזו הנשמה: לנשמה א / במדת: במדות ג /
החסד: הקב״ה ב / שאין ג ה / (ומתרומם) ו

לרוממותו ועל כן אנו אומרים על השמים כבודו זהו גוף השכינה.

ולאחר כך ברא הקב"ה דמות אחד בארבע יסודות כדמות אדם ממש והם ד'

65 מחנות שכינה והם מיכאל גבריאל אוריאל רפאל וכנויים חשמל ערפל

כסא הנוגה ואופן הגדולה. מיכ' של מיכאל הם שבעים שמות מל של חשמל

כמו כן ע' שמות סימן סוד ה' ליריאיו. וזהו שחלק הכתוב חש של

חשמל ואל של מיכאל וכשם שנעשים שוים נעשה מהם חשאל ר"ל חשות לאל

כבוד. קול ורוח ודבר. קול היא החקירה. רוח הוא השכל הקבוע בלב.

70 דבר הוא סוד הידיעה. ועל זה נאמר כמראה אדם עליו מלמעלה. ועוד

סימן חשמל ח' חכמה ש' שלום מ' ממשלה ל' לבוש. חכמה דכתיב והחכמה

מאין תמצא. שלום דכתיב עושה שלום במרומיו. ממשלה דכתיב המשל

ופחד עמו. לבוש דכתיב הוד והדר לבשת וזהו שכתבו רז"ל בחגיגה חשמל

הוא שלש מאות ושלשים ושמונה מיני מאורות והפחות שבכולן כזיו גלגל

75 חמה ואיכא דאמרי שע"ח כחשבונו וזהו שכתוב בספר מעין החכמה טוב

ומטיב והכל לו זאת ראשית תחלת המתנה פעלו שש מאות ועשרים הם ראש

מלולו שסימנו כתר והוא לשון המתנה הרי פירוש מיכאל וחשמל והוא

ענין אחד הנקרא יסוד המים הרי המחנה האחת. המחנה השנית גבריאל

והוא ערפל הוא יסוד האש והוא מתאחז בשרשי חשמל. כיצד כבר אמרנו

80 כי מל של חשמל הם ע' ומשתוים עם ע' של ערפל שהוא ע' שמות הרי אלו

---

63 כבודו (אעפ"י שמלא את כל הארץ) א / זהו: וזהו ו ה' א / השכינה: שכינה ז

64 ולאחר כך: ואח"כ ו / אחד: אחת ז   65 (והם) ה (נקראים) ו / וכנויים: ובגוים ד

ובגוום ה / מיכאל: מכאל ו   66 ואופן א והאופן ג ד ה ז / הגדולה: הגדול ג /

מיכ: מי' ה (מיכ של) א (מיכ) ג / הם: והם ה / שבעים: שבעה ה / (שמות) ו (מיכ של

מיכאל) א (של הק') ו   67 (שמות) ו / סימן: וסימן ב שנא' ז / (שחלק) ב

67-68 (חש... מהם) ה   68 וכשם שנעשים: וכשנעשים א וכשנעשים ו נעשים ז /

שוים: שווין א שנים ו / (מהם) ו / (חשות): חשיות ב ו   69 כבוד: כבודו ג / ורוח: רוח ו /

ודבר: ודבור ה ו / היא: הוא א ו / החקירה: החקיקה ג / (הוא) א ד ה   70 דבר: דבור

ג ה ו / (ועל זה): ועליו ה / זה: דמיון ד' יסודות אלו א / נאמר דמות ג

72-73 (ממשלה... עמו) ג ה ו   73 לבשת: לבושו ד ה ממשלה המשל ופחד עמו ג /

שכתבו: שאמרו ב ג (בו) א / רז"ל: רבותינו ד ז (רז"ל) ג ה במסכת א ה / חגיגה (רז"ל) ה /

(חשמל) ו   74 הוא: ההוא ו / שלש מאות ושלשים ושמונה: י"א ו"ל ו"ח ד י"ש ו'ל ז"ח

ה / ושלשים: ושבעים ג ושמונה (וזהו שכתוב מעיין החכמה) ו / מאורות: מראות ב ו /

והפחות: והקטן א / שבכולן: שבכלם א ד ה שבכולם ו / כזיו: כעין ב ז   75 חמה:

החמה ג ד / ואיכה: ואית ב / שע"ח: שלש מאות וחמשים ושלשים ושמונה ג שט"ח ה /

כחשבונו: בחשבונו ה (כחשבונו) א ג / וזהו: והוא ג / שכתבו: שכתבו א דכתיב ב דכתבו ד

שכתב ג / (בספר) ו   76 ומטיב: ומטוב ו / והכל לו: והכללו ג והכל שלו ה זה קללו ו /

זאת: זו ג / פעלו: פעליו ה מפעלו ו / (הם) ג   77 שסימניו: וסימניו ה (הוא) ג / לשון

המתנה: ראש המתגאה ו / המתנה: מתנה א המתכה ה / הרי: הוא ו / פירוש מיכאל:

פירושו של מיכאל ושל ג / והוא: הוא ב ו   78 (אחד) ו / (הרי המחנה האחת) א /

המחנה האחת: מחנה אחד ב ו ז מחנה אחת ג / האחת: האחד ה / השנית: השניה א שני

ו והשני ז (הוא מחנה) ג   79 הוא: והוא ב ג ו (הוא) א / מתאחז: מתאחד א ו /

בשרשי: בראשי ג / אמרנו: ביארנו ב   79-80 (כיצד... שמות) ג   80 הם שבעים

(משרתים) ב / ומשתוים: ומשתנים ו ומשתחוים ז / שהוא: שהם ו ז

בקרב אלו וזהו דכתיב במאמר שירו של ר' פנחס חסמא לז ללז אחוזים
בכנפי סוד תנועה כלומר זה כנגד זה אחוזים יסוד המים שהוא מיכאל
ויסוד האש שהוא גבריאל הרי טעם העי' של ערפל. טעם רפ"פ ר"פ
כשתוציא רל"ו מחשבון ר"פ שהם רמז למדת כסא

85 הכבוד ישאר מ"ד כשתוציא ב' ממ"ד לשים עם ל' של ערפל להיות ל"ב
ישאר מ"ב שהם סימן ה' בם וזהו סימן אסורה נא ואראה את המראה הגדל
הזה. וזהו גבריאל גבר עלינו אל. המחנה השלישית הוא האחדות עצמה
הוא אוריאל והוא יסוד הרוח והוא האויר והוא מאיר לצד מקום הנשמות
וסימנו קומי אורי כי בא אורך שהוא עתיד להאיר אפילתן של ישראל.

90 המחנה הרביעית הוא רפאל רופא האמת על כן נקרא יסוד הארץ כי הוא
ממונה על העפר האבוק מתחת כסא הכבוד והוא נקרא חומר כמו שאמר רב
האיי ז"ל ועלה במחשבה בריאת החומר הקדמון שממנו נאצלים כל
הנבראים וכן פירשו חכמי הטבע התקיפים הפילוסופים החריפים בחכמת
המחקר. ואחר אילו ד' מחנות שכינה הוא היחוד הנקרא היכל הקדש

95 ויש לו ד' פאות כנגד מזרח ומערב וכנגד צפון ודרום וכנגד מחנות שכינה.
עד כאן סדרא דמארי עלמא מכאן ואילך סדר מטטרון שמורה על ידיעת
בורא עולם בסדר אחר. דע שמטטרון הוא ממונה לפני היכל הקדש. טעם

---

81 דכתיב: שכתב א ב /במאמר: בזמר ז (במאמר) ג /(ר') ב /(חסמא) א /(לז) ה /
אחוזים: אחרים ג   82 (סוד) ג /תנועה: התנועה ג /כנגד: עם ב /זה (הם) א (זה) ו /
(שהוא) ד ה   83 ויסוד: סוד א יסוד ד ה מיסוד ו /(שהוא גבריאל) ה /הרי: והרי ב /
טעם (טעם) ה (טעם) ב /הע': ע' ב של ע' ה /(טעם) ב /רפ"ל: רפאל א ה מ"ל של חשמל ג
/(ר"פ) ו   84 (מחשבון... שהם) ו /ר"פ: ר"ב ג /שהם: שהוא א (רל"ו אלף פרסאות) ו
/(למדת) ז /למדת כסא: לכסא ו   85 לשים: צרף ו /עם: על א ה /ל': ע ז /(להיות)
א   86 שהם: שהוא ג (ה') א /וזהו: והוא ג /סימן: האויר ה (סימן) ו /(את) ו
87 וזהו: מהו ו (וזהו) ד ה /(גבר) ג /אל: האל ב /השלישית: השלישי ו /הוא: היא א ז
האחדות: אחדות א ב אחדותו ג   87-88 האחדות... אוריאל: אוריאל היא האחדות
עצמה ו   88 (והוא האויר) ד ה /(מקום) ו /הנשמות: הנפשות א   89 וסימנו:
וסימניו ה וסימנך ו /אורך וכבוד ה /אפילתן: אפלן א אפילתם ב אפלתם ד /ישראל
(לעתיד לבא) ג   90 הרביעית: הרביעי ה ז /הוא: היא ז (הוא) ד /כי הוא: שהוא
ו   91 האבוק: האבוקה ו /והוא: זהו ד ה /נקרא: הנקרא ג /רב: רבי ג ה רבינו ז
92 האיי (גאון) ו /(ז"ל) ב ד ה /ועלה: עלה ג /במחשבה: במחשבתו ו /בריאת: בבריאת
א   93 וכן: וכך ב /הטבע: מטבע ג (ז"ל) א /(הפילוסופים) ו (הפילוסופים החריפים)
ה   94 (אילו) ב /שכינה (אילו) ב /הוא היסוד שהוא א   95 (לו) ג /פאות: מראות
ו /ומערב: מערב א ו /ודרום: דרום א ו /מחנות: מחנות: מחנה ד ה ז (מחנות) ג   96 סדרא:
סדריא ב סדריה ג ד סדרי: ה ז /דמארי: דמרי א ז דמריה ד גמרי ד /עלמא: דעלמא ד
ה /(ואילך) ג /סדר: סדרי ב סוד ו ז (שמורה) ו   97 בורא: הבורא ו /אחר: אחד ד /
ממונה: הממונה ה   97-99 טעם... דתנן: והוא כסא הכבוד ועליו אמ' משה כי יד על
כסיה כ"ס שמונים הוא שמונים פילגשים שסידר מאריה דעלמא כולם מלכות ששים
המה מלכים ושמונים פילגשים הוא מטטרון שהוא פילגש לפני גבר' עוז ועליו אמ' משה
ע"ה ואת תדבר אלינו שהוא נות בית בתחלק של והוא נמי כסא הכבוד וכסא הנוגה
והיא אשת חיל הסובלת לבעלה ועליה יש לומר כסא כסא הכבוד וכס יה כ"ס הוא שמונים
פילגשים הרי לך ושמונים פילגשים מבואר היטב. סדר מטטרון מבואר היטב. סדר מטטרון עתה אני מתחיל לסדר
סדר מטטרון מפי ר' עזרא אות באות בתיבה. ג

אחר מפני שהוא סוף למעשה העליונים ותחילה ליסוד התחתונים. וטעם

אחר מפני שיעור הקבוע דתנן אמר הקב"ה למשה משה השמר מפניו שכבר

100 שמתיו משרת לפתח היכלי מבחוץ לעשות דין בכל פמליא של מעלה ובכל

פמליא של מטה ושמע בקולו ללמוד ממנו זכות אל תמר בו דרך הכוונה

לכוין לבך בשעת התפילה וזהו שאמרו חכמי המחקר כי חכמים היו

משימים דעתם בכל מסכתא ומסכתא לבאר רמזים מסתרי התורה ומטעמי

התורה ועל ענין הכוונה אחז"ל במס' ברכות כל המאריך באחד מאריכין לו

105 ימיו ושנותיו וכמה עד שימליכהו בשמים ובארץ ובארבע פנות העולם

וכל זה הוא רמז להמליך הקב"ה בכל כחותיו וההתחלה מן מטטרון וזהו מה

גדלו מעשיך /

ה' מאד עמקו מחשבותיך. מה גדלו מעשיך ה' אלו ד' מחנות. מאד עמקו

מחשבותיך הם /

הכחות האחרות. ועל זה נאמר ברוך כבוד ה' ממקומו שהוא מקום העולם

ואין העולם מקומו. ועוד מקום חשבונו קפ"ו ויהוה חשבונו קפ"ו כיצד י'

110 בחשבון עשרה כשתחשוב עשרה פעמים עשרה הם מאה. ה' בחשבון חמשה

כשתחשוב חמשה פעמים חמשה הם כ"ה. ו' בחשבון ששה כשתחשוב ששה

פעמים ששה הם ל"ו. וה' אחרונה של שם בחשבון כ"ה תמצא השם בחשבון

---

98 אחר: אחד ז/העליונים: עליונים ו/ותחילה: ותחילת ז 99 אחר (הוא) ב/אמר
(לו) ו ז/(משה) א ז/מפניו (ושמע בקולו) א 101-99 (שכבר... מטה) ג 100 דין:
דרך ו/ובכל: ולכל א (ובכל) ו 101-100 (ובכל... מטה) ה 101 ללמוד: ללמד ב/
(ללמוד ממנו זכות) ג/זכות (ושמע בקולו ללמוד ממנו זכות) ו/אל: ואל ה/בו (אל
תמירוני בו) א/בו (שכבר שמתיו משרת לפני פתח היכלי וכל יהוה שיהיה קמצי כמו זה
יהוה הוא אדון העולם וכל פתחי הוא מטטרון שהוא שוער המלך והוא נועל ופותח
והוא ראוי לעשות דין בכל פמליא של מטה ושמע בקולו ללמד ממנו זכות אל תמר [בו
אל] תמיראי בו כי) ג 102 לכוין: תן ו/לבך (בו) ב ה/התפילה: תפלה א ג ז/וזהו:
וזה ו/שאמרו (חז"ל ו) ג/חכמים: חז"ל א 103 משימים: שמים א/מסתרי: מ[נ]רי ב/
מספרי ג/התורה: תורה ב ג ה ז 104 התורה: תורה ב ה ז/(ענין) ו/במס' (שבת)
ב 105 וכמה: ועד כמה א/שימליכהו: שתמליכהו ג/פנות: רוחות ז 106 (הוא) ו
/להמליך (את) ד/הקב"ה: להקב"ה א ז (הקב"ה) ה ו/(בכל כחותיו) א/וההתחלה:
והסתי' א וכההתחלת ב והתחלה ד ו (היא) ג (הוא) ו/(מן) ה מן (מ"ם טית מט' מן) ב
(מ"ט) ד/מטטרון: מט"ט ג ממטטרון ה 107 (וזהו) ה/גדלו: רבו ה /מאוד...
מחשבותיך) ב (מאוד... מעשיך) ג ד ה/עמקו מחשבותיך: וגו' א/מעשיך (ה') ז/אלו: ואל
ה/עמקו: עמקרו ה/הם: והם ה 108 הכחות האחרות: כחות האחדות א/האחרות:
האחרונות ה/ועל: על ה/מקום העולם: מקומו של עולם ג 109 העולם: עולמו ג ד ז
/ויהוה: שם של ד' אותיות ו/וה': קפ"ו: בי בחשבון המרובעת הרחבה ג/(ויהוה חשבונו
קפ"ו) ה/(חשבונו) ה/קפ"ו: ו/קפ"ו: כן א/כיצד: כד ג (קפ"ו) א/(י') ה 110-109 (י'...
כשתחשוב) ו 110 (בחשבון) א/(בחשבון עשרה כשתחשוב) ג/(עשרה הם) ג/הם:
הרי א הן ו/(ה') א ה/בחשבון: חשבונו א ד ז 111-110 (ה'... כשתחשוב) ו/
(בחשבון... כשתחשוב) ג 111 (כשתחשוב) ה/(חמשה) ה (חמשה הם) ג הם: הן ו/(ו'
בחשבון ששה כשתחשוב) ו/בחשבון: חשבון א חשבונו ז (הם) ב/(בחשבון ששה
כשתחשוב) ג/(כשתחשוב) ה 112 (ששה) א (ששה הם) ג/הם: הן ו/וה': ה' פ'
ה' הן כ"ה ו /אחרונה... בחשבון: חמשה פעמים חמשה של שם בחשבון: ה' פעמים חמשה א
(של שם בחשבון) ה /בחשבון: חשבונו ז/כ"ה (כמו כן) ד (כראשונה) ז/תמצא: ונמצא ז /
תמצא השם: הרי כל ב /תמצא השם בחשבון: הרי ג (השם) ו /בחשבון: החשבון ו

קפ"ו. וזהו חשבון המרובע בכל מקום שתחשוב האות והתיבה עצמה
בחשבון תקונה. ועוד יכיר האדם את בוראו על זה העניין שכתבנו ובעניין
תפלתו כמו /

115 שכתבו חז"ל במס' ברכות כשאדם רוצה להתפלל כשהוא כורע כורע בברוך
וכשהוא זוקף זוקף /

בשם ר"ל כשהוא כורע יכוין לבו לשמים כדי ליחד שמו של הקב"ה בכל
כחותיו על הסדר שפירשנו וידע מדה ושיעור ומתכונת הגוף. מדה כמו
שאתה אומר וימודו בעומר. שיעור הוא כמו שאתה אומר משערין בזרת לידע
כמה /

ארכו וכמה רחבו. ומתכונת הגוף כדי שיתבאר לו שגוף הוא נאמר בכל

120 עניין נראה וניכר כמו שאתה אומר גוף הדא מילתא גופא אמר ר' פלוני
גוף עניין זה ולידע שגוף שכינה אינו ניכר ונראה אלא נסתר ונעלם.
והדברים שהגוף ניכר ונראה ממשותו מהם לשלול אותם מגוף
השכינה. כיצד עיני ה'. אזני ה'. ראשו כתם פז. קווצותיו תלתלים. חכו
ממתקים. ידיו גלילי זהב. שוקיו עמודי שש. רגלי ה'. חוטמו של ה'. וכל

125 אילו מפורשים בספר מכלל יופי. ר"ל עיני ה' הם כמו עין אדון עין
לבן שמורים על דמות עיני הכחות. אזני ה' כמו האזינו האזנת

---

113 וזהו: את יהוה מקום ג / חשבון: החשבון ב / בחשבון המתרבה הנקרא ג / שתחשוב:
כשתחשוב ה   113-114 (בכל... תקונה) ג / (שתחשוב... תקונה) ה   114 בחשבון:
כחשבון ז / תקונה: הקונה א תקומה ה / ועוד יכיר האדם: ויתרון האדם להכיר ג /
האדם: אדם א ו ז / על: ועל ד ה / זה: דרך ג / (זה) ב / (העניין) א / שכתבנו: אשר כתבנו
ו(להתפלל) ה / ובעניין: וענין א כענין ו / תפלתו: תפלה א / כמו שכתבנו וכמו ב שכתבנו
ג   115 שכתבנו: שאמרו ג שאמ' ה / שכתבו חז"ל: שאחז"ל ו / חז"ל: חכמים ב ד ז ז"ל
ג (חז"ל) ה / (במס') ו ז / ברכות: שבת ב (ז"ל) ה / (כשאדם... להתפלל) ו ז / (רוצה לתתפלל
כשהוא) ג כורע (בתפלתו) ג / וכשהוא זוקף: וכשזוקף ז   115-116 (זוקף... כורע)
ה   116 בשם (כורע) א / ר"ל: כלי ג / (כשהוא כורע) ד / (כדי) ו   117 על הסדר:
כמו ה / שפירשנו: שפירשתי א שאמרנו ז / וידע: לידע ו / מדה ושיעור: שיעור ומדה ו /
(ומתכונת הגוף) ו / הגוף: כגוף ה / מדה: הוא ו   117-118 כמו שאתה אומר: זש"ה
ג   118 (שאתה... שאתה) ו ז / משערין: משער ד ה / בזרת: בזוית (זו) ב בזרת) ו /
ומתכונת: מתכונת א ב / לו: לנו ג / שגוף: הגוף ה / (הוא) ה ו / נאמר: ואמרו ג   119 (וכמה) ו /
120 (נראה) ה / כמו שאתה אומר: כש"א ו / הדא: הכא ה / (מילתא) ג / גופא: גופה ז (ר')
ד ה / (פלוני) ג   120-151 (נראה... טוב) ב   121 עניין: עליו ד ה / (שגוף) ו / אינו:
אינה ו (אינו) א / (ונראה) ו / (אלא) ד   121-123 לידע... השכינה: לידע שגוף אדם
נראה וניכר והשם ית' אינו נראה וניכר ממשות וישותו מהם צריך לשלול אותם מגוף
שאין לשכינה שום דבר גופי ועל זה אמ' [   ]ש כי להללו יאותו לו מדות דומות לשלל.
ג   122 והדברים: וכדברים ו / (שגוף) ו / ניכר ונראה: נראה וניכר ו / ונראה: נראה ד
ה / ממשותו: ממשות ה / לשלול אותם: לשלמותם ז   123 השכינה: שבעה ד ה / (עיני
ה' אזני ה') ו (אזני ה') ה / פז (סוד המך כסאו) ג   124 חוטמו: חותמו ה / חוטמו של
ה': אף ה' ג / וכל: וכולם ו   125 אילו (הם) א / מפורשים: מפורשות ו [   ]לים) ג /
(ר"ל) ג ה ו ז / ה' (ר"ל) ו / (ר"ל עיני ה') ז / הם: ר"ל ג / (כמו עין) ה   126 שמורים:
שמורות ה שאמרים ו / על: כל ה / כמו (האזנתו) / האזנת: א / האזנתם א והאזנת א
האזנתי ד והאזנת ה

ופירושו שיקול המלה להבין עניינה וזהו מאזנים האזינה והדומים
לאילו. ראשו כתם פז הוא כסא כבודו כמו שהוא ראש לפעליו
כדכתיב כסא כבוד מרום מראשון ר"ל מרום מעלליו של שם. קווצותיו

130 תלתלים זהו שבעה אלה עיני ה' המה משוטטות בכל הארץ. טעם אחר
קווצותיו כמו קצות הארץ. חכו ממתקים זהו כח הממתיק לכל
מי שמתעסק בזו החכמה. וכלו מחמדים זהו יופיאל שמייפה לכל
הנבראים מאחדות השוה. ידיו גלילי זהב הם הגלגלים. שוקיו עמודי
שש הם זהרי חמה שמשתמשין בגלגל הרקיע העליון וזהו דכתיב ודמות

135 על ראשי החיה רקיע. רגלי ה' כמו שהוא אומר השמים כסאי והארץ הדום
רגלי הם חיילותיו כדכתיב רק אין דבר ברגלי אעבורה. חוטמו הוא
האף ועיקרו אחטם לך כלומר אסבך לך עניינים כדי שיתחטם גזר דיני
לבלתי יתפשט לחבל העולם כדתנן בספר מכלל יופי הקב"ה שם מלאך
בין וילון לרקיע ושמו דומיאל שהוא ממונה לסתום פיהם של מלאכי

140 חבלה כדי שלא יתפשטו בעולם לחבלו. טעם אחר אחטם לך אשקיע
כמו אז אשקיע מימיהם כלומר אשקיע העבירה ואגלה הזכות וכל זה למכוין
יחוד בכל משליו ואל יוציא דבר מגונה מפיו ויכוין לבו בהזכרת
השם להזכירו באלו שבעה נקודים באיזה מהם שירצה יְהוָה מֶלֶךְ יָהֹוָה
מָלָךְ יְהֹוָה יִמְלוֹךְ מחזה שדי יחזה. דרכיך ה' הודיעני וכך

---

127 ופירושו: ופירוש א (ופירושו) ג / שיקול: שיכיל ד / שיקול המלה: שכל המדה ה /
עיינה: עיינו ו / וזהו: מלשון א מהו ו / מאזנים: מאזני ד (מאזנים) ה (וזה אמרי) א
(האזינו) ו / (האזינה) ג / והדומים לאילו: והדומה לו ג (והדומים לאילו) ד והדומים:
ודומים ו   128   כבודו: כבוד א ג / כמו: דמות ז (כמו) א ג / ראש: ראשית ה (לכל) ג /
לפעליו: מפעליו ג פעליו ד ה   128-129 (כמו... כבוד) ו   129   (מראשון... שם) א /
(ר"ל מרום) ד ה / מעלליו: למעלליו ז / מעלליו של שם: שלשי מעלותיו ו / של: על ה
130   תלתלים זהו: אותיות ד ה / (בכל הארץ) א / טעם: וטעם ג   130-131   (זהו...
קווצותיו) ו   131   (קווצותיו) ג (תלתלים) ו ז / כמו: ר"ל ו / (זהו) ה / הממתיק: הממתק
ד   132   שמתעסק: שיתעסק ה / בזו: בזאת א ו / זהו: והוא א זה ו / שמייפה: שמו יפה
ה   133   מאחדות: מן אחדות ג / השוה: השגה ז   134   הם: הן ו / זהרי: והרי ה /
שמשתמשין: שמשמשים ה שמשתמשים ו / הרקיע: רקיע ו / וזהו: זהו ו / וזהו דכתיב:
הה"ד א / (ודמות) א ו ז   134-135   זהרי... רקיע: שש קצוון [ ] ג   135   החיה:
החיות ה ו ז / שהוא אומר: שנא' ג שאתה אומ' ה שאמר ו   135-136   (והארץ... הם)
א   136   רגלי (השמים כסאי) ג / כדכתיב: כמו א דכתיב ג / דבר ו / חוטמו:
חוטם ג וחוטמו ו / הוא: זה ה   137   ועיקרו: ועיקר ה (הוא) ו / אסבר: אסבב א אספר
ה אכובב ו / (עניינים) א / דיני: דינו א דין ד ה   137-138 (אחטם... לחבל) ג
138   כדתנן: כדכתיב ד ככתו' ה וכן כתי' ו   139   לרקיע: ורקיע ד ז / דומיאל: סמאל
ג / שהוא ממונה: שממונה ג   140   (כדי) א (אחר) ו / (אחר) א / (ותהלתי) אחטם לך (לבלתי הכריתך פי) ג (לך)
א   140-141 (אשקיע כמו אז) ג   141   (אז) ה ו / אשקיע (את) א ו / כלומר: כמו א
פי' ג כאלו ד כלו ה / אשקיע (כל) ג / ואגלה את ה / וכל זה: וזה ה / למכוין: למבין ד
לכוין ה   142   יחוד: יחוסו ד (יחוד) ו / משליו: מושליו ה / ואל: ולא ה / (מגונה)
ה   143   השם (ב"ה) ג / יהוה: א' א ז או ו (יהוה) ג ד / יהוה: או ו (יהוה) א ג ד ה
ז   144   יהוה: או ו (יהוה) א ג ד ה ז / מחזה: ומחזה א / מחזה: ומחזה א / וכך: וכן א ג
בכך ו כך ז

145 פירשו בעלי הלשון והקב"ה ידריכנו בדרך אחדותו לייחד שמו בכל
מפעלינו ודרך תבונות יודיענו. אמר ר' ישמעאל קראתי ושניתי זה
העניין לפני ר' נחוניא בן הקנה ואמר לי כל היודע רז זה ושונה
אותו במשנה בכל יום מובטח לו שהוא בן העולם הבא ונוחל שני
עולמות העולם הזה והעולם הבא ויתן לו הקב"ה משכר העולם הבא
150 כבוד לנחול בעולם הזה דכתיב כבוד חכמים ינחלו ותמימים ינחלו
טוב.

---

145 פירשו: פירש ה / בעלי לשון: לך ה / והקב"ה: הקב"ה א הב"ה ה / בדרך ⟨ישרה ב⟩ ג /
אחדותו: ייחודו ד ה   146 מפעלינו: מפעלים א מפעליו ה ו / יודיענו: תודיענו ג יורנו
ד ה ז / קראתי: קריתי ז   151-146 ⟨אמר... טוב⟩ ג   147 רז: רזה ה / ושונה: ושנה
ה   148 ⟨במשנה⟩ ד ה   149 עולמות: עולמים ד / ⟨העולם⟩ ה / ⟨והעולם⟩ ה / ויתן:
ונותן ה / ⟨הקב"ה⟩ ו / משכר ⟨טוב⟩ ו / העולם: לעולם ו   150 כבוד: כדי א ⟨כבוד⟩ ה /
בעולם: העולם ד / ⟨ותמימים ינחלו טוב⟩ ו

This is *The Book of Contemplation* that Rabbi Hammai, of blessed memory, the principal spokesman, composed on the topic of the Innermost. In it he revealed the essence of the entire existence of the Glory, which is hidden from sight. No creature can truly comprehend the essence of His existence and His nature, since He is in the state of balanced unity; for in His completeness the higher and lower beings are united. He is the foundation of everything that is hidden and revealed. From Him issues forth all that is emanated from the wondrousness of the Unity.[185] Rabbi Hammai explained all these matters according to the account of the Chariot and the explication of Ezekiel's prophecy, peace be upon him. This is the beginning of the treatise in proper order.[186]

Blessed and exalted is the Name, which is majestic in valor, for He is One, who unites with his powers, like the flame of a fire that is united with its colors.[187] Moreover, His powers emanate from His Unity like the light of the eye, which issues forth from the pupil of the eye.[188] These are emanated from those, like a scent from a scent or a candle-flame from a candle-flame, since this emanates from that and that from something else, and the power of the emanator is within that which was emanated. The emanator, however, does not lack anything.[189]

Thus the Holy One, blessed be He, before He created anything, He was primordial, inscrutable, and limitless,[190] without conjunction and without disjunction, without change and without movement.[191] He was hidden in the sustaining power. At the time when His priority was intellectualized, prior to all primal elements that issue forth from

---

185. Until this point, the text is the same as *Contemplation–Short* and *Contemplation–Long*.

186. See *Contemplation–Long*, p. 69.

187. See *Contemplation–Short*, p. 41.

188. Cf. *Contemplation–Long*, p. 78.

189. See *Contemplation–Short*, p. 41.

190. Cf. *Contemplation–Thirteen Powers*, p. 83.

191. Cf. R. Judah Barzeloni's *Perush*, 56: "without conjunction and without disjunction, without change and without movement."

the central emanation[192] He was hidden and able to exist by Himself, and His power was indiscernible.[193] When it arose in His mind to bring into being all of His action, His Glory appeared and His Glory and radiance were revealed simultaneously.[194]

The explanation of knowledge of Him is through five processes and they are: *tikkun*, combination, utterance, sum, and computation. The knowledge of these five processes is unique in the branches of the root of vocalization that is magnified in the root of the thirteen types of transformation. How is the *tikkun* [accomplished]? It derives the word through the utterance and the utterance through the word; the sum through the computation and the computation through the sum—until all the words are positioned in the font of the flame and the flame in the font—until there is no measuring or quantifying the light that is hidden in the superabundance of the secret darkness.[195]

Moreover, the knowledge of the Unity and Its root is this darkness, and its explanation is explicated herein, as R. Ishmael b. Elisha, the high priest, explained it in the Chamber of Hewn Stones.[196] As we teach,[197] R. Ishmael said, That day we were present, I and R. Akiva b. Joseph, before R. Nehuniah b. ha-Kanah. R. Hanina b. Taradion[198] was also there. I asked R. Nehuniah b. ha-Kanah, saying to him, Rabbi, show me the Glory of the King of the universe, in order that the knowledge of Him, like His other actions, will be clari-

---

192. *'azilut ha-mitmaza'*; cf. R. Meshullam's *Kabbalah*, below, p. 209 for the expression *ha-'ahdut ha-mitmaza'* (central Unity).

193. This passage is an abridgment of *Contemplation–Thirteen Powers*, p. 83, which in turn combines elements from either *Contemplation–Short* or *Contemplation–Long*.

194. See *Contemplation–Short*, p. 42.

195. This paragraph represents a slight reworking of material from the start of *Fountain*; see above, p. 50f.

196. Cf. *B. Berakhot*, 7a, concerning R. Ishmael's encounter with Divine angel 'Akatri'el. This episode was elaborated upon in the *hekhalot* corpus in similar ways to that of *Contemplation–Standard*; see P. Schafer, *Synopse zur Hekhalot-Literatur* (Tubingen 1981), 138, #309.

197. *De-tenan* is indicative of a quote from a mishnaic source, which in this case is fanciful. This entire section bears the influence of *hekhalot* literature; see specifically *Hekhalot Rabbati*, ch. 15, in *Battei Midrashot*, 1:90.

198. Cf. *Hekhalot Rabbati*, 80f.

fied in my heart. He said to me, Son of the proud,[199] come let us delve into the great ring[200] on which is engraved the name and *'aR'aRYeT'a*[201]

---

199. Cf. *Hekhalot Rabbati*, 90, and Schafer, *Synopse*, 170, #403.

200. Magic rings, engraved with Divine or angelic names, were a frequent component of *hekhalot* literature; see *Hekhalot Zutarti*, 32; *Hekhalot Rabbati*, ch. 25, p. 36; *Sefer ha-Razim*, 105; *3 Enoch*, 73 (Hebrew); *Sefer Razi'el*, 51b; *Merkavah Shelemah*, f. 26b; and M. Cohen, *The Shiur Qomah*, 231; as well as the Metatron material in Schafer, *Synopse*, 164, #389, and 166, #396. For a rabbinic narrative concerning King Solomon and a magic ring that was engraved with a Divine name, cf. *B. Gittin*, 68a.

201. The Divine name, *'aR'aRYeT'a*, is explained below as an acrostic related to the theme of Divine Unity. It appears to have been coined by the author of *Contemplation–Standard*. Scholem contended that it is found in two earlier sources; see *Origins*, 315 and n. 240 there. The magical text from the *hasidei 'ashkenaz* that he referred to is British Museum 752, f. 93b. Upon examination of this manuscript one discovers instead, the name *'aDDYT'a*. Furthermore, I was unable to locate anything comparable in the second source *Tefillah de-R. Hamnuna Saba*. An examination of Schafer's *Konkordanz zur Hekhalot-Literatur* (Tubingen 1986), 1:78, reveals the existence of the following letter combinations: *'aR'aYT* and *'aR'aR RR YH*; however, neither of these functions as an acrostic.
Nevertheless, it is possible that *'aR'aRYeT'a* stems from the *hasidei 'ashkenaz*, for in J.T.S. 1884, f. 20b, transcribed below, p. 203 this term is attributed to R. Meir of Germany and others, who seem to be connected with the *hasidei 'ashkenaz*. In this text *'aR'aRYeT'a* is explained in reference to the lion, *'arya'*, which in rabbinic literature (cf. *Yoma* 21b) was said to have been lying on the altar. Other interpretations include the commentary on The *Prayer of Unity of R. Nehuniah*, in which it is depicted as equaling the sum of the numerical values of the highest *sefirot*: *keter* (= 620), *hokhmah* (= 73), *binah* (= 67), the fifty "Gates of Understanding," and the three *matres* letters. This totals 813, as does *'aR'aRYeT'a*. Another interpretation is offered by R. Joseph of Hamadan (cited in Altmann, *K.S.* 40 [1964] 268) who comments, "and it is called *'aRaRYeT'a*, for from thence begins the light (*'or*).
In the text *Sod ha-Neshamot ha-Penimiyyot*, which Scholem attributed to R. Isaac Cohen, *Kabbalot*, 123, one reads about *'oratya*, which is explained as an acrostic for *'ozar* (treasure), *rahamim* (mercy) and *tif'eret* (beauty). It is likely that both *'aR'aRYeT'a* and *'oratya* were formulated as a result of their similarity to the Aramaic, *'orayyta*, signifying the Torah. For a specialized usage of *'orayyta* in the *Shi'ur Komah*, cf. M. Cohen, *The Shiur Qomah*, 187 and 189, n. 16.
Finally, it is interesting to note that *'aR'aRYeT'a* eventually made its way into the Jewish liturgy. In the evening service for the New Year a special

is His name, as well as the ring of the earth, which is *'aHV*.[202] I will show you everything.

I entered inside,[203] into the Outer Holy Palace,[204] and removed from there R. Nehuniah b. ha-Kanah's book, entitled *Book of the Celestial Palaces*,[205] and discovered the following, written at the start of the book.

Mighty within the rooms of grandeur[206] is He who sits on the wheels of His chariot, with the seal *'ehyeh 'asher 'ehyeh* (I will be who I will be), and with a great ring on which is engraved the name *'aR'aRYeT'a*, which is His name. It denotes: *O*ne, the *S*tart of His *U*nification, the *S*tart of His *U*nity, His *P*ermutation is *O*ne, Individual and Unique; Individual, Unique, One.[207] Also, with the ring of the earth that is *'aHV*, which is His name, denoting: *O*ne who *W*as *A*nd will be. The intermediary between both of them is He who is.

---

prayer for prosperity is recited. It concludes by referring to several Divine names from the magical tradition, including *'aR'aRYeT'a*; see *Maḥzor Rabba* (Jerusalem n.d.), 30.

202.   This too is explained below as referring to God's existential nature. The family of mss. comprised of Mousayeff 64 and Munich 408, offers a slightly different reading, which may actually represent the original. Mousayeff has *'aHVY* and Munich has a scribal misreading, *'aHNY*. Several other texts of the "Circle" discuss *'aHVY*, including *Fountain* and *Explanation of the Name 'aHVY*; see also R. Elhanan b. Yakar's *Perush Sheni*, Dan ed., *Tekstim*, 33, 37, and 39. The source for all of these texts is R. Judah ha-Levi's *Kuzari*, ch. 3:3, p. 221, and 4:25, pp. 266f, wherein ha-Levi contends that these four letters represent the basis of the Tetragrammaton.

203.   On the leitmotif of secrets hidden in the innermost chambers, cf. M. Cohen, *Shiur Qomah*, 119.

204.   See below, p. 125.

205.   Scholem assumes that this material represents an unknown, yet authentic text, *Origins*, 314. However, owing to the author's penchant for fabricating sources, one should be skeptical; furthermore, it must be considered in relation to R. Meshullam's *Kabbalah*, which influenced *Contemplation–Standard* and which likewise mimics *hekhalot* literature; see below, p. 208.

206.   This expression is found in *Ma'aseh Merkavah*, ed. G. Scholem, *Gnosticism*, 107. This text has recently been translated by N. Janowitz in *The Poetics of Ascent* (Albany 1989); see also Schafer, *Synopse* 212, #558.

207.   See Scholem's discussion of this expression, *Origins*, 342, n. 284.

"A word spoken appropriately" (Prov. 25:1). He was prior to when He created the world; He is in this world, and He will be in the world to come.[208] This is symbolized by: He did, He does, He will do.

In this orderly presentation, the root of all the essences are explained that are contained in the *Book of the Account of Creation.*[209] They are the counsel that is revealed from the Supreme Hiddenness that is concealed, which is called *'omen*, meaning the Father of Faith, from whose power faith was emanated. He, may He be blessed, is united with His powers and is elevated and exalted above them, such that there is no end to His exaltedness. He is unique amongst the thirteen powers. Each and every power has a well-known, distinctive name, and their position is one atop the other. The first is called Primordial Wisdom. The second is Marvellous Light. The third is *hashmal.* The fourth is *'arafel.* The fifth is Throne of Light. The sixth is Wheel of Greatness, which is called *hazhazit* (looking-glass), meaning the place of the source of the seers' vision. The seventh is called Cherub. The eighth is called Wheels of the Chariot. The ninth is the Encompassing Ether. The tenth is Celestial Curtain. The eleventh is Throne of Glory. The twelfth is Domain of the Souls, which is called Chambers of Greatness. The thirteenth is the Secret of the Supreme Configuration, which is called the Outer Holy Palace.

These thirteen powers are revealed together from the Supreme Hiddenness that is concealed, which is called *'omen*, meaning Father of faith, from whose power faith was emanated. And He, may He be blessed, before He created anything was called *'el*, that is to say, very strong. His power was not yet discernible. When He began to manifest His actions, He brought into being the two products of mystery and faith, in the balanced unity, and the essence that we can perceive through inquiry into the Creator of this world.

Know that the Master of the entire universe, may His name be blessed, is a living light, pure and refined, comprised of the radiance of the shining light, the brilliant light perceptible by none, bright like the image of the form of the soul, which is entirely imperceptible.[210] He, may His name be blessed, even though the splendor of His Glory is not perceptible, on account of the honor of His creatures He made

---

208. See R. Elhanan's *Sod ha-Sodot*, Dan ed., 3, in which the three *havayot* of the Tetragrammaton are: He was, He is, and He will be.

209. See above, p. 82, n. 144. This paragraph and the next are taken from *Contemplation–Thirteen Powers.*

210. See *Contemplation–Short*, p. 42.

for Himself a likeness,²¹¹ as if it were an actual body. For the honor
of Israel there is an angel appointed before the Holy One, blessed be
He, who blesses in the name of Israel each day, in order to sanctify
the name of the Holy One, blessed be He, in the glory of the sanctification of those that dwell below.

The Holy One, blessed be He, is unique amongst the seven
angels that sit in the first echelon in the kingdom of the supreme
heaven. They are: 'Orpani'el, Tigra'el, Danra'el, Palmi'el, 'Asimon,
Paska'el and Bo'el.²¹² Concerning them it is said, "The seraphs are
standing above Him, each one with six wings" (Isa. 6:2). This refers
to the camps²¹³ which surround Him, before and behind. They are
called souls, as we teach in the *Book of the Essential Sapphire Brick-
work.*²¹⁴ "The Holy One, blessed be He, is a soul for the soul."²¹⁵ All
these seven camps are called soul and the Master of all is a soul for
this soul. He is elevated through the attribute of mercy and is exalted,
until there is no end to His exaltedness. Therefore we say, "On the
Heavens is His Glory" (Ps. 113:4). This is the body of the Divine
Presence.²¹⁶

---

211. *dumiyyah.* Compare R. Eleazar b. Judah, *Ḥokhmat ha-Nefesh.*
"*Ḥokhmat ha-Demuyyot*"; see also below, n. 217. On *dumiyyah* as mystical
silence, cf. G. Scholem, *Gnosticism,* 33.

212. On the seven archangels, see above, *Contemplation–Short,* p. 45, n.
37. See also the *Book of True Unity,* which focuses on these seven "seraphs."
This list of archangels with slight variants is found at the end of *Ma'aseh
Merkavah,* also known as *Masekhet Hekhalot, Battei Midrashot,* 1:62. A better version of this text is found in Florence ms. 2:41/4, f. 161a.

213. The concept of the four camps of the Divine Presence is known from
classical sources, see below, n. 219. The association between the four angelic
categories and the seven archangels was already developed in
Contemplation–Short. Contemplation–Standard takes this one step further
by asserting that these seven archangels also correspond to camps.

214. No such work is known.

215. Based on Ibn Gabirol's *Keter Malkhut,* "for You are the soul of the
soul"; cf. G. Scholem "'*Ikvotav shel Gavirol,*" *Me'asef Sofrei 'Erez Yisra'el*
(1940), 163f. Although therein Scholem quotes *Contemplation–Standard* as
reading "soul of the souls," most manuscripts read "soul of the soul," which
is identical with Ibn Gabirol's poem.

216. *guf ha-shekhinah.* This expression is rooted in *hekhalot* literature. For
example, in *Masekhet Hekhalot* we read, "This is the body of the presence

Afterwards the Holy One, blessed by He, created an image[217] using the four primal elements,[218] like the image of a real man. These are the four camps of the Divine Presence.[219] They are: Michael, Gabriel, 'Uri'el, and Raphael, and their epithets are: *ḥashmal, 'arafel,* Throne of Light, and Wheel of Greatness. *Mikh*[220] of Michael corresponds to the seventy names;[221] *mal*[222] of *ḥashmal* also corresponds to the seventy names.[223] This is symbolized by "the secret of God is for those who fear Him" (Ps. 25:14). Thus Scripture divided *ḥash* from *ḥashmal* and *'el* from Michael, and since they are equivalent,[224] *ḥasha'el* was formed from them, that is to say, quickness[225] for the Glory of God.

---

of His Glory" (*shekhinat kevodo*), Parma ms. 3531, f. 2a, cited in Schafer, *Konkordanz*, 143. Moshe Idel traces it to the *Midrash 'Otiyyot de-R. Akiva,* wherein it is synonymous with *shi'ur komah,* Cosmic Measure, "'*Olam ha-Mal 'akhim be-Demut 'Adam*" in *Meḥkerei Yerushalayim be-Maḥshevet Yisra'el,* 3:1 (1984), 30 and n. 110; see also M. Idel, "*Bayn Tefisat ha-'Azmut le-Tefisat ha-Kelim,*" *Italia,* 3:103f. *Guf ha-shekhinah* is also found in R. Meshullam's *Kabbalah,* below, p. 210, referring to the four *yesodot,* primal elements.

217. *demut:* On R. Eleazar b. Judah's theory of *demut* as an archetype, see G. Scholem, *Origins,* 112, n. 114.

218. See above, p. 46f.

219. On the four camps of the *shekhinah,* cf. *Ma'aseh Merkavah,* in *Battei Midrashot* 1:59, *Pirkei de-R. Eliezer,* ch. 4, R. Ezra, *Perush le-Shir ha-Shirim,* 489, R. Azriel, *Perush ha-'Aggadot,* 73, R. Asher b. David, *Kabbalat,* Dan ed., 54 and R. Joseph Gikatilla, *Sha'arei 'Orah,* 1:56.

220. *Mikh* equals seventy.

221. See above, *Contemplation–Short,* p. 45, n. 40.

222. *Mal* equals seventy.

223. In *Contemplation–Short,* p. 45, the seventy names are discussed only in reference to the *'ayin* of *'arafel.* In *Contemplation–Thirteen Powers,* p. 86f., these names are also connected to the *mal* of *ḥashmal.* Here they are related in addition to Michael. Accordingly, we see a gradual expansion of this doctrine. See also, p. 209.

224. Namely *mal* and *mikh,* see above n. 220 and n. 222.

225. See above, *Contemplation–Thirteen Powers,* p. 86, n. 176.

Voice and breath and speech.[226] The voice represents inquiry. The breath is the intellect that is fixed in the heart.[227] Speech is the secret of knowledge. Concerning this[228] it is said, "like the appearance of a man above Him" (Ezek. 1:26).

Morever, *ḥashmal* is an acronym: *ḥet = ḥokhmah* (wisdom); *shin = shalom* (peace); *mem = memshalah* (dominion); *lamed = levush* (garment).[229] Wisdom, as is written, "And wisdom shall be brought into being from nothingness" (Job 28:12). Peace, as is written, "He makes peace in His exalted regions" (Job 25:2). Dominion, as is written, "Dominion and fear are with Him" (Job 25:2). Garment, as is written, "Glory and splendor have You worn" (Ps. 104:1). Thus our sages, of blessed memory, have written in *Ḥagigah*, "*Ḥashmal* represents 338 types of lights. The smallest of all of them is like the radiance of the solar sphere. In addition, there are those that say 378, corresponding to its numerical value."[230] So it is written in the book *The Fountain of Wisdom*, "The good and the better, for everything is His."[231] This is the start of His activity: 620 are the start of His utterance, symbolizing *keter* (crown).[232] This denotes waiting.[233] This is the interpretation of Michael and *ḥashmal* and comprises one topic,[234] which is called the element of water. Behold the first camp.

---

226.   *Sefer Yeẓirah*, 1:9, see above, p. 54 and 61f.

227.   *ha-sekhel ha-kavu'a ba-lev.* In *Mo'znei Zedek*, an early thirteenth-century Hebrew translation of a treatise by the Islamic philosopher-theologian al-Ghazali, we read (p. 152) "Know that the exaltedness of the intellect (*ha-sekhel*) is on account of its being a tabernacle for wisdom . . . and it is fixed (*kavu'ah*) within it."

228.   Namely, the "image" discussed above.

229.   This acronym is also found at the conclusion of *Contemplation–Long*.

230.   There is no such comment in *Ḥagigah*. In *Contemplation–Long*, where this statement also occurs, there is no such ascription to rabbinic literature. Its source is actually *hekhalot* literature, see above, p. 78, n. 140.

231.   Although there are two texts by this name–one of which being central to the "Circle"–in neither does this material appear.

232.   *Keter* equals 620; see above, p. 86, n. 173.

233.   See above, p. 85, n. 170.

234.   The association between the four powers, angelic camps and elements is rooted in R. Meshullam's *Kabbalah*, see below, p. 209.

The second camp is Gabriel and he is *'arafel*. He is the element of fire and he grasps the roots of *hashmal*. How so? We have already said that *mal* of *hashmal* represents seventy; it is equivalent to the *'ayin* of *'arafel*, representing the seventy names.[235] Behold these are amongst those. So it is written in the recited poem of R. Pinhas Hisma, "These are grasping those in the wings of the secret of movement."[236] That is to say, these opposites are grasping each other: the element of water, which is Michael, and the element of fire, which is Gabriel. Behold the explanation of the *'ayin* of *'arafel*.

The explanation of *resh peh lamed*. Consider *resh peh*.[237] When you subtract 236 from the value of *resh peh* (280), alluding to the measure of the Throne of Glory, forty-four remains. When you subtract two from forty-four, to put them with the *lamed* (30) of *'arafel*, yielding 32, then 42 remains. They are represented by "God is with them."[238] It is also denoted by "I shall turn and see this great vision" (Exod. 3:3).[239] Accordingly, Gabriel indicates God has triumphed (*gavar*) over us.

The third camp is Unity itself. It is 'Uri'el. He is the element of the spirit and the ether. He shines on the side of the domain of the souls. He is connoted by, "Arise my light (*'ori*) for your light has come," (Isa. 60:1) for in the future he will illuminate Israel's gloom.

The fourth camp is Raphael, the true healer (*rofeh*). Therefore, he is called the element of the earth, since he was appointed over the dust, pulverized from under the Throne of Glory. This is called matter, as Rabbi Hai, of blessed memory, said,[240] "And there arose in His thought the creation of primal matter,[241] from which were emanated all creatures." So it was also explained by the forceful physi-

---

235. See above, n. 223.

236. Another fanciful attribution, cf. *Origins*, 318, n. 245.

237. The following calculation is taken from *Contemplation–Short*, p. 45.

238. *bam* (with them) equals forty-two.

239. *ha-gadol* (great) is written without a *vav* and likewise equals forty-two.

240. Another fanciful ascription.

241. Some thirteenth-century kabbalists endorsed the Platonic theory of primordial matter, see R. Ezra's comments, in his critique of Maimonides, in G. Scholem, "*Te'udah*," 157f., and his *Perush le-Shir ha-Shirim*, 494. See also Nachmanides' discussion of *homer rishon* in his commentary of Gen. 1:1, *Perushei ha-Torah*, 1, p. 12; as well as I. Efros, *Studies*, 192.

cists, the keen philosophers of theoretical science.[242] After these four camps of the Divine Presence, there is the Unity, which is called the Holy Palace.[243] It has four corners corresponding to east and west, north and south, as well as the four camps of the Divine Presence.

Until this point has been the delineation of the Master of the universe, from here on is the delineation of Metatron, who teaches knowledge of the Creator of the universe, through a different delineation. Know that Metatron was appointed to serve in front of the Holy Palace. Another explanation is that he is the end of the supernal realm and the start of the lower elements.[244] Another explanation is on account of the fixed measure, as we teach,[245] "The Holy One, blessed be He, said to Moses, "Moses, beware of him" (Exod. 23:21), for I have posted him as an attendant outside the door of My palace, in order to administer the law, throughout the supernal domain and the lower domain. "Listen to his voice," (Exod. 23:21) in order to learn from him how to warrant merit. "Do not rebel against him" (Exod. 23:21)[246] through concentration, by directing your heart dur-

---

242. *ḥokhmei ha-meḥkar*. This term is frequently found in R. Azriel's writings, e.g., *Perush 'Eser Sefirot*, 1, *Perush 'Aggadot*, 87, and *Perush Sefer Yeẓirah*, 460. It usually refers to Neoplatonic material. See the discussion in I. Efros, *Studies*, 19. Scholem, *Origins*, 318, improbably interprets this passage as being a paraphrase of Erigena's *De Divisione Naturae*; see below, p. 182.

243. See above, p. 47, n. 55.

244. This discussion on Metatron is a reworking of *Contemplation–Short*, p. 48.

245. This passage is based on *Shi'ur Komah*; cf. M. Cohen, *Shiur Qomah*, 235f., and *'Otiyyot de-R. Akiva*, 352. See also the text from the circle of the Unique Cherub, published by J. Dan, "*Kavvanat ha-Tefillah me-Kabbalat ha-R. Y. Ḥ.*, *Da'at*, 10 (1983), 48-50, esp. p. 49, which has numerous parallels with this section of *Contemplation–Standard*.

246. See M. Cohen's comments, *Shiur Qomah*, 238, n. 7, on the play on words between *tammer* (rebel) and *tamir* (exchange) thereby warning against confusing Metatron with God. That Metatron's position was problematic is seen in the veiled comments at the end of *Contemplation–Short*, as well as the shifting of Metatron's status in *Contemplation–Long*; see above, p. 70. Other mid-thirteenth-century sources that reflect this concern are the *Perush le-Shi'ur Komah*, which condemns as heretical the association of Metatron and the Divine Presence; cf. Scholem, *Reshit*, 174, n. 2, and the *Introduction to Sefer ha-'Orah*, Milano ms. 62, ff. 85b-93b, which Scholem attributed to R. Jacob Cohen; cf. *Reshit*, 257. Therein (f. 93a) we read that one should direct one's thoughts to God and not Metatron when studying this treatise.

ing prayers." Thus the theoreticians have asserted that the sages used to fix their attention on each and every Talmudic tractate in order to explicate the allusions of the secrets of the Torah and the cantillation notes of the Torah. On this topic of concentration, the sages, of blessed memory, have said in *Berakhot*,[247] anyone who prolongs the recitation of the word "one," his days and years will be increased. How long (should he prolong it)? Until he has acknowledged His sovereignty in heaven and on earth, and the four corners of the world. All of this is an allusion to acknowledging the sovereignty of the Holy One, blessed be He, over all of His powers. The start is with Metatron. Thus it is written, "How great are Your deeds, Lord, exceedingly deep are Your thoughts" (Ps. 92:6). "How great are Your deeds, Lord," these are the four camps; "exceedingly deep are Your thoughts" are the other powers.

Concerning this it was said, "Blessed is the Glory of God from His place" (Ezek. 3:13). He is the domain (*makom*) of the world, but the world is not His domain.[248] Moreover, the numerical value of *makom* is 186, and the Tetragrammaton (*yud heh vav heh*) is also 186.[249] How so? *Yud* (= ten) as a multiple of ten, when you calculate ten times ten, it is 100. *Heh* (= five) as a multiple of five, when you calculate five times five, it is twenty-five. *Vav* (= six) as a multiple of six, when you calculate six time six, it is thirty-six. The final *heh* of the Name yields a sum of twenty-five. Accordingly, you shall find that the Name yields a sum of 186. This is the calculation which has been completely squared, when you calculate the numerical value of each individual letter and word in a correct computation.

Moreover, one can recognize his Creator through this subject about which we have written. Concerning the topic of prayer, it is as the sages, of blessed memory, have written in the tractate of *Berakhot*, "When one wants to pray, he should bow at the word "blessed" and straighten up at the Name."[250] That is to say, when he bows, he should direct his heart to Heaven in order to unite God's name with all of His powers, according to the order that we explained.

---

247. *B. Berakhot*, 13b.

248. *Bere'shit Rabbah*, 68:9.

249. This calculation of "squaring" the Tetragrammaton, thereby yielding the *gematria* of *makom* is found in R. Eleazar of Worms' *Sefer ha-Ḥokhmah*, in *Perush ha-Rokeaḥ*, Vol. 1 (Bnei Brak 1978), 33.

250. *B. Berakhot*, 12a.

He should know the measure and the dimension and the proportion of the body. The measure is, as you say, "and measure it with an omer" (Exod. 16:8). The dimension is, as you say, they measure with a *zeret* to know how long and how wide. Finally, the proportion of the body is in order that it will be clear to him that it is a body, about which it is said concerning everything that is visible and discernible–as you say, the "body" of this topic: *gufa'* (body), Rabbi so and so said this specific thing. Know moreover that the body of the Divine Presence[251] is neither discernible nor visible, but secret and hidden. Whatever is related to a body and has a substance, which is discernible and visible, one must negate these things from the body of the Divine Presence.

What about the eyes of God? the ears of God? His head is fine gold? His locks are braided? His palate is sweet? His hands are gold rods? His legs are marble pillars? the feet of God? the nose of God?[252] All these things are explained in the book *Consummate Beauty*.[253] Thus the eyes (*'aynei*) of God are like the color (*'ayin*) red or the color white, referring to the images of the colors of the powers.[254] The ears (*'oznei*) of god are like, "we have heard" (*ha'azinu*) or you heard, and its explanation is the weighing of a word in order to understand its meaning; hence, scales (*mo'znayim*), weighing, and similar expressions. "His head (*ro'sho*) is fine gold" (Cant. 5:11). This is the Throne of His Glory,[255] since it was the first (*ro'sh*) of His deeds, as is written, "The Throne of Glory is on high from the beginning" (Jer. 17:12) that is to say, the most exalted of the deeds of the Name. "His locks are braided" (Cant. 5:11). They are seven, being the eyes of God that roam over all of the earth.[256] Another explanation, His locks

---

251. *guf ha-shekhinah*; see above, n. 216.

252. In general, these anthropomorphic images are drawn from Canticles 5:11-16. These verses were discussed in the *Shi'ur Komah*, cf. *Sefer Razi'el*, f. 51a. Moshe Idel has convincingly demonstrated the indebtedness of this presentation to Ibn Ezra's commentary on Song of Songs, "*'Olam*," 21f.

253. Another fanciful work.

254. See G. Scholem, "Colours and their Symbolism," *Diogenes*, 108 (1979), 103.

255. So too in Ibn Ezra, *Perush le-Shir ha-Shirim*, 5:11.

256. Compare Ibn Ezra, *Perush*, 5:11; see also R. Moses Cordovero's utilization of this passage from *Contemplation–Standard*, *Pardes Rimmonim*, *Sha'ar Hekhalot*, ch. 4, f. 47b.

(*kevuzzotav*) like in the ends (*kazvot*) of the earth. "His palate is sweet" (Cant. 5:15). This is the power that offers sweetness to any who engages in this wisdom. "And He is altogether lovely" (Cant. 5:16). This is Yofi'el,[257] who beautifies all that was emanated from the balanced unity. "His hands are golden rods (*gelilei*)" (Cant. 5:14). These are the celestial spheres (*galgalim*).[258] "His thighs are marble pillars" (Cant. 5:15). These are the rays of the sun that shine in the sphere of the highest heaven, as it is written, "an image upon the heads of the creatures, a firmament" (Ezek. 1:22). The feet of God, this is as He says, "The Heavens are My chair and the earth is My footstool" (Isa. 66:1). Feet are His armies, as is written, "There is no harm, only let me pass on foot" (Num. 20:19). His nose (*hotmo*) is His anger. Its essence is "I will withhold from you (*'ehtam lekha*)" (Isa. 48:9). That is to say, I will explain matters to you, in order to withhold the execution of My judgment, so that it shall not spread out to destroy the world. So we teach in the book *Consummate Beauty*, the Holy One, blessed be He, placed an angel between the celestial veil and the heaven. His name is Dumi'el,[259] for he was appointed to shut the mouths of the angels of destruction, so that they would not spread out into the world to destroy it. Another explanation of *'ehtam lekha* is "I will set down," as in "I shall make their waters settle" (Ezek. 32:14). That is to say, I shall cause sin to settle and reveal merit.

All of this is for one who concentrates on the Unity in all his utterances and nothing improper issues from his mouth. Furthermore, he concentrates his heart on the pronunciation of the Name, by pronouncing it with these seven vocal marks,[260] whichever of them he chooses. *YeHVeH* is king (*melekh*); *YaHVah* ruled (*malakh*); *YiHVoH* shall rule (*yimlokh*).[261] "God, show me Your paths"

---

257. Compare *Hekhalot Zutarti*, 35; *Targum Pseudo-Jonathan* on Deut. 34:6; *Ma'aseh Merkavah*, G. Scholem ed., 108; and G. Scholem, *Gnosticism*, 12 and n. 7.

258. Compare Ibn Ezra, *Perush*, 5:14.

259. On Dumi'el, the Angel of Silence, in *hekhalot* literature, see the discussions by I. Gruenwald, *Apocalyptic*, 165 and G. Scholem, *Gnosticism*, 33.

260. This is referring to the vocalization in the next sentence.

261. It is unclear whether the original text contained the repetition of God's Name. This reading is only presented in a few mss., such as J.T.S. 1547; nevertheless, prior to the word *melekh* most mss. either have the Tetragrammaton or an *'alef*. It is conceivable that there was a gradual scribal censoring

(Ps. 25:4). So the linguists have explained. May the Holy One, blessed be He, lead us in the path of His Unity, in order to unify His Name in all our deeds. May He show us the path of Understanding.

R. Ishmael said,[262] I have read and rehearsed this subject before R. Nehuniah b. ha-Kanah and he said to me, Anyone who knows this secret and studies it repetitively,[263] each day, is guaranteed that he shall merit the world to come and shall inherit two worlds: this world and the world to come.[264] Furthermore, the Holy One, blessed be He, will give him the honor to inherit the reward from the world to come in this world, as is written, "Wise men shall inherit honor and the perfect shall inherit good" (Prov. 28:10).

I AM R. HAMMAI

One of the more popular writings of the "Circle" is the *Commentary on the Tetragrammaton*. This work frequently cites material from both *Contemplation* and *Fountain*. In many of the manuscripts in which it has been preserved, preceding the *Commentary* there is a short preamble the bulk of which is an abridgment of the opening sections of *Contemplation–Short*. Of interest is the purported discussion therein between R. Hammai and his mentor, R. Hammai the Elder.

The following transcription is based on J.T.S. 1805, with variants from Florence 2:41, f. 198b.

---

of this sensitive doctrine, involving the vocalization of the Tetragrammaton, and for this reason only a few mss. have preserved it.

The expression, "The Lord is King, etc." is found in several places in the liturgy; cf. *The Daily Prayer Book*, P. Birnbaum trans. (New York 1985), 58. The *Bahir* also discusses the pseudoverse and offers a slightly different, though comparable, vocalization. According to Aryeh Kaplan, its source is *Hekhalot Rabbati*, 31:4, and the *siddur* of R. Amram Gaon, *The Bahir* (York Beach 1989), 197, n. 116.

262. This concluding section is similar to material found in *Shi'ur Komah*; see *Sefer Razi'el*, ff. 49b and 51a; cf. M. Cohen, *Shiur Qomah*, 175f.

263. *be-mishnah*: cf. M. Cohen's discussion of this expression, *Shiur Qomah*, 223, n. 5.

264. In *B. Kiddushin*, 71a, this reward is granted to one who carefully preserves the tradition of the forty-two-letter Name. R. Eleazar b. Judah, in *Sefer ha-Ḥokhmah*, Bodleian 1568, f. 5b, applies this to one who knows the secret of *keter* (Crown) and Divine Presence.

I AM R. HAMMAI

1 אמר ר' חמאי ראש המדברים על ענין הפנימיות הכריחני ר'
חמאי הגדול שאפרש לו עקר כל מציאות הכבוד הנסתר מן העין אשר
אין כל בריה יכולה לעמוד על עיקר מציאותו ומהותו על הדרך האמיתית
כמות שהוא באחדות השוה שבשלמותו מתאחדים עליונים ותחתונים

5 וממנו יוצאים כל כתות הנבראים בדרך אצילות כריח מריח וכנר
מנר שזה מתאצל מזה וזה מזה וכח המאציל בנאצל ואין המאציל
חסר כלום. וזהו מחיבור שחיברתי אני ר' חמאי.

---

1 הפנימיות: פנימיות החכמה   2 שאפרש: שאי אפשר הכבוד: הדבור
4 שבשלמותו: שבהשלמותו   5 יוצאים: יצאו כתות: כתות (נ"א כחות)

Rabbi Hammai, the principal spokesman, said concerning the topic of the Innermost: Rabbi Hammai the Elder compelled me to explain to him the essence of the entire existence of the Glory, which is hidden from sight. No creature can truly comprehend the essence of His existence and His nature, since He is in a state of balanced unity; for in His completeness the higher and lower beings are united. From Him all the created powers issue forth by the process of emanation, like a scent from a scent or a candle-flame from a candle-flame; since this emanates from that and that from something else, and the power of the emanator is within that which was emanated. The emanator, however, does not lack anything. This is from a book that I composed. I am Rabbi Hammai.

THE BOOK OF UNITY OF R. HAMMAI

Among the most influential of all the writings of the "Circle" was the *Pseudo-R. Hai Responsa*.[265] Scholem contended that they were written in Provence around 1230;[266] however, in chapter 4 we shall discuss their relationship to the literary activity of R. Isaac Cohen, who lived during the latter half of the thirteenth century. R. Isaac was also the first to cite this text.[267]

As Scholem noted, this treatise was referred to by several late thirteenth-century kabbalists, including R. Isaac's disciple, R. Todros Abulafia and R. Bahya b. Asher.[268] It also was at the center of a philosophical controversy in Italy, which began at the end of the fifteenth

---

265. General discussions of this text are found in Scholem, *Origins*, 349-354, and G. Vajda, *Recherches sur la philosophie et la kabbale dans la pensée juive* (Paris 1962), 179-181.

266. G. Scholem, *Origins*, 349.

267. G. Scholem, *Kabbalot*, 86.

268. G. Scholem, *Origins*, 349, n. 297. The responsa's influence is also discernible in R. Meir ibn Sahula's fourteenth-century commentary on *Sefer Yeẓirah*, wherein he refers to the three ineffable, hidden *sefirot*; see Z. Galili, "*Le-She'elat Meḥabber Perush 'Or Ganuz*," *Meḥkerei Yerushalayim be-Maḥshevet Yisra'el* 4 (1985), 93. See also R. Joseph b. Shalom Ashkenazi, *Perush le-Parshat Bere'shit*, M. Hallamish ed. (Jerusalem 1985), 132, in which *keter* is divided into compartments, identified as the supernal lights. Subsequently, the responsa were referred to by R. Shem Tov ibn Shem Tov in his *Sefer ha-'Emunot*, 4:4, f. 28b.

century. In 1491, R. Isaac Mar Hayyim expounded upon the responsa in a series of letters.[269] Shortly thereafter, R. Elhanan Sagi Nahor wrote a rejoinder, and this was followed by R. David Messer Leon's exposition. Eventually, prominent kabbalists of the sixteenth century, such as R. Meir ibn Gabbai and R. Moses Cordovero, likewise discussed this work and its interpretation by renaissance scholars.[270]

The core of these pseudepigraphic epistles is a discourse by R. Hammai that R. Hai Gaon supposedly transmitted to his students. Although this short piece appears to be rather straightforward, it is quite radical, insofar as it asserts that within the Godhead there are three supernal lights.[271] From these lights emanated the three supernal *sefirot*, referred to by the epithets: Pure Thought, Knowledge, and Insight.

In addition to being a central component of the *Pseudo-R. Hai Responsa*, this text also seems to have circulated independently. R. David Messer Leon quoted it, in toto, in his *Magen David* and referred to it by the title, *The Book of Unity*.[272] Messer Leon's presentation of *Unity* is significant in that it was independent of Mar

---

269. The most important of these letters was published by Y. Nadav, "'Iggeret ha-Mekubbal R. Yizḥak Mar Ḥayyim 'al Torat ha-Ẓaḥzaḥot," *Tarbiẓ* 26 (1956-570), 440-458.

270. See E. Gottlieb's seminal discussion of all of these works, *Meḥkarim be-Sifrut ha-Kabbalah* (Tel-Aviv 1966), 397-412. More recent articles on this material include: M. Idel's "*Beyn ha-'Aẓmut*," 89-111; H. Tirosh-Rothschild, "Sefirot as the Essence of God in the Writings of David Messer Leon," *AJS Review* 7 and 8 (1982-83), 409-425; and S. Gershenzon, "A Tale of Two Midrashim: The Legacy of Abner of Burgos" *Approaches to Judaism in Medieval Times*, D. Blumenthal ed., 3 (1988), especially 137-142.
As Gottlieb demonstrated, R. David Messer Leon plagiarized much of Mar Hayyim's commentary. What is problematic is that R. Moses Cordovero, who was aware of Messer Leon's treatise, attributes this commentary as originating from an unknown R. Aaron. Although Gottlieb offered various solutions to this puzzle, the issue remains unresolved. It is significant that Mar Hayyim refers to a certain R. Yohanan, at the start of his commentary, (whom Moshe Idel asserted is R. Yohanan Alemanno, see "*Beyn*" 89). Perhaps, both R. Aaron and R. Yohanan are referring to the same individual and the name change is simply due to a scribal error.

271. On the issue of the possible influence of Christian theology, see above, p. 4, n. 6.

272. Halberstam 465 (now in Jew's College), f. 7b-8b.

Hayyim's epistle, which was Messer Leon's source for his commentary, but not the actual text. Not only does Mar Hayyim not preface his remarks with a full version of the text as Messer Leon does, but there are some minor variations between the two renditions of the treatise. This would substantiate their independence and offer support for the contention that in addition to its inclusion in the *Pseudo-R. Hai Responsa, Unity* was circulating as a separate text.

Given that *Unity* was known as an independent work in the sixteenth century, what was its origin? As a preliminary hypothesis, it seems reasonable to assume that *Unity* started as a separate text and that the *Pseudo-R. Hai Responsa* represent an expanded commentary, embedded within which is the original text. Moreover, this later reworking was connected with R. Isaac Cohen and his circle.

The following transcription is based on one of the manuscripts of the *Pseudo-R. Hai Responsa*, Florence 2:18, ff. 76b-77a. This text was compared to the versions cited by R. Isaac Mar Hayyim and R. David Messer Leon. There is virtual consensus among all of these witnesses; none of the variants are especially significant. The following translation is eclectic and based upon the best readings. Prefatory comments of Mar Hayyim and Messer Leon are also included.

THE BOOK OF UNITY OF R. HAMMAI

עוד הוסיפו לשאול חברת הגאונים ז"ל ה"ה מאת אדוננו הגאון ז"ל אם יש לו
ענין במה שכתב באור קדמון ובאור מצוחצח ובאור צח. והשיב להם אל
תטריחונו לשאלות שאין אנחנו יכולין להעמיק בהם בדרכי התשובות. רק
ארמוז לכם ענין אחד קבלנוהו מרבותינו הזקנים ז"ל גם מצאנוהו כתוב
בטופסי דרב חמאי. כי ג' שמות אלו כלם ענין אחד ועצם אחד דבקים דבוק
אמיץ בלי פרוד ובלי חבור בשרש כל השרשים כדמיון משל גשמי הלב והריאה
והטחול שרש אחד לכלם ולשאר האיברים שבכל החלל. ואור קדמון נמשכת
ממנו המחשבה הטהורה כמשך מחשבות הלב. ומן האור המצוחצח והצח בשתי
מעיינות נמשכות מהן המדע והשכל ובאמצעות השכל והמדע נתעצמו כל
השלהביות הרוחניות זה בזה וזה עם זה כעניני הלהבות הנאחזות בתוקף
הגחלים. ומה שיהיה גנוז ונסתר זה בתוך זה וזה בתוך זה עד שהגיע זמן רצון
הפועל הקדמון ויצאו מן הכח אל הפעולה הרוחנית ונאצל אצילות העולם
העליון עד יסוד האבן העשירית הנקראת בלשון חכמי רזים אור עב. ומרוב
העובי קראוהו גם כן חשך מעורב. כי כל כחות השלהביות מתערבות בה
ומשתנות בתוכה והיא יסוד כל העולמות הרוחניים והגשמיים וכמה מיני
גוונים מתעצמים בה. ומצטיירים בכחה מהם צורות רוחניות ומהם צורות
גשמיות כי היא חותם אחרון לכל החותמות. זה תוקף לשון רב חמאי המעמיק
והמקובל מפי תנאין ואמוראין בסדר הקבלה לחכמי ישראל הקדושים.

Pseudo-R. Hai Preamble

Furthermore, this same group of *ge'onim*, of blessed memory, asked our master, the *ga'on* (i.e., R. Hai) if he possesses something else related to what he wrote about the Primal Light, the Brightened Light, and the Bright Light. He responded to them, Don't bother us with such questions, since we cannot delve into them via responses; however, for your sake, I will but allude to one matter that we have received from our aged rabbis, of blessed memory. We have also found this written in the treatises of R. Hammai.

Mar Hayyim Preamble

... if he possesses something else related to what he wrote about the Primal Light, the Bright, and Brightened Light. He responded and revealed from his words that although he possesses something, he is unable to delve into it and to convey to them the profundity of the matter. He said, Don't bother me with such questions, since we cannot delve into them via responses, owing [to the injunction] "what is too marvellous for you, do not inquire etc."[273] Nevertheless, even though I am unable to delve fully into this, for your sake I will but allude to one matter that we have received from our aged rabbis, of blessed memory. We have also found this written in the treatise of R. Hammai Gaon, of blessed memory.

Messer Leon Preamble

This is what I found in the marvellous *Book of Unity* that R. Hammai composed.[274] ... and it is like what I will explain below from the responsum of R. Hai Gaon.[275]

Text

For these three names represent one thing and one essence, exceedingly bonded without any separation or any connection, with the root of all roots. Like the physical analogy of the heart and lungs and

---

273. *B. Ḥagigah*, 13a, quoting *Ecclesiasticus* 3:21.

274. Halberstam 465, f. 7b.

275. *Ibid.* f. 8a.

spleen–there being one root to all of them and the other limbs of the body. Pure Thought emanates from the Primal Light (*'or kadmon*), like the flow of the thoughts of the heart. From the Brightened and Bright Light (*'or ha-mezuhzah ve-ha-zah*) flow Knowledge and Insight, like two fountains. By means of Insight and Knowledge, all the spiritual flames became realized–this in that and this with that, like the flames that grasp tightly to the coals. That which was concealed and hidden, this in that and this in that, until the time of desire for the Primal Laborer had arrived.

They issued forth from potential into spiritual activity, and the emanation of the supernal realm was emanated up to the foundation of the tenth stone, which is called "Dense Light" in the language of the sages of mysteries. Owing to its exceeding density, they also called it "Mixed Darkness." For all the powers of the flames are mixed in it and transformed in it. She is the foundation of all the spiritual and physical realms. Different types of color are realized in her and formed within her power. Some of them are spiritual forms and some of them are physical forms–for she is the final seal of all seals.

Pseudo-R.Hai Postscript

This is the verbatim text of R. Hammai, the profound, who received [it] from the mouths of *tanna'im* and *'amora'im* (i.e., classical rabbinic authorities), by means of the regulated transmission (*kabbalah*) of the holy sages of Israel.

Messer Leon Postscript

Up until this point is the quotation from our rabbi, Rabbi Hammai Gaon, in the *Book of Unity*.

3

COSMOLOGICAL THEORIES OF THE "CIRCLE OF CONTEMPLATION"

THE COSMOLOGY OF *THE BOOKS OF CONTEMPLATION*

In the previous chapter we have presented the writings that constitute *The Books of Contemplation*. Now we are able to explore the rich theosophical texture of these works. The major theme of all of the recensions of *Contemplation* is how the cosmos came into being and its ensuing celestial structure. Although the various versions differ on specifics, they all share the same overall formulation. This particular presentation of cosmogony is something that is found only in these specific texts, and in later works from the "Circle" that are based on these treatises. Although the writers of the "Circle" undeniably drew heavily from classical and contemporary sources, they recast this material into a distinctive and original shape.

Before examining the actual cosmological doctrines of *The Books of Contemplation*, we must consider the intellectual milieu from within which these works were formulated. It can be readily observed that the impetus for writing such treatises followed contemporary trends. At precisely this time, in the first half of the thirteenth century, there was widespread interest in the dynamics of cosmogony. It is at this period that *The Book of Creation*, the classic Jewish cosmological treatise, becomes the subject of unparalleled, intense scrutiny. In the span of a few decades, major commentaries on this work, (which are still extant), were written by: R. Eleazar of Worms, the Pseudo-Saadia commentator from the Unique Cherub Circle, his colleague R. Elhanan b. Yakar, who wrote two distinct commentaries, as well as the kabbalists, R. Isaac the Blind, R. Azriel of Gerona, and Nachmanides. To be sure, interest in *Creation* was not confined to this period. There are the tenth-century commentaries by Saadia, Dunash ibn Tamin, and Shabbetai Donnolo, and in the twelfth century R. Judah b. Barzillai penned a mammoth exposition. Somewhat later, the savant R. Abraham ibn Ezra wrote his commentary and the poet-philosopher R. Judah ha-Levi included an extended discussion of *Creation* in his popular book, *Kuzari*. Nevertheless, in this span of a few decades from the thirteenth century, more commentaries were written on *Creation* than in the preceding centuries, since its composition. It is also significant that these writers were not confined to one specific geographical locale; they lived and wrote in Germany, northern and southern France, and Spain.[1]

Furthermore, *Creation* was not the only classic cosmological work then in vogue. Many centuries earlier, during the rabbinic period, a corpus of mystical treatises were composed which focused on the *hekhalot*, "celestial palaces." Only in the thirteenth century, however, did these works begin to circulate widely. This was at least partly owing to the efforts of R. Eleazar b. Judah to publicize the traditional esoteric writings and teachings that he had received. In 1217, following the passing of his teacher, R. Judah Hasid, as well as the loss of his only son in a Crusade massacre, R. Eleazar lamented that he had no one to whom to pass on these esoteric traditions. He therefore embarked on an ambitious literary project, devoted to the various branches of this heritage.[2] In his writings, especially *Secrets of the Mysteries*, there are large blocks of material drawn from *hekhalot* texts. In addition, entire *hekhalot* treatises were transmitted by his students and other members of the *hasidei 'ashkenaz*.[3]

The impact of R. Eleazar's writings was due in part to his stature as a scholar and sage.[4] Also, some of his students traveled south, coming in contact with Spanish mystics and thereupon transmitted this material to them. In a subsequent chapter we will discuss the influence of R. Eleazar on the "Circle," as well as the fact that one of its treatises is even attributed to him.[5] We shall also have occasion

---

1. See R. Abraham Abulafia's listing of twelve commentaries on *Creation* that he had studied; most were from the early thirteenth century. Among those mentioned that are no longer extant are expositions by R. Judah Hasid, R. Ezra of Gerona, R. Jacob (Cohen?) of Segovia and R. Isaac of Beziers; cf. A. Jellinek, *Beit ha-Midrash*, 3:xlii.

2. See R. Eleazar b. Judah, *Sefer ha-Ḥokhmah*, Introduction, cited by J. Dan, *'Iyyunim be-Sifrut Ḥasidei 'Ashkenaz* (Ramat Gan 1975), 45ff.

3. For example, Bodleian 1531.

4. Cf. E. Urbach, *Ba'alei Tosafot*, 321-341.

5. See below, p. 199f.

to present important texts, which stemmed from R. Eleazar's students and were seminal to the writings of the "Circle."[6]

There is one final feature of early thirteenth-century theosophical writing that warrants consideration. The first full-fledged literary figure among the kabbalists was R. Ezra of Gerona. In can be assumed that he was actively writing around 1230. In the introduction to his commentary on the *Song of Songs* he noted that he was growing old and that for many years he had restrained himself from setting down his esoteric doctrines; however, he could no longer refrain from doing so.[7] Although R. Ezra does not delve deeper into his motivations for writing, on reading his commentary one is struck by a theme which comprises the underpinning of the entire treatise, namely, the coming redemption. *Song of Songs*, which focuses on the relationship between the Shulamite and her lover, is interpreted by R. Ezra as a historical drama which is unfolding on two levels, the mundane, earthly realm and the intra-Divine. R. Ezra's basic interpretation of the text is that the figure of the Shulamite simultaneously corresponds to the standard rabbinic interpretation of the Congregation of Israel, as well as the kabbalistic concept of the lowest of the *sefirot, malkhut*, (Sovereignty) being synonymous with the *shekhinah* (Divine Presence). R. Ezra's perception of the immediacy of redemption was fostered by the approach of the year 1240, which corresponded to the start of the sixth millenium, the traditional commencement of the messianic era.[8] Ezra was not alone in functioning within a messianic framework; similarly R. Eleazar of Worms participated in the circulation of a messianic letter.[9]

Briefly summarized, the above-mentioned features related to early thirteenth-century trends point to: (a) an intense interest in the problems of cosmogony, as exemplified by the study of *The Book of Creation*, (b) the dissemination of *hekhalot* texts through the activities of the *ḥasidei 'ashkenaz*, (c) the breakdown of the barrier to keep esoteric material private, as seen in connection with R. Eleazar and R. Ezra,[10] and (d) an underlying impetus tied to burgeoning messianic

---

6. See below, pp. 200-210.

7. R. Ezra, *Perush le-Shir ha-Shirim*, 479.

8. See below, p. 198, n. 21.

9. See below, p. 199.

10. For other evidence of this phenomenon, see below p. 188.

expectations. All of these factors laid the groundwork for the writings of the "Circle," to which we can now turn our attention.

It is appropriate to begin any discussion of the cosmological doctrines of *Contemplation* with a methodical analysis of *Contemplation–Short*. This work represents the starting point of the corpus. It is the oldest recension and offers an intriguing exposition on the initial stages of the process of creation, not found in the later versions. Before we can investigate this specific topic, however, it is first necessary to turn to the body of this text.

The basic premise of *Contemplation–Short* is that the cosmos came into being by means of an emanational creative process, involving a succession of *koḥot* (powers), each one producing the next. "Thus, the Holy One, blessed be He, generated all of His powers, these from those, by the process of emanation."[11] The initial power is identified as Primordial Wisdom. "When it arose in His mind to create all His actions and display His power and produce all of His creations, He created one power. This power is called Primordial Wisdom."[12]

Primordial Wisdom is the source of all subsequent powers. "He is united with the Primordial Wisdom. From this wisdom that is called mystery, the Holy One, blessed be He, generated all the spiritual powers simultaneously."[13] Although herein the emanation of the other powers is said to have occurred simultaneously, later on the writer delineates a specific sequence. "At that moment the Holy One, blessed be He, emanated each power individually–one at a time. The first was Marvellous Light."[14] The treatise then proceeds to describe how *ḥashmal* (electrum) emanated from Marvellous Light, and from it seven other powers were formed in sequence: *'arafel*, Throne of Light, Wheel of Greatness, Cherub, Wheels of the Chariot, Encompassing Ether, and finally Celestial Curtain. It is possible that there is no real contradiction between the initial statement that the powers were generated simultaneously, and this subsequent successive enumeration: the sequencing is primarily intended to indicate the rank of the various powers in the celestial hierarchy and not chronological temporality.

---

11. See above, p. 41.

12. See above, p. 41.

13. See above, p. 42.

14. See above, p. 43.

Together these ten spiritual entities constitute the supernal realm. Moreover, they are subdivided into three distinctive groupings. The four middle powers–*hashmal, 'arafel*, Throne of Light, and Wheel of Greatness–"stand above like *yesodot*, (fundamental elements/foundations)."[15] They are also referred to as "the Inner Holy Palace."[16] The subsequent forces are also depicted as being part of the celestial palace. "Furthermore, everything is called the Palace of the Lord."[17] Since the middle powers constitute the "inner" palace, presumably the lower forces correspond to the outer aspects of the Divine abode.

Whereas the lower eight powers are clearly extra-Divine entities, as their names indicate, the initial two forces are more problematic. Primordial Wisdom is associated with God, as the manifestation of His power of creativity. Although an entity distinct from God, it was nonetheless infused with the Divine Spirit.

When it arose in His mind to create all His actions and display His power and produce all of His creations, He created one power. This power is called Primordial Wisdom, which is called mystery. Before He created this power, His power was not discernible, until His radiance was seen and His glory was revealed in this wisdom . . . for the Holy One, blessed be He, animated this wisdom itself.[18]

The second power, Marvellous Light, was generated from Primordial Wisdom, as noted above. The author of *Contemplation-Short* interprets these two forces in terms of the verse from *Psalms*, "'You are clothed in majesty and beauty' (Ps 104:1) . . . "Majesty" refers to the splendor of the Primordial Wisdom. "Beauty" is the Marvellous Light."[19] Accordingly, both of these are seen as constituting Divine garments.

From the above analysis we can see that there is a fundamental difference between the upper two powers and the lower eight. Primordial Wisdom and Marvellous Light represent the outer clothing

---

15. See above, p. 46f.

16. See above, p. 47, n. 55.

17. See above, p. 48.

18. See above, p. 41f.

19. See above, p. 43.

of the Divinity; as such, they reflect Divine majesty and beauty, for they are the primal manifestations of His creative power.[20] The lower eight, however, are merely the components of God's celestial domain.

Let us now consider why the author of *Contemplation–Short* formulated this schematization of ten celestial powers. Although individual elements of this doctrine were borrowed from a variety of sources, this particular configuration was either a product of the author of *Contemplation–Short*, or one of his unnamed teachers.

The basic concept, whereby the cosmos is structured in ten successive levels, belongs to a multifaceted tradition in both rabbinic literature, and Arabic and Judeo-Arabic philosophical writings.

A classical formulation is found in the rabbinic exposition, *Lessons of the Fathers*, "with ten statements the world was created."[21] This is followed by the assertion that decades constitute the basic pattern of history. "There were ten generations from Adam to Noah."[22] In the *Talmud*, the primal decade is associated with other groups of ten, notably the Ten Commandments, ten key praises in *Psalms*, and the ten stalwarts of the synagogue service.[23] The latter was a manifestation of the halakhic principle, requiring a quorum of ten for liturgical activities.[24]

Another talmudic statement that is germane, is the following:

> R. Zutra b. Tuvia said in the name of Rav, "By means of ten attributes (*devarim*) the universe was created: by wisdom, understanding, knowledge, power, reprimand, valor, righteousness, judgment, mercy, and compassion."[25]

---

20. Compare the theory of form (i.e., wisdom) and matter, as the two simple substances that constitute the initial stage of creation in Judeo-Arabic philosophy; see S. Stern, "Ibn Hasdai's Neoplatonist," *Oriens*, 13 (1961), 104f., and A. Altmann, "Creation and Emanation in Isaac Israeli," in *Studies in Medieval Jewish History and Literature*, I. Twersky ed. (Cambridge 1979), 1-15.

21. *'Avot*, 5:1. The "statements" (*ma'amarot*) refer to the Divine commands in the opening chapter of Genesis.

22. *'Avot*, 5:2.

23. See *B. Rosh ha-Shanah*, 32a, and *B. Megillah*, 21b.
On the association between the *ma'amarot* and the commandments, cf. Hippolytus, *Refutation of All Heresies*, 8:7, and Idel's comments, "*Ha-Sefirot sheme-'Al ha-Sefirot*," *Tarbiẓ*, 51 (1982), 274ff.

24. *B. Berakhot*, 21b.

25. *B. Ḥagigah*, 12a; cf. E. Urbach, *Ḥazal*, 173-174. A related statement

These two traditions,[26] namely, the ten *ma'amarot* and Rav's listing of ten attributes, were subsequently synthesized in the *Lessons of R. Eliezer.* "By means of ten statements was the world created ... and in three it is encompassed; they are wisdom, understanding, and knowledge."[27]

Of seminal importance in the formulation of medieval Jewish thought was the stress on the decade-based counting system in *The Book of Creation.* It begins by listing ten biblically rooted names of God and then focuses on the theory of the ten *sefirot*–ten primordial numbers, which functioned as cosmic building blocks.[28]

Later writers added to this matrix. The tenth-century philosopher Saadia, commenting on *Creation,* expounded on the ten names of God by illustrating how each corresponded to a different context in which the Deity manifested His presence.[29] He then related this to the ten Aristotelian categories[30] and also to the Ten Commandments. Another example of the elaboration of *Creation* is found in the early kabbalistic treatise *Bahir,* wherein *Creation*'s image of the *sefirot* as ten fingers is related to the upraised hands of the priests as they bless the people.[31]

There is another matrix of metaphysical concepts which stem from a Judeo-Arabic context. In the Pseudo-Bahya *Treatise on the Soul,* chapter 16 is devoted to an enumeration of the ten levels of created being. The first is referred to as the *shekhinah* (Divine Presence), corresponding to the Active Intellect followed by: the universal soul, nature, *hyle* (universal matter), the sphere, planets, fire, air, water, and finally earth.[32] This doctrine is clearly related to the formulation found in the ninth-century Islamic writings of the *Ikhwan*

---

is found in *'Avot de-Rebbe Natan,* Nusḥa A, ch. 37, Schechter ed., 110.

26. Cf. M. Idel, "*Sefirot*," 269.

27. *Pirkei de-R. Eliezer,* ch. 3.

28. *Sefer Yeẓirah,* ch. 1.

29. Saadia, *Perush 'al Sefer Yeẓirah,* in *Sefer Yeẓirah ha-Shalem,* J. Kapah ed. (Jerusalem 1972), 46; see also, R. Judah Barzeloni, *Perush 'al Sefer Yeẓirah,* 116f.

30. See Aristotle's *Categories,* J. Ackrill trans., ch. 4:5.

31. *Sefer ha-Bahir,* R. Margoliot ed., 55:124; cf. *Sefer Yeẓirah,* 1:3.

32. Pseudo-Bahya ibn Pakuda, *Kitab Maani al-Nafs,* I. Broyde trans. (1897).

al-Safa, Brethren of Purity, who divided the cosmos into nine "states of being." They are Creator, intellect, soul, *hyle*, nature, body, the sphere and its planets, the four primal elements and worldly beings.[33] Although the *Ikhwan al-Safa* usually designated the levels of being from one to nine, with one representing the Divinity, implicit in their writings is the contention that the number one corresponds to the Divine Being, and hence, the Divine Essence would be represented by zero.[34]

This metaphysical conception parallels a basic Islamic astronomical theory, which in turn was a modification of the Ptolemaic theory of the eight spheres. The Muslims propounded an additional ninth sphere to account for the precession of the equinoxes.[35] On the other hand, within Jewish philosophical writings, ten spheres were the norm. An example of this is found in R. Solomon ibn Gabirol's classic poem *Keter Malkhut*. Therein Ibn Gabirol discourses at length on the ten spheres, comprised of nine celestial configurations and the tenth, which is the *galgal ha-sekhel* (intellectual sphere).[36]

Another related doctrine, that was likewise transmitted from Arabic to Jewish philosophers, was the theory of the ten Separate Intellects. In the twelfth-century Jewish treatise *Gan ha-Sekhalim* by R. Natanel b. al-Fayyumi, the Intellects are categorized into nine levels corresponding to the nine cardinal numbers and are completed by the first creation, i.e., Divine wisdom, or the Universal Intellect, thus yielding ten.[37]

This theory of the ten Separate Intellects was also incorporated into Maimonides' *Guide*[38] and subsequently, it became a component of Jewish mystical writings. Even in the earliest stratum of the *kabbalah*, one finds evidence of these doctrines. In the *Bahir* mention is made of the ten spheres corresponding to the ten *ma'amarot*,[39] and

---

33. S. Nasr, *An Introduction to Islamic Cosmological Doctrines* (Boulder 1978), 51-52. For the study of the writings of the *Ikhwan* in Spain, see there, 36, n. 53.

34. *Ibid.*, 46.

35. *Ibid.*, 133; see also, Maimonides, *Guide*, 1:18.

36. Solomon ibn Gabirol, *Shirim Nivharim*, H. Schirmann ed. (Jerusalem 1966), 97-105.

37. R. Natanel b. al-Fayyumi, *Gan ha-Sekhalim*, J. Kapah ed. (1954), 3.

38. Maimonides, *Guide of the Perplexed*, 2:4.

39. *Sefer ha-Bahir*, 78:179.

in the writings of R. Isaac the Blind and his disciples, there is frequent use of the term *'olam ha-nifradim* (world of separated entities), which Scholem has traced to the "separate" intellects.[40]

The Arabic tradition from which this doctrine evolved can be readily traced. Of prime significance in this respect was al-Farabi's seminal metaphysical treatise, *Opinions of the Inhabitants of the Virtuous City*. Therein he discusses the superabundance of the Supreme Being, which resulted in the emanation of the primary intellect.[41] Through the act of self-intellection, a second intellect was emanated, and so on. "The separate intellects which come from the First are ten in number... each of these ten are unique in their being and degree."[42]

Ibn Sina adopted and modified al-Farabi's teaching. He propounded the equivalence of the hierarchy of Intellects (*uqul*) and the angelic pleroma (*malaika*).[43] In all, Ibn Sina posited three sets of angels: (1) archangels, corresponding to the Intellects, (2) emanated angels, who are the moving souls of the spheres, and (3) human souls or terrestrial angels. In his *Epistle on Angels* he assigned names to these archangels, several of which call to mind the various designations of the *sefirot*: Face of Holiness, Right Hand of Holiness, Royalty of Holiness, Nobility of Holiness, Rigor of Holiness, Brightness of Holiness, Sagacity of Holiness, Spirit of Holiness, and Servant of Holiness.[44]

It is within this context of the angelic hierarchy that one can consider Maimonides' discussion of the ten categories of angels, depicted as ten successive emanations.[45] This theory was subsequently adopted by thirteenth-century writers. An interesting example is R. Isaac ibn Latif's assertion in his *Gateway to Heaven* that the ten degrees of angels mentioned by Maimonides are in fact the Sepa-

---

40. G. Scholem, *Origins*, 282.

41. Cf. M. Fakhry, *A History of Islamic Philosophy* (New York 1970), 136f.

42. Al-Farabi, *Idées des Habitants de la cité verteuse*, R. Jaussen trans. (Cairo 1959), 39.

43. H. Corbin, *Avicenna and the Visionary Recital* (London 1960), 48. On Avicenna and the Ten Intellects, cf. *Philosophy in the Middle Ages*, A. Hyman ed., 234-235; Avicenna, *al-Risalat al-Arshiya*, in A. Arberry, *Avicenna on Theology* (London 1951), 36f.

44. H. Corbin, *Avicenna*, 46.

45. Maimonides, *Mishneh Torah*, "Yesodei ha-Torah," 2:7.

rate Intellects.[46] The influence of Maimonides' formulation on the "Circle of Contemplation" is also discernible. At the end of the *Book of True Unity*, ten categories of angels are listed, differing only slightly from Maimonides' enumeration.

A further development was the metaphysical theory of the gradation of Divine lights. Its earliest proponent was al-Ghazali in his *Mishkat al-Anwar*.[47] Subsequently, the Sufi theoretician Suhrawardi Maqtul synthesized all of the above doctrines and combined them with Oriental concepts, thereby developing his doctrine of *Ishraq*, Divine illumination. He posited that light was the root-principle of metaphysics.[48] Moreover, in his treatise on the Temples of Light he associated the Neoplatonic process of the emanation of the ten Intellects with the creation of the celestial light.[49]

Having considered all of this source material, we can readily understand why the author chose to express his cosmological doctrine in terms of ten celestial gradations. While it cannot be determined if the author of *Contemplation-Short* knew Arabic, knowledge of that language by a Jew living in Castile in the first half of the thirteenth century was not uncommon.[50] Moreover, at precisely this time, there were several individuals in Spain who were actively disseminating Arabic Neoplatonic writings. R. Abraham ibn Hasdai of Barcelona translated several of these works into Hebrew, including al-Ghazali's

---

46.   Vatican ms. 335, f. 22a.

47.   See A. Schimmel, *Mystical Dimensions of Islam* (Chapel Hill 1987), 259, and al-Ghazali, *Mishkat al-Anwar*, W. Gairdner trans. (Lahore 1952), 100. Moreover, even Ibn Sina depicted God as the source of everflowing light, cf. S. Nasr, *Introduction*, 213.

48.   See A. Schimmel, *Mystical Dimensions*, 260. One could speculate on the possible connection between Suhrawardi's theory of Divine illumination and the preponderance of light imagery in the early *kabbalah*. This motif is incorporated into the titles of so many of the classics, such as *Bahir* (Brightness), *Sha'arei 'Orah* (Gates of Light) and *Zohar* (Splendor), as well as the cosmological theories of light in the *Fountain of Wisdom* and related works of the "Circle."

49.   *Le Livre des temples de la lumière*, in *Quinze traités de Sohravardi*, H. Corbin trans., 50f.

50.   Some examples include R. Meir Abulafia, cf. B. Septimus, *Hispano*, 15, and R. Joseph Gikatilla, see his criticisms of al-Harizi's translation of the *Guide*, appended to *She'eilot...Yizhak Abarbanel* (Venice 1574) reprinted (Jerusalem 1967); see below p. 190f.

Mo'znei Zedek (Scales of Righteousness) and Israeli's *Sefer ha-Yesodot* (Book of Fundamentals). In addition, he incorporated Israeli's Neoplatonic source into his *Prince and the Nazirite* (chapters 32 to 35).[51] Another important figure is the above-mentioned R. Isaac ibn Latif. He was an accomplished Neoplatonist and well-schooled in the Arabic philosophical heritage, to which he constantly referred. His early works were written in Hebrew and date from the third and fourth decades of the thirteenth century.[52] They display a clear sympathy for kabbalistic concepts and Heller-Wilensky even asserts that Ibn Latif was in contact with the kabbalists of Gerona.[53]

Had the author of *Contemplation-Short* simply discussed these ten powers, then his presentation would seem rather pedestrian. It is, however, in the opening lines of the text that a different set of concepts is addressed, which point to a radical conception of the Divine infrastructure.

The treatise opens with assertion that its theme is *ha-penimiyyut*, the Innermost, or most hidden aspect of the Divinity. "This is *The Book of Contemplation* that Rabbi Hammai, the principal spokesman, composed on the topic of the Innermost."[54] This innermost dimension is immediately identified as pertaining to the Divine Glory, which is completely hidden and imperceptible. "In it (i.e., this treatise) he revealed the essence of the entire existence of the Glory, which is hidden from sight."[55]

The reason that the Glory is imperceptible is that this innermost aspect of the Divinity exists in a state of *'ahdut ha-shaveh*,[56] balanced

---

51. See S. Stern, "Ibn Hasdai's Neoplatonist," *Oriens*, 13 (1961) 58-120.

52. See S. Heller-Wilensky, "Isaac ibn Latif–Philosopher or Kabbalist," in *Jewish Medieval and Renaissance Studies*, A. Altmann ed., esp. 215, n. 216 and S. Heller-Wilensky, *"Le-Heker ha-Mekorot...,"* *Divrei ha-Kongres ha-'Olami ha-Revi'i*, 2 (1969), 324.

53. S. Heller-Wilensky, "Isaac ibn Latif," 211. Ibn Latif refers cryptically to "the secret teaching of Rabbi A.," which Heller-Wilensky interprets as referring to R. Abraham of Gerona.

54. See above, p. 37.

55. See above, p. 37.

56. On this seminal concept in *Contemplation*, see above, p. 39, n.10.

unity, that is to say, absolute undifferentiation. Concerning such a state no knowledge is possible, for all knowledge is predicated on a distinction between the knower and what is known.[57]

> No creature can truly comprehend the essence of His existence and His nature, since He is in the state of balanced unity, for in His completeness the higher and lower beings are united.[58]

This Divine hypostasis is also the root of everything. "He is the foundation of everything that is hidden and revealed."[59]

The next few lines are crucial. Using the same general frame of reference as is found in the body of the text, the initial stages of the cosmogony are depicted as stemming from an emanative process. What is significant is that the first emanation occurs intradivinely.

> From Him issues forth all that is emanated from the wondrousness of the unity, and all the powers that are revealed from the Supreme Hiddenness, which is called *'aman*. The explanation is that from Him, the sustaining power emanated, which is called the Father of Faith, since faith was emanated from its power.[60]

These two sentences, which are crucial to the entire text, are very different from the rest of the treatise. Whereas the remainder of the work is readily understandable, these lines present a series of technical terms, whose meanings must be nuanced from other parts of the text. Only after a very careful reading of the entire treatise, can these lines be properly comprehended.

When one reduces these statements to their basic components, the following pattern emerges. There is an initial category, referred to as *'aman* (or possibly vocalized *'amen*). From this state *'av 'emunah*, Father of Faith, was emanated. Thereupon, Father of Faith generated faith (*'emunah*). Each of these three stages is also described

---

57. This idea is also expressed in *Fountain*; see above p. 55f. The source of both of these texts was undoubtedly Maimonides, *Mishneh Torah*, "Hilkhot Yesodei ha-Torah," 2:10.

58. See above, p. 38f.

59. See above, p. 39.

60. See above, p. 39f.

in a second set of terms: *'aman* is identified as Supreme Hiddenness; Father of Faith is associated with the sustaining power; and in a subsequent passage, faith is equated with Primordial Wisdom.[61]

It is also apparent that the first state, *'aman* or Supreme Hiddenness, is synonymous with the previously discussed Divine Glory, which likewise was described as being hidden and imperceptible. In order to appreciate the significance of the second level, one must take the initial statement–namely, that it is called Father of Faith, for it generated faith–and juxtapose this with a later comment. "Accordingly, this wisdom was called faith, for the Holy One, blessed be He, animated this wisdom itself."[62] Thus the progenitor of wisdom/faith is identified as the Holy One, blessed be He. Lest the significance of this passage be misinterpreted, the author of *Contemplation–Short* adds, "Therefore, the Holy One, blessed be He, is called God of faith."[63] Clearly this designation, "God of faith," is equivalent to the earlier epithet, Father of Faith. From this we see that the standard rabbinic designation for God, namely, the Holy One, blessed be He, is explicitly associated with the second hypostasis, Father of Faith, and is therefore secondary to *'aman!* Thus, according to *Contemplation–Short*, God created Himself.

An initial question that comes to mind is why did the author express his theories in such a peculiar fashion? He sets forth a linear sequence, involving the relationship between three elements, but he only defines these terms in a piecemeal fashion. Previously we noted, in relation to *Contemplation–Short*'s treatment of Metatron, that the author was very sensitive to the radical nature of his formulations.[64] As a result, he wrote esoterically by somewhat masking his views. Since he was careful in his presentation of Metatron, how much more so when discussing the most sublime topic, God's innermost nature.

It is worth emphasizing that in terms of the recensions of *Contemplation*, it is only in *Contemplation–Short* that this theory of the intra-divine emanation is found. In *Contemplation–Long* the distinction between the Glory and the Holy One, blessed be He, is blurred, and a hypostasis, which bears the characteristics of both, is the only one discussed. We have noted above *Contemplation–Long*'s revision

---

61. See above, p. 42.

62. See above, p. 42.

63. See above, p. 42.

64. See above, p. 48, n. 62.

of the role of Primordial Wisdom and suggested that it represented a shying away from controversy.[65] We see here a second rejection of a radical doctrine and can conclude that it too exemplifies a "conservative" tendency on the part of the author of *Contemplation–Long*. Moreover, both *Contemplation–Thirteen Powers*, as well as *Contemplation–Standard*, address this issue textually. Through a simple modification, the key statement now reads, "*'Omen* means Father of Faith."[66] Thus the two hypostases that were differentiated in *Contemplation–Short* have been compressed together into one state.

In considering the sources of these conceptions we shall focus on several theological constructs: Divine Hiddenness[67] and its connection with the concept of Divine Glory, as well as theories of intradeical emanation, which is sometimes expressed as Divine autogenesis.

The classical Jewish source for the concept of Divine Hiddenness is Moses' encounter with God in Exodus 33. In verse 18 Moses petitions, "Please show me Your Glory (*kevodekha*)." God demures and states, "You cannot see My face" (verse 20). This is then qualified in verse 23, "And you shall see My back, but My face will not be seen." However one interprets the terms face and back,[68] this passage unambiguously affirms that there are two aspects to the Divinity: one is imperceptible, and the other is perceptible.

Wolfson asserted that Philo was the first philosopher to explicitly formulate the doctrine of Divine unknowability.[69] Philo contended that Moses prayed for a knowledge of God's essence and that God answered him that only His existence could be known, and it could be known only from the world, but that His essence could not

---

65.   See above, p. 70, n. 97.

66.   See above, p. 83 and p. 103.

67.   The monograph by S. Balentine, *The Hidden God* (Oxford 1983), offers an exhaustive study of biblical references to God hiding His face–usually in response to human sin; however, it does not address the theological construct of Divine unknowability.

68.   R. Abraham b. David of Posquières' comment on Maimonides' *Mishneh Torah*, "Hilkhot Yesodei ha-Torah," 1:10, cited in Karo's *Kesef Mishnah*, is intriguing. Rabad concludes by asserting that the terms "face" and "back" represent a "great mystery" that cannot be revealed; cf. I. Twersky, *Rabad*, 289, n. 11.

69.   H. Wolfson, *Philo* 2 (Cambridge 1947), 119.

be known by any created being.[70] He based this theory on the above-mentioned biblical passages.

> "Thou shalt see what is behind Me, but My face thou shalt not see" (Exod. 33:23). It means that all below the Existent, things material and immaterial alike, are available to apprehension ... but He alone by His very nature cannot be seen.[71]

This theme of Divine incomprehensibilty was also espoused by Gnostics,[72] middle Platonists,[73] and Neoplatonists,[74] and was subsequently adopted by theologians and philosophers of Christianity, Islam, and Judaism. One can see its impact on such Christian writers as Augustine,[75] Pseudo-Dionysius,[76] and John Scotus Erigena.[77] Beginning with Al-Kindi, Islamic philosophers also adopted this position. For Al-Kindi, Divine incomprehensibility results from the assertion that God represents a pure and simple unity, which possesses no attributes and is therefore undefinable.[78] Al-Kindi

---

70. *Ibid.*, 86.

71. Philo, *De Mutatione Nominum*, 5, F. Colson trans. (Cambridge 1968), 147.

72. See *The Nag Hammadi Library*, 100 and 449, and E. Norden, *Agnostos Theos* (Darmstadt 1974), 65ff.

73. Cf. H. Wolfson, "Albinus and Plotinus on Divine Attributes," *Harvard Theological Review*, 45 (1952), 115-130, and J. Dillon's criticism of Wolfson's assertions that the unknowability of God was alien to Greek thought and that Philo introduced this concept, in *Two Treatises of Philo of Alexandria*, D. Winston and J. Dillon eds. (Chico 1983), 217f.

74. Plotinus, *Enneads*, 5:3:13 and 6:8:11; see also, E. Dodd, "The Unknown God in Neoplatonism," in his Proclus, *The Elements of Theology*. (Oxford 1963), 310-13.

75. Cf. W. Tolly, *The Idea of God in the Philosophy of St. Augustine* (New York 1930), 124ff.

76. For example, Dionysius the Areopagite, *On the Divine Names and the Mystical Theology*, C. Rolt trans. (London 1920), 191-194.

77. For example, John Scotus Erigena, *Periphyseon*, M. Uhlfelder trans. (Indianapolis 1976), 3.

78. *Al-Kindi's Metaphysics*, A. Ivry trans. (Albany 1974), 112.

assumed a Neoplatonic stance, in contradistinction to his Mutazilite predecessors, and contended that God relates to the world by means of the process of emanation.[79] Al-Farabi reiterated these formulations[80] and stressed the limitation of human knowledge in comprehending the Divinity.[81]

Jewish Neoplatonists also adopted this position. Although in his surviving writings Isaac Israeli does not deal extensively with the concept of God,[82] there is the following passage in his *Book of Substances*. "The power of the Creator, may He be exalted, is infinite, and its scope has no limits, and intellects do not encompass it with their knowledge."[83] As Altmann has noted, this theme is clearly expressed in the writings of Israeli's student, Dunash ibn Tamim.[84] "Men are incapable of conceiving His essence; their intellect is insufficient."[85]

One also finds this theory expressed by Solomon ibn Gabirol in both his philosophical writings and his poetry.[86] He writes, "It is impossible to know the essence of the Primal Being, except through the contemplation of His creations."[87] The impossibility of true knowledge of God "is because His essence transcends everything and is infinite."[88]

Other medieval Jewish philosophers also endorsed this position. Saadia asserted, "As for the Creator Himself, however, there is no means whereby anybody can see Him. Aye, that is in the realm of

---

79. *Ibid.*, 187, n. 160.

80. Cf. Al-Farabi, *Idées des habitants de la cité verteuse* (Cairo 1949), 19ff.

81. See R. Hammond, *The Philosophy of Alfarabi* (New York 1947), 18f.

82. Cf. A. Altmann and S. Stern, *Isaac Israeli* (Oxford 1958), 151.

83. *Ibid.*, 92; see also Altmann's discussion of this passage, p. 157.

84. *Ibid.*, 157.

85. G. Vajda, "*Commentaire kairouanis sur le livre de la création,*" *Revue des Études Juifs*, 110 (1949), 76.

86. See for example, "*Keter Malkhut*" in *Selected Religious Poems of Solomon Ibn Gabirol* (Philadelphia 1974), 83, lines 29f. and 84, lines 39f., and lines 44f.

87. Solomon ibn Gabirol, *Mekor Ḥayyim*, A. Zefaroni ed. (Israel n. d.), 10.

88. *Ibid.*, 10.

the impossible."[89] Joseph ibn Zaddik argued that unknowability was the necessary conclusion of the problem of Divine attributes.[90] Moreover, this issue was thoroughly analyzed by Maimonides in the *Guide*. He begins by discussing the germane verses from Exodus 33 and asserts that Moses made two requests, to know God's essence and His attributes.

> The answer to the two requests that He, may He be exalted, gave him consisted in His promising him to let him know all His attributes, making it known to him that they are His actions, and teaching him that His essence cannot be grasped as it really is.[91]

The early kabbalists also adopted this position on ultimate Divine incomprehensibility. For example, R. Isaac the Blind refers to the highest aspect of the Godhead as "that which thought cannot conceive."[92] In addition, the concept of the *'ayn sof*, the infinite, inexpressible aspect of the Divinity, is likewise rooted in this assumption of the fundamental unknowability of God.[93]

Not only does the doctrine of Divine incomprehensibility have a lengthy tradition, but it is specifically associated with the concept of the Glory, mentioned in Exodus 33:18. In the midrash *Sifra'* we read, "R. Akiva says, Behold He states, "For man cannot see Me and live" even the Exalted Creatures do not see the Glory."[94] Similarly, in the *Lessons of R. Eliezer* it is written, "Moses said to the Holy One, blessed be He, "Please show me Your Glory." The Holy One, blessed be He, replied, "You cannot see My Glory, so that you will not die."[95]

---

89. Saadia, *The Book of Beliefs and Opinions*, S. Rosenblatt trans. (New Haven 1948), 130f.

90. Joseph ibn Zaddik, *Sefer ha-'Olam ha-Katan* (Bratzlav 1903); cf. J. Guttmann, *Philosophies of Judaism* (New York 1964), 117.

91. Maimonides, *Guide*, 123.

92. R. Isaac the Blind, *Perush*, 1, l. 7

93. For a study of the evolution of this doctrine, see D. Matt, "Ayin," 43-47.

94. *Sifra', Va-Yikra'* 2; cf. manuscript cited and discussed by R. Elior, *Hekhalot Zutarti*, 64, lines 85-99.

95. *Pirkei de R. Eliezer*, ch. 46.

Both Ibn Ezra[96] and Maimonides interpreted this usage of Glory (*kavod*) as referring to the Divine essence. Maimonides writes, "Then he asked for the apprehension of His essence, may He be exalted. This is what it means when he says, 'Show me I pray Thee, Thy Glory.'"[97]

Accordingly, when the author of *Contemplation–Short* depicted the hidden aspect of the Divinity in terms of the Glory, he was simply reflecting a basic Jewish theological conception.[98] Moreover, the specific formulations that he used also have their antecedents. *Contemplation–Short*'s expression "the Glory, which is hidden from sight"[99] is quite similar to the phrasing "His Glory, which is hidden from us," found in *Hekhalot Zutarti* and used in conjunction with a discussion of several biblical verses related to prophetic visions, principally Exod. 33:20.[100] *Contemplation–Short* also refers to Supreme Hiddenness (*seter 'elyon*). This expression is from Psalms 91:1 and had already been adopted by R. Azriel,[101] whose influence on *Contemplation–Short* will be discussed in chapter 5.

Although *Contemplation–Short*'s depiction of Divine incomprehensibility in terms of an imperceptible Glory is well-rooted in classical Jewish sources, its concept of intra-deical emanation warrants serious consideration. One finds this doctrine explicitly formulated in *The Fountain of Wisdom*, the other seminal text from the "Circle." Therein it is stated,

---

96.   Commenting on Exod. 33:18.

97.   Maimonides, *Guide*, 124.

98.   Although Saadia's theory of a divinely created, perceptible Glory is commonly portrayed as being the predominant medieval Jewish doctrine, cf. J. Dan, *Torat ha-Sod*, 104ff., numerous medieval luminaries rejected Saadia's formulation. See Ibn Ezra's short commentary on Exod. 33:18 and the references cited above, p. 38, n. 9 to R. Judah Hasid, *Bahir* and Nachmanides. Even R. Eleazar of Worms, who was the most forceful proponent of Saadia's theories among the *ḥasidei 'ashkenaz*, was ambivalent on this issue. His discussion of the Glory in *Sodei Razayya*, "*Hilkhot Ha-Kavod*" (Bilgoria 1836), 30f., is concerned with a transcendent, Divine entity. Accordingly, a reconsideration of this entire topic is necessary.

99.   See above, p. 37f.

100.   *Hekhalot Zutarti*, 25; P. Schafer, *Synopse zur Hekhalot-Literatur* (Tubingen 1981), 148f., #352.

101.   See above, p. 39, n. 12.

Know that the Holy One, blessed be He, was the first existent being. Only that which generates itself is called an existent being. Since He generated Himself, we can comprehend and conduct an investigation into His existence.[102]

This idea of Divine autogenesis is subsequently reiterated in a discussion of the Aramaic translation of Exodus 33:23, wherein the terms "My Back" and "My Face" are rendered as *de-vatrai* and *de-kadamai*. These expressions connote both temporal and spatial relationships, and in *Fountain* they are interpreted temporally.

That is to say, what preceded Me you will be unable to perceive. . . . Accordingly, you will not possess knowledge of this Darkness that is the focal point of My existence. However, from here on you shall know everything. That is to say, from this Darkness and what is below it, you shall know [all], even the creation of My essence and the essence of My Name and My Glory.[103]

Some of *Fountain*'s phraseology was derived from the opening lines of Maimonides' *Mishneh Torah*, wherein God is described as the "first existent being," on account of His causing all creatures to come into being. Although this passage does not necessarily advocate Divine autogenesis, there is a later statement that is more suggestive. It focuses on Exodus 33:18, "What was it that Moses requested to perceive when he said, 'Please show me Your Glory?' He requested to know the truth of *hemaz'o* of the Holy One, blessed be He."[104] Although the passive infinitive form *hemaz'o* can simply be translated as "His existence," were one predisposed, it could be literally rendered as "His being brought into existence." This would then imply an intra-deical process and this is certainly how the author of *Fountain* interpreted Maimonides' statement.

Kabbalistic interpretations of the opening line of Genesis may have also influenced the writers of *Contemplation–Short* and *Fountain*. The initial word *bere'shit* (in the beginning of . . .) was associated with the upper *sefirot*[105] and the name *'elohim* (God), with the

---

102. See above, p. 55f.

103. See above, p. 57f.

104. Maimonides, *Mishneh Torah*, "*Yesodei ha-Torah*," 1:10.

105. Cf. Nachmanides, *Perush 'al ha-Torah*, 11.

third *sefirah*. Accordingly, it was asserted that the initial words of Genesis connote that the upper *sefirot* generated (i.e., *bara'*) the next *sefirah*. This is stated explicitly in a text which is claimed to have been Nachmanides' initial draft of his Torah commentary and was preserved by his students. "For Wisdom (*hokhmah*) emanated *'elohim* (= *binah*), together with the Heavens (= middle *sefirot*)."[106]

This is also depicted in symbolic terms in an exposition which is found in R. Ezra of Gerona's commentary on the *'aggadah* and elsewhere. In some manuscripts it is ascribed to R. Isaac the Blind, and this attribution seems credible.

> *Bere'shit* (in the beginning of): the *beit* (i.e., the initial letter of the word) corresponds to the Exalted Depth (*'omek rom*, i.e., the first *sefirah, keter* [crown]). *Reshit* (the beginning) corresponds to the Primordial Torah (i.e., *hokhmah*) . . . *'elohim* (God) corresponds to the return (*ha-teshuvah* = *binah*) that precedes everything.[107]

The theme of Divine self-actualization is also alluded to in Nachmanides' introduction to his Torah commentary. He notes that the entire Torah is comprised of Divine names, and this would be evident were one to divide the words differently. The example he offers is a radical reformulation of the initial three words of Genesis "*be-rosh yitbara' 'elohim*.[108] Thus the transitive verb *bara'* (He created) has been transformed into a reflexive verb. Accordingly, this would yield the translation "in the beginning, God created Himself."

This doctrine was also elaborated upon in the opening section of the *Zohar*, which offers a novel interpretation of the initial words of Genesis 1:1. The most exalted element of the Divinity is described as the "Hidden of Hidden beings." This Hiddenness caused *reshit* (beginning) to disseminate, and thereafter, He made a palace for His

---

106. G. Scholem ed., *Kiryat Sefer* 6 (1929), 415.

107. Cf. J.T.S. 1187, f. 29a; J.T.S. 2194, f. 69a; and Vatican 294, f. 37a. Since *beit*, the second letter of the alphabet, corresponds to the first *sefirah*, presumably *'alef*, the first letter, would correspond to *'ayn sof*, Divine Infinitude. On the association of *teshuvah* (return) and *binah*, cf. R. Isaac's *Perush le-Sefer Yezirah*, 15, line 333; and R. Asher b. David, *Kabbalat*, 18, l. 40, and the assertion in l. 43 that *teshuvah* preceded creation.

108. Nachmanides, *Perush*, 1:6.

Glory. "This palace is called *'Elohim*, and this is the secret significance of 'With the beginning He created *'Elohim*.'"[109]

I am unaware of classical Jewish sources that expound the theory of Divine autogenesis; however, Gnostic writings abound with
this conception.[110] There are also discussions related to the Glory,
which we have not yet referred to, that may have contributed to this
doctrine. R. Nathan of Rome, in his classic Talmudic lexicon, the
'Arukh, composed around 1100, developed Saadia's theory of two
Glories.[111] R. Nathan contrasts Exodus 33:20, which states that man
cannot see God, with Isaiah 6:1, describing Isaiah's vision of God.
R. Nathan then proposes the following solution to this apparent
contradiction.

> There is a Glory that is above the Glory. And the Glory,
> which is the great splendor and closely connected with the
> Divine Presence, man cannot see it. Concerning this it is
> stated, "For man shall not see Me and live" (Exod. 33:20).[112]

This theory of the "Glory that is above the Glory" was subsequently adopted by some of the writers of the *hasidei 'ashkenaz*,
including R. Eleazar of Worms,[113] whose teachings had a great influence on the writers of the "Circle." Thus, the author of
Contemplation–Short synthesized this construct of a hidden Glory
with the radical concept of intra-deical emanation.[114]

---

109. *Zohar*, 1:15a; cf. the commentary on this passage in D. Matt, *Zohar: The Book of Enlightenment* (New York 1983), 210.

110. Cf. *The Nag Hammadi Library*, index entries on Autogenes, p. 480, and Self-begotten One, p. 489.

111. For Saadia's theory, cf. R. Judah Barzeloni, *Perush le-Sefer Yezirah*, 20f.

112. R. Nathan of Rome, *'Arukh ha-Shalem*, 6 (Jerusalem 1969), 110.

113. Cf. R. Eleazar of Worms, *Sefer ha-Yihud*, Casanatense ms. 179, f. 98; R. Abraham b. Azriel, *'Arugat ha-Bosem*, E. Urbach ed., 1 (Jerusalem 1939), 200, and see below, p. 203.

114. An interesting discussion pertaining to Divine self-generation that appears to have been influenced by the *Fountain of Wisdom* and the theory of the two Glories is *Zohar* 2:155; cf. G. Scholem, *Le-Heker*, 76f.

In considering the cosmological doctrines of *The Books of Contemplation*, there is a further issue that must be addressed. In comparing *Contemplation–Short* with the last two recensions, one notices an obvious difference. In *Contemplation–Short*, as well as *Contemplation–Long*, ten koḥot (powers) are discussed; however, in the later two recensions thirteen powers are enumerated. This shift is very significant and can be linked to the relationship between the "Circle" and *kabbalah*.

Although the author of *Contemplation–Short* was acquainted with some of R. Azriel's writings and appropriated specific terms from R. Azriel, he expressed no interest in the theory of the *sefirot* (intra-Divine states), which Azriel developed therein.[115] A plausible explanation for this occurrence is that the author of *Contemplation–Short* based his theories on a system that developed independently of the *kabbalah*–though, to be sure, both shared common antecedents. It is clear that "Circle" was primarily interested in material adapted from *hekhalot* literature, for example, R. Meshullam's *kabbalah*. Moreover, it seems likely that *Contemplation–Short* was written soon after R. Azriel's writings began to circulate in Castile. Accordingly, it was prior to the time when *kabbalah* had become the predominant articulation of medieval Jewish theosophy. Thus, one of the most important characteristics of *Contemplation–Short* is that it offers an alternative to the *kabbalah*, and thereby attests to the vitality of Jewish mysticism during the early thirteenth century.

Contemplation–Thirteen Powers, however, was written sometime later–though prior to 1260. It contains unmistakable references to the kabbalistic doctrine of the *sefirot*. Nevertheless, it is ironic that a text which endorses the theory of the ten *sefirot* transforms its central doctrine from ten to thirteen powers. We have previously noted several other puzzling features of this text. It insists that its teachings stem from *The Book of Creation* yet argues that *Creation* really intended thirteen *sefirot* and not ten, as is explicitly mentioned there. Moreover, when this writer discusses the most exalted levels of the *sefirot*: keter (Crown), ḥokhmah (Wisdom), and so on, he buries this material in the midst of a discussion of one of the lowest of *Contemplation*'s powers. This is unexpected and quite inappropriate.[116]

All of these "peculiarities" are understandable within the context of contemporary events. Precisely at this time there was tremen-

---

115. See below, p. 199.

116. See above, p. 85.

dous tension and fragmentation within Jewish intellectual circles. The most significant manifestation was the Maimonidean controversy, which had reached fever pitch during the third and fourth decades of the thirteenth century. While the connection between the controversy and the flourishing of the *kabbalah* is unclear, it is evident that *kabbalah* was under pressure, both internally and externally.[117] Internally there was the attempt by some to restrict it to those who had been privately trained. This is illustrated by R. Isaac the Blind's letter to Nachmanides and R. Jonah Gerondi, condemning the publicizing of the *kabbalah*.[118] Although it may be just coincidence, nevertheless, these two recipients of the letter played prominent roles in the controversy. R. Isaac's admonitions seemed to have been taken seriously by both, for R. Jonah never discussed *kabbalah* in his writings and Nachmanides did so very cautiously.[119]

External criticism of the *kabbalah* during this period is exemplified by R. Meir b. Shimon's polemical treatise, *Commanded War*, which contains a lengthy denunciation of what R. Meir viewed as heretical theology. It should not be assumed that R. Meir was an uninformed outsider. His use of kabbalistic terminology, as well as his description and critique of specific liturgical practices, correspond to theories attributed to the early kabbalists, R. Jacob the Nazirite and R. Abraham b. David of Posquières.[120] R. Meir is even quoted

---

117. Given the volatile atmosphere of the Maimonidean controversy, and the heightened sensitivity of the later writers of the "Circle," one can understand the rationale for including antiphilosophical polemics in such texts as *Pseudo-R. Hai Gaon Responsa* and *Pseudo-R. Eleazar Responsum*. On the relationship of these two texts to R. Isaac Cohen, see chapter 4.

118. See above, p. 26. Moreover, even the activities of R. Ezra and R. Azriel were muted. We noted at the start of this chapter that R. Ezra refrained from writing until he reached old age. In addition, R. Meshullam b. Solomon, a poet and disciple of R. Ezra and R. Azriel, commented, "They know the number and *shi'ur* (measure) of their Creator, but they refrain from talking in public about the Divine Glory and discussing this matter, on account of heretics," H. Brody ed., *Yedi'ot ha-Makhon*, 4 (1938), 92.

119. This position was also adopted by Nachmanides' successor, R. Solomon ibn Adret; cf. R. Shem Tov ibn Gaon, *Baddei 'Aron*, 1:5, cited by S. Munk, *Zeitschrift fur Hebraeische Bibliographie* (1908), 12:50.

120. See G. Scholem, *Reshit*, 73f. Interestingly, a major source that R. Meir used in his attack on anthropomorphism was R. Abraham b. David's *Ba'alei Nefesh*, J. Kapah ed., 127. On the relationship of R. Abraham and the *kabbalah*, see I. Twersky, *Rabad of Posquieres* (Cambridge 1962), 286ff.

in the kabbalistic writings of another product of Provence, R. Asher b. David, R. Abraham's great-nephew.[121] Nor were R. Meir's efforts against the spread of the *kabbalah* confined to a literary assault. Together with his uncle, R. Meshullam b. Moses, a prominent Talmudist, they circulated a letter condemning the *kabbalah* and encouraging kabbalistic texts to be burned–an interesting counterpart to the alleged Maimonidean book-burning.[122]

This external pressure was even reflected in the writings of the kabbalists themselves. R. Asher b. David, the nephew of R. Isaac the Blind and his designated emissary to Gerona, writes poignantly about the campaign waged by certain individuals to discredit the kabbalists. These sages were the targets of slander and persecution, and they were being unjustly referred to as heretics.[123]

Whereas *Contemplation–Short* was probably written prior to this strident condemnation of the *kabbalah, Contemplation–Thirteen Powers* was most likely written in its wake.[124] Its author, who seems to have been sympathetic to the *kabbalah*–as evidenced by his references to it–was nevertheless cautious. Accordingly, he only mentions the *sefirot* in passing, toward the end of the treatise. Presumably not

---

121. *Kabbalat R. Asher b. David*, 15.

122. After listing several kabbalistic commentaries composed by Rabbis Ezra and Azriel, R. Meir admonishes his readers, "Inquire and investigate thoroughly, and if they are in your midst extirpate it from the earth so that it shall not be a stumbling block for you, for indeed we have extirpated those that were found in our midst . . . We have written all of this with the approval of our master the great Rabbi, light of Israel, our teacher, R. Meshullam, the son of the great Rabbi, R. Moses, may the Merciful protect him, and other sages of the land" cited in A. Neubauer, "The Bahir and the Zohar," *Jewish Quarterly Review* 4 (1892), 358; cf. G. Scholem, *Origins*, 397ff. See also B. Septimus, "Piety and Power," in *Studies*, I. Twersky ed., 202, and B. Septimus, *Hispano-Jewish*, 165, n. 4 This is a significant forerunner to the subsequent, alleged burning of Maimonides' oeuvre. It is also interesting to consider a comment by Abba Shalom of Bonn, incorporated into a liturgical commentary by the *ḥasidei 'ashkenaz*, in which he mentions that he defended God's unity by burning unspecified "heretical" books, *Siddur Rabbenu Shlomoh*, M. Hershler ed., 22; J. Perles, *Jubelschrift . . . H. Graetz*, (1887), 16; cf. J. Rosenthal, "*Kara'im ve-Kara'ut be-'Eropah ha-Ma'aravit*," in "*Sefer ha-Yovel le-R. Ḥanokh Albeck* (Jerusalem 1963), 441.

123. J. Dan ed,. *Kabbalat*, 4, lines 24-26.

124. Concerning a possible textual influence of R. Meir's polemic on *Contemplation-Thirteen Powers*, see above, p. 84, n. 156.

wishing to be accused of heretical tendencies, he reformulated the radical theories of *Contemplation–Short* and *Fountain*, vis-à-vis Divine autogenesis and the intra-deical states. Finally, he transformed the theory of the ten powers into thirteen. On the one hand, this prevents the possible misconception that the powers are synonymous with the *sefirot*, and on the other hand it implicitly links this doctrine with the biblically formulated theory of the thirteen attributes of mercy. This association is made explicit in the later version of this recension.

The actual motivation behind the author of *Contemplation–Thirteen Powers'* decision to move away from the theory of ten *sefirot* and adopt instead a doctrine of thirteen powers cannot be determined with any certainty. Nevertheless, there are other writers that likewise reflect this tension, between enumerating ten or thirteen hypostases. The Provençal kabbalist, R. Asher b. David, who has been mentioned above, tried to reconcile the two positions. Somewhat later the Castilian kabbalist, R. Todros Abulafia, likewise considered the problem of these two competing doctrines.[125] Moreover, the *Book of Unity*, an essential component of the R. Hammai corpus, synthesized ten and thirteen by arguing that in fact there were three supernal lights, followed by ten *sefirot*.[126]

If our hypothesis is correct, and there is a sociopolitical factor that was prompting the transformation of *The Book of Contemplation*, this might also account for another basic difference between the earlier and later recensions of the text. In the earlier versions pseudepigraphy plays a very minor role and is confined to the attribution of the work to R. Hammai. On the other hand, *Contemplation–Standard* and other writings from the "Circle" are replete with fanciful references to rabbinic sages, as well as offering numerous quotations from nonexistent exotic works. This can be viewed as a concerted attempt by these later authors to authenticate and validate their works through the imprimatur of traditional authority. In an age of controversy, such an endeavor is readily understandable.

---

125. This issue was discussed at length by J. Dan, *Ḥugei*, 2-20. Another solution to this problem was proposed by R. Isaac Cohen, who argued that there were ten *sefirot* and three lower entities; cf. G. Scholem, *Kabbalot*, 86.

126. See above, p. 114ff.

THE COSMOGONY OF *THE FOUNTAIN OF WISDOM*

The Fountain of Wisdom, together with *Contemplation–Short*, constitute the cornerstones of the "Circle of Contemplation." In Appendix II it will be demonstrated that *Contemplation–Short* influenced *Fountain* and hence is prior; nevertheless, the points of contact between these two works are minimal, and *Fountain* is essentially an independent composition. Although it deals with cosmogony, how the universe came into being, *Fountain*'s unraveling of the cosmic mysteries is far more elaborate and creative than that offered in *Contemplation–Short*. *Fountain* truly deserves its status as one of the most significant treatises of the Jewish mystical tradition.[127]

Although *Contemplation–Short* and *Fountain* each offer a distinctive theosophical schematization, soon after their composition these two texts became intertwined. Virtually every other treatise related to the "Circle of Contemplation" draws on both of them. This is even the case with all subsequent recensions of the *Contemplation*.

The Fountain of Wisdom is the most complex of the writings of the "Circle." Although *Fountain* has been printed several times, Scholem is basically correct when he disparaged these editions as "extremely corrupt, such that this significant book has become totally unintelligible in them."[128] This treatise has also been preserved in some thirty manuscripts. Disparities and inconsistencies abound here as well. Accordingly, the complexities of this treatise are almost impossible to decipher. Not until a critical edition of this work has been prepared (a formidable task to be sure) will this marvellous text begin to reveal all of its mysteries. What follows is, of necessity, tentative.

One of the major problems in trying to understand *Fountain* is that throughout the text, specific terms and concepts are equated with other epithets or depicted as being their products. Whenever one charts these conceptual relationships, whether it be based on a specific manuscript or published edition, eventually one comes to a point where the equations no longer work and the logic breaks down. It would seem inappropriate to blame these inconsistencies on the writer. In general, he was quite methodical in mapping out his cosmological theories. It seems more likely that the problems in comprehension stem from errors in scribal transmission.

---

127. See the sources referred to above, p. 49.

128. G. Scholem, *Reshit*, 256.

This is born out by the fact that there are at least two distinct families of manuscripts that offer consistently different readings of pivotal terms. In Florence 2:18 and Bologna 2914, which are representative of a majority of the manuscripts, one finds mention of both *'avir kadmon* (Primal Ether) and *'or kadmon* (Primal Light), which appear to present two distinct concepts. In Zurich 177 and Jerusalem 8⁰ 330 *'avir kadmon* is used almost exclusively. There are several other terminological differences between these families. Of potential significance is the use of the term *'ikkar* ("root- principle"). Both families concur that Primal Ether is a product of the Ether (*ha-'avir*), and in both one finds the assertion that "the Ether is the root-principle." Although in Florence-Bologna there is the similar statement that "Primal Ether is the root-principle," in Zurich-Jerusalem Primal Ether is labeled as "a root-principle" and the definite article is reserved for the Ether. This latter rendering seems favorable.

Having touched upon some textual issues, we can now focus on the major themes of the work. The treatise is composed of two distinct, yet parallel and interrelated sections. The first section is concerned with the generation of Divine names as a product of basic patterns of the Hebrew language. As such, it represents a conscious development of the cosmological linguistic theories of *The Book of Creation*. The second section is an exposition on theosophical physics. It depicts the process of creation as sequences of emanated supernal lights. At various points in both sections of the work, the author refers to parallels elsewhere in the treatise, thereby underscoring the cohesiveness of the work as a whole.

Upon a careful reading of the text, we can clearly see that both sections are built upon an identical mathematical pattern, which can be represented as: zero (= the root-principle), one, two, four, five, ten, thirteen, and finally twenty-six.[129]

In the first section of *Fountain*, this mathematical sequence is presented as follows. The base element is the *yod* (i.e., the tenth letter of the alphabet),[130] which produces the *'alef* (i.e., the first letter).

---

129. The thirteenth-century Italian philosopher R. Jacob Anatoli likewise depicts the hierarchical structure of the universe mathematically; cf. A. Ravitzky, "*Ha-Hyposte'zah shel ha-Hokhmah ha-'Elyonah*," *Italia* 3 (1982), 25f.

130. Not only is *yod* the tenth letter and hence an appropriate symbol for the base-ten counting system, but also it is the smallest letter of the alphabet and looks like a dot with a tail; hence it has graphic significance, as well. For an interesting discussion of the *yod*, cf. R. Jacob Cohen, "*Explanation of the Letters*," in J. Dan, *Early Kabbalah*, 161f.

"Moreover, the circle we derived from the *'alef* and the *'alef* from the *yod*. The *yod* is the fountain."¹³¹ The *'alef* then doubles and quadruples.

> When you open your mouth to say "ah," behold two
> vocalizations [result]. These two vocalizations are two letters
> *'a, 'a.* And if you pronounce *'a, 'a,* they divide into four: *'a 'a*
> *'a 'a.*¹³²

These four are really five.

> If you place two at the start and two at the end, you will
> discover that there is some ether between them. You are
> unable to assert that this ether is not an *'alef,* nor is it less
> than this. Accordingly, there are five: *'a 'a 'a 'a 'a.*¹³³

As it is in the nature of each *'alef* to double, so too the set of five become ten. "Since an *'alef* is never less than two, when you calculate them (i.e., the five *'alefim*), you will discover that they are ten, corresponding to the *yod,* (i.e., the tenth letter)."¹³⁴ The series temporarily concludes with the assertion that thirteen is necessarily inferred. This is based on the observation that the numerical equivalency of the word *'eḥad* (one) is thirteen.

> The one corresponds to thirteen and the thirteen to one. This
> is like the calculation of ten. How so? The *'a* is two, as we
> said. The five *'a 'a 'a 'a 'a* all double, yielding ten. If you
> divide these ten into three groups, one will remain. This one
> is the *'alef.* Moreover, the numerical value of [the word] *'eḥad*
> (one) is thirteen. This is the *'a.*¹³⁵

---

131. See above, p. 53.

132. See above, p. 51.

133. See above, p. 51.

134. See above, p. 51.

135. See above, p. 54f. It is only toward the end of the second section of the text that the sequence continues with twenty-six. "And how each of the thirteen sources was divided into two sources, eventually yielding twenty-six attributes," p. 62. The reader has already been prepared for this step in that we have just been informed that the Tetragrammaton (*YHVH*) is the root-principle and its numerical value is twenty-six.

The sequence in the second part of the treatise, which is concerned with the generation of cosmic ethers and lights, develops as follows. The root-principle is identified as the Ether. "The Ether is the root-principle."[136] The Ether in turn generated the Primal Ether.

> Prior [to all of the above] there was the Ether, which is the root-principle. From it emerged a light, more refined than a thousand thousands thousands and ten-thousand myriads of varieties of light. This is the Primal Ether. It is the root-principle. Accordingly, it is called the Holy Spirit.[137]

This primordial ether then gives rise to two sources, one representing light and the other, darkness.

> At that time, Moses began to gaze upon the Primal Ether, which is the root-principle, as we have already stated, and discovered that it is obscured by two things, pertaining to two sources. From the first flows light and from the second, darkness.[138]

These two sources possess four distinct colors, which result in five color manifestations.

> From one source flows light which is divided into two colors. They are those that we have already mentioned, the color of white and red. From the second source flows the darkness. It is mixture of three colors: green, blue and white. Behold, there are five colors for the two sources that are transformed and change their colors as they are emanated.[139]

The text continues by describing how these five colors are transformed into ten hues and colors.

> These five colors constitute the flame that emerges from the Ether. They divide in their movement. For we have

---

136.　See above, p. 56.

137.　See above, p. 56.

138.　See above, p. 58.

139.　See above, p. 58f. Although there are ostensibly five colors, in actuality there are four, as white is listed twice.

previously stated that the two outpourings are one thing that
stems from the Primal Darkness. It teaches about form and
creation. This form, when it is transformed, is portrayed in
numerous hues and colors. There are ten hues. There are also
ten individual colors.[140]

These ten colors are depicted as celestial lights, bearing such names
as Marvellous Light, Hidden Light, and Sparkling Light.

The sequence concludes with thirteen doubling into twenty-six,
the latter corresponding to the numerical value of the Tetragrammaton, *YHVH*. In completing the pattern, the author ties together the
material from both sections of the treatise.

> This is the *tikkun*, by directing your heart upon these four
> letters which constitute the Ineffable Name. In them is hidden
> a flowing stream and an overflowing fountain. They divide
> into several parts and run like lightning. Their light continues
> to increase and grow stronger. The root-principle of all of
> them is *YHVH*. It has the numerical value twenty-six,
> corresponding to the twenty-six movements that emerged
> from the Primal Ether which divided into two parts–each part
> separate unto itself. Each part has the numerical value
> thirteen, corresponding to the thirteen sources that separated
> from *'a*.[141]

Although the bulk of *The Fountain of Wisdom* is devoted to a
delineation of the processes outlined above, there are several significant features of the text that have not yet been treated. Of particular
importance is a passage found in the middle of the text, which forms
a bridge between the two sections. It offers a remarkable discussion
on the impact of creation upon God Himself.

> Know that the Holy One, blessed be He, was the first existent
> being. Only that which generates itself is called an existent
> being. Since He generated Himself, we can comprehend and
> conduct an investigation into His existence.[142]

---

140. See above, p. 59.

141. See above, p. 61.

142. See above, p. 55f.

Thus there is the contention that since God is designated as the first existent being, this presupposes that He caused Himself to come into existence. Furthermore, this necessary precondition of Divine self-actualization having been fulfilled, there is now a subject (i.e., God's existence) which can be analyzed and investigated.

As we noted above, when we had the opportunity to briefly discuss this material in conjunction with *Contemplation–Short*'s theory of Divine autogenesis, the designation of God as "the first existent being" (*ha-maẓui ha-rishon*) is found in the opening lines of Maimonides' *Mishneh Torah*. Therein, however, God merits this ascription because "he causes all that exists to come into existence."[143] Accordingly, God is the 'first existent being" owing to his role as Creator. This is fundamentally different from the statement under consideration in *Fountain*. Whereas Maimonides is discussing consequences that are external to the Divinity, *Fountain* is concerned with God Himself.

Interestingly, a later text from the "Circle," the *Commentary on the Book of Contemplation*, develops this theme and discusses the designation of God as being necessarily existent. It asserts that the Divinity derives His existence from internal dynamics, as opposed to external factors.

> For His existence depends upon Himself, that is to say, He is caused by Himself and He does not have any cause that is extrinsic to Himself. Everything whose existence is dependent upon itself is considered to be necessarily existent.[144]

Having affirmed that God's existence is subject to investigation, *Fountain* starts the exploratory process as follows:

> How did it (i.e., God's manifestation) begin? By what way did it proceed or stand? By which path was it? Was it one lane or many lanes, or numerous divisions, or by which modes did it proceed?[145]

This rather convoluted passage is then explained in the following manner.

---

143. Maimonides, *Mishneh Torah*, "*Yesodei ha-Torah*," 1:1; see above p. 139.

144. Vatican ms. 290, f. 63b.

145. See above, p. 56.

What was it? That is to say, [was it] either a road (*derekh*), lane (*netiv*), or path (*shevil*)?–for the paths are narrow and short, the lanes are bigger, and the roads are wider still. The paths are like children, the lanes are like mothers, and the roads are engraved in the [primal] image of male and female.[146]

Although the author of *Fountain* had led us to believe that he would be discussing God's existence, he appears to be pursuing another topic, namely, the process of creation. This is confirmed by the choice of imagery that is offered, namely, various types of path-ways. Such a tack, however, is not that surprising. Since the connection between *Fountain* and *The Book of Creation* is well attested in other parts of the treatise, it is reasonable to assume that what we have here is an implicit discourse on the opening of *Creation* which commences, "By means of thirty-two marvellous lanes (*netivot*) of wisdom did God create the universe."[147]

Nor is it unreasonable for *Fountain* to discuss the notion of Divine existence in terms of creation. Since God manifests His being through this process, *Fountain* contends that it is first necessary to grasp the mechanics of the creative act, and this will eventually lead to consideration of the Divine being per se.

Not content to simply echo *Creation* in its use of the term *netivot* (lanes), *Fountain* differentiates between three distinct types of pathways: road, lane, and path, indicative of the varied course of Divine creativity. Each has a particular gender association, corresponding to its gender as a noun, as well as its function. Path is narrow and short, like a son. Lane is expansive, like a mother, and road is broad and ambisexual.[148]

A similar discussion is found in R. Isaac the Blind's commentary on *Creation*, though in a much more abbreviated manner. Discussing the relationship between the terms *netivot* (lanes) and *derakhim* (roads), he notes,

And the lanes are the mothers of the roads, for a lane is the mother of a road. Concerning this it is stated, "God

---

146. See above, p. 56.

147. *Sefer Yezirah*, 1:1.

148. *Derekh* (road) is one of the rare Hebrew words that alternates between masculine and feminine gender.

understood her road" (Job 28:23)–He understood the roads and the lanes that she possesses."[149]

An interesting footnote to this topic is found in R. Isaac of Acco's commentary on *Creation*, written in the early fourteenth century. After mentioning R. Isaac the Blind's interpretation, R. Isaac of Acco notes that Nachmanides had reversed the relationship between these elements.

> *'Netivot'–netiv* refers to a big and wide path *(shevil)*. *Derakhim* refer to narrow and small paths that branch out from the *netiv* in any direction. R. Moses b. Nachman (i.e., Nachmanides), of blessed memory, in his commentary on *The Book of Creation* explained this contrariwise. He stated that the *derekh* is large and the *netivot* are narrow paths.[150]

Let us now turn to two of the most prominent terms of the treatise, *'avir* (Ether) and *'avir kadmon* (Primal Ether). As Scholem has pointed out, *'avir* is a Hebraization of the Greek primal element, *aer*.[151] Margoliouth, in his pioneering essay on the significance of ether in the *kabbalah* and in particular in the writings of R. Moses de Leon, has identified *Creation*, as the source of this term in Jewish esoteric literature. Therein reference is made to "ether that cannot be grasped," which Margoliouth rendered "impalpable ether."[152]

The *Book of Creation* was not alone among early theosophical writings, in its usage of *'avir*. In *Hekhalot Zutarti* mention is made of "radiance of the ether of the marble stones."[153] Similarly, in the

---

149. G. Scholem, *Kabbalah be-Provence*, Appendix 1.

150. G. Scholem, "*Perusho shel R. Yizhak de-min 'Akko*," *Kiryat Sefer* 31 (1956), 383; see also Nachmanides' commentary likewise edited by Scholem, *Kiryat Sefer* 6 (1929), 402.

151. G. Scholem, *Jewish Gnosticism*, 33; see also J. Levy, "*Seridei Mishpatim be-Shemot Yevaniim be-Sefer Hekhalot Rabbati*," *Tarbiz*, 12 (1941), 165, and S. Lieberman, *Ha-Yerushalmi ki-Feshuto* (Jerusalem 1935), 1:221.

152. *Sefer Yezirah*, 2:5; G. Margoliouth, "The Doctrine of the Ether in the Kabbalah," *Jewish Quarterly Review* 20 (1908), 830.

153. *Hekhalot Zutarti*, 23. On other, related usages of *'avir* in *hekhalot* literature, cf. P. Schafer, *Konkordanz*, 1:21.

Talmud, in connection with a discussion of the Divine Presence being located in the west, a homiletical etymology is offered for the word *'orayah*, west, linking it to *'avir yah*, namely, "God's ether."[154] Also, in the Mandaean text, *The Secret Adam*, one finds the Mandaean counterpart in the term *ayar*, as found in the phrases *ayar-ziwa*, "the shining ether"; *ayar-rba*, "the great ether;" and *ayar-dakia*, the "pure ether."[155]

Another important, though later, source was Saadia's cosmological speculations. In his commentary on *Creation* he discusses how Divine speech penetrated the *'avir* during the process of creation.[156] In addition, Saadia's older contemporary, R. Isaac Israeli, associated *'avir* with the primordial state of the cosmos.[157]

The technical term *'avir kadmon* ("Primal Ether") is not evidenced in classical literature.[158] In chapter 5 we shall present a significant passage from a fourteenth-century manuscript, J.T.S. 1884. This text discusses the theories of various Jewish mystics active during the thirteenth century. One of the individuals identified in this text is an enigmatic figure, R. Meshullam the Zadokite, whose teachings were extremely influential in the development of the "Circle." In J.T.S. 1884 there is a reference to the doctrine discussed above of "the Glory above the Glory." This is immediately followed by an analysis of Exodus 34:6, "the latter [name] (i.e., the second reference to *YHVH*) refers to the Primal Ether, according to the *kabbalah* of R. Meshullam the Zadokite."[159] Thus it is possible that R. Meshullam, who was linked to the *ḥasidei 'ashkenaz*, was the source of the term *'avir kadmon*.[160]

---

154.   B. *Baba' Batra'*, 25a.

155.   E. Drower, *The Secret Adam* (Oxford 1960), 15 and 25.

156.   Saadia, *Perush*, 110f.

157.   See R. David Kimhi on Gen. 1:2, cited in *Sefer ha- Yesodot*, S. Fried ed., 46 (German section).

158.   Among the writings in the latter part of the thirteenth century that used the term *'avir kadmon*, presumably under the influence of *Fountain*, are R. Abraham Abulafia, *Ve-Zot le-Yehudah*, 17, and R. David ha-Lavan, *Masoret ha-Brit*, G. Scholem ed., *Koveẓ 'al Yad*, 1 (1936), 36.

159.   See below, p. 203.

160.   Mention can also be made of R. Elhanan b. Yakar, who was a member of the Unique Cherub circle, which appears to have been operating in Northern France in the first half of the thirteenth century. R. Elhanan refers to

In the recensions of *Contemplation*, *'avir* appears as *'avir ha-sovev*, "the encompassing ether." It is one of the lower powers, coming after the Wheels of the Chariot. In only one version of *Contemplation-Thirteen Powers*, namely, its incorporation into the *Midrash of R. Simon*, do we find that Primal Ether is listed as the first of the powers.[161] A similar contention is evidenced in other, later writings from the "Circle." For example, in *The Prayer of Unity Rabban Gamliel*, there is a lengthy description of Primal Ether as the primordial power. The key statement reads,

He is emanator of the entire unity from a single power that He created prior to everything. This is the Primal Ether which is called supreme exaltedness (*rom ma'aleh*), because it is first and the intelligence of everything that is emanated, above and below. Moreover, it is the source of all supernal blessings.[162]

An interesting aside is found near the end of the aforementioned *Commentary on the Book of Contemplation*. After discussing the doctrine of *Creation* concerning the *matres* letters: *'alef, mem*, and *shin*, which correspond to the primal elements,[163] the *Commentary* continues, "know that this ether is the Primal Ether that is mentioned in the book, *Midrash on Sciences (ḥokhmot) and Proof*."[164] The identification of this treatise is unclear, unless either *The Fountain of Wisdom* or perhaps the *Midrash of R. Simon* are intended.[165]

As we have just seen, some of the writings from the "Circle" follow *Fountain* by characterizing Primal Ether as the most sublime

---

"the initial, primordial light" (*'or ha-rishon ha-kadmon*) *Sod ha-Sodot* in J. Dan ed., *Tekstim*, 8. In addition, the Provençal kabbalist, R. Asher b. David, used the term "hidden ether" (*'avir ha-ne'elam*); see *Kabbalat R. Asher*, 21.

161. See above, p. 211.

162. Vatican ms. 185, f. 185a.

163. *Sefer Yeẓirah*, 3:3.

164. Vatican ms. 290, f. 64.

165. Moshe Idel has suggested to me that perhaps the text in question is R. Judah ha-Cohen's *Midrash ha-Ḥokhmah*, the manuscripts of which are currently inaccessible to me. Interestingly, in the Institute's microfilm 6812 (Guenzburg), ff. 38b-39b, one finds a kabbalistic critique of *Midrash ha-Ḥokhmah*, composed by a father and son. For a study of R. Judah, see C. Sirat, "*La qabbale d'apres Juda b. Salomon ha-Cohen*," in *Hommage à G. Vajda* (Louvain 1980), 191-202.

power. As Scholem has noted, however, there are other writings that follow *Contemplation*'s positioning of the ether near the bottom of the celestial hierarchy.[166] Specifically, Scholem partially cites a passage from the conclusion of the *Secret Knowledge of Existence* which ends,

> Why is it (i.e., Primal Ether) called primal? It is not because there are no other powers which preceded it–rather because it is primal. It is a cause of the created entities that subsequently emerged.[167]

Accordingly, Primal Ether is characterized as being primal, only with respect to the created universe, which emanated from it; nevertheless, there are numerous other "powers" that preceded it.

Furthermore, the author of this treatise previously contended that Primal Ether was "the external power in which exists the unity of the name of the exalted Holy One, blessed be He."[168] It was this force that was the focus of all prophetic visions. Thus it is considered "external" in terms of the external dimension of the Divinity. Accordingly, the *Secret Knowledge of Existence* represents a synthesis of the teachings of *Fountain* and *Contemplation*. It has interpreted Primal Ether in the same fashion as Encompassing Ether was presented in *Contemplation*, namely, at the lower end of the celestial hierarchy.

Although much of the material from the second section of *Fountain* is open to interpretation, it appears that the author equates three terms: Primal Ether, Primal Darkness, and the Light That Is Darkened From Illuminating–leading us to the theme of primordial darkness. This concept is found in two passages that warrant quoting at length. The first focuses on its profound imperceptibility.

> This corresponds to the Primal Darkness that ushered forth from the Ether. Do not hasten to investigate or contemplate it, for even Moses, our Rabbi, of blessed memory, was not allowed to ask questions about it. . . Then he (i.e., Moses) asked his pointed question, as is stated, "Please, inform me of

---

166. G. Scholem, *Reshit*, 170.

167. Schocken Kabbalah ms. 6

168. *Ibid.*

your ways" (Exod. 33:18). The Holy One, blessed be He, responded to him concerning this matter, "You cannot see My Face" (Exod. 33:20): that is to say, the knowledge of this Darkness that you are requesting, for it was all of Me and My source. . . Accordingly, you will not possess knowledge of the Darkness that is the focal point of My existence. However, from here on you shall know everything. That is to say, from this Darkness and what is below it you shall know [all], even the creation of My essence and the essence of My Name and My Glory.[169]

In order to crystallize his knowledge of the "image of the Holy One," Moses petitioned to comprehend the primordial darkness. This request was denied, for only the lower levels of the Divinity are perceptible. Within this remarkable discussion is the unequivocal assertion that the Primal Darkness was one of the sources and progenitors of the Holy One, blessed be He. This calls to mind the earlier discussion on Divine self-actualization. It parallels the perspective of *Contemplation–Short* in positioning the Holy One, blessed be He, as a lower stage of the Divinity.

The conclusion "even the creation of My essence and the essence of My Name and My Glory," comprises what God is said to have granted Moses, despite refusing to reveal His Face. The latter part of the phrasing of this statement is rooted in the verse from Isaiah, "Anyone that is called by My Name and whom I have created for My Glory" (Isa. 43:7). It also seems likely that the author of *Fountain* had read R. Judah Barzeloni's commentary on *The Book of Creation*. Therein, as in *Fountain*, there is a discussion of Moses' request to see the Divine Glory. In characterizing God's refusal, R. Judah writes, "And the Creator replied to him, 'You will not be able to see into the light of My Glory and the essence of its beginning.'"[170] This is the continuation of the following statement. "This is the great light that no creature can perceive its beginning . . . for the essence of this light is in its beginning."[171]

Despite the similarities in phrasing, there is a fundamental difference between *Fountain* and Barzeloni's formulations. R. Judah contended that Moses was denied perception of the created Glory in

---

169. See above, p. 57f.

170. R. Judah Barzeloni, *Perush*, 17.

171. *Ibid.*

its initial brilliance, but was granted an afterimage. On the other hand, in *Fountain* Moses sought to perceive God in His primordial state and was shown instead a lower state, namely, the Glory.

Quite similar to *Fountain*'s position, however, is that formulated by R. Elhanan b. Yakar in his *Secret of Secrets*, in a passage based loosely on Ibn Ezra's Torah commentary.

> And thus R. Abraham Ibn Ezra said, "You shall see My Back, but My Face will not be seen." He designated extant entities as "behind," whereas the unique corner that is infinite was referred to as "face." The explanation of "my back" refers to entities that I emanated or that I created afterwards, namely, the Glory and the Chariot.... The explanation of "and My face shall not be seen" comprises entities that were before everything else. This refers to the Spirit of the Living God, may He be blessed.[172]

The second, extended selection from *Fountain* that warrants consideration concerns Primal Darkness. It emphasizes that it was not so-named owing to any absence of light.

> It (i.e., Primal Darkness) is [also] called the Light That Is Darkened From Illuminating, for it is hidden and impossible to know the essence of the existence of this darkness. Accordingly, it is called Darkening Darkness; not because it resembles murk, but because no creature can look at it. Even the angels seated in the front row of the Kingdom of Heaven lack the power to look at it. It is like a human who lacks the power to look at the eye of the harsh sun. Moreover, all of the lights emerge from it, and therefore, it is only called Darkening Darkness because it is exalted, hidden, and concealed from all perception by the prophets.[173]

In seeking precursors to *Fountain*, one can find in the Pseudo-Bahya *Treatise on the Soul*, written around 1100, a lengthy discussion on the differentiation between the quality of darkness that is simply

---

172. Cited in J. Dan, *Hugei*, 127.

173. See above, p. 59f.

an absence of light, and darkness as a primal element.[174] The kabbalists of Gerona discussed darkness as a primordial element and the source of light. As Moshe Idel noted, "R. Ezra utilizes the symbol of darkness as the place of the *havayot* (essences) prior to their emanation."[175] R. Ezra writes to R. Abraham,

> From absolute darkness He emanated the *havayot* that were in darkness. 'And light dwells with Him' (Dan. 2:22)–He removed light from darkness as is written, 'and darkness was on the face of the depths and God said, Let there be light' (Gen. 1:3).[176]

Additionally, the concept of primordial darkness was expressed by R. Ezra's colleague, R. Azriel, as "the darkness that once was."[177]

Finally, in R. Azriel's prayer commentary one finds a statement that was probably the source of *Fountain*'s rather awkward term "The Light That Is Darkened from Illuminating." Commenting on the expression "and He creates darkness," R. Azriel remarks, "the hidden light that is darkened from illuminating is called darkness."[178]

In summation, we have noted that numerous texts prior to *The Fountain of Wisdom* address the theme of darkness as a primal element that functioned as one of the roots in the process of creation. To be sure, this is an important feature of *Fountain*'s cosmogony.

---

174. Pseudo-Bahya, *Kitab Ma'ani al-Nafs*, I. Broyde, ch. 3, pp. 7 and 8. See also Maimonides' discussion of darkness as the nonluminous primal element fire, *Guide*, 2:30.

175. M. Idel, *"Sefirot,"* 242; cf. the sources listed by Idel there, n. 17, and in his *"Homer Kabbali,"* 181, n. 58. This concept of darkness is already evident in the writings of R. Isaac the Blind, see his commentary on *Sefer Yezirah*, 10, as well as the text *'Inyan Ma'aseh Bere'shit*, J.T.S. 1187, f. 29, attributed either to R. Isaac or R. Ezra. For darkness as a primordial element in the writings of R. Elhanan b. Yakar, see J. Dan, *Hugei*, 133. On R. Azriel, see A. Altmann, "The Motif of the Shells . . . ," *Journal of Jewish Studies*, 9 (1958), 74ff. In R. Azriel's writings darkness is related to limitation and differentiation. This parallels Nachmanides' discussion of darkness and *zimzum* (contraction), *Perush le-Sefer Yezirah*, G. Scholem ed., 402.

176. G. Scholem, *"Te'udah Hadashah,"* 158.

177. R. Azriel, *Perush ha-'Aggadot*, 86.

178. R. Azriel, *Perush ha-Tefillah*, Bodleian ms. 1938, f. 213a. This term is ultimately based on Isa. 5:30, *'or hashakh* (the darkened light).

The significant theological component of *Fountain*'s speculation on the origin of the cosmos is absent, however, from these sources, and therefore, *Fountain* breaks new ground in this regard.

There is one final topic in *The Fountain of Wisdom* that warrants our attention. It is the presentation of the five processes associated with the Divine Name. These concepts appear throughout the text and were subsequently incorporated into later versions of *Contemplation* and other texts from the "Circle."

The primary explication of these terms is found in the opening of the treatise,

> These are the *tikkun*, combination, utterance, sum, and computation of the explication of the Ineffable Name–unique in the branches of the root of vocalization that is magnified in the thirteen types of transformation.
> How is the *tikkun* [accomplished]? It derives the word through the utterance and the utterance through the word; the *tikkun* through the combination and the combination through the *tikkun*; the sum through the computation and the computation through the sum–until all the words are positioned in the font of the flame and the flame in the font–until there is no measure or quantifying the light that is hidden in the superabundance of the secret darkness. Then everything is brought forth through the concluding operation, by means of the thirteen types of transformation.[179]

Although employing somewhat different terminology, it is likely that the author of *Fountain* was influenced by the passage in *The Book of Creation*, which describes the various processes that the primordial letters underwent.

> Twenty-two letters. He engraved them, hewed them, weighed them, exchanged them, refined them and created out of them the soul of every creature and the soul of everything that would be created in the future.[180]

---

179. See above, p. 50f.

180. *Sefer Yezirah*, 2:2.

The expressions that *Creation* utilizes are connected with quar-rying blocks of stone. They are being used metaphorically to describe the process of creation. Accordingly, there is no need to try and inter-pret them further. In *Fountain*, however, the author appears to have specific procedures in mind for each of these expressions. Unfortu-nately, he does not provide sufficient information to the reader such that we can be certain of what he intended. Scholem explicates this passage as depicting five activities which lead to the "gnosis" of the Glory. He interprets *tikkun* as placing the letters in harmony, *zeruf* as permutating the letters, *ma'amar* as forming them into a words, *mikhlal* as collecting all possible combinations, and *ḥeshbon* as calcu-lating their numerical value.[181]

In a similar vein, though not as specific, Dan comments,

> I will not pretend to explain, within this framework, exactly what the author intended with each of these concepts, which seem to have derived their roots from *Book of Creation* and its numerical-mathematical exegesis. . . . These five functions exhibit something "dry," concerning number-combinations and calculations, *gematriot, notarikonim*, and the calculation of the value of the letters of the alphabet in various ways.[182]

Both Scholem and Dan assume that the author intended specific "mathematical" processes through his usage of these terms. Presum-ably, these scholars were influenced in their interpretation by Abulafia's usage of terms like *zeruf* (combination), thereby designat-ing permutations of letters, in his letter-based meditative practices. The author of *Fountain*, however, gives no such indication that this is what he actually means. On several occasions, later on in the text he discusses *tikkun* and the other concepts in a very different man-ner. For him, *tikkun* is the state of preparation and concentration that one must undergo, who desires to properly contemplate some-thing, especially the Divine unity.

> This is the *tikkun* that we began to speak about. It is necessary for the act to be regulated (*tikkun*) in order to comprehend something fully and its existence within the unity of the Holy One, blessed be He.[183]

---

181. G. Scholem, *Origins*, 313.

182. J. Dan, *Ḥugei*, 42.

183. See above, p. 61.

He continues, "This is the *tikkun*, by directing your heart upon these four letters that constitute the Ineffable Name." Finally, toward the end of the treatise, he reiterates and amplifies–in order to make himself better understood. In the following passage not only is *tikkun* explained in terms of sincere concentration, but so too are the other procedures.

> This matter will be elucidated and clarified by means of its *tikkun*. The *tikkun* about which we have spoken is the start of everything. It is the direction of the heart, intention of the thought, calculation of the viscera, purification of the heart, until the mind is settled and logic and language are formed. From language [stems] clarification, and from clarification the word is formed. From the word is the utterance and from the utterance is the deed. This is its beginning.[184]

Admittedly, despite the author's sincere attempt to elucidate this issue, what he means is still rather obscure. Nevertheless, we get a sense of what he is driving at. It is surely more basic and yet more transcendent than mundane letter permutations, though this may be a part of it.

Later writers of the "Circle" transformed this doctrine. The compiler of the *Midrash R. Simon* interpreted *tikkun* as a method of arranging biblical verses in order to obtain Divine names. The specific example that he offers is the seventy-two-letter name[185] based on the verses from Exodus 14:19-21. The writer directs the adept to form letter permutations from beginning to end utilizing the first verse; end to beginning with the second; and beginning to end with the third.[186] Similarly, in the *Commentary on the Tetragrammaton* this issue is specifically related to the first forty-two letters of *Genesis*.[187]

Having analyzed the important doctrines and terms of *Fountain*, we can conclude our discussion by briefly considering its time of composition. It is significant that we find in the case of *Fountain* the same pattern of influences emerging as we noted above in con-

---

184. See above, p. 62.

185. See Rashi, *B. Sukkah*, 45a; Ibn Ezra on Exod. 14:19; and *Bahir* #110.

186. *Midrash R. Shimon ha-Zaddik*, in *Sefer Yezirah*, f. 39a.

187. *Perush Shem ben 'Arba' 'Otiyyot*, Florence ms. 2:41, f. 199b.

junction with *Contemplation–Short*. The term *'avir kadmon* was connected with R. Meshullam the Zadokite. Other evidence of influence from the *ḥasidei 'ashkenaz* entails the designations *'or zah* (bright light) and *'or mezuḥzah* (brightened light), found in R. Eleazar of Worms's writings and incorporated into *Fountain*. Parallels were also noted with the kabbalists of Gerona, and especially R. Azriel and his comments on primordial darkness. If in fact all of these writers influenced the author of *Fountain*, then one would have to conclude, as we shall in the case of *Contemplation–Short*, that it was composed after 1230. Moreover, in Appendix II we shall demonstrate that *Contemplation–Short* influenced *Fountain*. Nevertheless, *Fountain* was not simply an offshoot of *Contemplation–Short*–it was essentially independent, yet part of the same intellectual heritage.

4

HISTORICAL DIMENSIONS

Having presented and discussed the array of texts connected with *The Books of Contemplation*, we are now in a position to assemble the historical data that is available, in order to pinpoint the time and place of composition of these works. In so doing, we shall have occasion to reconsider the basic assumptions that Gershom Scholem made concerning the historiography of the early *kabbalah* in general and about the "Circle of Contemplation" in particular. In so doing, we shall offer alternative hypotheses.

SCHOLEM'S HISTORIOGRAPHY OF EARLY *KABBALAH*

In attempting to place the writings of the "Circle of Contemplation" within the framework of medieval Jewish mysticism, it is necessary at the outset to consider the theories of Gershom Scholem. Prior to his death in 1982, Gershom Scholem was widely acknowledged to be the world's foremost expert of Jewish mysticism. Arguably, he was also the most influential scholar in the field of Jewish studies. A prolific writer for over sixty years, Scholem published more than forty books and some 700 articles.[1]

Singlehandedly, Scholem forged the discipline of modern scholarship of Jewish mysticism. When he began his research in the early 1920s, much of this vast literary legacy consisted of thousands of medieval manuscripts that had been ignored and unread for cen-

---

1. A readable and edifying presentation of Scholem's scholarly achievement is the recent monograph by Joseph Dan, *Gerschom Scholem and the Mystical Dimension of Jewish History* (New York 1987); for an interesting intellectual biography of Scholem, see, D. Biale's *Gerschom Scholem: Kabbalah and Counter-History* (Cambridge 1982).

turies. Scholem's lengthy and productive career at Hebrew University in Jerusalem spanned more than half a century. During that time he scoured the great libraries of the world–identifying, cataloguing, and analyzing many of these texts. He once characterized his achievement as having started out by being confronted with a myriad of scattered and tattered folios, which he then transformed into history.[2] Scholem also trained three successive generations of researchers, many of whom have likewise made significant contributions to the field by carrying on this colossal enterprise.

The focus of his research was an exhaustive study of the earliest stage of kabbalistic writings. According to his own determination, this occurred from the middle of the twelfth century to the middle of the thirteenth. He viewed this as the formative period, during which time the basic doctrines and themes of medieval Jewish mysticism were conceived.

It is worth noting that Scholem began his lifelong project as a graduate student at the University of Munich, where he chose the *Bahir* as the topic for his Ph.D. dissertation. At the time there was considerable disagreement as to which treatise constituted the earliest evidence of the specialized theosophy characteristic of the *kabbalah*. Scholem forcefully contended that pride of place belongs to the *Bahir*. This assumption concerning the priority of the *Bahir* constitutes the cornerstone of Scholem's historiography of the evolution of medieval Jewish mysticism. Insofar as Scholem's views on the *Bahir* colored his perspectives on the "Circle," it is imperative to consider this topic at some length.

Like many of the treatises of the "Circle," the *Bahir* is also written pseudepigraphically. It appears to be the record of a series of discussions between various rabbis and sages from ancient times. Some of these are historical figures, though from different periods, and other characters are clearly fictitious. The work is commonly ascribed to R. Nehuniah b. ha-Kanah, the initial speaker, who was a rabbi from the early second century C.E. and played a prominent role in *hekhalot* literature. Owing to the obvious problems of historicity as well as the appearance of radical theological doctrines, such as the feminine aspect of the Godhead, cosmic dualism, and the transmigration of souls, Scholem and others concluded that it was a medieval work.

Furthermore, Scholem contended that the *Bahir* originated at some indeterminate time and place in the Middle East and that it surfaced in western Europe, specifically Provence, around the middle

---

2. Cited by J. Dan, *Scholem*, 2.

of the twelfth century.[3] Thereupon it was revised and philosophical concerns were incorporated into it. As it began to circulate in Provence and later on in Spain, its radically innovative theosophy, with veiled references to a dynamic stratification of the intra-Divine realm, began to influence contemporary Jewish mystics. Accordingly, Scholem viewed the *Bahir* as the catalyst behind the great outpouring of kabbalistic literature that occurred at the beginning of the thirteenth century.

Although subsequent researchers in the field of Jewish mysticism have accepted Scholem's hypothesis, it is far from proven. Whereas Scholem was forced to concede that the parallels to medieval Jewish philosophy that are found in the *Bahir* indicate that it must have been redacted in the mid- twelfth century,[4] he also noted numerous other parallels to Maimonides' writings which he consistently dismissed as not indicative of influence.[5] This methodological inconsistency is obviously problematic; however, it was necessitated for two reasons. First, Maimonides wrote in Egypt at the end of the twelfth century and his work did not circulate in western Europe until the start of the thirteenth century. Furthermore, Heinrich Graetz, the protean nineteenth-century Jewish historian, had asserted that the *kabbalah* was simply a pietistic reaction against Maimonidean philosophy. Scholem was very critical of Graetz and rejected his contentions. Accordingly, he was forced to deny Maimonidean influence, thereby enabling him to sustain his hypothesis that the *Bahir* was the earliest work of the *kabbalah*. As opposed to Graetz who viewed *kabbalah* as an unwelcome by-product of medieval Jewish philosophy, Scholem championed the intrinsic integrity of Jewish mysticism.

Although the issue of Maimonidean influence on the *Bahir* has not yet been systematically investigated, it can be noted in passing that Maimonides' influence on even the earliest writings of the "Circle" is undeniable. For example, *The Fountain of Wisdom*'s pivotal discussion of Divine self-generation, analyzed previously, repre-

---

3. On the indeterminate, oriental origins of the *Bahir*, see Scholem's discussion in *Origins*, 59f.

4. G. Scholem, *Origins*, 62f.

5. For example, he noted that the exact moralistic etymology of "Satan" is found in the *Bahir* and in Maimonides' *Guide*, and Scholem felt compelled to explain why "this need not be a borrowing" in *Origins*, 150.

sents an intriguing reformulation of Maimonides' statements in the opening chapter of his law code, *Mishneh Torah*.[6]

It should also be noted that the initial references to the *Bahir* are found in writings of Rabbis Ezra and Azriel, presumably composed around 1230 in Gerona, an important Jewish enclave just north of Barcelona. Scholem did not convincingly demonstrate that the earlier Provencal kabbalists were likewise influenced by the *Bahir*. None of these individuals, such as R. Isaac the Blind, whose work was discussed extensively by Scholem, use the terminology characteristic of the *Bahir* or focus on the same theosophical interests.

The earliest statement concerning the composition of the *Bahir* is that by R. Meir b. Shimon in his mid-thirteenth century polemic, *Commanded War*, discussed in the previous chapter. This text appears to have been written in 1245, although Scholem maintains an earlier dating of 1230-35.[7] R. Meir was a Talmudist. His personal connections with the preeminent family of Provençal kabbalists notwithstanding, he included a scathing denunciation of the *Bahir* in his treatise. R. Meir wrote,

> And we have heard that he has already composed (ḥbr) for them a book (and) he entitled it *Bahir* (i.e., Radiance), which we have referred to previously. They have seen no light in it. This book has just come into our possession and we discovered that they attribute it to R. Nehuniah b. ha-Kanah, Heaven forbid. There is no truth to this for never did this righteous individual falter in such a manner, nor among the sinners is he to be counted. The diction of this book and all of its topics demonstrate that it was from an individual that was ignorant of proper rhetoric and style. There are numerous examples of heresy. Moreover, we have heard that he also composed (ḥbr) for them a commentary on the *Song of Songs*, the *Book of Creation* and *Hekhalot* . . .[8]

This passage was originally published and translated by A. Neubauer. Neubauer's translation, which is similar to the preceding,

---

6. See above, p. 139 & p. 151.

7. See the *Encyclopedia Judaica*, 11:1255 and G. Scholem, *Origins*, 42.

8. This text was preserved in a Parma ms., de Rossi 155, and was published by Neubauer, "Bahir," 358.

was challenged by Scholem on linguistic grounds.[9] Scholem argued that the verb *ḥbr* is spelled defectively and should be rendered in the passive tense, i.e., *ḥubbar* as opposed to *ḥibber*. Accordingly, Scholem translates the opening sentence, "And we have heard that a book had already been written for them, which they call *Bahir*." Were this the only such occurrence of this verb, Scholem's reading would be plausible, though unproven. However, the parallel usage of *ḥbr* toward the end of the quotation clearly indicates that it is referring to the literary activity of a specific individual, who has also composed kabbalistic commentaries on biblical and classical texts. Although the identification of this individual is problematic, R. Meir b. Shimon seems to be indicating either R. Ezra or R. Azriel of Gerona. Not coincidentally, these two are the earliest adducers of the *Bahir*.[10]

Aside from external evidence concerning the composition of the *Bahir*, there are recent analyses of conceptual parallels between material in the *Bahir* and early kabbalistic writings. Moshe Idel has pointed to pertinent material in the writings of R. Asher b. David,[11] and others are currently investigating parallels with the writings of R. Judah b. Yakar, who died in Barcelona around 1217.[12] Nevertheless, none of this research points to examples of actual literary borrowing. Hence, even if it appears that there was influence, it cannot as yet be determined whether the *Bahir* was prior and therefore influenced these early kabbalists, or vice versa. Owing to the lack of any evidence to the contrary, the possibility that the *Bahir* did not achieve its final form as a kabbalistic text until after 1225 must be seriously considered.[13]

---

9. G. Scholem, *Origins*, 43, n. 74.

10. Scholem's assertion that *The Book of Contemplation* was one of the principal targets of R. Meir's polemic is unfounded; cf. *Origins*, 314.

11. M. Idel, *Kabbalah*, 141f.

12. Both Elliot Ginsburg and Elliot Wolfson have graciously discussed their current research on this issue with me.

13. This ascription of a thirteenth-century dating to the *Bahir* applies to the work as it now stands. Admittedly, Scholem has produced evidence that there existed a proto-version of the *Bahir*; see *Origins*, 106-123. What is significant, however, is that this earlier text did not exhibit the kabbalistic doctrines of the current work. Accordingly, it seems that someone in the thirteenth century appropriated this earlier treatise and transformed it into a kabbalistic treatise by introducing radically new theosophical concerns.

Not only does Scholem assign a relatively early dating to the *Bahir*, he likewise assumed that the writings of the "Circle" also originated in Provence "between 1200 and 1225."[14] Hence, according to him the "Circle" preceded most of the early kabbalists. Obviously, if this were in fact the case, the "Circle" would assume major significance as a forerunner of the *kabbalah*. In general, Joseph Dan, Scholem's successor, concurs on this early dating of the "Circle."[15] Presumably, it is for this reason that in Dan's recent anthology of kabbalistic texts in translation, selections from the "Circle" are positioned at the start of the book, even preceding the *Bahir*.[16]

Shortly, we shall present considerable evidence which indicates that, in fact, these writings stemmed from Castile and were directly influenced by the kabbalist R. Azriel of Gerona. Therefore, they actually postdate 1230, the presumed time of R. Azriel's activity.

SCHOLEM'S HISTORIOGRAPHY AND R. ISAAC COHEN'S LEGENDS

One can see in Scholem's linear sequencing of the development of the *kabbalah* a reflection of his personal propensity to arrange material in an orderly manner.[17] This approach, however, is an oversimplification. Joseph Dan has persuasively demonstrated that the early kabbalistic centers overlapped and were relatively contemporaneous.[18] As opposed to Scholem's contention that the *kabbalah* emerged after a protracted period and in successive locales, the evidence indicates that within the two decades from 1215 to 1235, all

---

14. G. Scholem, *Origins*, 327.

15. Dan designates the "Circle's" time frame as "the beginning of the twelfth to the mid-thirteenth century," *Hugei*, 59.

16. J. Dan, *Early Kabbalah*, 43-56.

17. An interesting example of the combination of Scholem's fastidiousness with his scholarly acumen was the methodical way in which he arranged the items in his vast personal library. In conversation, Joseph Dan remarked that Scholem's book arrangement was a decisive indication of how Scholem conceived the development of the mystical tradition. Thanks are also due to Moshe Idel for pointing out to me, in general terms, the "unilinear" dimension of Scholem's historiography.

18. This is the central thesis of *Hugei*. A summary of this position is found in a lengthy footnote in Dan's *Scholem*, 186f., n. 50.

of the esoteric writings of R. Eleazar of Worms, R. Isaac the Blind, and R. Ezra and R. Azriel of Gerona were composed, as well as the *Bahir*, the Ur-text of *The Book of Contemplation* and *The Fountain of Wisdom*.

What prompted Scholem to construct his linear hypothesis concerning the origins of the *kabbalah*? Aside from his love for order and precision, it seems that a second factor was the underlying assumption, formulated in his formative years of study, that the *kabbalah* had ancient roots. This argument was critical, for it validated *kabbalah* as an authentic component of traditional Judaism, in the face of its general disparagement by prominent nineteenth-century Wissenschaft scholars, like Graetz. A good example of this tendency was Scholem's championing the cause of the classical origins of the *Zohar*, in his inaugural lecture at Hebrew University.[19] Eventually, he revised his views on the *Zohar* and concluded that indeed it was the product of the late thirteenth-century Castilian writer, R. Moses de Leon.[20]

Although Scholem radically changed his views concerning the ancient authorship of the *Zohar*, throughout his career he tenaciously maintained that the *Bahir* had indeterminate, oriental origins.

> The conclusion remains clear: the Book *Bahir* was not composed as a result of a completely new inspiration of a gnostic character. On the contrary, it took over sources, in part reconstructed and in part inferred by our analysis. These sources, which are not homogeneous, came from the Orient. . . . Sometime between 1130 and 1170 the leaves of the original *Bahir* arrived in Provence, where they were subjected to a final revision and redaction into the form in which the book has come down to us.[21]

The only historical testimony that Scholem offers to substantiate this theory concerning the oriental source of the *Bahir*, and by

---

19. This lecture was published in *Mada'ei ha-Yahadut*, 1 (1926), 16-29.

20. See Scholem's comments on this development in *Trends*, 159. Although for half a century de Leon's authorship of the *Zohar* has been an axiom of scholarship, in recent years this question is once again being reexamined; see especially Y. Liebes' repercussive essay "How the Zohar was Written" [Hebrew], *Jerusalem Studies in Jewish Thought*, 8 (1989), 1-71.

21. G. Scholem, *Origins*, 123.

extension the *kabbalah* in general, is a comment attributed to the Castilian kabbalist R. Isaac Cohen, who was active in the latter half of the thirteenth century. It is recorded in a late fourteenth-century work.

> [The *Bahir*] came from Palestine to the old sages and *hasidim*, the kabbalists in Germany, and from there it reached several of the old and eminent scholars among the rabbis of Provence, who went in pursuit of every kind of secret science, the possessors of a higher knowledge. However, they only saw a part of it and not the whole of it, for its full and complete text did not come into their hands. In any case, it came to them from a distant land, whether from Palestine or from abroad, from old sages and holy kabbalists, who possessed a well-ordered tradition [*kabbalah*] transmitted to them orally by their fathers and forefathers.[22]

Thus, according to R. Isaac, the *Bahir* was composed in Israel, and was eventually transmitted to the German pietists and from thence to Provence. This statement, the veracity of which is essentially accepted by Scholem, is but one of many made by R. Isaac concerning the origins of various texts. Insofar as R. Isaac was an important conduit for the writings of the "Circle of Contemplation," and as shall be argued shortly, a probable author of some of its treatises, it is necessary to consider his assertions in some detail. This will entail the examination of a number of different, yet interrelated texts.

In his *Treatise on the Left Emanation* on the demonic forces, R. Isaac offers a lengthy account of how he learned about these doctrines. He writes,

> Now we shall speak about the system of evil powers which are in heaven, of those which were created and then annihilated suddenly. When I was in the great city of Arles, masters of [the *kabbalah*] showed me a booklet, a very old one, the writing in it being rough and different from our writing. It was transmitted in the name of the Rabbi and *ga'on* (i.e., exalted rabbinic authority) [whom they] called Rabbi Mazliah, for the old *ga'on*, our Rabbi Pelatiah, was from the holy city of Jerusalem, and it was brought by a great scholar and pietist

---

22. *Ibid.*, 41.

called Rabbi Gerschom of Damascus. He was from the city of Damascus and lived in Arles about two years . . . and I copied some things from it.[23]

R. Isaac Cohen's account bears remarkable similarities to a discourse on the *sefirot, Pseudo-R. Eleazer of Worms Responsum*, which Scholem ascribed to the "Circle." It has been preserved in two sources: it is found in Shem Tov ibn Gaon's *Baddei 'Aron*, as well as in a kabbalistic collection preserved in Berlin Or. Qu. 833, which offers significant additional material. The text purports to be the esoteric tradition of a R. Kashisha Gaon, originally from the Babylonian academy in Mata Mehasia, who taught in Apulia, Italy. Insofar as the term *kashisha* is Aramaic for "old man," presumably, this is simply a fictitious epithet.[24] (Interestingly, later kabbalists changed this name to the famous R. Sherira Gaon.)[25] One of his supposed students was R. Judah b. Aha from Corbeil. The latter in turn transmitted this material to his student, R. Eleazar of Worms, who subsequently publicized it.

A second and more complicated version of the process of transmission is found at the end of the Berlin manuscript's version. Therein it is claimed that the actual messenger was R. Berachiah from Damascus, who transmitted it directly to R. Eleazar the elder from Worms. It continues with an account by an anonymous reporter who had been told by a certain R. Solomon b. Mazliah of Arles in the name of the latter's father that in the days of R. Elhanan of Provence there was an aged scholar, who was head of the *sanhedrin* (rabbinical court) in Lunel. On behalf of this unnamed rabbi, R. Eleazar wrote a short treatise entitled *Sefer ha-Razim* (Book of Mysteries).

---

23. See G. Scholem, *Kabbalot*, 86f., and J. Dan, *Early Kabbalah*, 169f.

24. The use of an Aramaic term as a pseudepigraphic epithet has already been discussed above (p. 1) in connection with the supposed author of *The Book of Contemplation*, and as such seems to represent a stylistic feature of Castilian *kabbalah*. This might also have some relevance to discussions of the composition of the *Bahir*, wherein similar names, such as Ruhammai, are evident.

25. Cf. R. Moshe Cordovero, *Pardes Rimmonim*, 5:1, 23b, referring to Shem Tov ibn Shem Tov's *Sefer ha-'Emunot*, 4:11. A different approach to the identification of this individual was advocated by E. Urbach, who cites a rabbinical decree that refers to a certain R. Karshavya in *Ba'alei Tosafot* (Jerusalem 1968), 130.

The anonymous reporter continues by claiming that a certain R. Nataniel from Montpellier traveled "to our country" with a book from his uncle, R. Zechariah of Montpellier, who had spent time in Greece. While there he met a philosopher, who forsook his studies and instead sought out R. Hasdai ha-Nasi, of Davidic descent, who taught him about the mysteries of the *nekuddot*, supernal points. (An important clue to the identity of the author is the likelihood that "our country," namely, the author's domicile, refers to Spain.) [26]

Scholem eventually concluded that the author of the *Pseudo-R. Eleazar Responsum* was in fact R. Isaac Cohen. In support he noted,

> The text of the epistle is already partly transmitted in the
> writings of one of his relatives, Shem Tov ibn Gaon. The style
> of narration that ties pieces together, and the manner in
> which diverse sources are juxtaposed, conform in every
> respect to his style and procedure in similar epistles on the
> doctrine of the emanation of the "left," preserved in his name.[27]

Scholem is undoubtedly correct in his assumption that R. Isaac was responsible for this text, though his substantiation is rather vague. It is fascinating to observe that almost all of the names and places that are found in *Pseudo-R. Eleazar* are mentioned by R. Isaac in his *Treatise*, except in different combinations. In both accounts the material is conveyed by a messenger from Damascus, eventually it reaches Arles, and the name Mazliah is equally prominent.

---

26. Scholem interprets this passage likewise; see *Origins*, 379.

27. *Origins*, 355. For somewhat different reasons, Joseph Dan likewise determined that this text emanated from the circle of the Cohen brothers, *'Ofiyo u-Mekorotav shel Sefer Baddei ha-'Aron* (Jerusalem 1977), 60. More recently, Dan has discussed this text and modified his conclusions by attributing authorship to the early fourteenth-century kabbalist, R. Shem Tov ibn Gaon; cf. J. Dan, "*'Iggeret Garmeza u-v'ayyat ha-Pseudo-'epigrafiyah ba-Kabbalah ha-Kedumah*," *Mehkerei Yerushalayim be-Mahshevet Yisra'el,* 3:1 (1984), 111-138. While this proposal is worth considering, it is clear that *Pseudo-R. Eleazar* is connected with other writings from the "Circle," such as *Pseudo-R. Hai* and the *Responsa of R. Yehushiel*. All of these texts were either quoted directly by R. Isaac Cohen or in the case of *Pseudo-R. Eleazar*, by his disciple, R. Todros Abulafia, in *Sha'ar ha-Razim*, Munich ms. 209. These citations occurred in the thirteenth century, many decades prior to R. Shem Tov's activities.

To complicate matters even further, the important treatise from the "Circle," the *Pseudo-R. Hai Gaon Responsa*, offers significant parallels to the Berlin version of the *Pseudo-R. Eleazar* text. *Pseudo-R. Hai* concludes with a discussion of a sage from Sicily, who traveled to Montpellier. This unidentified individual recounted meeting a Moroccan scholar, who was living in Sicily and earning a living as a doctor to the king of Sicily. This luminary composed a treatise in Aramaic attacking philosophy, as well as teaching the significance of the twenty-four *nekuddot* (supernal points), connected with the Tetragrammaton. The parallels between these two accounts include a prepossessing figure, critical of philosophy, who lives in Greece or Sicily, and teaches the mysteries of the *nekuddot*. Furthermore, Montpellier functions as the point of transmission for both of these narratives.

As we concluded above, R. Isaac Cohen is probably the author of the *Pseudo-R. Eleazar Responsum*, owing to parallels with his personal reminiscences. Immediately preceding this testimony is an exposition, which includes the earliest datable reference to the *Pseudo-R. Hai Responsa*.[28] It would therefore not be unreasonable to conjecture that R. Isaac had a hand in this text, as well.

R. Isaac also seems to have penned another of the treatises of the "Circle," the *Responsa of R. Yehushiel*.[29] Like the *Treatise on the Left Emanation*, it too focuses on the cosmic drama involving evil and especially the archdemon, Samael. Each text constructs a narrative within an eschatological and messianic framework. Both sources view evil primarily in terms of jealousy and make the radical assertion that evil is hierarchically structured, paralleling the *sefirot*. In each work, evil is rooted below the third *sefirah, binah* (Understanding). It is interesting that when R. Isaac describes this process, he refers to *binah* by its epithet, Repentance.[30] This calls to mind R. Yehushiel's assertion that the cosmic goat is sacrificed on an altar "which stands before Repentance." A noteworthy stylistic feature is the penchant in both texts to use uncommon angelic names with the Divine suffix =*el* or =*iel*, in fact even the name Yehushiel fits this pattern. Furthermore, at key conjunctures in each text, there is the assertion that the source of esoteric knowledge comes from unidentified *ḥakhmei ha-kabbalah*, masters of the kabbalistic tradition.

---

28. G. Scholem, *Kabbalot*, 86. On the connection between R. Isaac and the material attributed to R. Hasdai ha-Nasi, see Scholem's discussion there, p. 31.

29. Most of this text was published by Scholem in *Le-Ḥeker*, 136-138.

30. See, J. Dan, *Early Kabbalah*, 166.

Not only are there compelling doctrinal reasons for ascribing the *R. Yehushiel Responsa* to R. Isaac, his student colleagues, R. Moses of Burgos and R. Todros Abulafia, were the first to cite it.[31] Moreover, the ascriptions found in the *R. Yehushiel Responsa* are similar to those already observed in the *Treatise on the Left Emanation*, as well as the *Pseudo-R. Eleazar Responsum*. R. Yehushiel is depicted as a sage from Germany. According to the text's preface he purportedly sent this composition to the pietist, R. Solomon of Corbeil, who passed it on to the great R. Yedidyah of Marseilles. A second and more complicated version of the process of transmission is found at the end of the text. Therein this material was supposedly conveyed by the sage R. Ezekiel of Africa to the seminary in Worms, and from thence, it was transmitted to the seminary in Lunel.

This rather convoluted investigation of the probable connection between R. Isaac Cohen and a number of the writings of the "Circle" has been undertaken for a specific purpose. Scholem constructed his historiography of the early *kabbalah* based on R. Isaac's statement concerning the oriental origins of the *Bahir* and its European transmission via Germany. Clearly, R. Isaac's unsubstantiated claim must be considered in the light of similar claims that he made in his *Treatise on the Left Emanation* and the related treatises from the "Circle," which likewise refer to sages from the east who transmitted their esoteric doctrines by means of the *ḥasidei 'ashkenaz* to Provence.

While R. Isaac may have been consistent in his exploitation of a basic motif, is there any historical value to these assertions? Although the underlying pattern is the same in every one of these works, virtually all of the details differ and cannot be reconciled. Of the numerous individuals referred to in these legacies, only R. Eleazar of Worms consistently appears. Not coincidentally, he is the only identifiable historical figure. Most, if not all, of the other individuals are fictitious or fictionalized. None of the sages that are referred to in these texts can be substantiated from other sources.[32] Like Hammai, the purported author of *The Book of Contemplation*, these rabbinic epithets constitute inventive Aramaicisms.

Whereas R. Isaac was active in the latter half of the thirteenth

---

31. See Scholem's references to these sources in *Kiryat Sefer*, 1:291.

32. Ephraim Urbach, however, assumed that there is a historical kernel embedded in the *Pseudo-R. Eleazar Responsum*. He comments, "The historical facts which have been collected in these statements, in which a hodgepodge of fictitious and historical names are utilized, have not been adequately clarified" in *Ba'alei Tosafot*, 130. Urbach equates the figure R. Judah

century, it must be stressed that none of the kabbalistic writings from the first half of the thirteenth century make comparable claims. Nowhere in the considerable literary corpus produced by R. Isaac the Blind, R. Asher b. David, or the Gerona kabbalists (R. Ezra, R. Azriel, Nachmanides) and others is there any corroboration of R. Isaac Cohen's contentions concerning the origins of the *kabbalah*. This leads to the obvious question of whether they were simply the product of his imagination.

It appears that in these writings of R. Isaac Cohen we are not dealing with history per se, but rather fanciful amplifications of legends connected with the mysterious ninth-century figure, Abu Aaron of Baghdad.[33] According to these accounts Abu Aaron was trained in a Babylonian rabbinical seminary and, being compelled to wander, he journeyed to Italy. There he taught some form of esoteric wisdom—although there is no indication that it corresponds to medieval, theosophical *kabbalah*. This legend was synthesized with the German pietists' family traditions concerning their esoteric heritage and has been recorded by R. Eleazar of Worms. As will be discussed in the next chapter, the writings and personality of R. Eleazar were quite influential on the "Circle" and other Castilian mystics, including R. Isaac Cohen.

Moreover, it is quite likely that R. Isaac encountered a disciple of R. Eleazar of Worms and the *ḥasidei 'ashkenaz* in his travels through Provence, and learned from him about the pietist's esoteric

---

b. Aha with the tosafist, R. Judah of Corbeil, the brother of another tosafist, R. Jacob of Corbeil. He tries to make sense of the name R. Judah b. Aha by suggesting a strained textual emendation: "R. Judah b. . . . , and our Rabbi, his brother (*'aḥiv*) of Corbeil."

For Urbach, the most intriguing element in the text is the contention "that the *beit midrash* (study hall) of the two brothers was a center for esoteric study." It must be pointed out that this is without corroboration from anything else that is known about their activity. It is also interesting to juxtapose Urbach's deductions with Scholem's bald assertion, "One can say with certainty that the authors of the entire literary corpus of *The Book of Contemplation* were not *talmidei ḥakhamim* (i.e., rabbinic scholars)," *Le-Ḥeker*, 261. It should also be noted that the "Circle's" R. Yehushiel was probably modeled after the early 11th-century sage, R. Hushiel, founder of the great rabbinical seminary in Qairawan, North Africa; see Abraham ibn Daud, *The Book of Tradition*, G. Cohen ed. (Philadelphia 1967), 64.

33. Discussions of Abu Aaron include: G. Scholem, "Has a Legacy been Discovered . . ." [Hebrew], *Tarbiz*, 32 (1963), 252-265, and J. Dan's entry "Aaron of Baghdad," in *Encyclopedia Judaica*, 2:21, which contains important bibliographical references.

tradition.[34] Although the identity of this individual is unknown, it is conceivable that there may be a direct connection between him and the enigmatic R. Meshullam the Zadokite, who will be discussed in the next chapter. This problematic figure, purportedly from Brittany, is connected with R. Eleazar. His theories were extensively utilized by the writers of the "Circle of Contemplation" and his assertions about the miraculous powers of R. Eleazar to teleport himself are identical with claims made by R. Isaac Cohen. Is it possible that R. Meshullam was R. Isaac's source of the pietistic legends and traditions?

Whatever the answer to this question, from the preceding analysis it is clear that the historical value of R. Isaac's contentions is severely mitigated. Yet this material forms the basis and heart of Scholem's historiography of the early *kabbalah*! Accordingly, Scholem's linear hypothesis concerning the origins of the *Bahir* and the *kabbalah* in general owes more to legend than reality and must be questioned.

THE "CIRCLE OF CONTEMPLATION"

Having analyzed Scholem's theories concerning the evolution of early *kabbalah*, we can now consider his treatment of the "Circle of Contemplation." The literary corpus of the "Circle" is vast. Scholem assigned some thirty-two texts to this category, and we have already considered a number of other works, which also warrant inclusion.[35] Despite the large number of treatises, it is exceedingly difficult to ascertain either their time or place of origin. Until this task has been accomplished with some degree of success, it may well be impossible to evaluate if this material truly represents the product of a *hug* (circle), as so conceived by Scholem–that is, a group of interdependent writers.[36]

---

34. In particular, R. Isaac discussed his encounter with a *hasid* (pietist) that he met while visiting Narbonne; cf. J. Dan, *Early Kabbalah*, 166.

35. Especially the different recensions and subtexts of *The Book of Contemplation*.

36. Hitherto, the only critique of Scholem's construct of the "Circle of Contemplation" is found in a lengthy footnote by Israel Weinstock. "In respect to the authorship of these treatises, Scholem attributes them to an anonymous group of kabbalists, who were active, according to his estimation, in

depiction of the Divine infrastructure. Although this approach was not adopted by the later kabbalists, it is fundamental to the writings of the "Circle." Accordingly, he concluded that these texts must stem from the earliest stratum of thirteenth-century theosophical works.[44]

Scholem's *terminus ad quem*, 1225, is based on two assumptions. He hypothesized that the major texts of the "Circle" predated R. Azriel, whose literary career he dates at this time.[45] This critical hypothesis will be challenged in the next chapter. Furthermore, Scholem contended that *Contemplation–Standard* was influenced by John Scotus Erigena's *On the Division of Nature*. Although Erigena composed his magnum opus in the ninth century, Scholem noted that it enjoyed considerable popularity toward the end of the twelfth and beginning of the thirteenth century. It was condemned at the Council of Paris in 1210, and Honorious III ordered all copies burned in 1225.[46]

In this connection Scholem refers to two passages in *Contemplation–Standard*. In the opening section mention is made of "the light that is hidden in the superabundance of the secret darkness." Scholem comments, "This world of images does not appear to me far removed from that of John Scotus Erigena and Pseudo-Denys the Areopagite."[47] This concept of the primordial darkness from which light emanated was not confined to *Contemplation–Standard*. It appears in other recensions of *Contemplation* and is a central theme of *Fountain*, as well. In addition, analagous material is found in the writings of all of the early kabbalists.[48] Furthermore, this notion did not originate among the Christian theologians that Scholem mentioned, for it is evidenced in earlier Gnostic writings.[49] Accordingly, pinpointing the source of *Contemplation–Standard*'s comments on this topic cannot be readily accomplished until a thorough investigation of this material has been undertaken.

---

44. G. Scholem, *Origins*, 316f.

45. G. Scholem, *Reshit*, 166.

46. G. Scholem, *Origins*, 314.

47. *Ibid.*, 314.

48. See above, pp. 158-159.

49. See, for example, *The Books of Jeu and the Untitled Text in the Bruce Codex*, C. Schmidt ed. (Leiden 1978), 235, and the numerous references to "Darkness" listed in the Index to *The Nag Hammadi Library* (San Francisco 1977), 481.

Scholem also focused on a passage involving a pseudepigraphic ascription to R. Hai Gaon. The text refers to the topic of hylic matter and then continues, "so it was also explained by the natural scientists and the metaphysical philosophers." Scholem asserts that this passage "reads like a paraphrase of the title and the metaphysical content of Erigena's work."[50] Unfortunately, this contention is too impressionistic to be conclusive.

In summation, we have seen that although Scholem dates the major texts of the "Circle" between 1200 and 1225, he offers no evidence that would compel us to accept this assertion. To be sure, the "Circle"'s relationship with R. Azriel is pivotal, but as shall be argued later on, there are strong indications that R. Azriel influenced the "Circle" and not vice versa.

Scholem also discussed works stemming from the middle of the thirteenth century, which warrant consideration. There are two anonymous texts from this period which exhibit clear connections to the "Circle." A lengthy citation from *Contemplation–Long* is found in a prayer commentary, that Scholem dated as having been composed prior to 1260.[51] This provides a *terminus ad quem* not only for *Contemplation–Long*, but also for the preceding recension, *Contemplation–Short*. Another significant source is an anonymous letter sent to Nachmanides, which Scholem dated around 1240.[52] The writer sought Nachmanides' advice concerning the study of *kabbalah*. The body of the letter is devoted to a presentation of concepts that the author had learned from his teacher, R. Joseph b. Mazah. These doctrines are permeated with technical terms peculiar to the "Circle." Accordingly, the letter represents an early attempt to reconcile the cosmological hierarchy of *Contemplation* with the theory of the *sefirot*.

In this letter one finds entire phrases lifted from *The Books of Contemplation*, though without any attribution. For example, in discussing the fourth *sefirah*, Nachmanides' correspondent writes, "and *'ofan ha-gedullah* (Wheel of Greatness) is called *ḥazḥazit* (speculum), meaning the place of the source of the seers' vision."[53] Although similar expressions are found in all of *Contemplation*'s recensions, these exact words appear in the *Midrash of R. Simon* and *Con-*

---

50.   G. Scholem, *Origins*, 318.

51.   G. Scholem, *Origins*, 345, n. 291.

52.   *Ibid.*, 391.

53.   G. Scholem, *Kiryat Sefer*, 6 (1930), 418.

templation–Standard.[54] There is also a close paraphrase of a statement from *Contemplation–Short.* The anonymous student writes, "for His Name represents the marking of the border–in order to indicate the magnitude of His exaltedness and beauty, may He be blessed."[55] Similarly, in *Contemplation–Short* we read, "the four letters of the Tetragrammaton, that is to say, the marking of the border–in order to indicate the magnitude of His beauty and the mighty valor of the Holy One, blessed be He."[56]

Were one to accept Scholem's dating of this letter, it would imply that *Contemplation–Short* was written prior to 1240. Although there is no compelling reason to reject this hypothesis, it should be noted that Nachmanides did not leave Spain for Israel until 1265. Accordingly, it is conceivable that the letter was written somewhat later.

Turning now to the literary activity of the Castilian kabbalists who utilized texts from the "Circle," it can be noted that even a cursory survey of R. Jacob Cohen's writings yields evidence of his acquaintance with these texts. R. Jacob's *Commentary on Ezekiel's Chariot* incorporates material from the *The Secret Knowledge of Existence,* which in turn was based on *The Book of Contemplation* and *The Fountain of Wisdom.*[57] Furthermore, another work plausibly ascribed by Scholem to R. Jacob is an exposition of *Sefer ha-'Orah.*[58] This treatise explores the theory of seventy-two, secret Divine Names and utilizes *The Secret of the Seventy-Two-Letter Name,* which frequently quotes from *Contemplation–Standard.*

R. Jacob Cohen was the first major literary figure among the Castilian kabbalists. Were one able to date his literary activity with precision, one could establish an important endpoint for many of the writings of the "Circle." Unfortunately, as is the case for most of the kabbalists of that period, there is a paucity of biographical data about him as well as his brother R. Isaac Cohen. Scholem contended that

---

54. See above, p. 103.

55. G. Scholem, *Kiryat Sefer,* 6 (1930), 418.

56. See above, p. 47.

57. Compare the discussion of *'avir kadmon* in *Perush Mirkevet Yeḥezkel,* A. Farber ed. (Jerusalem 1978), 50, and *Sod Yedi'at ha-Meẓi'ut,* cited in G. Scholem, *Reshit,* 169. On other influences of the "Circle" on R. Jacob, see Farber, *"Mavo',"* 14; 77, n. 6; 79, n. 15; and 80, n. 4.

58. G. Scholem, *Reshit,* 257.

R. Jacob died between 1270 and 1280 and that he was writing around 1270.[59] Until more precise information is uncovered, this approximate dating must suffice.

R. Jacob's younger brother was R. Isaac Cohen, whose writings we discussed at length earlier in this chapter. Not only did R. Isaac cite numerous texts from the "Circle," but, we argued, he likely composed several of them. In respect to R. Moses of Burgos, the disciple of the Cohen brothers, some noteworthy data has been preserved. R. Moses' writings exhibited numerous connections with texts from the later strata of the "Circle," as shall be discussed below.[60] By way of dating R. Moses' activity, Scholem has noted that another kabbalist, R. Isaac of Acco, wrote on several occasions, "I heard directly from R. Moses."[61] Insofar as R. Isaac came to Spain in 1305, this would indicate a relatively late date for R. Moses' sphere of activity. On further investigation, however, it appears that when R. Isaac of Acco refers to R. Moses, he is simply quoting from one of his literary sources, probably R. Shem Tov ibn Gaon's *Keter Shem Tov*. It should be noted that R. Shem Tov, in his *Baddei 'Aron*, remarked that although R. Jacob and R. Isaac had already passed on, in his youth he met R. Moses.[62]

A new datum pertaining to R. Moses is found in J.T.S. 1777. This codex contains a compendium of R. Moses' writings. Prefacing a selection from R. Moses' *haftorah* commentaries, the compiler asserts that this text was written in 1289.[63]

From the preceding analysis it is clear that by 1270, at the latest, various recensions of *The Book of Contemplation* had been cited by individuals living in Castile. In the next chapter we shall demonstrate that the authors of these versions had read R. Azriel's writings. Although ascribing specific dates to R. Azriel's activity is problematic, it seems likely that he was writing around 1230.[64] Therefore, until more specific data is forthcoming, we must hypothesize that sometime between 1230 and 1270 *Contemplation*'s recensions

---

59. G. Scholem, *Encyclopedia Judaica*, 9:1219.

60. See below p. 216 and p. 227.

61. G. Scholem, *Kabbalot*, 7.

62. *Ibid.*

63. See J.T.S. ms. 1777, f. 28b.

64. See below, p. 198.

were composed. Furthermore, it is reasonable to assume that the earliest version, *Contemplation–Short,* was composed around the time of R. Azriel's propagandizing activities, whereas the last recension, *Contemplation–Standard,* was composed at the end of this time frame.

Place of Composition

Scholem's Hypothesis. Scholem contended that these texts emanated from southern France, namely Provence. He noted,

> All of the treatises that mention names of places never once refer to places in Spain but rather to Corbeil, Montepellier, Worms, Toulouse and even London, and the great Yeshivah in Apulia, Italy. There is a noticeable tendency to form a literary connection with the *ḥasidei 'ashkenaz* and France. I have no doubt that most of these treatises, if not all of them , were written in Provence, although it is not impossible that individuals connected to this group lived in Burgos and Toledo.[65]

In assessing Scholem's contention that the writings of the "Circle" are primarily a product of Provence, one must first consider the sources of Scholem's historical data. Although he does not cite specific references, when one peruses the corpus, one discovers that the geographical locales to which he has referred are concentrated in a few treatises. The *Pseudo-R. Eleazar Responsum* mentions Worms, Corbeil, and Apulia; the *Responsa of R. Yehushiel* refer to Corbeil, Marseilles, Worms, and Lunel; Toulouse is mentioned in a responsum by R. Yekutiel, which Scholem discusses in connection with the "Circle"[66] but, for an unknown reason, did not include in his listing of the texts; and finally, the *Pseudo-R. Hai Responsa* refers to Montpellier.

Even a cursory examination of these writings reveals that, with the exception of the *Pseudo-R. Hai Responsa,*[67] they have a very tenuous connection with the "Circle." They exhibit little if any of the characteristic terminology or theosophy of the core texts. In no way,

---

65. G. Scholem, *Reshit,* 163.

66. G. Scholem, *Origins,* 327, n. 263.

67. Concerning the *Pseudo-R. Hai Responsa,* see above, p. 114f.

can they be considered to be mainstream works. This is born out by the fact that Scholem virtually ignores them in his extended discussions of the "Circle" in *Origins of the Kabbalah*. Moreover, as we discussed above, and at some length, these treatises may have been composed by R. Isaac Cohen, a Castilian kabbalist, who was active during the latter half of the thirteenth century. Accordingly, Scholem's assertions concerning the origins of the "Circle" in early thirteenth century Provence are highly suspect.

The Castile Thesis. We have seen that Scholem's hypothesis that the writings of the "Circle of Contemplation" were composed in Provence is based on peripheral texts, which appear to have been composed by a Castilian kabbalist. When one peruses the treatises that formed the core of the "Circle," such as *The Books of Contemplation, The Fountain of Wisdom*, and the *Midrash of R. Simon the Righteous*, one does not find any reference to a specific locale. Nevertheless, there is a significant amount of external, albeit circumstantial, evidence that warrants consideration. These indicators point to Spain and specifically Castile.

All of the earliest references to *The Books of Contemplation* and the other writings of the "Circle" are found in treatises by Castilian kabbalists. Moreover, all of the important Castilian kabbalists, such as R. Jacob Cohen, R. Isaac Cohen, R. Moses of Burgos, and R. Todros Abulafia, frequently cited works from the "Circle." Significantly, outside of Castile there was no awareness of the "Circle" until the late thirteenth century.

In this connection, R. Isaac Cohen's comments about "R. Hammai's book" are noteworthy, "Concerning R. Hammai's book in all of Provence I saw it in the possession of three pietists . . . one in Narbonne . . . and two in Arles."[68] Although Scholem interprets this passage as a confirmation of his theory that R. Hammai's book, (presumably one of the recensions of *Contemplation*), was composed in Provence, just the opposite appears to be the case. R. Isaac is clearly surprised that in all his travels throughout Provence he only noticed three copies of this text with which he was obviously familiar. It is difficult to imagine that *Contemplation*, which comprised an entire corpus of recensions and subtexts and was the catalyst for the vast body of writings of the "Circle," could have been such a rarity, had it been a product of Provence. Were one to assume, however, that *Contemplation* originated in Castile and that R. Isaac was familiar

---

68. G. Scholem, *Kabbalot*, 83.

with it and its significance there, then his comments are perfectly understandable.

Let us now consider what is known about Jewish mystical activity in Castile in the first half of the thirteenth century, in order to assess if it is compatible with our hypotheses concerning the composition of *Contemplation*. In the introduction to his seminal *Treatise on the Left Emanation*, R. Isaac Cohen noted that only a few of his predecessors had ever engaged in this branch of theosophy: "They are the ancient elders, the sages of Spain."[69] Although these Spanish forerunners go unnamed, from several letters published by Scholem, we can identify specific individuals who were active in Castile in the first part of the century. There is an anonymous letter from the mid-thirteenth century which lists a number of mystics. Among others, mention is made of: R. Abraham Hasid, R. Judah the Pietist of Germany, R. Eleazar of Worms, and the pietist R. Judah ibn Zizah of Toledo.[70]

Moreover, in the mid-thirteenth-century letter to Nachmanides that was discussed above, the anonymous writer states that he studied *kabbalah* under the instruction of R. Joseph b. Mazah. Scholem has pointed out that the Mazah family was prominent in Toledo and that archival evidence exists, concerning a judge named Samuel b. Joseph ibn Mazah.[71] What is significant for our purposes is that the doctrines discussed in this letter stem from the "Circle" and there are even direct quotes from *The Book of Contemplation*.

---

69. *Ibid.*, 82. Some scholars also refer to R. Abraham ha-Yarhi's *Sefer ha-Manhig*, written in Toledo circa 1200, as possibly referring to kabbalistic teachings; cf. B. Septimus, *Hispano-Jewish Culture in Transition* (Cambridge 1982), 136, n. 87, and the sources mentioned therein. Although this material does not appear to reflect the theory of the *sefirot*, if in fact it does, then it would be one of the earliest literary references to the kabbalistic doctrines–particularly noteworthy as it occurs in a book written in Castile. Additionally, Scholem presents some circumstantial evidence of kabbalistic activity in Castile in the 1230s in *Origins*, 405.

70. G. Scholem, *"Ikvotav shel Gavirol ba-Kabbalah," Me'asef Sofrei 'Erez Yisra'el* (1940), 175-176. In the manuscripts of this letter, the name listed is slightly different. In the Bodleian ms. it is R. Yuda ibn Zuga and in the Vatican ms. it is R. Yehudah ibn Ziva; cf. Scholem, *Ibid.* 176, n. 77. Mention can also be made of R. Jacob Cohen's attributed teacher, R. Abraham de PR'aVYS (Perais?); see G. Scholem, *Kabbalot*, 6 and 9.

71. G. Scholem, *Origins*, 391.

In the next chapter we shall have the opportunity to analyze the relationship between R. Azriel of Gerona's writings and the "Circle." For now it suffices to note that one of R. Azriel's treatises was a mystical epistle that he composed specifically for the community of Burgos, around 1230.[72] The writers of *The Book of Contemplation* quoted numerous passages from this letter. This suggests that they probably lived in Burgos, or other neighboring cities of Castile.[73]

R. Azriel clearly intended to transform the *kabbalah* from an esoteric discipline, known only to an small clique of mystical theologians, into a more widely accessible topic of study. He went so far as to claim, "*Kabbalah* should be made available to those outside our circle. I myself have corresponded with the kabbalists of Burgos. In addition, I have written a small work which clearly explains the principles of *kabbalah* to the wider public."[74] Presumably, the "small work" that R. Azriel refers to is his catechetical treatise, known as *Gate of the Inquirer*, wherein the reader is supplied with correct responses should he be challenged about the basic doctrines of the *kabbalah*.

Finally, in connection with R. Azriel's efforts to publicize the *kabbalah*, mention should be made of R. Isaac the Blind's famous letter to R. Jonah and Nachmanides in Gerona. R. Isaac was distressed to hear that certain acquaintances of his, (presumably R. Azriel and R. Ezra), were publicly disseminating esoteric teachings. He continues, "And I have also heard from the lands neighboring yours, and from the city of Burgos, that they are openly preaching in the marketplace and streets."[75]

In light of this evidence of intense mystical activity in Castile in the first half of the thirteenth century, we must take seriously the frequent comments found in *Contemplation–Short*, wherein the author asserts that specific doctrines were learned from his teachers.[76]

---

72. Published by Scholem, *Kabbalot*, 71-78.

73. Interestingly, in many of the manuscripts which contain R. Azriel's letter, it is found immediately following *Contemplation–Standard*; cf. Bodleian 1822, 1833, 2240, 2296, 2456; British Museum 752; Vatican 236.

74. Cited by S. Blickstein, *Between Philosophy and Mysticism* (Jewish Theological Seminary dissertation 1983), 17, n. 45.

75. G. Scholem, *Te'udah Ḥadashah*, 143; see above, p. 26.

76. For an overview of the Jewish mystical activity in Castile during the second half of the thirteenth century, see M. Idel, *Kabbalah*, 211.

LINGUISTIC EVIDENCE

In addition to these historical indications of a link between the writings of the "Circle" and Castile, there is significant linguistic evidence as well. In the important treatise *Secret Knowledge of Existence*, the relationship between God and His powers is described in a rather startling image. It is compared to a creature possessing a protective shell and is identified as "*kalpako*, in the vernacular."[77] This is a reference to the Castilian *galapago* meaning turtle. It is likewise related to *kalabbak*, and is ultimately derived from Arabic.[78]

In *Contemplation-Short*, the proto-text of *Contemplation*, there is an enigmatic passage which is comprehensible if one assumes that the writer knew Spanish. It occurs during a discussion of the two powers, *hashmal* and *'arafel*. *Hashmal* is associated with the archangel Michael, who is also called *'orpani'el* (Light of God's Face) and is positioned on the right side, that is, the side of life. *'Arafel*, being *hashmal*'s counterpart, is located on the left–the side of death. Moreover, *'arafel* generates a power that is designated "*nogah*'s (light) throne". Since *nogah* must precede its throne and since *'arafel* is identified as the source of "*nogah*'s throne," therefore, by implication, *'arafel* and *nogah* are synonymous. This, however, is very problematic–for the Hebrew word *'arafel* signifies fog and darkness, whereas *nogah* refers to brightness and light. The author of *Contemplation-Short* deals with this dilemma in the following statement: "This comprises the topic of *'arafel*. And thus they referred to

---

77. Schocken ms. *Kabbalah*, 6. The entire passage reads, "There is a certain creature named *kalzum* (?) that is called *kalpako*, in the vernacular, which has a covering from bone." The unidentified word *kalzum* is written in an unsteady hand, possibly indicating that the scribe was unsure of what to write. Perhaps it is related to the Greek, *chelone*, turtle. Bernard Septimus has also suggested that this analogy is similar to the *kamza'* (snail), mentioned in *Bere'shit Rabbah* 21:5, in relation to Gabriel.

78. Cf. *Diccionary Catala-Valencia-Balear*, A. Alcover (1935), 2:758. Thanks to my colleague, Felisa Heller, for bringing to my attention J. Corominas, *Breve Diccionario Etimologico de la Lengua Castellana* (Madrid 1973), 287, wherein *galapago* is derived from *calappacu*. The Spanish kabbalists commonly used the vernacular; cf. R. Azriel's *Commentaire sur la Liturgie*, G. Sed-Rajna trans., 31, also his *Perush ha-'Aggadot*, 5, and R. Ezra, *Perush le-Shir ha-Shirim*, 481, as well as *Kabbalat R. Asher b. David*, J. Dan ed. (Jerusalem 1980), 27.

nogah, that is to say, as it is written in Hebrew characters."[79] This confirms that *'arafel* was equated with *nogah*. Moreover, this latter term is specified as being written in Hebrew letters. This statement would make sense were one to assume that by *nogah*, the author was actually referring to the Spanish word *noche*, i.e., "darkness" and "night," but spelled in Hebrew letters. This would then resolve the apparent contradiction between *'arafel* = darkness and *nogah* = light.[80]

Another example of foreign language usage in the "Circle" is found in *The Commentary on the Forty-Two-Letter Name*. Therein one finds a discussion of *ḥesbonot* (sums). The author notes parenthetically that in the vernacular this word is rendered *suma*. Scholem, who published this text, annotated this passage *summa*, thereby indicating that the author was referring to Latin.[81] While Scholem's hypothesis may be correct; nevertheless, it should be noted that there is the comparable Spanish or Castilian derivative *suma*. The author could just as easily be referring to Spanish as Latin. Interestingly, he continues by appending the Arabic counterpart of this word. This

---

79. See above, p. 46.

80. This contention is born out in the Ladino translation of the Torah wherein *ha-laylah* (night) in Gen 1:16 is rendered *nogy*; cf. *Ladino Pentateuch*, M. Lazar ed. (Labyrinthos 1988), 3.
Bernard Septimus, however, has suggested a different interpretation of this passage that warrants consideration. *B. Pesakhim* opens with a discussion of the Mishnaic use of the term *'or* (light). After much debate it is concluded that in this particular context it refers to evening. R. Huna expresses this concept using the Aramaic *naghe*. Accordingly, Septimus suggests that the passage in *Contemplation–Short* is referring to R. Huna's phrasing. This explanation, however, would not account for *Contemplation–Short*'s qualification that the specific term must be written in Hebrew characters. This implies that it would normally not be the case and yet Aramaic shares the same characters. Therefore it must be referring to another language.
It is also significant that in the thirteenth century the word *nogah* acquired a negative connotation, being associated with darkness, death, and evil. This is apparent not only in *Contemplation–Short* but also in *Gate of Concentration*; see Scholem, *Origins*, 416-419; as well as in the writings of R. Joseph Gikatilla, *Sha'arei 'Orah*, 1:36 and 212, and the *Zohar* on *kelipat ha-nogah*; cf. I. Tishby, *Mishnat ha-Zohar*, 1:300f. and 323ff. What is common to all these works is that they were written in Spain. By assuming that these authors knew Spanish, one can readily understand why they found this term appropriate for this novel doctrine.

81. G. Scholem, *Kitvei Yad ba-Kabbalah*, 216, n. 11.

supplies further evidence of the knowledge of Arabic by these individuals.[82]

A final linguistic example underscores the difficulty in trying to trace the apparent Spanish influence on the writings of the "Circle." In the important work *Commentary on the Tetragrammaton*, there is an interesting analogy of a master builder whose work is incomparable. One day he is tricked by two of his apprentices who learn his secrets and then go into business for themselves. They succeed by marketing their wares at a much lower rate. "What he used to do for a *dinar*, they would do for six *pashitim*."[83] Although these coins are mentioned in rabbinic literature, the latter in particular is used infrequently. It is conceivable that they were chosen, over numerous other possible terms, owing to their resemblance to the Spanish coins, *dinero* and *peseta*.[84]

What we have seen in the preceding examples are various cases of foreign language usage, traced to Spanish or Castilian, in a significant number of the writings of the "Circle," including *Contemplation–Short* itself. There is likewise some evidence of knowledge of Arabic by these authors. All of this material corroborates the assertion that these writings stemmed from Spain, and Castile in particular. Conversely, Scholem's theory of a Provençal origin of the "Circle" would not be able to account for this usage of Spanish. Also, the knowledge of Arabic by Jews in Castile of the period is attested and understandable in light of the cultural heritage of once Moslem Spain, but this too is problematic were one to assume that these works stemmed from Provence.

We can now relate our conclusions concerning the dating and the place of composition of the writings of the "Circle of Contemplation" to general theories of the historiography of the *kabbalah*. As we noted at the start of this chapter, according to Scholem, the history of the *kabbalah* is linear: kabbalistic doctrines were transmitted from Provence to Gerona and finally on to Castile. To each of these regions there is a corresponding time frame: Provence, late twelfth to early thirteenth centuries; Gerona, second quarter of the thirteenth century; and Castile, second half of the thirteenth century. Since

---

82. See p. 130; this may also be cited in support of Amos Goldreich's thesis concerning the Arabic origins of the "Circle's" terminology, *"Me-Mishnat."*

83. Florence ms. 2:41, f. 199b.

84. See also my comments in "The Development of *Yihudim* in Spanish Kabbalah," *Jerusalem Studies in Jewish Thought*, 8 (1989), 26, n. 4.

Scholem dates the major treatises of the "Circle" "around 1200," in order to conform to his general theory, they must of necessity have been written in Provence.

A significant revision of Scholem's linear conceptualization of the evolution of the *kabbalah* is found in Joseph Dan's Hebrew study, *The Circles of Early Kabbalists*.[85] Therein Dan focuses on doctrinal commonalities found in the writings of a number of distinct theosophical groups, all functioning in the early thirteenth century. The picture that emerges from Dan's exposition is that simultaneously throughout western Europe there was a flourishing of mystical theology and that one must look horizontally rather than vertically.

The evidence discussed previously indicates that significant activity was also occurring at this time in Castile. This would necessitate a fundamental reconsideration of the place of Castile within the development of the *kabbalah*. It has always been clear, though never sufficiently stressed, that during the latter half of the thirteenth century Castile was the most important center for the study of *kabbalah*, both in terms of numbers of kabbalists as well as the significance of the writings produced. With the exception of sixteenth-century Safed, such concentrated activity is unparalleled in Jewish history. Moreover, in considering the case of Safed it should be noted that most of its sages had been trained elsewhere, including Alkabetz, Karo, and even Luria. Thus Safed was primarily a refuge and haven, wherein Jewish mysticism and spirituality flourished. The Castilian kabbalists, on the other hand, were all indigenous. Although one cannot deny that some traveled and studied elsewhere, or were influenced by outside teachings; nevertheless, if there had not been a rich tradition for studying Jewish theosophy in Castile, one would be hard-pressed to explain its broad-based activity there.

---

85.   J. Dan, *Ḥugei*.

5

Historical Connections

The writings of the "Circle of Contemplation" were not composed in an intellectual vacuum. Rather, they display points of contact with other contemporary groups of Jewish mystical theologians, active in the early thirteenth century. In this chapter we shall investigate connections with the kabbalists of Gerona as well as the *ḥasidei 'ashkenaz*. These linkages vary from textual similarities to doctrinal borrowings. Previously, we have ascertained that these texts were written prior to 1270–stemming from our forthcoming discussion of R. Azriel's relationship to the "Circle," we shall be able to pinpoint this dating even further.

There is some circumstantial evidence linking *Contemplation* to Gerona.[1] The name, R. Ezra, appears in one of the subtexts of *Contemplation–Standard*. This is possibly a reference to the kabbalistic savant R. Ezra of Gerona, although it is likely that this particular allusion stems from a scribal error.[2] A second connection with Provence or Gerona is the text *Contemplation–Standard/Inner Attributes*. This is a version of *Contemplation–Standard* that concludes with material penned by R. Asher b. David, who served as a theosophical emissary to Gerona.[3] Even though both of these attribu-

---

1. There are even some textual affinities between the writings of R. Isaac the Blind and the "Circle." For example, the gender-related discussion of the various terms for path that is found in R. Isaac's commentary of *Sefer Yeẓirah*, is similar to that found in *Fountain*, see above, p. 152. Moreover, Scholem contended that the pivotal term, *ḥokmah kedumah* (Primordial Wisdom) occurs in a text composed by R. Isaac; cf. *Origins*, 287. This ascription, however, is highly doubtful, as the text seems to be a later composition; see above, p. 41, n. 18. A translation of this text appears in J. Dan, *Early Kabbalah*, 73-99.

2. See below, p. 232.

3. Moshe Idel, in a recent paper entitled "Nahmanides: Kabbalah, Halakhah and Spiritual Leadership" delivered at the J.T.S. conference on

tions are interesting; nevertheless, they are connected only with the last recension of *Contemplation* and hence are not overly significant.

R. AZRIEL AND *THE BOOKS OF CONTEMPLATION*

By far the most complex issue is the connection of R. Azriel to the "Circle." As Scholem has noted, R. Azriel "is the only one of the group whose work is connected in style and content with the writings of the circle of *The Book of Contemplation*."[4] Others have also been sensitive to this association. Isaiah Tishby, in his pioneering research on R. Azriel's commentary on the *'aggadah*, wrote,

> The largest and most significant part of the terms and
> concepts that I have indicated as being particular to R. Azriel,
> in the Gerona circle, are found in the anonymous,
> pseudepigraphic writings of the Circle of Contemplation. A
> careful comparison and basic analysis of the relationships
> between these writings and those of R. Azriel could shed light
> on several obscure points in the history of the beginning of
> the *kabbalah*.[5]

So complicated is this issue that Scholem was unable to determine who influenced whom. Writing about the text, *The Secret Knowledge of Existence*, Scholem commented,

> The language of its opening is comparable in practically each
> of its expressions to the style of R. Azriel in his letter to
> Burgos, and it seems to me that there is some kind of special
> connection between R. Azriel and the author of this treatise,
> even though it is clear from its content that R. Azriel himself
> cannot be considered to be its composer.[6]

In general, Scholem assumed that the major texts of the "Circle" predated R. Azriel. Two factors contributed to this determination.

Jewish Mystical Leadership has challenged the common assumption that R. Asher was actually sent by R. Isaac the Blind to Gerona.

4.　G. Scholem, *Kabbalah*, 49.

5.　I. Tishby, "*Kitvei ha-Mekubbalim*," *Sinai*, 16 (1945), 178.

6.　G. Scholem, *Reshit*, 256; see also *Origins*, 327, end of n. 263.

First, Scholem assumed that the writings of the "Circle" stemmed from Provence. According to his conception of the development of the *kabbalah*, Provence represented the original home of the *kabbalah*; only later did it shift south to Gerona.[7] Second, Scholem noted that R. Azriel was the only early kabbalist who used the same idiosyncratic terms, as are found in the "Circle." Although somewhat vexed by the question of who influenced whom, Scholem noted that whereas R. Azriel used these terms in a consistent manner, in the writings of the "Circle" they are employed haphazardly. Scholem assumed that this indicated that the "Circle's" authors originated these terms, but that it was R. Azriel who reworked this material into a cohesive matrix. Thus he "succeeded wherein they failed: to build a conceptual structure from the scattered bricks that he had found."[8]

None of Scholem's arguments vis-à-vis R. Azriel are compelling. In the previous chapter we presented considerable evidence demonstrating that the major works of the "Circle" were written in Castile and not Provence. Also, it seems more reasonable to assume that the one who originated a set of terms would use them consistently, whereas later writers would be prone to transform their meaning. Accordingly, R. Azriel's consistency is an indication of his priority.

It should be noted that R. Azriel was conceptually consistent; however, he did not always express himself uniformly. For example, to convey the concept of the harmonious balancing of forces within the Divine Unity, he refers to: *hashva'ah*, (equalized), *shaveh*, (equal), *'ahdut*, (unicity), *'ikkar*, (principle), and *yihud*, (unity), and forms countless combinations of these terms.[9] On the other hand, the writers of the "Circle" favor the expression *'ahdut ha-shaveh* (balanced unity), used only rarely by R. Azriel.[10] Since the author of *Contemplation–Short* selected this specific phrase from R. Azriel's grab bag of expressions, the subsequent redactors simply followed suit.

More than terms were shared. Based on the evidence of common phrases and even sentences, the only plausible conclusion is that the "Circle" borrowed from R. Azriel and not vice versa. For exam-

---

7. See above, p. 170.

8. G. Scholem, *Reshit*, 165.

9. I. Tishby, *Ḥikrei ha-Kabbalah* (Jerusalem 1982), 18.

10. *Ibid.*, 18; see above, p. 39, n. 10; for a discussion of another important term that appears to have been coined by R. Azriel, see above, p. 39, n. 12.

ple, in R. Azriel's commentary on *Creation*, he describes the emanation of the second *sefirah* from the first as, "spirit from spirit: the
explanation is that just as a scent is emanated from a scent and a
candle-flame from a candle-flame, so too was the spirit emanated
from the spirit."[11] Similarly, in *Contemplation–Short* the process of
the emanation of the powers is described as follows, "Furthermore,
all of them (i.e., the powers) are revealed by the process of emanation, like a scent from a scent or a candle-flame from a
candle-flame."[12]

Another obvious parallel is found in R. Azriel's letter to Burgos.
Therein he notes, "and the hidden light is united with the flame of
fire in its colors."[13] Similarly, in *Contemplation–Short*, we read,
"Moreover, He is united with them like the flame of fire, which is
united with its colors."[14]

R. Azriel's letter influenced the other recensions of *Contemplation* as well. Another line from R. Azriel's letter states, "Indeed it is
encumbent upon me to give praise and thanks for the marvel of marvels, that are in the secrets of the hidden actions that are called distant counsels."[15] Similarly, in *Contemplation–Long* it is stated, "and
the marvel, marvellously causing marvels, that are in the secrets of
the hidden actions called counsels."[16]

In addition, the expression from R. Azriel's letter, "all of the
acts and the entities and objects that are revealed from the Supreme
Hiddeness that is concealed,"[17] calls to mind the statement from
Contemplation–Thirteen Powers, "These thirteen powers are revealed
together from the Supreme Hiddeness that is concealed"[18]

Before considering the implications of these parallel occurrences, two observations are warranted. First, it should be noted that
the connections between R. Azriel's writings and *Contemplation* are
not confined to any one recension. The examples we have chosen are

---

11. R. Azriel, *Perush*, 1:10.

12. See above, p. 41.

13. G. Scholem, *Kabbalot*, 72, n. 2.

14. See above, p. 41; see also p. 47, n. 56.

15. G. Scholem, *Kabbalot*, 72.

16. See above, p. 72.

17. G. Scholem, *Kabbalot*, 72.

18. See above, p. 83.

passages that are unique to each of the versions. Accordingly, we have eliminated the possibility that the influence was just on the earliest of the recensions and that it was simply repeated in the later ones. Moreover, this connection between R. Azriel and the "Circle" is also noticeable in other writings. For example, Azriel's influence on *Fountain* was noted above.[19] It is also important to realize that although R. Azriel wrote extensively, almost all of the identifiable parallels stem from his letter to Burgos. This is significant, for it offers additional support to the theory that the "Circle" was based in Castile and not in Provence.

Obviously, the expressions and sentences that are found in both the writings of R. Azriel and the recensions of *Contemplation* cannot be dismissed as mere coincidences. Four alternatives suggest themselves: (1) R. Azriel himself composed *The Books of Contemplation*; (2) R. Azriel had in his possession all of these writings and copied different parts of them (this would obviously necessitate that *Contemplation* predate R. Azriel); (3) R. Azriel and the authors of the "Circle" possessed a third work and independently utilized it;[20] (4) the authors of *Contemplation* received R. Azriel's letter and made use of it.

The first option can be immediately dismissed. R. Azriel's theosophy and in particular his advocacy of the kabbalistic doctrine of the *sefirot* is alien to *The Books of Contemplation*. Furthermore, it is difficult to sustain the second alternative. The exact parallels between R. Azriel and the "Circle" are not confined to any one recension but are evidenced in all of them. This would necessitate the hypothesis that R. Azriel possessed all four recensions and selected material from each. Such a theory, however, does not fit with other data that we possess concerning *The Books of Contemplation*, for R. Azriel was

---

19. See above, p. 159.

20. This common source theory was originally suggested to me by Bernard Septimus and has been elaborated upon in a recent article by Amos Goldreich, "*Me-Mishnat*," see especially 142, n. 8. Goldreich's erudite paper seeks to show that the critical term *'aḥdut ha-shaveh* (balanced unity) originated in early medieval Ismaili circles. Although he demonstrates that a parallel concept was formulated by this group, there is no evidence that the actual Hebrew term derived from this source. Moreover, the process of transmission from early medieval Yemen to thirteenth-century Spain is rather vague. In addition, even accepting Goldreich's thesis, this is no way accounts for the sentences that are common to R. Azriel's letter to Burgos and *Contemplation*.

active around 1230 and the last recension is not attested to before 1270. Moreover, since no one outside of Castile seemed to be aware of the "Circle" until the latter part of the thirteenth century, how was R. Azriel able to monopolize this extensive literary corpus, while his numerous contemporaries in Gerona and Provence did not have access to these texts?

The third option is more fascinating, but nonetheless problematic. It presupposes that there was a missing link, a common source shared by R. Azriel and the "Circle," which has subsequently become lost. Not only is there no evidence that such a text ever existed, but neither do R. Azriel nor the writers of *The Books of Contemplation* give any indication of utilizing such a work. Were one to adopt the law of parsimony–by making the least number of assumptions–then one would have to reject the missing text theory out of hand. Naturally, should such a text unexpectedly emerge, it would be necessary to revise these conclusions.

The most plausible approach is the assumption that the "Circle's" writers, who were living in Castile, had read R. Azriel's letter that he sent to Burgos around 1230.[21] Accordingly, we could date the earliest recension, *Contemplation-Short*, to this period or shortly thereafter. This would have enabled Nachmanides' correspondent, writing around 1250, to have access to it. It would also provide a time frame for the subsequent recensions to develop, ending with *Contemplation-Standard*, prior to 1270.

Although in terms of the time sequence there appears to be good reason for assuming that the authors of *The Books of Contemplation*

---

21. Owing to the paucity of biographical data on the early kabbalists, it is impossible to pinpoint precisely when they composed their works. Scholem assumes that both R. Isaac the Blind (cf. *Kabbalah*, 45) and R. Ezra of Gerona (cf. *Origins*, 371) died around 1235. Moreover, he assumes that R. Isaac wrote his letter which condemned the activities of unnamed colleagues–whom Scholem identified as R. Ezra and R. Azriel–"at the close of his life" (*Kabbalah*, 46). Accordingly, R. Azriel's letter to Burgos could be plausibly dated around 1230. One of the few pieces of information provided by the kabbalists themselves is R. Ezra's assertion in the introduction to his commentary on *Song of Songs* that he waited until reaching old age before feeling compelled to reveal these esoteric teachings. Furthermore, as Ehrenpreis has noted long ago, R. Ezra's emphasis on the imminent redemption that underlies his commentary is connected to the start of the sixth millenium, which occurred according to Jewish calculation in 1240; see M. Ehrenpreis, *Die Entwickelung der Emanationslehre* (Frankfurt 1895), 25. This tends to corroborate Scholem's assumptions.

were influenced by R. Azriel's letter to Burgos, there is a glaring problem with this hypothesis, as was pointed out by Amos Goldreich.[22] We have already indicated above that R. Azriel was a committed kabbalist, who advocated, at times dogmatically, the theory of the *sefirot*. Goldreich wonders how it was possible that the writers of the "Circle" could have been seriously influenced by R. Azriel's writings and yet completely reject his theosophical premises? One has only to glance at R. Azriel's letter to Burgos, to realize that nowhere in this text is there any overt reference to the doctrine of the *sefirot*. This is uncharacteristic of any of his other writings and presumably was a conscious decision on his part. One can only speculate that such a tack was undertaken as a preliminary stage in an orchestrated campaign to cautiously disseminate esoteric teachings.[23]

THE *HASIDEI 'ASHKENAZ* AND THE "CIRCLE"

In considering other contemporary connections with the "Circle," it is significant to note that of its many treatises bearing pseudepigraphic ascriptions, only one contemporary historical figure is referred to, i.e., R. Eleazar of Worms.[24] All other ascriptions are either to fictional characters, such as R. Hammai, or classical rabbinic personalities, such as R. Nehuniah b. ha-Kanah, Rabban Gamliel, and R. Simon the Righteous. This affords a clue to the special relationship between the "Circle" and the German pietist, R. Eleazar.

To be sure, the efforts of the *hasidei 'ashkenaz* and R. Eleazar, in particular, in disseminating Jewish mystical theology were well-known throughout Europe. There is evidence of R. Eleazar's involvement in a messianic campaign, which extended as far as North Africa.[25] Also, according to later folklore, an aged R. Eleazar miracu-

---

22. A. Goldreich, *"Me-Mishnat,"* 143.

23. On R. Azriel's activities as a publicizer of the *kabbalah*, see above, p. 188.

24. R. Eleazar was accredited with transmitting two of the "Circle's" writings: *Book of True Unity* and *Pseudo-R. Eleazar Responsum*.

25. G. Cohen, "Messianic Postures of Ashkenazim and Sephardim," *Leo Baeck Memorial Lecture*, 9 (1967), 15.

lously journeyed to Spain, in order to teach Nachmanides *kabbalah*.[26] Thus, it is understandable that R. Isaac Cohen asserted that the early kabbalistic classic *Bahir* reached Spain via Germany.[27]

Beyond these general occurrences, can one establish whether there is any substantive link between the "Circle" and the *hasidei 'ashkenaz*? At the outset it can be affirmed that R. Eleazar of Worms directly influenced the "Circle." This conclusion is based upon an analysis of a text entitled *Treatise on Unity* by R. Eleazar of Worms.[28] This work exhibits numerous parallels with the basic theology of the *hasidei 'ashkenaz*, and Scholem contended that is it authentic.[29] In its numerous descriptions of supernal lights, such as "the bright light, brilliant and shining," and the depiction of the Divine Presence as "the great, brilliant whiteness, a shining light," one can readily see a source for the similar terminology in *The Fountain of Wisdom*. R. Eleazar's treatise also influenced other works of the "Circle," such as *Book of True Unity*, which was even attributed to R. Eleazar, but which bears unmistakable evidence of being a later, derivative work.[30]

Furthermore, in the course of my research I have discovered two, interrelated texts that offer concrete confirmation of the impact of the *hasidei 'ashkenaz* on the "Circle of Contemplation." The first of these is found in the Jewish Theological Seminary ms. 1884. This fourteenth-century codex also contains the version of *Contemplation–Standard*, with the additional material attributed to R. Ezra, discussed above. This text, which was partially water-damaged and difficult to decipher,[31] focuses on the significance of the celestial name *'aR'aRYeT'a*. It connects its explication to the teachings of an unidentified R. Meir of Germany. It should be emphasized

---

26. See I. Kamelhar, *Rabbenu Eleazar me-Garmeza* (Rzeszow 1930), 43f.

27. G. Scholem, *Origins*, 39ff. The problematic nature of R. Isaac's assertions were discussed in the previous chapter.

28. It has been preserved in various manuscripts, such as Casanatese 179, f. 98a, and Cambridge 644, f. 35-36.

29. G. Scholem, *Kiryat Sefer*, 6 (1929), 275.

30. *Ibid.*

31. I am extremely grateful to my colleague, Elliot Wolfson, who examined this manuscript under ultraviolet light and was thereby able to decipher two, key words that were otherwise illegible.

that the individuals referred to in this text, such as R. Meir[32] or R. Peretz of France, are not known to us from other sources. Nevertheless, this important text may one day prove to yield the identity of historical figures behind the anonymity and pseudepigraphy of the early *kabbalah*.

Note that the designation, *'aR'aRYeT'a*, and the definition given herein are identical with that found in *Contemplation–Standard* and numerous other treatises of the "Circle." The following is a transcription and translation of this text.

---

32. In various compendia of magical material there are techniques attributed to an unidentified R. Meir, for example in Vatican 243, f. 4b, which presents an amulet to aid in "opening one's heart" to improved study. Interestingly, in Paris 776/5, f. 175a, there is an oracular procedure attributed to R. Meir and a prophylactic technique attributed to R. Judah Hasid, f. 175b.

ידיעתו וחקירתו על מה ולמה שנקרא אֲרַאֲרָיְתָא כלו' זה שאמרו חז"ל אריא
היה רובץ על גבי המזבח למעלה מחוט הסיקרא אראריתא שמה וזהו "כי
ברא ה' חדשה בארץ נקבה תסובב גבר" הוא אויר הקדמון והיא מיוחסת אצל
חכמי קדם נקודה אחרונית פעמים נאצלת ופעמים אוצלת פעמים נשפעת
ופעמים שופעת והיא דו פרצופין עץ החיים ועץ הדעת ממנה מתחדשים
רוחניים ומורגשים ושרשי היסודות אשר אצולות וערוכות ונמשכות והולכות
לכל עבר ועבר והוא רמז בתורה "ועל הארץ הראך את אשו הגדולה" וה"ר
מאיר מאלמאניה זצ"ל קרא שמו אור הקדמון מזה השם הטהור והקדוש
וסימנו אחד. ראש. אחדותו. ראשון. ייחודו. תמורתו. אחד. וה"ר פרץ מצרפת
זצ"ל קרא שמו מעלה עשירית שהעומר עשירית האיפה הוא והיא רמז גדול אל
ספירת העומר והרמז הוא זה סימנו "דמעב איש ולויות" ויש בזה סוד הכרובים
רמז למבין זש"ה "זכר ונקבה בראם... ויקרא את שמם אדם ביום הבראם" כל
כך וקראו שמו גם כן אנשי הדת הפנימית כבוד למעלה מכבוד וזה הרמוז של
"ויעבר ה' על פניו ויקרא ה' ה'" האחרון הוא אויר הקדמון מקבלת הרב ר'
משולם הצדוקי מן טְרַיסָא שהיא במלכות אשכנז וחכמי הקבלה קבלו מה"ר
משה ב"ר נחמן זצ"ל על אויר הקדמון שהיא נקראת אם כלאה וזהו ש"ה "כי
אם לבינה תקרא" והיא הספירה השלישית הנוסף באדם.

The knowledge and insight into why He is called *'aR'aRYeT'a*, that is to say, that which the sages, of blessed memory, stated, "A lion (*'arya'*) was crouched on top of the altar [attached] by a red chord."[33] Its name was *'aR'aRYeT'a*. This [alludes to] "for the Lord created something new in the land: a woman shall encircle a man" (Jer. 31:22). This is the Primal Ether (*'avir ha-kadmon*). She is ascribed by the ancient sages to be the final point—sometimes she is emanated and sometimes she emanates; sometimes she is influenced and sometimes she influences. She is two-faced: the tree of life and the tree of knowledge. From her are created spiritual entities and sensual beings, as well as the roots of the fundamental elements that are emanated and arranged and drawn out and proceed in every direction. This is alluded to in the Torah, "And upon the earth He showed you His great fire" (Deut. 4:36).

R. Meir of Germany, blessed is the memory of the righteous, called its name Primal Light (*'or kadmon*), from this pure and holy name. It corresponds to: One, His unity, First, His unicity, His transformation, One. R. Peretz of France, blessed is the memory of the righteous, called its name Tenth Level, for the *'omer* is a tenth of an *'ephah*. This is a profound allusion to the counting of the *'omer*. This is its sign, "[Cherub, lions, and palms] according to the spacing of each, and wreaths [encircling]" (1 Kings 7:36). There is in this the secret of the Cherubs: an allusion to one who understands what is written in Scripture—"male and female He created them . . . and He called their name Adam, on the day He created them" (Gen. 5:2), so it is.[34]

Similarly, the proponents of interior religion called its name, the Glory above the Glory.[35] This is the hidden meaning of "And the Lord passed before him, and he called out, 'Lord, Lord'" (Exod. 34:6). The latter [name] refers to the Primal Ether, according to the *kabbalah* of R. Meshullam the Zadokite of Terayusah, which is in the kingdom of Germany. The kabbalist sages received [a teaching] from

---

33. See *B. Yoma*, 21b, where this notion is discussed, though not in these exact words.

34. On the Cherubs being male and female, see below in R. Meshullam's *Kabbalah*. This concept is rooted in *B. Yoma*, 54a-b.

35. This expression has been discussed above, p. 141.

R. Moses b. Nachman concerning Primal Ether, that it is called a mother like Leah. Thus, it is stated in Scripture, "If you shall call out to understanding (*binah*). . ." (Prov. 2:3). She is the third *sefirah*, which has been added to Adam.

R. MESHULLAM THE ZADOKITE

Toward the end of this text, there is mention of the *kabbalah* of R. Meshullam the Zadokite of "Terayusah, which is in the kingdom of Germany." This enigmatic figure is claimed to have taught about the *'avir kadmon*, "Primal Ether." This term is at the heart of *The Fountain of Wisdom*, and hence, this is an extremely significant reference.[36]

Furthermore, in the Ambrosiana library in Milan there has been preserved a treatise entitled *The Kabbalah of R. Meshullam the Zadokite*, "from the city of Tréport, which is in the kingdom of Brittany." In the preface to this text it refers to the magical practices of R. Eleazar of Worms. As has already been seen, this work contains significant material, which was incorporated into key writings of the "Circle."[37] Hitherto, there has been very little discussion of this pivotal individual.[38] Similar to mystical and magical traditions attributed to R. Meir that were discussed above, we find several references to an unidentified R. Meshullam that may be germane. For example, Bodleian 2282 is a fourteenth-century Ashkenazic manuscript with large blocks of material emanating from the *ḥasidei 'ashkenaz*. Included in this compendium is a homiletical discussion, attributed to an unidentified R. Meshullam, on the angelic hosts that participated in the revelation at Mt. Sinai.[39]

---

36.   See above, p. 153f.

37.   See above, p. 44, n. 34. Accordingly, R. Meshullam's *Kabbalah* provided the doctrinal foundation for the middle part of *Contemplation–Short*, was quoted extensively in the *Midrash of R. Simon*, and is alluded to in *The Secret Knowledge of Existence*.

38.   See the brief comments of M. Idel in *Mystical Experience*, 159, n. 146, as well as Scholem, *Kiryat Sefer*, 11 (1934), 189.

39.   Bodleian 2282, f. 13a. Interestingly, this codex was owned by a certain R. Meir from *TROPA* (?), perhaps likewise Tréport.

Another text is headed "from the *kabbalah* of R. Meshullam of France."[40] Therein mention is made of magical techniques derived from "the book that is called *Razi'el*." This is potentially significant for *Razi'el* was an important collection of *hekhalot* material stemming from the school of the *hasidei 'ashkenaz*. Also, there is an unidentified R. Meshullam who was active in the *hasidei 'ashkenaz* as a rabbinic authority.[41]

The longest and the most interesting of these fragments is found in Vatican 211, which contains significant material from the Gerona kabbalists.[42] This codex ends with a letter partially preserved by "the sage, R. Meshullam, of blessed memory." R. Meshullam mentions herein that he had visited "*migdol*" (castle). As this is a common Hebrew designation, the specific locale cannot be determined. Nevertheless, it is quite plausible that it refers to a place in Spain.[43] The letter focuses on a dream that R. Meshullam had, during which he was informed of the secret significance of *'arayot* (forbidden relations).[44] He discusses human reproductivity in connection with the well-springs that irrigated the world during the seven days of creation and argues that since Cain and Abel stemmed from this primordial epoch, they were permitted to marry their sisters. This treatment is

---

40. Bodleian 123/4 f. 70b-71a. Moshe Idel has briefly commented on this text and argued that possibly the designation "R. Meshullam *zarfati*" (from France) was the authentic epithet, and that it was eventually corrupted into *zadoki* (Zadokite) in the Ambrosiana manuscript, *Mystical Experience*, 159, n. 146.
Another brief "*kabbalah*" attributed to a R. Meshullam is Ancona 23/3 f. 51b, which offers a list of efficacious "names" that promote health, and so on.

41. See Cambridge Or. 786/4, f. 174b. Therein R. Meshullam transmits a ruling in the name of R. Abraham Haldik, one of the halakhic authorities of the *hasidei 'ashkenaz*. On this latter figure, see E. Urbach, *'Arugat ha-Bosem*, 4 (Jerusalem 1963), 124f.

42. Part of this text was translated in French and annotated; see G. Vajda, *Le Commentaire d'Ezra de Gerone sur le cantique des cantiques* (Paris 1969), 395-400.

43. When I discussed this text with Frank Talmage, of blessed memory, he noted that it could either refer to a locale in Spain or Italy.

44. See M. Idel's discussion of this topic in "We Have No Kabbalistic Tradition on This," in *Rabbi Moses Nahmanides: Explorations in His Religious and Literary Virtuosity* I, Twersky ed. (Cambridge 1983), 56.

quite similar to that found in the *Responsa of R. Yehushiel*, mentioned in the previous chapter in connection with R. Isaac Cohen.[45]
The exact relationship between these texts needs to be evaluated
further.

Turning now to the actual text of R. Meshullam's *Kabbalah*, it
can divided into three uneven sections. Only the first part is germane
to the "Circle" and will be transcribed and translated. Owing to the
doctrinal inconsistencies between the first part and the latter two
parts, it is likely that these latter sections were appended by a later
author. For example, in the first part Michael is identified with the
element fire, and Gabriel with water, whereas in the second section
Michael is associated with air and Gabriel with fire. There are even
inconsistencies between parts two and three. In the second part,
Michael is associated with the vowel *kamez*, whereas in the conclusion, he is connected with the vowel *hirik*. In addition to this internal
evidence suggesting that parts two and three are from later writers,
there is also external support for this thesis. It is significant that all
of the writings of the "Circle" mentioned above that utilized R.
Meshullam's *Kabbalah* only cite material from the first section of the
work. This corroborates the suggestion that only the first part of the
text stems from the original source.

The first paragraph focuses on the figure of R. Nehuniah b.
ha-Kanah, who discovered a *Sefer Hekhalot* (*Book of the Celestial
Palaces*) in the Temple. Thereupon he transmitted the secret of the
Divine Name to his worthy students. This motif forms an integral
part of *Contemplation–Standard*, which likewise discusses R.
Nehuniah and the *Sefer Hekhalot*, as well as an esoteric Divine
Name.

In the second paragraph the four divisions of the *merkavah*
(Divine Chariot) are discussed. They are: *hashmal*, *'arafel*, Throne of
Light, and Wheel of Greatness. These four terms constitute a major
building block in the enumeration of the celestial powers within all
of the recensions of *The Books of Contemplation*. Moreover, the latter
three-quarters of this paragraph appears verbatim at the end of the
Midrash of R. Simon.[46] Accordingly, R. Meshullam's *Kabbalah* was
avidly studied by the writers of the "Circle," and constituted one of
their major sources.

---

45. One of the R. Yehushiel responsa is even devoted to "the secret of the
mysteries of *'arayot*," and likewise discusses Cain and Abel; cf. Casanatense,
180, f. 60a, and G. Scholem, *Le-Heker*, 136-138.

46. This follows the text transcribed below on p. 215.

MILANO 62, F. 109B

קבלה משם המפורש שחבר הרב ר׳ משולם הצדוקי נר״ו מעיר טריפא במלכות בריטנה וחברו מספר היכלות שמצא ר׳ נחוניא בן הקנה בהיכל ה׳ בימי יהוידע הכהן ומסרו בקבלה לחכמי דורו הראויין לעמוד בהיכל מלך ומשרתי אלהינו ושימש הרב הגדול ר׳ אליעזר מגרמשא עם זה השם שהיה מקובל בו ורכב על ענן פעמים רבות כשעלה ר׳ עקיבא לסולם החכמה הזהיר לתלמידיו הראויין לעמוד בהיכל מלך מלכי המלכים הקב״ה בני הזהרו בדבריכם שמא תחובו חובת גלות בדבריכם השם שלא כהוגן כי הואיל שתהיו בקיאין לשמש ושתדעו השם כהוגן תדעו המעלה האותיות אזי תצליחו שנא׳ ״אשגבהו כי ידע שמי״ כי כל אות ואות הוא מורה כנגד הכחות של מעלה והנקודות כנגד הכחות של מטה. וכשתדע כל אות ואות מהו מורה אזי תהיו נשמעים ונכתבים לפניו. ודעו בני כי חשמל וערפל הם שני כחות ״זכר ונקבה בראם... ויקרא את שמם אדם״ כלו׳ האדם הוא היודע קריאתם חשמל הוא הכרוב הגדול והוא מתהפך פעמים לזכר ופעמים לנקבה ועל כן תמצא בנבואת יחזקאל חשמל וחשמלה שהיא נקבה ועל זו אמרה אמ׳ משה ״את הכרובים ואת להט החרב המתהפכת״ והוא מורה על סוד האמונה שהיוד מהשם מורה עליו שהוא בורא עולם ועל כן נקראין תיסק כרביה שהבריה קם מהיוד חשמל ״חיות אש ממללות״ פי חשות מל האיש כעניין מל הם שבעים שמות וזהו ״סוד ה׳ ליריאיו״ שורש וענף ופני יוד הא ואו הא ופני הפרי ה״א אחרונה למעלה הוא שכינה שהיא השכינה הפרי פניו של אדם למזרח ולבו למערב ששם שכינה שורה וידמה בדעת ובדבר שמיוסד על יסודות ארבעה שמהם מתפשטים הנבראים ואלו הן המחלוקות הבאים ארבעתם בסוד האחדות המתמצע שהוא מקום הכל. חשמל ערפל כסא הנוגה אופן הגדולה וכל אחד מד׳ חלקים כיצד דעו תלמידיו חשמל חלק אחד מיכאל חלק שני יוד של ד׳ אותיות חלק שלישי אורפניאל חלק רביעי זהו כח האש שנא׳ ״כי באש ה׳ נשפט״ הכח השני ערפל ד׳ חלקיו הוא כעצמו חלק אחד גבריאל בה״א של ד׳ אותיות ג׳ תגראל אוסף קדושה עליות לצד האחדות ד׳ זה כח הימים זהו והימים והמים אשר מעל השמים הכח השלישי כסא הנוגה ארבע חלקיו הוא עצמו אחד אוריאל ב׳ דנהאל ג׳ וו של ד׳ אותיות ד׳ כח הרוח שנא׳ ״מד׳ רוחות בואי הרוח״ הכח הד׳ והאופן הגדולה ד׳ חלקיו הוא עצמו אחד רפאל ב׳ פמליא ג׳ ה׳ אחרונה של ד׳ אותיות הרי לך ד׳ יסודות שהם יו למעלה כנגד מה שלמטה והם נקראין גוף השכינה ועל זה נאמ׳ ״שמע ישראל ה׳ אלהינו ה׳ אחד״.

R. Meshullam's *Kabbalah*, based on Milano 62, and manuscript versions of the *Midrash of R. Simon the Righteous*:

[This is] a *kabbalah* (i.e., a transmitted teaching) about the Ineffable Name, composed by the rabbi, R. Meshullam the Zadokite–may the Merciful One protect and deliver him–from the city of Tréport, which is in the kingdom of Brittany. He transcribed it from the *Book of Celestial Palaces* (*Sefer Hekhalot*) that R. Nehuniah b. ha-Kanah found in the Temple (*hekhal*) of the Lord, in the days of Yehoyadah the priest. He passed it on by means of the transmitted teaching to the sages of his generation, who were worthy to stand in the Palace (*hekhal*) of the King and the servants of our God.

The great rabbi, R. Eleazar of Worms, conjured this Name that he had received and rode on a cloud, many times. When R. Akiva ascended the ladder of wisdom, he warned his students who were worthy to stand in the palace of the King of kings of kings–the Holy One, blessed be He: My sons, be careful in your words lest you are penalized with the penalty of exile owing to speaking the Name improperly. When you shall be expert at conjuring and know the Name properly, you will know the exaltedness of the letters; then you shall succeed, as is said "I shall upraise him, for he knows My Name" (Ps. 91:14). For each letter corresponds to the supernal powers and the vowels correspond to the lower powers. When you know the significance of each letter, then you will be heard and inscribed before Him.

Know, my sons, that *hashmal* and *'arafel* are two powers: "male and female He created them . . . and He called their name Adam/man" (Gen. 5:2)–that is to say, the man who knows how to pronounce them. *Hashmal* is the great cherub: sometimes it is transformed into a male and sometimes into a female.[47] Accordingly, you will find in Ezekiel's prophecy [both] *hashmal* and *hashmalah*, which is the feminine. Concerning this word Moses said, "the cherubs and the flaming sword that revolved" (Gen. 3:24). Moreover, it refers to the secret of the faith[48]–for the *yod* from the Name indicates that He created the universe. Therefore, they are called "you shall ascend like youths,"[49] since the created beings emanated from the *yod*. *Hashmal*

---

47. See above, n. 34.

48. On the esoteric significance of "faith," see above, p. 40, n. 15.

49. Thanks to Ze'ev Gries for helping to clarify this problematic passage; cf. *B. Sukkah*, 5b, *B. Hagigah*, 13b and *Tanhuma*, S. Buber ed., 25.

[refers to] creatures of fire that speak;[50] [   ] silent,[51] a quick word.[52] This is related to *mal* (= seventy), which corresponds to the seventy Divine Names. Thus, "the secret (*sod* = 70) of the Lord is for those that fear Him" (Ps. 25:14).[53]

The root and the branch and the face: *YOD, H'e, V'AV, H'e*[54]–and the face is the fruit, which is the final *heh*. Above it is the Divine Presence, for the Divine Presence is the fruit. [Therefore] a man [praying] should face east and his heart should be in the west–that is where the Divine Presence resides.[55]

It appears in thought and word that it (i.e., the Name) is based on four foundations, [like the *'alef*][56] from which the created beings[57] are disseminated. These are the four divisions, which come from the mystery of the central Unity that is the domain of everything: *hashmal, 'arafel*, Throne of Light, and Wheel of Greatness, as well as each of their four parts.

How so? Know, students, *hashmal* is one part. Michael is the second part. The *yod* of the Tetragrammaton is the third part. 'Orpani'el is the fourth part. This is the power of fire, as it is stated, "for by the fire shall the Lord judge" (Isa. 66:16).

The second power is *'arafel*. Its four parts are: it itself is the first part. Gabriel is the second. The *heh* of the Tetragrammaton is the third. Tagra'el is the fourth. It is the mystery of the sublime holiness associated with the Unity. This is the power of water. Thus, "the seas and the waters that are above the Heavens" (cf. Gen. 1:7).

The third power is the Throne of Light. [These are] its four parts: it itself is the first. 'Uri'el is second. Danra'el is third. The *vav*

---

50.   Herein, *hashmal* is interpreted as a contraction of the phrase: *hayyot 'esh memallelot*.

51.   All of the versions of this imcomplete passage disagree; nevertheless what is intended is another interpretation of *hashmal*: silent = *hashot*.

52.   A further interpretation of *hashmal*: involving *hish* (quick) and *millah* (word). Other variants utilize *millah*'s other connotation: "circumcision."

53.   See above in *Contemplation–Short* for a comparable discussion, p. 45.

54.   The numerical value of this particular spelling of the Tetragrammaton is 45, which corresponds to *'adam*, i.e., primordial human.

55.   See *B. Baba' Batra'*, 25a.

56.   This addition is found in the *Midrash of R. Simon*.

57.   The *Midrash of R. Simon* reads instead "limbs."

of the Tetragrammaton is fourth. It is the power of air (*ruaḥ*), as it is stated, "from the four winds, come spirit (*ruaḥ*)" (Ezek. 37:9).

The fourth power is the Wheel of Greatness. These are its four parts. It itself is one. Raphael is the second. Pamali'el is the third. The final *heh* of the Tetragrammaton is fourth.

Behold these are the four foundations which are sixteen above, corresponding to what is below. They are called the body of the Divine Presence.[58] Concerning this it is stated, "Hear, Israel, the Lord our God, the Lord is one" (Deut. 6:4).

---

58. *Guf ha-shekhinah*, see above, p. 104, n. 216.

APPENDIX I: CONTEMPLATION'S SUBTEXTS

In chapter 2 we presented the array of the major recensions of *Contemplation*. In addition to these fundamentally different texts, all claiming to represent the authentic teachings of R. Hammai, there are at least ten other works that are also part of the same family of writings. These constitute significant variants of the third and fourth recensions. When all of these works are considered together, one can obtain a precise picture of the dynamism of this central faction, within the broader corpus of writings of the "Circle." As we have seen in chapter 5, it is difficult to date these writings with absolute precision; nevertheless, almost all of them are products of the latter two-thirds of the thirteenth century. Below are transcriptions from subtexts of the third recension: *Contemplation–Thirteen Powers*–texts 3:1 to 3:5, and the fourth recension: *Contemplation–Standard*–texts 4:1 to 4:5.

3:1 *MIDRASH OF R. SIMON THE RIGHTEOUS*

The *Midrash of R. Simon the Righteous* is one of the more important works of the "Circle." It is essentially a compendium of the earlier writings. It commences with material from *Fountain* and most of the second half of the *Midrash* consists of a presentation, in toto, of *Contemplation–Thirteen Powers*. The concluding section of the *Midrash* is a lengthy quote from R. Meshullam the Zadokites' *Kabbalah*. One significant difference between the *Midrash* and its sources is evident. Whereas in *Contemplation–Thirteen Powers* and virtually every other version of *Contemplation*,[1] the initial power is Primordial Wisdom, in the *Midrash* it is Primal Ether, and Primordial Wisdom

---

1. The only other text, related to *Contemplation*, that likewise lists Primal Ether is J.T.S. 1547, but one of the manuscripts of *Contemplation–Standard*.

is relegated to second position. This feature indicates the influence of *Fountain*, wherein Primal Ether plays the dominant role.

The *Midrash of R. Simon* has been preserved in two distinct formats.[2] It is found in several manuscripts as an independent text, and it was also quoted in its entirety in R. Moses Botareil's commentary on *The Book of Creation*, which exists in manuscripts as well as appearing in the standard printed edition of *Sefer Yeẓirah*.

The transcription that follows is only that section of the *Midrash* containing *Contemplation–Thirteen Powers*. It is based on five sources: ב refers to R. Moses Botareil, *Commentary on the Book of Creation*, printed in *Sefer Yeẓirah* (Jerusalem 1965), f. 39; ג refers to a manuscript of R. Botareil's commentary, Vatican 441, ff. 154b-155b; מ refers to the *Midrash*, as found in Munich 54, f. 293a; נ refers to the *Midrash*, as found in Munich 215, ff. 205-207 and ק refers to the *Midrash*, in Casanatense 179, f. 94b. From a perusal of the variants, it can be readily seen that the two Munich manuscripts form a family, as do the versions from R. Botareil's commentary. The Casanatense text vacillates between these two groupings.

---

2. A partial commentary on the *Midrash*, composed toward the end of the thirteenth century, is found in J.T.S. 1777, immediately preceding the commentary on the *Midrash ha-Konen*, which Scholem ascribed to R. Isaac the Blind, though this attribution is suspect; see above, p. 41, n. 18.

MIDRASH OF R. SIMON THE RIGHTEOUS

1   ועוד שהוא עיקר כל ההויות הנכללות בספר מעשה בראשית וכל זה העניין
הוא רמז לי"ג כחות רוחניים שהזכיר בעל ספר יצירה והם ספר וספר
וספור וי' ספירות בלימה שהם סוד אח"ד שכל אלו הי"ג כחות יש לכל אחד
ואחד מהם שם ידוע בפני עצמו וכולם מעלתם זו למעלה מזו. הא' האויר
5   הקדמון. הב' נקרא חכמה קדומה. הג' אור המופלא. הד' חשמל. הה'
ערפל. הו' כסא הנוגה. הז' אופן הגדולה הנקרא חזחזית פירוש מקום
מוצא חזיון החוזים. החי' כרוב. הט' גלגלי המרכבה. הי' אויר
הסובב. הי"א פרגוד זהו כסא הכבוד. הי"ב מקום הנשמות הנקרא חדרי
גדולה. הי"ג סוד המערכה העליונה הנקרא היכל הקדש העליון. ואלו
10   הי"ג כחות הם מתגלים כאחד מסתר עליון הנעלם הנקרא אומן פי' אב
האמונה שמכחו האמונה נאצלת והוא ית' קודם שברא שום דבר היה יחיד
ומיוחד באין חקר ובלי גבול אפשר לעמוד בעצמו בכח קיום לכך נק'
שמו אל ר"ל חזק חזק ולא היה כחו ניכר ועלה בדעתו להמציא כל
פעליו וברא כח אחד ראשון וקראו אותו חכמה הקדומה ממנה תוצאות
15   התעלומה ותוצאות האמונה נקראת קדומה שממנה נאצלו שנים עשר כחות
הנזכרים. ושקולה היא כנגד העשרה בהשואת האחדות הם עשר ספירות
בלימה וזהו שכתו' והחכמה תעוז לחכם מעשרה שליטים. החכם הוא יתברך
ויתעלה כד"א מי כהחכם ומי יודע פשר דבר וממשות כח זה הנקרא
חכמה הקדומה הוא אור חיים זך ומזוקק כתם טוב נכתב ונחתם בזיו
20   שפריר העליון הנקרא אין הנשלל בכל המושג וזהו סוד והחכמה מאין
תמצא זה הצד העליון הוא רצון באין גבול ולמה נקרא רצון מפני

---

1 ההויות: הסודות ב החיות נ"א הסודות ג החיות מ נ /וכל מ נ   2 (הוא רמז)
ק   2-3 (שהזכיר... בלימה) ב ג מ נ   3 שכל אלו: וכל אלה ק /הי"ג כחות: הכחות
ב ג/(יש) ק   4 (ואחד) ב/(בפני עצמו) מ/מעלתם: למעלתם ב ג מעלה ק /הא'
(הוא) ב ג /האויר: אויר ב ג   5 קדומה: הקדומה ב ג/אור: האור ב ג   6 הנוגה:
הערוגה ב ג /הגדולה: הגדול מ/הנקרא: הנקראת ק /חזחזית: חזחזית ב חיזזית נ"א
חזיזי ג חזית ק   6-7 (פירוש מקום מוצא) ק   7 החי' (נקרא) ב ג/הט' (נקרא) ב ג
/הי' (נקרא)   8 הי"א (נקרא) ב ג /זהו: זה ב ג/והוא ב ג /מקום (מקום) נ   9 הנקרא:
נקרא ק   10 הי"ג: י"ג מ נ /כאחד: באחד מ ק/מסתר: מכתר ב ק/עליון: העליון מ
נ ק   11 ית': יתע' ק/דבר: דבר מ/היה (הוא) ג/והיה (הוא) ב   12 ומיוחד: מיוחד ג ק /ובלי
גבול אפשר לעמוד: ובלא תכלית וגבול לעמוד ב ג (אפשר) ק   13 (חזוק) ב ג/כחו:
כח נ"א אז (כחו) ב/(כחו) ב/ועלה: ועלתה ב ג /בדעתו: לדעתו ג   14 פעליו: פעליו ק/
(אחד) ב ג ק /(אותו) ב ג ק /ממנה: וממנו ק   15 התעלומה: תעלומות ב תעלומה ג /
שממנה: שממנו ק /נאצלו שנים עשר כחות: נאצל כח י"ג כחות ב ג   16 העשרה
עשרה מ נ /הם: והם ב ג הן מ   17 וזהו שכתו': וזה מה שאמ' ק /מעשרה שליטים:
וגו' מ נ (אשר היו בעיר) ב ג /(החכם) ג/(החכם) ק/יתברך (הוא אור) ב ג   18 (ויתעלה) נ ק
(ויתעלה... דבר) ב ג /כד"א: כמה דאת אומר מ/(ומי) מ נ /(פשר דבר) מ נ /ממשות:
וממשלת ק/הנקרא: נקרא ק   19 חכמה: החכמה מ נ /הקדומה: קדומה ק /חיים:
החיים ב ג /כתם: כתב ק/נכתב: נכתבו מ נ /בזיו: כזיו נ   20 המושג: מושג נ
21-20 (המושג... גבול) מ   21 הצד העליון: צד עליון ק

שבמאמרו נמצא היש מאין גם הוא אור מזהיר ונקרא כבוד ה' על זה
נאמר עוטה אור כשלמה שהוא מתאחד באורו ובזיוו כלהב אש המתאחד
בגווניו ומתעלה עד לאין סוף. ונקרא אחד על שהיה קודם לכל הקדומים
25 הנאצלים מפליאת אחדותו וזאת החכמה היא עליונית לי' ספירות
ומתחלקת לו' קצוות ימין ושמאל פנים ואחור מעלה ומטה. ימין הוא
כח קיום בלי ממשות פועל פעולות בכל יום וזהו ימין ה' עושה חיל
תוספת רוח הקדש. שמאל כח מושכל בלי ממשות ויש בו מהות והוא צד
אמצעי משפיע כחותיו לכל צד ולא ינטה מאמצעותיו ומעליו ר"ל שלא
30 יאצל ממנו רוח הקדש לצד אחד מצדדיו וזהו יד ה' פירוש מכת סילוק
רוח הקדש. פנים שני כחות שהם הכרה לכל הכחות המתגלים מסתר עליון
שאמרנו ונקראים חן וחסד שהם פנים של רחמים. אחור עוצם החכמה שפע
הבינה תכלית השגת החקר והוא כח בעצמו ומתפשט לכח מוטבע לצייר
צורות ולהבדיל כח מכח. מעלה כח הנקרא כתר עליון והוא לשון המתנה
35 והוא צד עליון מתרבה עד אין סוף ממציא כל הנמצאים והוא לשון הדר
כמו ברוב עם הדרת מלך. ועוד מורה לשון כתר שכל המשיג שום דבר
בידיעה זו מתוך חקירתו ומעלים ומכסה הוד מעלין עליו כאילו עטרו
להקב"ה ועליו נאמר אשגבהו כי ידע שמי יקראני. והאמת כי לא ישיג
שום נברא ידיעת דבר זה על אמתת ידיעה אבל ישלול ממנה כל הגלוי
40 וכל המושג ועל זה נקרא המוצא הראשון ר"ל החכמה הקדומה תעלומה
שהיא נעלמת מלהשיגה על אמתתה ועל השואת אחדותה. ועוד כתר בחשבונו
עולה /

תר"ך עמודי אור שהם יקד יקוד. ונקראים שרשי החכמה הקדומה. מטה
הוא כח הנקרא אמונה והוא מדת הדין והוא סבת השמש והירח והמשכת

---

22 שבמאמרו: שבאמרו נ /(אור) ק /ונקרא: שנקרא ב ג 23 ובזיוו: וזיוו ב ג וזיו ק /
(אש) נ 24 בגווניו: בגוונים מ נ /לאין: אין מ ק /(על) ק /הקדומים: הקדמונים מ נ
קודמים ק 25 מפליאת: מפליאות ב ג /וזאת: וזאת ק /ומתחלקת: 26 ומתחלקת:
ומתחלקות מ ומתחלקין נ מתחלקות ק 27 וזהו: וזה ב ג (שנאמר) ב ג /עושה חיל וגו'
מ נ 27-28 (פועל... ממשות) ק 28 תוספת: תוספות מ /הקדש: קודש נ /צד:
הצד ב ג 29 אמצעי: האמצעי ב ג האמצע ק /מעליו: ומעליו ק /כחותיו ב ג /כחותיו: רוחותיו נ
/מאמצעותיו: מאמצעיתיו ק /ומעליו: ומעליו ב ומעלה נ"א ומעליו ג 30 יאצל: נאצל
ב ג /מכת: מדת ב מדה ג מכה ק /סילוק: וסילוק ק 31 פנים (שהם) מ נ /הכרה:
הברה ק /מסתר: מכתר ק 32 עוצם: עצם ב ג /שפע: שפני ב ג 33 לכח: לכל צד
ק 34 כח מכח: מכח לכח ק /המתנה: הוד ב ג (כתר לי זעיר) ק /מעלה כח: מעלה
הוא ב ג /כתר: סתר ג 35 מתרבה: מתוכה מ /סוף: חקר ב ג /ממציא: וממציא ב ג
מאציל ק (כל כי) ב ג /הנמצאים (נאצלים מצד השפעתו) ב ג 36 (שהשכל) ק /שום:
שם ק 37 ומעלים: ומכלים נ /ומעלים (ומעלים) ב ג /הוד: סודו ב ג סוד מ נ /מעלין: מעלה
ג /(עליו) ק /(צבא מעלה) נ"א זכות מעלה) ג /כאילו (עשאה) ב (עשה) נ /עטרו להקב"ה:
עטרה לו ב עטרה להקב"ה ג 38 (יקראני) ג 39 אמתת: אמת ק /ישלול: ישליל נ /
(כל) ב ג 40 נקרא: נאמר על ב נאמ' ג /ר"ל: כלומר ב ג /(תעלומה) ב ג
41 אחדותה: אחדות ק /(כתר בחשבונו) מ נ /(עולה) ב ג 42 תר"ך: תדיר ק /אור:
אויר ק /יקד יקוד: יקרים ב ג /ונקראים: ונקרא מ נ 43 כח: הכח ק /והוא: והיא ק
/השמש (זה) נ

[refers to] creatures of fire that speak;[50] [   ] silent,[51] a quick word.[52] This is related to *mal* (= seventy), which corresponds to the seventy Divine Names. Thus, "the secret (*sod* = 70) of the Lord is for those that fear Him" (Ps. 25:14).[53]

The root and the branch and the face: *YOD, H'e, V'AV, H'e*[54]–and the face is the fruit, which is the final *heh*. Above it is the Divine Presence, for the Divine Presence is the fruit. [Therefore] a man [praying] should face east and his heart should be in the west–that is where the Divine Presence resides.[55]

It appears in thought and word that it (i.e., the Name) is based on four foundations, [like the *'alef*][56] from which the created beings[57] are disseminated. These are the four divisions, which come from the mystery of the central Unity that is the domain of everything: *hashmal, 'arafel*, Throne of Light, and Wheel of Greatness, as well as each of their four parts.

How so? Know, students, *hashmal* is one part. Michael is the second part. The *yod* of the Tetragrammaton is the third part. 'Orpani'el is the fourth part. This is the power of fire, as it is stated, "for by the fire shall the Lord judge" (Isa. 66:16).

The second power is *'arafel*. Its four parts are: it itself is the first part. Gabriel is the second. The *heh* of the Tetragrammaton is the third. Tagra'el is the fourth. It is the mystery of the sublime holiness associated with the Unity. This is the power of water. Thus, "the seas and the waters that are above the Heavens" (cf. Gen. 1:7).

The third power is the Throne of Light. [These are] its four parts: it itself is the first. 'Uri'el is second. Danra'el is third. The *vav*

---

50. Herein, *hashmal* is interpreted as a contraction of the phrase: *hayyot 'esh memallelot*.

51. All of the versions of this imcomplete passage disagree; nevertheless what is intended is another interpretation of *hashmal*: silent = *hashot*.

52. A further interpretation of *hashmal*: involving *hish* (quick) and *millah* (word). Other variants utilize *millah*'s other connotation: "circumcision."

53. See above in *Contemplation-Short* for a comparable discussion, p. 45.

54. The numerical value of this particular spelling of the Tetragrammaton is 45, which corresponds to *'adam*, i.e., primordial human.

55. See *B. Baba' Batra'*, 25a.

56. This addition is found in the *Midrash of R. Simon*.

57. The *Midrash of R. Simon* reads instead "limbs."

of the Tetragrammaton is fourth. It is the power of air (*ruaḥ*), as it is stated, "from the four winds, come spirit (*ruaḥ*)" (Ezek. 37:9).

The fourth power is the Wheel of Greatness. These are its four parts. It itself is one. Raphael is the second. Pamali'el is the third. The final *heh* of the Tetragrammaton is fourth.

Behold these are the four foundations which are sixteen above, corresponding to what is below. They are called the body of the Divine Presence.[58] Concerning this it is stated, "Hear, Israel, the Lord our God, the Lord is one" (Deut. 6:4).

---

58. *Guf ha-shekhinah*, see above, p. 104, n. 216.

תנועותה בלילה וזהו שאומרים אמת ואמונה בלילה וזהו שכתוב כי

45   עשית פלא עצות מרחוק אמונה אומן. פלא ממשות הכח עצות מרחוק הם

העניינים הרוחניים המתגלים לעין וכל זה מאמונה אומן. עניין החכמה

הקדומה מבואר מקצתו בזה. פי׳ חשמל חיות אש ממללות. פ״א חש מל

פרמזל ר״ל מהירות וזהו פי׳ חשמל והכריתה פי׳ מל והכוונה חבור שני

עניינים זה הפך זה בהתבונן שני הצדדים מלמעלה ולמטה על דרך הדמיון

50   וכבר העירו אותנו פעם אחרת שהוא נגזר מן הדבור ומן השתיקה ואמרו

פעמים חשות פעמים ממללות וכי׳ חשות מל החיש בעניין מל הם ע׳

שמות והוא סוד ה׳ ליריאיו.

---

44 תנועותה: תנועותיה ק / בלילה: בכל לילה ב ג / וזהו: זה ק / (שאומרים) ק / שכתוב:

שאמ׳ ק   45 עצות: עשות נ / (עצות... אומן) ק / (אומן) מ / פלא: בלי ב / ממשות:

ממשלת ק / (הכח) ק עצות: העוצות ק   46 העניינים: פנינים ק / מאמונה: האמונה

ק   47 מקצתו בזה: מקצותיו כזה ב ג (ונקשר זה הסוד הנפלא בסוד החשמל) ב

ג   52-47 (פ״א... וכו׳) ב ג ק   51 מל החיש: מלה חיש מ נ מל החישות ק / בעניין:

כעין ב ג כעניין ק / הם ע׳ שמות: שמו ב ג שמו סוד מ נ

3:2 *COMMENTARY ON THE THIRTEEN ATTRIBUTES*

Contemplation–Thirteen Powers has also been cited in toto in the *Commentary on the Thirteen Attributes.* Although no author is ascribed to this work, the angelology of the latter part of this text has numerous parallels with that of R. Moses of Burgos' *Commentary on Zechariah's Candelabrum.*[3] Accordingly, it is reasonable to assume that either he, or someone closely connected with him, is the author of this text as well. This would also tie in with R. Moses' involvement with *Contemplation–Standard,* which will be discussed later. Whoever the author, this version is also significant for its influence on the next treatise, *Thirteen Powers.*

The *Commentary on the Thirteen Attributes* has been preserved in two manuscripts, Cambridge Dd. 10.11.2.4., ff. 33b–35a, designated by ק, and Florence 2:38, f. 101b–102a, designated by פ. These manuscripts differ only occasionally. Until line 65, (corresponding to the end of the material from *Contemplation–Thirteen Powers*), the following transcription is derived from both of these manuscripts. After that point, it is based solely on Florence 2:38, which is all that is currently available to me.

---

3. See G. Scholem, *Kabbalot,* 126. Furthermore, in another of his writings, R. Moses enumerates a series of angels, which also parallels this material (*ibid.,* 172) and therein he notes that this is only one of the lists that he received, thereby indicating a multiplicity of traditions. This would account for specific disparities among the various listings.

COMMENTARY ON THE THIRTEEN ATTRIBUTES

1 פי׳ שלש עשרה מדות על דרך קצרה בסתם ופשוט לכל מבין.
יש לנו לדעת מה תועלת יש בחילוף אותיות יג מידות ולמה אין ה׳
יוצא כמשמע האותיות ופשוטן כי בתחלה החליפו היוד בעבור מם וההא
בצדי והו בפה והא בצדי כבר למדנו כי היוד כנגד הדבר המתעלם
5 והנסתר ועל כן צורתה קטנה. ובחלופה במם בא ללמד ולגלות עקר הדבר
יותר ומי שיש לו לב להבין ועינים ולראות יבין מתוך מם למה נקראת
המחשבה בלשון טהורה ולא בלשון טהור ויבין סוד הפסוק שאמ׳ ועתה
פן ישלח ידו ולקח גם מעץ החיים ועוד אותיות מנצפך למה הן
נקראות בסוף התיבה ולא בתחילה והנני אומר על המם שבשם הראשון של
10 יג מדות שהיא מצפץ דעת עליון וכתר עליון ועל כן תמצא שאמ׳ החכמה
בלשון תמצא ולא ימצא ויש עלינו לדעת למה נקראת החכמה בלשון נקבה
ולא בלשון זכר וכן התשובה אבל כלל כל הדברים ועיקרם מפורש במ״ם
ועל כן היא נקודה פתח ולא קמץ ומכאן יש לנו ראייה למה שאמ׳ הנביא
וזרקתי עליכם מים טהורים וטהרתם ועל כן אמרו רז״ל מחשבה טהורה
15 ולא אמרו קדושה והרי אתה לומד סוד מם העליונה וסוד מם התחתונה
והעדות בדעתו תהומות נבקעו. וזה סוד עץ הדעת ועל כן היוד עם המם
הוא לשון ים ועל כן נמצא כתו׳ ומעין יוצא מבית ה׳. ועוד כתו׳
אחר אמ׳ יהי מקור נפתח לבית דוד. ולא לזרע דוד אלא בלשון בית
וזה מאמ׳ הנביא ע״ה באומרו כי עזבו מקור מים חיים את ה׳ וסוד
20 הדברים האלה הם נקבה תסובב גבר. מצאתי לך ה׳ הגדולה והגבורה
ובענין פי׳ המפרש ובאר עקר ההויות הנכללות בספר מעשה בראשית ועל
זה הענין רמז ליג כוחות רוחניות שהזכיר בעל ספר היצירה והם ספר
ספר וספור עשר ספירות בלימה. וכל אלו הי״ג כוחות יש להם לכל אחד
ואחד מהם שם חלוק בפני עצמו. ומעלתם זו למעלה מזו. הראשון נקר׳
25 חכמה קדומה השני אור מופלא השלישי חשמל הרביעי ערפל החמישי כסא
הנוגה הששי אופן היא אופן היא אופן הגדולה הנקראת חזית פי׳ מוצא חזיון
החוזים השביעי כרוב השמי׳ גלגל המרכבה התשיעי האויר הסובב העשירי
פרגוד היא כסא הכבוד היב מקום הנשמות הנקר׳ חדר גדול היג סוד
המערכת העליונה הנקר׳ היכל הקודש העליון ואלו יג הכחות מתגלין
30 מסתר עליון הנעלם. אומן הוא הנקרא פירושו אב האמונה שמכחו האמונה
נאצלת והוא ית׳ קודם שברא שום דבר היה יחיד ומיוחד באין חקר ובלי
גבול איפשר לעמוד ולהתקיים בעצמו בכח קיום לכך נקרא שמו אל חזוק
חזק נ״א חזק תקיף ולא היה נכר אלא לעצמו ועלה בדעתו להמציא כל
פעליו יש מאין וברא כח אחד ראשון וקראו חכמה הקדו׳ ממנה תוצאות

---

1 (ופשוט) פ /מבין (פשוט) פ   3 ופשוטן: ובפשוטו ק   8 מעץ: מעין פ
10 שהיא: שהם פ   12 אבל: מכל פ /עיקרם: עיקרים ק   13 ולא קמץ: וקמץ
פ   14 ועל כן אמרו רז״ל: אמל(?) פ   15 לומד: למד פ   19 (באומרו) פ
21 ובענין: וכענין ק   22 ליג: לג ק   27 המרכבה: המחשבה ק   28 חדר: אדר
ק   31 שום: משום ק   33-32 (חזוק חזק נ״א) פ

תעלומה ותוצאות האמנוה ונק' הקדומה שממנה נאצלו יב כוחות הנזכרים   35
ושקולה היא כנגד העשרה בהשואת האחדות הם עשר ספירות וזה שכתו'
החכמ' תעוז לחכם מעשרה שליטים וג' החכם הוא ית' כמו' דתימ' מי
כהחכם וממשות כח זה הנק' חכמה קדומה היא אור החיים זך ומזוקק כתר
טוב נכתב ונחתם בזיו ושפריר הצד העליון הנקרא אין הנכלל מכל המושג.

וזהו סוד והחכמה מאין תמצא זה הצד העליון הוא רצון באין גבול ולמה   40
נקרא רצון שבמאמרו וברצונו נמצא היש מהאין גם הוא אור מזהיר ונקרא
כבוד ה' על כן נאמר עוטה אור כשלמה שהוא מתאחד בגווניא ומתעלה עד
לאין סוף ונקר' אחד על שהיה קדם לכל הקדומים הנאצלים מפליאת
אחדותו זאת החכמה היא עליונית לעשר ספירות ומתחלקת לשש קצוות ימין

ושמאל פנים ואחור מעלה ומטה. ימין הוא כח הקיום בלי ממשות פעול   45
פעולות בכל וזהו ימין ה' עושה חיל תוספת רוח הקודש. שמאל כח מושכל
בלי ממשות ויש בו מהות והוא צד אמצעי המשפיע כוחותיו לכל צד ולא
ינטה מאמצעותיו ומעליו וכל שלא נאצל ממנו רוח הקודש לצד אחד
מצדדיו וזהו יד ה' כי הוא כח חלוף רוח הקודש. פנים שני כוחות שהם

הכנה לכל הכחות המתגלין מסתר עליון שאמרנו ונקראים חן וחסד שהם   50
פנים של רחמים. אחור עצם החכמה שפע הבינה הוא תכלית השגת החקר
והוא כח בעצמו ומתפשט לכח מוטבע לצייר צורה ולהביא כח מכח. מעלה
כח הנק' כתר עליון והוא צד עליון מתרבה עד אין סוף ממציא כל
הנמצאים והוא לשון אדר ברוב עם הדרת מלך. ועוד מורה לשון כתר

לשון המשיג שום דבר בידיעה מתוך חקירתו ומעלים ומכסה הודו מעלין   55
עליו כאילו עטרו של הקב"ה ועליו נאמ' אשגבהו כי ידע שמי והאמת כי
לא ישיג שום נברא דעת על אמתת ידיעה אבל ישאל ממנה כל
הגלוי וכל המושג ועל זה נקרא המוצא הראשון מהכל חכמה קדומה
תעלומה נעלמת מכל השגה על אמתתה ועל תשואת אחדותה. ועוד סתר

בחשבונו שש מאות וששי' עמודי אור שהם יקד יקוד ונקראי' שרשי   60
החכמה הקדומה. מטה היא כח הנק' אמונה והיא מדת הדין והיא סבת
השמש והירח ומהמשכת תנועותיה בלילה וזהו שאמ' אמת ואמונה בלילה.
וזהו שכתו' עצות מרחוק אמונה אומן. פלא ממשות הנה עצות מרחוק
הדברים והעניניי' הרוחניים המתגלים לעין וכל זה מאמונה אומן

ענין החכמה הקדומה מבואר מקצת בזה. תם. שמות עשר הספירות שהם   65
עשרה במניין הקדושים הנא' בתוכה. אהיה יה יהוה אדני שדי צבאות
אל אלהים אל עליון. ומלבד אלו הי' שמות יש להם שמות אחרים על
דרך ההויות כאשר זכרתי ואלו הם הי' שמות יַהֲוַהַהָא יָהֻהֲוָה וְהַהֲאָה
יאהֹוֹהֹ יָהֲהָא הֲוַו יַוֵהֹ יֵוָהֹ אַהֵ יְהָאַיֵהֲ יַאֲהֲוֹהֹי וְאַל כל העשרה שמות הם

---

35 (הנזכרים) פ   37 כמ' דתימ': כמו אמר ק   38 כהחכם: כחכם פ   40 באין:
מאין ק   41 היש מהאין: יש מאין ק כשלמה (אורה) ק/(שהוא) פ/(עד) פ
43 שהיה: שהוא ק   47 מהות: מיתות ק/אמצעי': ממציא פ   49-48 (לצד אחד...
הקודש) ק   50 הכנה: הבנה פ   51 הוא: היא ק   52 והוא: והיא פ
54 ברוב: כרוב ק   56 (של הקב"ה) פ   57 דבר זה: דבורה פ   61 אמונה:
ממונה פ   63 פלא: על א ק   64 הרוחניים: המחניים פ/המתגלים: המתגלגלים ק

נכללים בשלשה שמות אלו יְהוָה יַהוָה יְהוֹה כמו שהעשר ספירות נכללים 70
בשלשה שני ה' בחכמה יסד ארץ כונן שמים בתבונה בדעתו תהומות
נבקעו הרי לך בשלשה נכלל הכל שהם החכמה התבונה הדעת ועלו כולם
למספר אחד שהם י"ג כנגד י"ג מדות של רחמים וזהו ה' אחד ועתה
מודיעך גם כן סוד יג מדות וסוד שמותם ואכלול בתוכם סוד אותיות

האלפא ביתא דע כי עשר האותיות שהם מהאלף עד היוד כולם נקראים 75
יהוה מפני שבזה המערכת נמצאים אותיות השם שהם אהוי ולא מכף עד
תיו ולא עד צ שהיא סוף כל המערכות ועוד כל חשבון אותיות השם
במבטה שהם יוד הא ואו הא למה הא ועם האותיות שהם י הרי נה בחשבון
אותיות אבגדהוזחטי שהוא כולל הכל כי הכל הוא נה ועל אלי האותיות
עשר נקראים יהוה. ואלו הם השמות של יג המדות. הראשון פלא שהוא 80
נקרא יהוה הגדול והוא אות הכף. השני הוא נקר' מטטרון שהוא נקרא
יהוה הקטן והוא אות הלמד. שלישי הוא נקרא מיכאל שהוא נקרא אל
והיא אות נון וזאת המדה שבקש משה להשיג. הרביעי גבריאל והוא
נקר' רחום וזה השגתו שהשיג משה ע"ה והוא נקר' אות פא והוא הנקר'
אות סמך מסך הפרכת. החמישי צדקיאל הוא הנק' חנון וזה השגתם של 85
נביאי' והוא נק' אות צדי והוא האות הנקרא עין עינים רואות. הששי
אורפניאל והוא הנק' ארך אפים והוא האות הנק' קוף והוא נקר' ו
פתחו שערים. השביעי סנדלפן, והוא הנק' רב חסד והוא אות ריש והוא
אות הנק' ץ צדיק יסוד עולם. השמיני שלמיאל והוא הנק' אמת והוא
האות הנק' שין. התשיעי טוביאל הוא הנקרא נוצר חסד לאלפים והוא 90
אות הנקר' תיו. העשירי אוריאל והוא הנק' נושא עון והוא אות ך.
היא ברופיאל והוא הנק' פשע והוא אות ס. היב חסדיאל והוא הנק'
חטאה והיא אות מם. שלשה עשר תמיאל והוא הנקר' נקה והוא האות ק.
תם פירוש שלש עשרה מידות.

3:3 *THIRTEEN POWERS*

Thirteen Powers has been preserved in several manuscripts, notably
Mousayeff 63, f. 12a-12b, designated by א; Munich 24, f. 199a, designated by מ⁴; Munich 92, ff. 74a-75b, designated by ג; Florence 2:38,
f. 98a, designated by פ; and Cambridge (Institute #23112), f. 35a designated by ק. Of these, only Mousayeff 63 offers a complete version
of the treatise and is the basis of the following transcription.[5] In general, this treatise is the same as *Contemplation–Thirteen Powers*; however, interpolated into this work is material related to the Thirteen
Essences (*havayot*). It seems likely that the redactor of *Thirteen Powers* was influenced by the previous text, *Commentary on the Thirteen
Attributes*, for therein one finds reference to most of these Essences.
Nevertheless, in the *Commentary*, we find that *Contemplation–Thirteen Powers* is presented intact, and only afterward are the
Essences discussed, whereas in *Thirteen Powers* this new material has
been integrated into the body of the text itself.

Thirteen Powers is first cited in *Foundation of the World*, written
around 1300 and commonly attributed to Hananel b. Abraham.[6]

---

4.   At times variants listed only as מ are also shared by ג, פ and ק; unfortunately, these designations are lacking owing to the incompleteness of my
transcriptions of these manuscripts.

5.   The other versions break off at line 48, except פ which ends at line 16.

6.   Guenzburg 607, f. 56a. Ascribing this work to Hananel does not fit with
R. Shem Tov ibn Gaon's assertions in *Baddei 'Aron* that *Yesod 'Olam* was
part of the library of Hananel's father, Paris ms. 840, facsimile edition, D.
Loewinger ed. (Jerusalem 1977), 1.

THIRTEEN POWERS

1 אלה הם שלשה עשר כחות הנקראים כחות החכמה הקדומה.
לך ה׳ הגדולה והגבורה והתפארת והנצח וההוד כי כל בשמים ובארץ לך
יהוה הממלכה והמתנשה לכל לראש. בענין זה פירש המפרש ובאר עיקר
ההויות הנכללות בספר מעשה בראשית וכל זה הענין רמז לי״ג כחות

5 רוחניות שהזכיר בעל ספר יצירה והם ספר ספר וספור עשר ספירות
בלימה. עשר ספירות וספר וספר וספור הם יג כחות רוחניות וכל
אילו הי״ג כחות יש להם לכל א׳ וא׳ מהם שם ידוע וחלוק בפני עצמו
בשני פנים. הפן הא׳ על דרך החכמה והפן השני על דרך ההויות. אלו
הן השמות שהם על דרך החכמה. א׳ חכמה קדומה. ב׳ אור מופלא. ג׳

10 חשמל. ד׳ ערפל. ה׳ כסא הנגה. ו׳ אופן הגדולה הנקרא׳ חזחזית פי׳
מוצא החזיון. ז׳ כרוב. ח׳ גלגל המרכבה. ט׳ האויר הסובב. י׳
הפרגוד. יא׳ כסא הכבוד. יב׳ מקום הנשמות הנקרא חדרי גדולה. יג׳
כחות סוד המערכה העליונה הנקרא היכל הקדש החיצון. ואלה שמותם על
דרך ההויות. א יַהֲוַהֲהֲא. ב יָהֲוָאֲוָה. ג יְהֲהָאֲוָה. ד יאהֹהֹהֹה. ה יָאֲהְוָהֲ.

15 ו יָהֲאֲהֲוָ. ז יֲוֲהֲאֲהֲ. ח יָהֲאֲהֲהֲ. יְהֹוֹהֹא. י יָאֲהֹוָה. יא יְהֹוָה.
יב יַהֹוֹהֹ. יג יְהֹוָה. כבר נשלמו שמות יג כחות החכמה הקדומה ותמצא
בם ע״ב אותיות כנגד ע״ב שמות של שלשה פסוקים ויסע ויבא ויט
ואילו הי״ג כחות מתגלים מסתר עליון הנעלם הנקרא אמן. ופירושו
אב האמונה שמכחו האמונה נאצלת. והוא יתי׳ קודם שברא שום דבר היה

20 יחיד מיוחד באין חקר ובלי גבול איפשר לעמוד ולהתקיים בעצמו ממש
בכח ניכר קיום ומציאות עצמו. לכך נקרא אל ר״ל חזק תקיף ולא היה
ניכר אלא לעצמו. ועלה במחשבתו לברוא ולהמציא כל פעליו יש מאין.
ובָרא כח ראשון א׳ וקראו חכמה קדומה ממנה תוצאות תעלומה ותוצאות
האמונה. ונקראת קדומה מפני שממנה נאצלו שנים עשר כחות הנזכרים

25 ושקולה היא כנגד העשרה בהשואת האחדות הם עשר ספירות. וזהו שכתוב
החכמה תעוז לחכם מעשרה שליטים אשר היו בעיר. החכם הוא יתי׳ כמו
שנאמ׳ מי כהחכם ומי יודע פשר דבר. וממשות כח זה הנקרא חכמה קדומה
היא אור החיים זך ומזוקק כתם טוב נכתב ונחתם בזיו ושפריר הצד
העליון הנקרא אין הנשלל מכל המושג. וזהו סוד והחכמה מאין תמצא

30 וזה הצד העליון הוא הנקרא רצון באין גבול. ולמה נקרא רצון מפני

---

1 אלה: אילו מ/(הנקראים כחות) פ (כחות) ק   3-2 (לך... לראש) מנפק/בענין:
כענין מ   4 בספר: זה ק/(מעשה) פ   6 (בלימה) מנפק/ספירות בלימה מנפק/
הם: הרי פ/(כחות) פ   7 לכל: וכל מ   8 הפן: האופן פ/אלו הן: ואותן מ
10 (אופן... החזיון) פ   11 (המרכבה) פ   12 חדרי: חדר פ   13 (כחות) מנפק
עשר נ/החיצון: העליון מ/ואלה: ואלו מ   14 ההויות אילו הכתובות הנה ברמז
מ   16 כבר: וכבר מ/שמות: הנה בציור מ/הקדומה על דרך ההויות מ   17 בם:
בה ק/של: על מ   55-16 (כבר... הרוחניים) פ   18 מסתר: מכתר מ   19 אב:
לב מנק   21 (ניכר) מנק/עצמו: עצמי מ/נקרא שמו מנק/תקיף: ותקיף מ
22 ניכר אלא: נברא לא מ   23 (ובְרא) מ/   ראשון א׳: אחד ראשון מ
30 (הוא) מ

שבמאמרו וברצונו נמצא היש מאין. גם הוא מזהיר ונקרא כבוד יהוה.
על זה נאמר עוטה אור כשלמה נוטה שמים כיריעה. לומר שהוא מתאחד
באורו וזיוו כלהב אש המתאחד בגווניו ומתעלה עד אין סוף. ונקרא
אחד על שהיה קודם לכל הקדומים הנאצלים מפליאת אחדותו וזאת החכמה
היא עליונית לעשר הספירות ומתחלקת לשש קצוות ימין ושמאל פנים ואחור   35
מעלה ומטה וזהו פירושם ועיקרם. ימין הוא כח הקיום בלי ממשות פועל
פעולות בכל יום וזהו ימין יהוה עושה חיל ר"ל תוספת רוח הקדש. שמאל
הוא מושכל בלי ממשות ויש בו מהות צד אמצעי משפיע כחותיו לכל צד
ולא ינטה מאמצעותה ומעלייה ר"ל שלא נאצל ממנו רוח הקדש אלא לצד
אחד מצדדיו וזהו יד ה'. כי הוא מכח חלוף רוח הקדש. פנים הם שני   40
כחות שהם הכנה לכל הכחות המתגלים מסתר עליון שאמרנו ונקראים חן
וחסד שהם פנים של רחמים. אחור הוא עצם החכמה שפע הבינה היא תכלית
השגת החקר והוא כח בעצמו ומתפשט לכח מוטבע לצייר צורה ולהביא כח
מכח. מעלה כח הנקרא כתר עליון והוא צד עליון עולה ומתרבה עד אין
סוף. ממציא כל נמצאים. והוא לשון הדר. ברב עם הדרת מלך. ועוד   45
מורה לשון כתר לשון המשיג סוף דבר בידיעה מתוך חקירתו ומעלים
ומכסה הודו מעלין עליו כאלו עטרו להקב"ה ועליו נאמ' אשגבהו כי
ידע שמי. והאמת כי לא ישיג שום נברא דבר זה על אמתתו לידע אותו
ידיעה אמתית אבל ישליל ממנה כל המושג וכל הגלוי ועל כן נקרא המוצא
הראשון מהכל חכמה קדומה תעלומה נעלמת מלהשיגה על אמיתתה ועל   50
השואת אחדותה. וסוד כתר בחשבונו שש מאות ושרים עמודי אור שהם
יקוד. ונקראים שרשי החכמה הקדומה. מטה הוא כח הנקרא אמונה.
והוא מדת הדין. והוא סבת השמש והירח ומתמשכת תנועות בלילה וזהו
שאנו אומרים אמת ואמונה בלילה. וזהו שכתוב אמונה אומן העצות
הרוחניים.   55

31 שבמאמרו: שבאמרו מ/הוא אור מנק   33 (באורו וזיוו כלהב אש) מנק/בגווניו:
בגוונא מ בגוונה נ   34 וזאת: וראות מ וראה נ וראת ק/החכמה: בחכמה מ
35 לעשר: בעשר מ/קצוות: מצוות מ   36-37 (ועיקרים... בכל) ק   38 מושכל:
מושל מ/מהות: מתות נ   39 ר"ל: וכל מ/(אלא) מ   40 מכח: כח מ/הם: בהם
מ   43 לצייר: ולצייר מ   45 הדר: אדר מ/ועוד: ועד מ   46 סוף: שום מ/
מעלים: ומעלין מ ועלין נ ומעליו ק   47 ומכסה: ומרבה מ/מעליו: מעליו נ (עליו) ק
/עטרו של נ   48-55 (והאמת... הרוחניים) מנק

3:4 *THE SECRET OF THE THIRTEEN ATTRIBUTES OF MERCY*

This text represents an even later stage of development. Its title suggests influence from the circle of the *Zohar*,[7] thereby placing it in the late thirteenth or early fourteenth century. It has been preserved in Cambridge 505, designated as ק, British Museum (Gaster) 10682, designated by ג, and published in *Shushan Sodot* (Koretz 1778), f. 34a, designated by ש. The following transcription is drawn from all of these sources. Although only the first part of the text concerns us here, the latter part offers a lengthy commentary on *The Prayer of Unity of R. Nehuniah b. ha-Kanah*.

---

7. For example the *Zohar* begins with a discussion of the thirteen Attributes of Mercy. This terminology is also found in R. Joseph Gikatilla's writings; cf. *Sha'arei 'Orah*, 2:107. Interestingly, this phrasing is not found in R. Moses de Leon's Hebrew writings; cf. E. Wolfson, *Sefer ha-Rimmon*, 1:28, 30, and 42, n. 126.
See also the text *Sod Yud-Gimel Middot she-ha-Torah Nidreshet ba-Hem*, Jerusalem 8° 488, f. 38b-39a, which links R. Ishmael's hermeneutical rules to the *sefirot*. This text likewise is connected to R. Moses de Leon, both terminologically, as well as in its philosophical bent.

THE SECRET OF THE THIRTEEN ATTRIBUTES OF MERCY

1 סוד י"ג מכילתי דרחמי בשמותם ובהוייתן הרומזים אל כ"ע ונרשמים
בחכמה ומפורשים בבינה ויצאו לפועל בי"ג מדות שנאמרו למשה רבינו
ע"ה ואלה שמותם. א חכמה קדומה. ב אור מופלא. ג חשמל. ד ערפל.
ה כסא הנוגה. ו אופן הגדולה הנקראת חזחזית פי' מוצא החזיון.

5 ז כרוב. ח גלגל המרכבה. ט האויר הסובב. י הפרגוד. יא כסא הכבוד.
יב מקום הנשמות הנקרא חדר גדולה. יג סוד המערכה העליונה הנקראת
היכל הקדש העליון ואלה שמות הוויתן.

בינה	[ ]	כ"ע		
יהוה	חכמה קדומה	יְהַוַהַאַ	ה"א	
יהוה	אור מופלא	יְהַיַאַוַהַ	ה"ב	10
אל	חשמל	יְהַהַאַוַהַ	ה"ג	
רחום	ערפל	יַאַהַוַהַ	ה"ד	
וחנון	כסא הנוגה	יַאַהַוַהַ	ה"ה	
ארך אפים	אופן הגדולה	יְהַאַהַוַהַ	ה"ו	
רב חסד	כרוב	יַוַוַהַאַהַ	ה"ז	15
ואמת	גלגל המרכבה	יְהַאַוַהַ	ה"ח	
נוצר ח"ל	האויר הסובב	יהווהא	ה"ט	
נושא עון	הפרגוד	יַאַהַוַוַהַ	ה"י	
ופשע	כסא הכבוד	יְהֹוָה	הי"א	
וחטאה	חדר גדולה	יְהֹוָה	הי"ב	20
ונקה	היכל הקדש	יְהֹוָה	הי"ג	

הנה לך מבוארים י"ג מכילתי דרחמי הרומזי' בהוייתן בכ"ע וברשימתן
בחכמה ובמדתן בבינה הפועלת בהם ע"י אב המון ראש הבנין כי כל י"ג

25 מדות כלם מדות הרחמים אין בהן אחת שמורה על הדין כי אל הוא גם
הוא רחמים כמו שכתו' אלי אלי למה עזבתני כי לא שאל למה עזבהו
מדת הדין וראוי שתדע שבכל י"ג ההויות לא נחסר מתוכן יהוה הרומז
לקו המאצעי רק נוסף עליו אהו לפעמים אה ולפעמים או וסודו
למשכיליו ינעם וברוך מגלה עמוקות מני חשך כי הוא אמר ויהי.

───────────────

1 מכילתי: מכילתא ש / בשמותם: בשמותן ש   2 ומפורשים: ומפורש ק
4 חזחזית: חזיז ש   5 הסובב: הרוכב ג   6 הנקרא חדר גדולה: הנקראת חדר
הגדולה ש / יג: היג ק   7 שמות הוויתן: שמותם בהוויתן ש   8 [ ]: ש"ה ש
16 גלגל: גלגלי ש   20 גדולה: הגדולה ש   22 מבוארים: מבואר ג / מכילתי:
מכילתא ש / (הרומזי') ג / וברשימתן: ונרשמין ג   23 הפועלת בהן: הפעולות בהם ש /
(ראש הבנין) ג   24 כלם מדות: כלם במדת ש / בהן: בהם ש / שמורה: שתורה ק / (על
הדין) ג / (הוא) ש   25 עזבהו: עזבתני ש   26 מדת הדין: מה"ר ש   27 (לפעמים
אה) ש   28 ינעם: יונעם ש טעמו ג

3:5 *PSEUDO-RABAD'S TWELVE ATTRIBUTES*

One of the most important conduits for the transmission of the *kabbalah* was the fifteenth-century Spanish scholar, R. Shem Tov ibn Shem Tov. Included in his writings is a short citation from a work ascribed to Rabad. This refers to R. Abraham b. David of Posquières, one of the leading Talmudists of the twelfth century and ostensibly one of the pioneering kabbalists.[8] The material attributed to Rabad consists of an enumeration of twelve of the thirteen powers.[9] If this ascription is authentic, it would necessitate a complete reassessment of our dating of *Contemplation*. However, in none of R. Abraham's voluminous writings is there anything resembling this text, and accordingly, its authenticity must be challenged. It is also significant that the designation for the final power, "Outer Holy Palace," is only found in the later versions of *Contemplation*, such as *Thirteen Powers* and *Contemplation–Standard*. This corroborates our assumption that this text represents a later development.

The following transcription is taken from D. Ariel's dissertation, *Shem Tob ibn Shem Tob's Kabbalistic Critique* (Brandeis Dissertation 1982), 112f.

---

8. On the issue of Rabad as a kabbalist, compare G. Scholem, *Origins*, 205-227, and I. Twersky, *Rabad*, 286-330.

9. Twelve corresponds to the twelve compass points, enumerated in *Sefer Yezirah*, 5:1.

PSEUDO–RABAD'S TWELVE ATTRIBUTES

ומצאתי לשון זה בשם הראב"ד ז"ל והשם המורה על מהותה בי נשבעתי נאם י'
רמז לי"ב גבולי אלכסון כלומ' י"ב מדו' מושפעות מאלו המעיינות. ואלו
שמותם. האור המופלא חשמל ערפל כסא הנוגה אופן הגדולה כרוב גלגל
המרכבה אויר הסובב פרגוד כסא הכבוד. מקום הנפשות הנקרא חדרי הגדולה
היכל הקדש החיצון. ואלו הן ענפי תולדות הספירות.

4:1 *CONTEMPLATION–BURGOS*

The earliest citations from *Contemplation–Standard* are the most problematical. They are found in the writings of R. Moses of Burgos. In all, R. Moses presents about half of the text. Whereas most of the material corresponds to our text, the delineation of the thirteen powers contains unique statements. Among the additional material, not found in any other version of *Contemplation–Standard* are theories and terms particular to the teachings of R. Isaac Cohen[10] and his students, such as the division of the thirteen powers into ten *sefirot*, plus three lower entities,[11] as well as the term *'olam ha-mitboded* (World of Separation).[12] One could therefore postulate that this text represents R. Isaac's transcription and commentary on *Contemplation–Standard*, (or possibly R. Moses' own version of the text based on his teacher's doctrines).

This text was partially published by Scholem.[13] The following transcription is based primarily on Parma de Rossi 68, f. 67a, designated by פ, as well as Mousayeff 63, f. 5b-6b, designated by מ, and J.T.S. 1777, f. 28b-29b, designated by נ.[14]

---

10. There is also some connection between this material and the *Responsa of R. Yekutiel.*

11. Cf. G. Scholem, *Kabbalot*, 86.

12. See G. Scholem, *Le-Ḥeker*, 52-54.

13. G. Scholem, *Kabbalot*, 128, and G. Scholem, *Le-Ḥeker*, 185.

14. Only in Parma de Rossi is the material found in this sequence. In both Mousayeff and J.T.S., lines 60 to 96 precede the first section.

CONTEMPLATION–BURGOS

1 ואקדים בתחילה מה שמצאתי בספר העיון שחיבר רב חמאי ז"ל א"ר
ישמעאל בן אלישע כהן גדול בלשכת הגזית א"ר ישמעאל אותו היום
היינו מצויין אני ור' עקיבה בן יוסף לפני ר' נחוניא בן הקנה
והיה שם ר' חנינה בן תרדיון ושאלתי לר' נחוניא בן הקנה ואמרתי

5 לו הראיני כבוד מלכו של עולם כדי שיתבאר ידיעתו בלבי כשאר פעליו
אמ' לי בן גאים תא ונעסוק בעיזקתא רבתא דחתימין בה שמאיה
ואראריתא שמיה ובעזקתא דארעא ההיא אהו ואראה לך הכל ונכנסתי לפני
ולפנים בהיכל הקודש החיצון והוצאתי משם ספרו של ר' נחוניא בן
הקנה הנקרא ספר היכלות ומצאתי כתו' בתחילת הספר כך אדיר בחדרי

10 גדולה היושב על רום גלגלי מרכבתו בחתימת אהיה אשר אהיה ובעזקתא
רבתא דחתימין ביה שמיא שמיה אראריתא סימן אחד ראש אחדותו ראש
יחודו תמורתו אחד יחיד ומיוחד אחד חי העולמים ובעזקתא דארעא די
שמי' אהו וסימן אחד היה ויהיה והמתמצע בין שניהם הוה דבר דבור
על אופניו היה קודם שברא העולם הוה בעולם הזה ויהיה לעולם הבא

15 והסימן פעל פועל יפעל סימן ה' מלך הוה ה' מלך היה ה' ימלוך
יהיה מלך בעולם הזה מלך קודם העולם הזה ימלוך לעולם הבא. ובזה
הסדר מפורשים שרשי כל ההויות הנכללות בספר מעשה בראשית שהם
סתרים יתגלו מסתר עליון הנעלם הנקרא אומן פי' אב האמונה כמה
דכתי' אמונה אומן שמכחו האמונה נאצלת ופי' אומן ר"ל אמונה ממנו

20 נאצל ובעבור שהאמונה חותם תבנית שהאדון היחיד הנעלם מהכל חתם בה
כל ההויות וכל הפעולו' קראה חפצי בה היא ראשית במחשבת האדון
הנעלם והיא אחרית לכל האצילו' המתבודד והיינו הא דכתי' אני ראשון
ואני אחרון והאדון הנעלם ית' מתאחד בכחותיו ומתרומם מהם עד שאין
סוף לרוממותו והם יג כחות שבהם מתגלה האדון היחיד ויש לכל אחד

25 ואחד שם ידוע בפני עצמו ומהם נראים פעולות יג מידות האמורות
בתורה משה עבד ה' וכל מעלה על גבי מעלה זו למעלה מזו. הראשון
אור מופלא שהוא האור הנסתר ומכוסה מעין כל בריה ומתרגמינן כי
יפלא ארי יתכסי היפלא מה' דבר היתכסי. השנית פליאות חכמה גם
כן מתעלמות ומתכסות כל פליאות מיני האצילות המתאצלים בה מהאור

---

1 (שחיבר רב חמאי ז"ל) נ   2 בן: א"ר פ /(א"ר ישמעאל) נ /(אותו) נ   3 מצויין:
מצואין מ /(בן הקנה) פ   4 (בן הקנה) פ   5 (כבוד) פ /מלכו: מלכותו מ נ   6 ונעסוק (עמך)
מ נ/שמאיה: וארא מ /(שמאיה) נ   7 הכל: מכל מ נ   9 ספר (היכל) נ /(הספר)
נ   11 (רבתא) מ נ שמיא: שמיה מ /(שמיא) נ /אחדותו ראש: אחדותו ראשית מ
אחדותו (ראש) פ   12 (אחד) פ   13 הוה: היה פ   14 שברא העולם הוה: שבא
לעולם הזה פ /הזה (היה) מ נ   15 (סימן) נ פ   16 (ה') ימלוך מ נ   17 שהם
סתרים: שסתרים פ   18 יתגלו: נתגלו פ יתגלו (לו) מ נ   19 אמונה: אמונת פ /ופי'
(ר"ל) מ פ /אומן: אמן מ נ /(ר"ל) מ פ   20 (בה) פה   22 אחרית: האחרית פ /
והיינו הא דכתי': והדא הוא דכתי' מ והדה"ד נ   23 ית' מתאחד: מתנשא מתייחד מ /
שאין (לו) פ   24 היחיד: האחד מ פ   25 (ואחד) מ נ   26 עבד ה': עבדי פ
27 שהוא: הוא פ /(ומתרגמינן... דבר היתכסי) פ   29 מיני: מבין מ מנון נ

המופלא. השלישית אור צח שהוא מצחצח כל מיני האצילות הגנוזים בו   30
ומוציאם מן הכח אל הפועל באמצעות המאור. הרביעית הוא חשמל
ופירושו חסדו שמים מלאכים. החמישי ערפל מידת הדין הגדולה שבו
מתעלה ומתנשא החשמל בשעת הראותו בתוקף אצילות הגבורה להוציא
הפעלים מן הכח גם הוא באמצעות שר הגבורה שהוא גבריאל וגם הוא
נקרא ערפל כי הוא דמות מחיצה עומדת לפני מידת הגבורה והוא סוד   35
ומשה ניגש אל הערפל אשר שם האלהים ועל הערפל הנעלם שהוא מתעלם
בערפל הנראה לנביאים ע"ה על שניהם רמזו חז"ל בתפילת ר"ה ונגלית
עליהם בערפלי טוהר. שני מיני ערפל הם האחד נעלם והשני נראה ועל
הראשון הנעלם נרמז באיוב ולא ידע בפש מאד. השישי אופן הגדולה
ונקרא כן כי הוא מכלל יופי לז' פנים הנוראי' והוא מכלל הז' הוא   40
הנקרא חזקית כי הוא מוציא חזיון החוזים. השביעית חדרי הנשמות
כי ממנו פורחות נשמות הצדיקים. השמיני והתשיעי הם גלגלי המרכבה.
העשירית הוא הנקרא כרוב שבו מתפאר הרוכב בשמי שמי קדם ועליו נאמ'
רצונו לומר על הרוכב ועל הכרוב וירכב על כרוב ויעוף. האחד עשר
כסא הכבוד שהוא כדמות כסא לכבוד העשירי ועוד נקרא היכל הקודש   45
הפנימי. השנים עשר היכל הקודש התיכון. השלש עשרה הוא היכל הקודש
האחרון ושלשתן הם היכלות לכבוד השכינה שהיא מעלה עשירית. ובספר
מעיין החכמה שמצאתי מפרש שם כי אלה שלשה היכלות שפי' רב חמאי יש
להם שמות אחרים ידועים ואלה שמותם שלשתן על שם מדת המלכות היכל
הקודש הפנימי הוא שר העומד לפני כתר מלכות ושמו מלכיאל היכל   50
הקודש התיכון עיטוריאל ונקרא כן על שם העטרה הגדולה שהוא כדמיון
הזהב הנמשל למידת הדין היכל הקודש החיצון שמו נשריאל על שהוא
משולה לנשר שנא' כנשר יעיר קנו ע"כ מס' מעין החכמה ועתה אשוב
להשלים בפי' רב חמאי מס' העיון מה שהחלותי אילו היג כחות הם
מתגלים כאחד מכח סתר עליון האחד הנעלם הנקרא אומן ופי' אב האמונה   55
שמכחו האמונה חביבה לפניו והוא האחד המתנשא על הכל נקרא סתר
עליון קודם שברא הנבראי' עליוני עליוני ועליוני תחתונים בעבור
כי הוא היה לבדו אחד נעלם ונסתר עד שברא עולם המתבודד ושאר
העולמים ונתייחד כבודו בעליוני' ובאומה יחידה בין האומות

30 (שהוא) פ /(בו) פ   31 הוא: שהוא מ (הוא) נ   32 מלאכים: מלאים פ /
הגדולה: הגדול פ   33 ומתנשא: ומתכסה פ   34 הוא: הן מ נ   35 והוא סוד:
ז"ס נ   36 אל הערפל (הנראה לנביאי') פ /מתעלם: מתעלה פ /   39 (הנעלם) פ /
הגדולה: הגדול פ   40 כי הוא: על שהוא מ נ   41 חזקית: חזית פ
42 נשמות: נפשות מ נ   44 (רצונו... הכרוב) פ   45 (כדמות) נ /ועוד נקרא: ונקרא
פ   46 (הוא) פ   47 (הם) פ   48 שמצאתי: מצאתי נ   49-52 על שם... היכל
הקודש החיצון: על שם מידות היכל הקודש התיכון עיטוריאל ומלכיאל היכל הקוד' הפנימי הוא
שר העומד לפני כתר מלכות ושמו מלכיאל היכל הקודש החיצון פ   52 שהוא
משולה: שם שמשולה פ   53 (מס' מעין החכמה) פ   55 (ופי') פ   57 שברא:
שנבראו פ   58 (הוא) פ /(ונסתר) פ   60-59 (בין... בשם) פ

60   המיוחסות בשם ישראל ע"כ. עוד מצאתי שם בשם רב חמאי ז"ל ענין
נכבד בענין שרפי' עומדי' ממעל לו וז"ל הקב"ה מתייחד בז' מלאכים
היושבים ראשונה במלכות שמים העליונים ואילו הם אורפניאל תיגריאל
דנדאל פלמיאל אסימון פסכאל בואל ועליהם נאמר שרפים עומדים ממעל
לו שש כנפים מלשון מטות כנפיו והם מחנות שמסובבות פנים ואחור

65   והם נקראים נשמות כדתנן בספר לבנת הספיר ועי' כתוב שם הקב"ה הוא
נשמה לנשמה שכל אלו הז' מחנות הם הנקראות נשמה ואדון הכל נשמה
לזו הנשמה והוא מתעלה במידת החסד ומתרומם עד שאין סוף לרוממותו
ועל כל אנו אומרים על השמים כבודו זהו גוף שכינה שהוא כדמיון
לנשמה והם כדמות גוף ובנא הקב"ה דמות אחד כדמות ד' יסודות

70   שהשכינה בתוכם כדמות נשמה והם כדמות גוף דמות אדם והם ארבע מחנות
שכינה והם מיכאל גבריאל אוריאל רפאל. מיכאל יסוד המים גבריאל
יסוד האש אוריאל יסוד הרוח רפאל יסוד העפר וכינויים חשמל ערפל
כסא הנוגה ואופן הגדולה מיכ' של מיכאל שבעים בגימ' כנגד ע' שמות
מל של חשמל כמו כן ע' שמות סימן סוד ה' ליראיו וזהו שחלק הכתו'

75   חש של חשמל ואל של מיכאל ונעשה מהן חשאל ר"ל חשיות לאל כבוד והוא
מלשון גם אני ידעתי החשו וזהו פי' ולך דומיה תהילה אלהים ועל זה
נאמר ודמות כמראה אדם עליו מלמעלה. ועי' סימן חשמל חכמה שלום
ממשלה לבוש. חכמה דכתי' והחכמה מאין תמצא שלום דכתיב עושה שלום
במרומי ממשלה דכתי' המשל ופחד עמו לבוש דכתי' הוד והדר לבשת

80   וזהו שדרשו רז"ל במסכתא חגיגה חשמל הוא שלש מאות ושלשים ושמונה
מיני מראות והפחות שבכלם כזיו גלגל החכמה ואיכ' דאמ' שע"ח
כחשבונו וזהו שכתו' בספר מעיין החכמה טוב ומטיב והכל לו זאת
ראשון תחלת פעלו שש מאות ועשרים הם ראש מילולו חשמל הוא מיכאל
מיכאל הוא חשמל הנה זאת מעלה אחת ויסוד אחד הנק' יסוד המים והוא

85   מחנה אחת. המחנה השנית גבריאל והוא ערפל והוא יסוד האש והוא
מתאחז בשרשי חשמל כיצד מל של חשמל הם ע' ומשתוים עם ע' של ערפל
שהיא שבעי' שמות הרי אילו בקרב אילו וזהו דכתיב במאמר שירו של
ר' פנחס חסמא לז ללז אחוזים בכנפי סוד תנועה כלומר זה כנגד זה
הם אחוזי' יסוד המים שהוא מיכאל ויסוד האש שהוא גבריאל. המחנה

90   השלישית הוא אוריאל והוא יסוד הרוח והוא האויר והוא האמצעי
המאיר לצד היסוד שמשם מקור הנשמות וסימנו קומי אורי כי בא אורך
שהוא עתיד להאיר אפלתן של ישר'. המחנה הרביעית הוא רפאל רופא

---

60 (ע"כ) פ / מצאתי שם: מ"כ נ   61-60 (ענין נכבד) פ   63 דנדאל: דנראל פ /
(ממעל לו) פ   66 (אלו) פ / (הם ה) נקראות פ / נשמה: נשמות מ   67-66 (נשמה
לזו הנשמה ו) הוא פ   67 סוף לרומימותו: לרוממותו סוף פ   69 (והם בדמות גוף)
מ נ / אחד: אדם פ / כדמות: בדמות מ   70 כדמות: כדמיון נ   71 (והם) פ
73 בגימ' כנגד: בענין מ כענין נ   74 (כן) פ   75 (חש של) פ / ונעשה: ועשה נ
76 (אלהים) פ   79 לבשת: לבושו נ   80 שדרשו... חגיגה: שאחז"ל בגמ' אין
דורשין פ   81 (שבכלם) פ   83-82 (זאת ראשון... מילולו) מ פ   84 (הנק')
פ   86 מתאחז: מתאחד פ / (של חשמל) פ   87 (דכתיב ב) מאמר (שירו) פ כתי'
בשירו מ   88 פנחס (בן) פ / כלומר: פי' פ   91 מקור: יסד פ

האמת יסודו יסוד העפר כי הוא ממונה על העפר האבוק שהוא מתחת כסא
הכבוד והוא נקרא חומר קדמון כמו שאמר רב האיי גאון ז"ל ועלה
95 במחשבה בריאת החומר הקדמון שממנו נאצלים כל הנבראים אחר אצילות
המעלות הנעלמות מעיני כל חי עד הנה מספר העיון.

---

93 על: עד פ

4:2 *CONTEMPLATION–J.T.S. 1884*

The oldest manuscript containing part of *Contemplation–Standard* is J.T.S. 1884, ff. 17a-19a, which is an early fourteenth-century collection of *kabbalah*, now partially water-damaged. As part of an extended exposition on the Divine Chariot, it quotes some two-thirds of *Contemplation–Standard*, from lines 50 to 146 of the Hebrew text, although without acknowledging its source. In general, this version is the same as *Contemplation–Standard*, with two notable exceptions. There is an expanded discussion of Metatron centering on the novel and startling image of Metatron as God's *pilegesh* (concubine),[15] which includes a reference to R. Ezra. If this were to be a reference to R. Ezra of Gerona, it would be significant for it would provide a rare link between the "Circle" and contemporary kabbalists. Nevertheless, it is more likely that this is simply a scribal error, which should have read "R. Akiva." The latter is orthographically close, and this material parallels a passage cited at the end to *Contemplation–Short* based upon the *'Otiyyot de-R. Akiva*. The second difference is found in lines 121 to 123 and is related to the discussion of the term *guf ha-shekhinah* (body of the Divine Presence).[16] Although J.T.S. 1884 offers a different reading, the thrust of the argument is the same.

What follows is a transcription of the text from J.T.S. 1884, f. 18a, on Metatron, with the parallel material from *Contemplation–Standard*, p. 94f.

---

15. This is based on Exod. 17:16 and Cant. 6:8. For a somewhat different interpretation of this material, cf. R. Joseph Gikatilla, *Sha'arei 'Orah*, 1:131.

16. See above, p. 94, for a transcription of this passage in the apparatus of *Contemplation–Standard*.

CONTEMPLATION–J.T.S. 1884

1 ... עד כאן סדריה דמארי עלמא. מכאן סדר מטטרון שמורה על ידיעת
בורא עולם בסדר אחר. דע שמטטרון הוא ממונה לפני היכל הקדש והוא
כסא הכבוד ועליו אמ׳ משה כי יד על כס יה כ״ס שמונים הוא שמונים
פילגשים שסידר מאריה דעלמא כולם מלכות ששים המה מלכות ושמונים
5 פילגשים הוא מטטרון שהוא פילגש לפני גבר׳ עוז ועליו אמ׳ משה ע״ה
ואת תדבר אלינו שהוא נות בית תחלק שלל והוא נמי כסא הכבוד וכסא
הנוגה והיא אשת חיל הסובלת לבעלה ועליה יש לומר כסא הכבוד וכס
יה כ״ס הוא שמונים פילגשים הרי לך ושמונים פילגשים מבואר היטב.
סדר מטטרון עתה אני מתחיל לסדר סדר מטטרון מפי ר׳ עזרא אות באות
תיבה בתיבה. אמ׳ הקב״ה למשה השמר מפניו ושמע בקולו אל תמר בו
10 שכבר שמתיו משמרת לפני פתח היכלי. וכל יהוה שיהיה קמצי כמו זה
יְהֹוָה הוא אדון העולם וכל פַּתחי הוא מטטרון שהוא שוער המלך והוא
נועל ופותח והוא ראוי לעשות דין בכל פמליא של מטה...

CONTEMPLATION–STANDARD

עד כאן סדרא דמארי עלמא מכאן ואילך סדר מטטרון שמורה על ידיעת
בורא עולם בסדר אחר. דע שמטטרון הוא ממונה לפני היכל הקדש, טעם אחר
מפני שהוא סוף למעשה העליונים ותחלה ליסוד התחתונים. וטעם אחר שפני
שיעור הקבוע דתנן אמר הקב״ה למשה משה השמר מפניו שכבר שמתיו משרת
לפתח היכלי מבחוץ לעשות דין בכל פמליא של מעלה ובכל פמליא של מטה...

4:3 CONTEMPLATION–STANDARD/INNER ATTRIBUTES

This version is identical with *Contemplation–Standard*,[17] except that a few lines from the end it breaks off into a new discussion that continues at some length. This new material, which is concerned with the *middot ha-penimiyyot*, "Inner Attributes," among other topics, bears a strong resemblance to the conclusion of R. Asher b. David's *Commentary on the Thirteen Attributes*.[18] Accordingly, one may posit that in fact R. Asher composed this material,[19] and that owing to a scribal error or whim, two distinct treatises were wedded together.

The latter part of this text is ascribed to an anonymous kabbalist from *BLDRS*. Presumably this is a reference to Beziers, although I am not aware that it is ever spelled with a *lamed*.[20]

Altogether, this version appears in five manuscripts: Hebrew University 8° 2930, designated by י ; British Museum 10682, designated by ב; British Museum (Gaster) 749, designated by ג; Jewish Theological Seminary 1837, designated by נ; and Frankfort 116, which is incomplete and designated by פ. J.T.S. and Gaster are virtually identical, with Hebrew University only rarely diverging from these two. Only British Museum 10682 offers the occasional variant, none of which are significant, except for the added colophon. The following transcription is the conclusion of this text, wherein it differs from *Contemplation–Standard*.

---

17. It is part of the family of *Contemplation–Standard* manuscripts, represented by Bodleian 1610.

18. A comparison with R. Asher b. David's *Commentary* reveals numerous parallels; see *Kabbalat R. Asher b. David*, J. Dan ed. (Jerusalem 1980), 47f.

19. From an in-passing comment, it is apparent that Scholem also assumed that R. Asher composed this material, although he does not elaborate upon this assumption; cf. *Origins*, 393, n. 70.

20. Perhaps there is some connection between this place name and *R. Yekutiel*, who is said to have come from *LONDRS*, i.e., London.

CONTEMPLATION-STANDARD/INNER ATTRIBUTES

1 ... וכלו מחמדים זהו הנטוע עם השרש במקום יניקתו שיונקים משם
כדי להשפיע להם ולכל היצורים כולם ומדתם מדה בלא מדה באין סוף
ותכלה והכל מתאחד למעלה באחדות השלמות הוא עילת העילות וסיבת
הסיבות. ע"כ כל מדה ומדה מהם אפשר להקרא בשם המיוחד שכולם
5 מתאימות להתברך משפע הברכה הבא מאין סוף בלי הפסק וגם יש מדות
מוגבלות שהן מזומנות להשתלח בשליחות המדות הפנימיות הנקראות ג"כ
מדותיו של הב"ה אע"פ שהן מדות נפרדות ומוגבלות וג"כ נביאיו
ועבדיו וכהניו נקראו בשמו ומרכבתו ובשם מלאכיו אז"ל קודם שנברא
העולם לא היה אלא הוא ושמו ברוך הוא ומבורך שמו של חי העולמים
10 שרצה לעשות פמליא שלפניו לפארו ולהדרו ולהמליכו לפי שנאצלו מזיו
הדרו ומשפע אורו לפי שאם אין מלך אין צבא ואם אין צבא אין מלך
וגם רצה לבנות עולם השפל מסיבת גלגל מרומו והגלגל הסובב לו מכח
עצמו אלא שהוא מסבבו וכל עילה וסיבה היוצאת מהם בכח תנועתם ברא
מהם האדם ושתף בו כוחותם וכח הממציאים כדי להזכיר בוראם ולפאר
15 ליוצרם ולהגיד מעשיו ולספר נפלאותיו ולהשכיל על כוחות מדותיו
ולהמליכו עליהם לשמור מצותיו חקיו ומשפטיו ותורותיו וללכת בדרכיו
ולהדבק ביראיו ועבדיו למען ידעו ויבינו וישכילו על זאת כי הוא
חברם בד' יסודות ונפח באפם נשמת חיים וברוח הפנימי עטרם ובכבוד
עליון הכתירם ובעת שיקיימו תורתו ויעשו רצונו עד בא בא פקודתן
20 תשובנה כל הסבות לקדמותן והרוח תזכה והברה היא הנפש הפנימית
הטהורה תשוב אל האלהים אשר נתנה ותהיה צרורה בצרור החיים לאור
באור החיים באותה המדה שתדבק בה לעשות רצון קונו עד בא חליפתה
גם היא תשוב לסיבתה ותחזור חלילה סולו סולו המסילה עד כלות מספר
אותותיו במחקר אותותיו ותבוא במצרף מכל שבע מדותיו אם לא קיים
25 אותם או שנטה מדרכם דכתיב כי שבע יפול צדיק וקם וסימן לדבר נוצר
חסד לאלפים והמשכיל יבין. מכאן ואילך כל דבר ודבר על מקומו יבא
בשלום. העושה במתניו שלום ישפיע לנו ברחמיו ברכה ושלום אמן סלה.
כל זה פירש חכם מקובל מרבותינו הקדושים מעיר בלדרש.

---

2 להשפיע (למעלה) ב / ולכל: וכל ב / סוף: קץ ב   3 (למעלה) ב / השלימות: השלימה
ב י / הוא (סוף) י   5 בלי: בלא ב   6 שהן: שהם ב   9 (שמו של) נ
10 ולהדרו: ולהאדירו ב   11 הדרו ומשפע: כבודו משפע י   12 גלגל: גלגלי ב /
מכח: מסיבת י   14 מהם: מהן ב / ושתף: נשתתף נ / להזכיר: להכיר ב   15 על: כל
ב   18 באפם: באפיו ב   19 שיקיימו: אשר יקיימו ב / בא פקודתן: בוא עת
פקודתם ב   22 שתדבק: שידבק נ ג שדבק י   23 (מספר) ב   24 אותותיו:
אותיותיו ב   27 במתניו שלום: שלום במרומיו ב / ושלום: (עד בלי די) ב   28 כל
זה פירש: ע"כ מצאתי בהעתיק פ / מרבותינו הקדושים: מאבותינו הגדולים ב / (חכם) ג /
בלדרש: בלדירש נ / בלדרש (ע"כ מצאתי בלדרש בזה הספר השי"ת יזכינו לקרות בו
ולהבין סתריו ורמזיו אכי"ר ע"ה דוד נטף יצו') ב

4:4 CONTEMPLATION-STANDARD/MAGIC

The early fourteenth-century manuscript, British Museum 752, has been previously mentioned in connection with *Contemplation-Standard*. Toward the end of this codex, f. 151a-b, there is an interesting synopsis of *Contemplation-Standard*. In it, the angelic names contained within the book are emphasized, and others are added. This results in the transformation of *Contemplation-Standard* into a magical treatise, to be recited for its curative powers.

CONTEMPLATION–STANDARD/MAGIC

1 ה"א חכמה קדומה. ה"ב אור מופלא. ה"ג חשמל. ד ערפל. ה כסא
הנוגה. ו אופן הגדולה חזיחזית. ז נקרא כרוב. ח נקרא גלגלי
המרכבה. ט אויר הסובב. י פרגוד. יא כסא הכבוד. יב מקום שמות
הנקרא חדרי גדולה. יג סוד מערכה גדולה העליונה. היכל החיצון.

5 פניא׳ תיגרא׳ דנרא׳ פלמיא׳ אסימון פסכא׳ בוא׳ והן נשמרת ונ"ל.
ולאחר מיכך אמס מגאר׳ וכנוים חע׳ כסא הנ׳ ואהג׳. קול רוח דבור. ק.
הוא שכל הק׳ דבור הוא בזק [ספק] ידיעה מי׳ חש׳ מי׳ גכ׳ אש׳ עב׳.
ארי רוח רפא׳ עפר ד"א אי ר׳ מח׳ שכ׳ היכל הקדש מטטרן לפ׳ שיר ק׳
ק׳ כי ג אב אב אב אבר אבר אברא אברא אברא אבראק אבראק
אבראק /

10 אבראקל אבראקל אבראקל אבראקלא אבראקלא אבראקלא יה יה יה יהו
יהו /
יהו יהוה יהוה יהוה אהיה אהיה אהיה שדי אלהים צבאות. מטטרון
אכתריאל מיכאל וגבריאל רפאל תנו רפואה לפלוני בן פלוני מהאש
ומהקדחת שבו. אאא ססס. אחר. א אב אבר אברק אברקי אברקיא
אברקיאל אברקיא אברקי אברק אבר אב א משביע אני אתם מלאכים
שתרפאו /

15 פלו׳ בן פלונית אמן אמן אמן אמן סלה.

---

1 מיכאל, גבריאל, אוריאל, רפאל.
2 חשמל, ערפל
3 כסא הנוגה
4 ואופן הגדולה

4:5 R. HASDAI'S *BOOK OF CONTEMPLATION*

A clear testimony to the influence of *Contemplation* is its surfacing in the writings of fifteenth-century scholars from Yemen.[21] An interesting characteristic of these references is that *Contemplation* is ascribed to R. Hasdai and not R. Hammai. Recently, the treatise of one of these individuals, the rabbinic scholar and doctor, R. Zechariah b. Solomon, was published.[22] M. Havazelet, its editor, noted the appearance of several references in the text to R. Hasdai and correctly concluded that this material does not correspond to *Contemplation*.[23]

The identification of the Yemenite references to R. Hasdai's *Book of Contemplation* can now be made by considering Ben Zvi ms. 3239. In fact, *Contemplation–Standard* does appear in this Yemenite manuscript, f. 14a-17b. The text commences, "This is the *Book of Explanation* (*sefer ha-bi'ur*) that Rabbi Hasdai, the principal spokesman, composed . . ." The text of *Contemplation–Standard* follows. There is also a marginal notation on f. 15a asserting that this material has been copied from *The Book of Contemplation*. Later on in this codex there is a kabbalistic anthology entitled *Likkutim Gan ha-Melekh*. Therein one finds a discussion of the thirty-eight-letter name that is attributed to R. Hasdai and which R. Zechariah likewise quoted.[24] Accordingly, what we find is that in Yemen, *Contemplation* had become incorporated into a larger corpus of writings, all of which were attributed to an unknown Rabbi Hasdai.

---

21. See the references in Y. Tobi's "*Ketav Yad Ḥadash*" in *Tagim* 5-6 (1975), 80.

22. R. Zechariah b. Solomon, *Midrash ha-Ḥefeẓ*, M. Havazelet ed. (Jerusalem 1981).

23. *Ibid.*, 21f., and especially 22, n. 22.

24. Compare Ben Zvi 3239, f. 28a, and *Midrash ha-Ḥefeẓ*, 202.

APPENDIX II: TEXTUAL RELATIONSHIPS

In chapter 2 and Appendix I we have presented more than a dozen treatises, all associated with *The Book of Contemplation*. The problem that confronts us now is to delineate, as precisely as possible, the connection between these treatises. Two issues are paramount. First, what is the relationship between the four major recensions? Second, what is the connection between the subtexts that comprise the latter two recensions?

Obviously, this presupposes that there are four recensions; however, even a cursory survey of these texts will bear out that, on the basis of shared material, they fall into four groupings. For example, it is indisputable that *Contemplation–Thirteen Powers* is cited virtually in toto in the *Midrash of R. Simon*, and in *Commentary on the Thirteen Attributes*. Moreover, the text referred to simply as *Thirteen Powers* shares most of its material with the *Commentary*. Hence, all four of these texts are linked together in a special relationship that is not exhibited by works associated with any other group.

Furthermore, now that the material related to *Contemplation–Thirteen Powers* has been collected, we must consider: (1) how it relates to the other recensions? (2) whether *Contemplation–Thirteen Powers* is the parent of this family of texts or merely a product of one of the treatises wherein it appears? and (3) how do the other subtexts relate to one another?

The analysis that follows must of necessity be based on internal evidence. There are no original manuscripts of any of the texts; all have been preserved in later copies. Moreover, none of these works are readily attributable to historical figures, and although some were cited in works stemming from the mid-thirteenth century, this only indicates a *terminus ad quem*. Finally, as all of these treatises are totally concerned with theosophy, it is understandable that none refer to specific historical events that would aid in their dating. Although solid external data is lacking, the task of ordering these works can be undertaken, with the understanding that conclusions are presumptive and may have to be revised should new material emerge.

In reading these texts with an eye to ordering them, one must bear in mind two considerations. How does the text read on its own? Does it seem to be a self-sufficient work, written independently, or are there indications that it is a reworking of earlier material? This impression that one receives can then be tested, by comparing it to the other writings which are somehow related to it. For example, when reading *Contemplation–Short* one discovers a coherent and cohesive work that can easily stand on its own. In contrast, *Contemplation–Standard* offers a pastiche of distinct blocks of material on a variety of topics. Thus our initial impression would lead us to posit that *Contemplation–Short* was earlier than *Contemplation–Standard*. This hypothesis can then be investigated through a comparative study of selected passages from the texts themselves.

A COMPARATIVE STUDY OF THE RECENSIONS

At the outset it should be noted that the four major recensions can be paired off on the basis of their listing of the *koḥot* (celestial powers). *Contemplation–Short* and *Contemplation–Long* posit ten powers, whereas *Contemplation–Thirteen Powers* and *Contemplation–Standard* enumerate thirteen. Accordingly, we shall utilize this natural division by first considering the relationships that exist between the members of these pairs.

Contemplation–Short and *Contemplation–Long*

The text that is referred to as *Contemplation–Short* appears to be the proto-text of *The Books of Contemplation*. It is relatively compact and cohesive. It focuses entirely on one theme, a schematization of cosmogony. The work proceeds systematically. There are no tangents, speculative wanderings, or excessive elaborations. Significantly, it is the only text that does not offer an initial listing of the various powers. The impression given is that whereas the author of *Contemplation–Short* simply set down his theory of successive powers, subsequent redactors listed these powers, as a skeleton upon which to build. This hypothesis is supported by the fact that in all the other versions, this enumeration appears at or near the start of these treatises.

The cohesiveness and conciseness of *Contemplation–Short* is in sharp contrast to the expansive nature of *Contemplation–Long*. Whereas *Contemplation–Short* moves methodically from one power to the next, *Contemplation–Long* presents a diffuse excursus on the initial three stages. It then abruptly aborts the endeavor of writing an extensive treatise on the remaining powers.

Although, in general, *Contemplation–Long* is more expansive than *Contemplation–Short*, there are specific instances where the author of *Contemplation–Long* compressed or reworked material. For example, in respect to the pivotal discussion of the relationship between God and His powers, *Contemplation–Short* offers a systematic exposition:

> He is the primal emanator, for He preceded all the primordial elements that were emanated from the wondrousness of His unity. Furthermore, all of them are revealed by the process of emanation, like a scent from a scent or a candle-flame from a candle-flame; since this emanates from that and that from something else and the power of the emanator is within that which was emanated. The emanator, however, does not lack anything. Thus, the Holy One, blessed be He, generated all of His powers, these from those, by the process of emanation. Moreover, He is united with them like the flame of fire, which is united with its colors, and He ascends above in His unity and is exalted, such that there is no end to His exaltedness.

In *Contemplation–Long*, this material has been chopped up. Toward the beginning of the text we read,

> by the process of emanation, like a scent from a scent, or a candle-flame from a candle-flame, since this emanates from that and that from something else, and the power of the emanator is within that which was emanated.

Then follows a discussion of Divine Providence and other matters. Finally, this section concludes,

> All the powers that are extant are equivalent in His Unity, in one equality. He ascends and is hidden in the secrets of the actions and activities undertaken by the hidden power. He is united like a flame that is united with its colors.

It can thus be seen that the author of *Contemplation–Long* had other concerns and reworked material from *Contemplation–Short*, in an attempt to integrate it into a novel exposition. At times, however, this procedure resulted in sacrificing the clarity of the original formulation.

Contemplation-Thirteen Powers and *Contemplation-Standard*

Not only are *Contemplation-Thirteen Powers* and *Contemplation-Standard* related in that each enumerates thirteen powers, but the lines immediately following the listing of these powers are also particular to them. In comparing the two, it is evident that *Contemplation-Thirteen Powers* is relatively cohesive, whereas *Contemplation-Standard* is eclectic. At times the material that is shared by both texts is presented in a coherent fashion in *Contemplation-Thirteen Powers*, but not in *Contemplation-Standard*. For example, after the powers are enumerated in *Contemplation-Thirteen Powers*, it is stated:

> These thirteen powers are revealed together from the Supreme
> Hiddenness that is concealed, which is called *'omen*, meaning
> the Father of Faith, from whose power faith was emanated.
> And He, may He be blessed, before He created anything He
> was singular and unique, inscrutable and limitless, able to
> stand and exist by Himself, through the sustaining power.
> Accordingly, He is called *'el*, that is to say, "very strong."
> When His power was not yet discernible, except to Himself, it
> arose in His mind to manifest all of His actions.

Herein the flow of the discussion is quite understandable. We learn that God referred to as *'el* is indicative of strength, on account of His ability to exist independently.

The parallel section in *Contemplation-Standard* reads,

> These thirteen powers are revealed together from the Supreme
> Hiddenness that is concealed, which is called *'omen*, meaning
> Father of Faith, from whose power faith was emanated. And
> He, may He be blessed, before He created anything was called
> *'el*, that is to say, very strong. His power was not yet
> discernible. When He began to manifest His actions, He
> brought into being the two products of mystery and faith. . .

This statement lacks intelligibility. Is God referred to as strong because His power was not yet recognized? Furthermore, the key statement that God was able to exist independently is indeed found in *Contemplation-Standard*, but instead, in the opening section of the treatise wherein God's primordial nature is discussed. This would support the contention that the author of *Contemplation-Standard* reworked this material–not always successfully–for his own purposes.

Contemplation–Standard as the Last Recension

It is clear that *Contemplation–Standard* is a derivative text. When one compares it with *Contemplation–Short* and *Contemplation–Long*, one finds that blocks of material have been expropriated from both. Its opening lines follow *Contemplation–Short*, then shift into material from *Contemplation–Long*, and then back again into *Contemplation–Short*. To this has been added a pastiche of material from *Fountain* on the five processes associated with the Divine Name, as well as quasi-*hekhalot* passages, and finally the enumeration of powers from *Contemplation–Thirteen Powers*. All of the above is evidenced on the first page alone. The fact that the author of *Contemplation–Standard* drew from so many diverse sources accounts for the seeming lack of cohesiveness of the work. Nevertheless, one should not assume that this writer did not have a methodology, for it is clear that he was operating by association. During the presentation of a topic that he felt was related to something in another text, he would simply interject this second block of material. An example of this is the inclusion of the opening section of *Fountain* in connection with a discussion of the Divine Name.

Moreover, the quasi-*hekhalot* section on R. Ishmael and R. Nehuniah b. ha-Kanah, which seems to be irrelevant to the thrust of the treatise, is actually an elaborate preamble–setting the stage for the enumeration of the powers. The redactor was undoubtedly aware that these powers were drawn primarily from *hekhalot* literature, and therefore, he fabricated his own *hekhalot* text in order to provide a dramatic introduction for this material.

Contemplation–Thirteen Powers and *Contemplation–Short*

Hitherto it has been argued that *Contemplation–Short* preceded *Contemplation–Long* and that *Contemplation–Thirteen Powers* preceded *Contemplation–Standard*. Let us now consider the relationship between the two progenitor texts.

At the outset one notices that despite their similarities, there is a fundamental difference between the two works. *Contemplation–Short* is an independent, speculative treatise, whereas *Contemplation–Thirteen Powers* is essentially a commentary on several statements from the *Book of Creation*. The thirteen powers in this text are introduced as follows: "This entire topic is an allusion to the thirteen spiritual powers, to which the author of the *Creation* refers, and they are '*sefer* and *sefar* and *sippur* and the ten *sefirot* without substance.'"

Moreover, the latter half of this work is a running commentary on the six directional points mentioned in *Sefer Yeẓirah* 1:13.

This intrinsic connection to *Creation* is all the more intriguing when one realizes that the basic doctrine of thirteen celestial powers is inconsistent with the theory of the ten *sefirot*, which is at the heart of what is propounded in *Creation*. This is in marked contrast to the ten powers of *Contemplation–Short*. Were one able to establish that *Contemplation–Thirteen Powers* was derived from *Contemplation–Short*, one could speculate that the author of *Contemplation–Thirteen Powers* felt the need to validate his teaching of thirteen powers, as opposed to ten. To do so he directly confronted the issue by focusing on *Creation*, which constitutes the single, most important formulation of the doctrine of the ten spiritual forces and boldly asserting that thirteen is the real meaning of *Creation*.

A compelling reason supporting the contention that *Contemplation–Short* is the progenitor of these texts is that it methodically treats each of the powers. *Contemplation–Thirteen Powers*, on the other hand, in an effort to harmonize its teachings with *Creation*, does not seriously discuss any of the powers, other than the highest: Primordial Wisdom.

An example of how *Contemplation–Thirteen Powers* has expropriated material from *Contemplation–Short* and reworked it to fit into its format of commenting on *Creation* is evident in the treatment of cosmogony. *Contemplation–Short* offers a well-developed theory of the initial phase of the process of creation. (An analysis of this material appeared in chapter 3.) Part of its exposition centers on the expression "sustaining power" (*koah kiyyum*).

> The explanation is that from Him the sustaining power was
> emanated, which is called Father of Faith, since faith was
> emanated from its power. He is the primal emanator, for He
> preceded all the primordial elements that were emanated from
> the wondrousness of His unity.

In *Contemplation–Thirteen Powers* this material has been reformulated.

> Moreover, it is called One for it was prior to all the
> primordial elements that were emanated from the
> wondrousness of His Unity. This Wisdom is exalted above the
> ten *sefirot* and is divided into six directions: right and left,
> before and behind, above and below. Right. This is the
> sustaining power, without substance.

In comparing these two distinct uses of the expression "sustaining power," we can see that in *Contemplation–Short* it is associated with the Divine state, the Father of Faith. This is fitting, for Father of Faith is depicted as being the source of all emanations. Turning to *Contemplation–Thirteen Powers*, we find that sustaining power is now applied to a lower stage of the celestial hierarchy, namely, the Right Side, according to the six-sided formulation of *Creation*. This Right Side is then associated with the Holy Spirit, and so one can appreciate why the author has utilized the concept of sustaining power, in a very different manner.

Contemplation–Long and *Contemplation–Thirteen Powers*

Let us finally consider the relationship between *Contemplation–Long* and *Contemplation–Thirteen Powers*. Since *Contemplation–Long* is closely connected to *Contemplation–Short*, which is the oldest recension, and since *Contemplation–Thirteen Powers* is connected to *Contemplation–Standard*, the latest version, there is an inherent rationale for the assumption that *Contemplation–Long* preceded *Contemplation–Thirteen Powers*. In surveying these texts we find at least two passages that are shared by *Contemplation–Long* and *Contemplation–Thirteen Powers*, yet not found in the other recensions. This allows us to properly assess their interdependence.

Contemplation–Long begins with a discussion of God's unity. One of the topics treated is providence. In this context we read: "He is unified in the Unity, which does not change, except through His determination. He influences his powers on every side and brings down and balances without deviating from the middle of His supremacy." Almost identical phrasing is noticeable in *Contemplation–Thirteen Powers*; however, there it appears in isolation, without the context of a sustained presentation: "It is the middle aspect whose powers influence each side. It does not deviate from its middleness or superiority."

It is noteworthy that this discussion on Divine Providence in *Contemplation–Long* concludes with the statement, "He comprises all sides, hidden and revealed. He begins above and ends below, and concludes before and behind, and right and left." This is based on the six directional points of *Sefer Yeẓirah* 1:3 and, as previously noted, forms the core of *Contemplation–Thirteen Powers*.

Also in *Contemplation–Long* there is a protracted exposition on Primordial Wisdom. One facet is concerned with its basic incomprehensibility, as expressed in the epithet "Supremely Holy Hiddenness"

(*seter ha-kedoshah ha-'elyonah*). This leads into the comment
"Accordingly, if you want to perceive Him, you will not perceive
Him; therefore, you will deny that there is any perceiving or revealing
of Him." On the other hand, in *Contemplation–Thirteen Powers* the
parallel statement comes in the midst of the discussion about the six
directions. The topic is once again Primordial Wisdom, but now as
it relates to the kabbalistic term "Supreme Crown" (*keter 'elyon*),
"The truth is that no creature can perceive the knowledge of this
thing through true knowledge for it is devoid of any revelation of
conceptualization."

Although Primordial Wisdom is the highest of the powers in all
of the recensions of *Contemplation*, surprisingly, in *Contemplation–Thirteen Powers* it is discussed in the context of the directional
points, i.e., the lower powers. Thus it appears to be misplaced. Also,
basing an exposition involving Divine incomprehensibility on the
term *keter 'elyon* ("Supreme Crown"), as we find in
Contemplation–Thirteen Powers, is not nearly as appropriate as
Contemplation–Long's exposition on *seter ha-kedoshah ha-'elyonah*,
"Supremely Holy Hiddenness."

Finally, in addition to the kabbalistic term *keter 'elyon*, one
finds other allusions to the theory of the *sefirot* in *Contemplation–Thirteen Powers*,[1] but not in *Contemplation–Long*. In general,
evidence of this doctrine in the writings of the "Circle" indicates a
later stratum.

Summation

By methodically examining the interrelationships among the recensions, we have demonstrated that *Contemplation–Short* was the basis
of the other versions. Next came *Contemplation–Long*, which was
essentially an expansion of the first part of *Contemplation–Short*.
Contemplation–Thirteen Powers was the third recension. It focused
on the central theme of *Contemplation*, namely, the emanation of the
powers, but transformed this theory into thirteen entities, instead of
ten. In doing so, it paradoxically sought authoritative support from
The Book of Creation. The final recension was *Contemplation–Standard*. It is the most variegated of the versions and constitutes a pastiche of the previous works.

---

1. An example is the following statement: "Essence of Wisdom, the profusion of Understanding." Concerning *Contemplation–Thirteen Powers'* ambivalent attitude toward the *kabbalah*, see pp. 142-145.

The Family of *Contemplation-Thirteen Powers*

Any consideration of *Contemplation-Thirteen Powers* must determine if it is, in fact, what it appears to be: the progenitor of the family. Since it appears in its entirety in the *Midrash of R. Simon the Righteous*, it is conceivable that the *Midrash* is its ultimate source, and only subsequently did it become an independent treatise. First, it should be noted that *Contemplation-Thirteen Powers* is referred to as being an independent work in *Commentary on the Thirteen Attributes*, which was probably written by R. Moses of Burgos in the latter half of the thirteenth century. This indicates that it stems from a relatively early period in the "Circle's" development. Second, in the *Midrash*, the listing of the powers begins with Primordial Wisdom, a term borrowed from *Fountain*. This is an anomaly and is not found in any other text, either within this recension or in the next. It seems quite unlikely that the progenitor of a recension would exhibit a central doctrine that is rejected by all of its descendants. Finally, there is evidence that the writer of the *Midrash* appropriated blocks of material from other texts as well. The *Midrash* begins with a lengthy citation from *Fountain*, and immediately after the section corresponding to *Contemplation-Thirteen Powers*, it continues with a lengthy quote from R. Meshullam the Zadokites' *Kabbalah*.

The Books of *Contemplation* and *The Fountain of Wisdom*

The final question for consideration is what is the relationship between *Contemplation* and *Fountain*? Can we discern direct influences of one on the other? It is clear, and has been documented in the notes to the translations, that *Contemplation-Long*, *Contemplation-Standard*, and many of the subtexts were heavily influenced by *Fountain* and incorporated material from it into the body of their respective texts. Of critical importance is the determination of the relationship between *Contemplation-Short* and *Fountain*.

The limited overlapping between these two texts is a strong indication that they were written essentially independently of each other. Nevertheless, there are a few examples of shared material. The second of the powers in *Contemplation-Short* is identified as Marvellous Light (*'or mufla'*) Similarly, this designation appears at the start of *Fountain*'s enumeration of ten primordial lights. This epithet was not commonly used prior to the composition of these texts and it is improbable that two contemporary writers would independently coin the same expression. Accordingly, it is likely that this is an example of influence, though the exact direction is still ambiguous.

Another compelling example of influence is discernible in shared phrasing. *Contemplation-Short* asserts that Divine potency was manifest subsequent to the creation of the first power, Primordial Wisdom. Thus we read, "until His radiance appeared and His glory was revealed in this Wisdom." Similarly, toward the end of *Fountain* there is a description of the primordial fountain, "(its) radiance appeared and its glory appeared and was revealed." Yet, here too it is difficult to determine which text borrowed from which.

A more instructive example is the contention in *Fountain* that the primordial and preeminent force, *'avir kadmon* (Primal Ether) most assuredly preceded *'arafel, hashmal, pargod,* and other celestial powers. This statement appears in the heart of *Fountain*, toward the start of its most important discourse on the significance of Primal Ether. What is startling is that virtually all of the celestial entities that it lists correspond to *Contemplation-Short*'s enumeration of the ten powers, though in somewhat different order. A plausible interpretation of this passage is that the author of *Fountain* had read and rejected *Contemplation-Short*; instead he asserted that his own theosophical formulation was far superior to that found in *Contemplation*.

Assuming that *Fountain* represents a reaction to *Contemplation-Short*, we can also understand why a discussion about *hashmal* occurs at the end of *Fountain*, almost as an afterthought. Since *hashmal* plays such a prominent role in *Contemplation-Short*, presumably the author of *Fountain* felt compelled to indicate how this critical concept related to his own theosophical configuration. If our hypothesis concerning *Fountain*'s dependence upon *Contemplation-Short*, is correct then *Contemplation-Short* must have predated *Fountain*. Accordingly, pride of place would belong to it, as the starting point of the "Circle of Contemplation."

SELECTED BIBLIOGRAPHY

Altmann, Alexander. "The Motif of the Shells in Azriel of Gerona." *Journal of Jewish Studies* 9 (1958): 73-80.

Basser, Herbert. "The Rabbinic Attempt to Democratize Salvation and Revelation." *Studies in Religion* 12:1 (1983): 27-33.

Cohen, Martin. *The Shuir Qomah*. Lanham, 1983.

Corbin, Henri. *Avicenna and the Visionary Recital*. London, 1960.

Dan, Joseph. "'Anafi'el, Metatron ve-Yozer Bere'shit." *Tarbiẓ* 52 (1983): 447-457.

―――. *The Early Kabbalah*. Mahwah, 1986.

―――. *Ḥugei ha-Mekubbalim ha-Rishonim*. Jerusalem, 1980.

―――. *'Iyyunim be-Sifrut Ḥasidei 'Ashkenaz*. Ramat Gan, 1975.

―――, ed. *Kabbalat R. Asher b. David*. Jerusalem, 1980.

―――. "Kavod Nistar." In *Dat ve-Safah*, edited by M. Hallamish, 71-79. Ramat Gan, 1982.

―――. *'Ofiyo u-Mekorotav shel Sefer Baddei ha-'Aron*. Jerusalem, 1977.

―――. *Tekstim be-Torat ha-'Elokut shel Ḥasidut 'Ashkenaz*. Jerusalem, 1977.

―――. *Torat ha-Sod shel Ḥasidut 'Ashkenaz*. Jerusalem, 1968.

Efros, Israel. *Philosophical Terms in the Moreh Nebukim*. New York, 1924.

―――. *Studies in Medieval Jewish Philosophy*. New York, 1974.

Elior, Rachel, ed. *Hekhalot Zutarti*. Jerusalem, 1982.

Farber, Asi. *Perush Merkavat Yeḥezke'l le-R. Ya'akov b. Ya'akov ha-Kohen*. Hebrew University Thesis, 1978.

Fishbane, Michael. *Biblical Interpretation in Ancient Israel*. Oxford, 1985.

Galili, Ze'ev. "Le-She'elat Meḥabber Perush 'Or Ganuz." *Meḥkerei Yerushalayim be-Maḥshevet Yisra'el* 4 (1985): 83-96.

Goetschel, Roland. *Meir ibn Gabbai.* Leuven, 1981.

Goldreich, Amos. *"Me-Mishnat Ḥug ha-'Iyyun."* *Meḥkerei Yerushalayim be-Maḥshevet Yisra'el* 6:3 (1987): 141-156.

Gottlieb, Efraim. *Ha-Kabbalah be-Sof ha-Me'ah ha-Yud Gimel.* Jerusalem, 1979.

_____. *Meḥkarim be-Sifrut ha-Kabbalah.* Tel Aviv, 1976.

Gruenwald, Ithamar. *Apocalyptic and Merkavah Mysticism.* Leiden, 1980.

Halperin, David. *The Faces of the Chariot.* Tubingen, 1988

Heller-Wilensky, Sarah. "Isaac ibn Latif–Philosopher or Kabbalist." In *Jewish Medieval and Renaissance Studies,* edited by A. Altmann, 185-223. Cambridge, 1967.

Idel, Moshe. *"Beyn Tefisat ha-'Aẓmut le-Tefisat ḥa-Kelim ba-Kabbalah be-Tekufat ha-Renesans."* *Italia* 3 (1982): 89-111.

_____. *Kabbalah: New Perspectives.* New Haven, 1987.

_____. *The Mystical Experience in Abraham Abulafia.* Albany, 1988.

_____. *"'Olam ha-Malakhim be-Demut 'Adam."* *Meḥkerei Yerushalayim be-Maḥshevet Yisra'el* 3:1 (1984): 1-66.

_____. *"Sefirot she-me-'Al ha-Sefirot."* *Tarbiẓ.* 51 (1982): 239-280.

_____. "We Have No Kabbalistisc Tradition On This." In *Rabbi Moses Nahmanides: Explorations,* edited by I. Twerksy. Cambridge, 1983.

Janowitz, Naomi. *The Poetics of Ascent.* Albany, 1989.

Jellinek, Adolf. *Ginzei Ḥokhmat ha-Kabbalah.* Leipzig, 1853.

Kaplan, Aryeh. *The Bahir.* York Beach, 1989.

_____. *Meditation and Kabbalah.* York Beach, 1985.

Lanier, Michal. *Tefisat ha-'Ayn Sof: Hashva'ah beyn Mekubbalei Ḥug ha-'Iyyun le-Veyn R. Azriel me-Gerona.* Tel Aviv University Thesis, 1979.

Liebes, Yehuda. *"Keẓad Nithabber Sefer ha-Zohar."* *Meḥkerei Yerushalayim be-Masheṿet Yisra'el* 8 (1989): 1-71.

_____. *"Hashpa'ot Noẓriyyot 'al Sefer ha-Zohar."* *Meḥkerei Yerushalayim be-Masheṿet Yisra'el* 2:1 (1982/3): 43-74.

_____. *Perakim be-Millon Sefer ha-Zohar.* Jerusalem, 1977.

Marcus, Ivan. *Piety and Society.* Leiden, 1981.

Margaliot, Reuven. *Mal'akhei 'Elyon.* Jerusalem, 1964.

Matt, Daniel. "Ayin: The Concept of Nothingness in Jewish Mysticism." *Tikkun* 3:3 (1988): 43-47.

Nadav, Yael. *"'Iggeret ha-Mekubbal R. Yiẓḥak Mar Ḥayyim 'al Torat ha-Ẓaḥzaḥot."* *Tarbiẓ* 26 (1956-57): 440-458.

Neubauer, Adolf. "The Bahir and the Zohar," *Jewish Quarterly Review* 4 (1892): 357-368.

Newman, Louis J. *Jewish Influences on Early Christian Reform Movements.* New York, 1925.

Newsom, Carol. "Merkabah Exegesis in the Qumran Sabbath Shirot." *Journal of Jewish Studies* 38:1 (1987): 11-30.

Pines, Shlomo. *"Ve-Kava' el ha-'Ayin ve-Nivaka'."* *Tarbiẓ* 50 (1981): 339-347.

Ravitzky, Aviezer. *"Ha-Hypostezah shel ha-Ḥokhmah ha-'Elyonah."* *Italia* 3 (1982): 7-38.

Schafer, Peter. *Kondordanz zur Hekhalot-Literatur.* Tubingen, 1986.

_____. *Synopse zur Hekhalot-Literatur.* Tubingen, 1981.

Scholem, Gershom. *"'Ikvotav shel Gavirol ha-Kabbalah."* In *Me'asef Sofrei 'Ereẓ Yisra'el,* 160-178 (1940).

_____. *Jewish Gnosticism, Merkavah Mysticism and Talmudic Tradition.* New York, 1965.

_____. *Kabbalah.* New York, 1978.

_____. *Kabbalot R. Ya'akov ve-R. Yiẓḥak ha-Kohen.* Jerusalem, 1927.

_____. *Le-Ḥeker Kabbalat R. Yiẓḥak b. Yaakov ha-Kohen.* Jerusalem, 1934.

_____. *Major Trends in Jewish Mysticism.* New York, 1972.

_____. "The Name of God." *Diogenes* 79 (1972): 59-80; 80: 164-194.

_____. *Origins of the Kabbalah.* Princeton, 1987.

_____. *Reshit ha-Kabbalah.* Jerusalem, 1948.

_____. *"Te'udah Ḥadashah le-Toldot Reshit ha-Kabbalah."* In *Sefer Bialik,* edited by Y. Fikhman, 141-162. Tel Aviv, 1934.

_____. *"Zur Frage der Entstehung der Kabbala."* *Korrespondenzblatt des Vereins zur Grundung und Erhaltung einer Akademie für die Wissenschaft des Judentums* 9 (1928): 4-26.

Sed-Rajna, Gabrielle. *"L'Influence de Jean Scot sur la doctrine du kabbaliste Azriel de Gerone."* In *Jean Scot Erigene et l'histoire de la philosophie*, 453-463. Paris, 1977.

Septimus, Bernard. *Hispano-Jewish Culture in Transition*. Cambridge, 1982.

———. "Power and Piety in Thirteenth-Century Catalonia," In *Studies in Medieval Jewish History and Literature*, edited by I. Twersky, 197-230. Cambridge, 1979.

Shahar, Shulamit *"Ha-Katarizm ve-Reshit ha-Kabbalah."* *Tarbiẓ* 40 (1971): 483-507.

———. "The Relationship between Kabbalism and Catharism in the South of France," In *Les Juifs dans l'histoire de France*, edited by M. Yardeni, 55-62. Leiden, 1980.

Tishby, Isaiah. *Ḥikrei Kabbalah u-Sheluḥoteha*. Jerusalem, 1982.

———. *"Kitvei ha-Mekubbalim R. Ezra ve-R. Azriel me-Gerona."* *Sinai* 16 (1945): 159-178.

———, ed. *Perush ha-'Aggadot le-R. Azriel me-Gerona*. Jerusalem, 1945.

Trachtenberg, Joshua. *Jewish Magic and Superstition*. New York, 1987.

Twersky, Isadore. *Introduction to the Code of Maimonides*. New Haven, 1980.

———. *Rabad of Posquieres*. Cambridge, 1962.

———. *Studies in Jewish Law and Philosophy*. New York, 1982.

Urbach, Ephraim. *Ba'alei Tosafot*. Jerusalem, 1968.

Vajda, Georges. *Recherches sur la philosophie et la kabbale dans la pensée juive*. Paris, 1962.

Verman, Mark. "Classifying the *Hug ha-'Iyyun*." In *Proceedings of the Tenth World Congress of Jewish Studies*, 57-64. Jerusalem, 1990.

———. "The Development of Yihudim in Spanish Kabbalah." *Jerusalem Studies in Jewish Thought* 8 (1989): 25-41.

———. *Sifrei ha-Iyyun*. Harvard University Dissertation, 1984.

Weinstock, Israel. *Be-Ma'aglei ha-Niglah ve-ha-Nistar*. Jerusalem, 1969.

Wertheimer, Shlomoh, ed. *Battei Midrashot*. 2 vols. Jerusalem, 1980.

Wolfson, Elliot. *The Book of the Pomegranate*. Atlanta, 1988.

———. *Sefer ha-Rimmon*. Brandeis University Dissertation, 1986.

Zunz, Leopold. *Ha-Derashot be-Yisra'el*. Jerusalem, 1954.

INDEX

Aaron, 115n. 270
Abba Shalom of Bonn, 144n.122
Abraham bar Hiyya, 41n.18. 43n.29
Abraham b. Azriel, 141n.113
Abraham b. David (Rabad), 24, 25,
    134n.68, 143, 144, 225
Abraham de PR'aVYS, 187n.70
Abraham Ḥasid, 187
Abraham ha-Yarhi, 187n.69
Abraham of Gerona, 131n.53, 159
Abu Aaron of Baghdad, 21, 177
Abulafia, Abraham, 18, 122n.1,
    154n.158, 161
Abulafia, Meir, 40n.15, 130n.50
Abulafia, Todros, 114, 145,
    174n.27, 176, 186
'Adam (primordial human), 209
    n.54. See also Biblical
    figures: Adam
Adler, Shulamit, xi
Agrippa, Cornelius, 2 n.4
Akiva (b. Joseph), 137, 208
    and mysticism, 15-18, 48, 100,
    232. See also 'Otiyyot de-R.
    Akiva
Alcover, A., 189n.78
'Alef, 'alefim (letter), 5-55, 61,
    111n.261, 140n.107, 147,
    148, 155, 209
Alemanno, Yohanan, 115n.270
Al-Farabi, Abu Nasr Muhammad,
    129, 136
Al-Ghazali, Abu Hamid, 107n.227,
    130
Al-Harizi, Judah, 130n.50

Alkabetz, Solomon, 192
Al-Kindi, Abu Yusuf, 135, 136
Alter, Robert, 6n.13
Altmann, Alexander, 77n.135,
    101n.201, 126n.20, 136,
    159n.175
Amram Gaon, 112n.261
Anatoli Jacob, 147n.129
Angel, angels, 43-45, 56, 59, 75,
    129, 130
    'Akatri'el, 100n.196
    'Anafi'el, 75n.122
    Angel of the Divine Presence,
    50n.68
    'Arafi'el, 44n.33, 48n.59, 75, 76
    archangels, 44n.36, 45n.37,
    104nn.212-213, 129
    'Asimon, 104
    Bo'el, 104
    Cherub, 47, 70, 77, 83, 103, 124,
    203, 208
    Danra'el, 104, 209
    Dumi'el, 111
    emanated, 129
    Gabriel, 46, 105, 107, 189n.77,
    206, 209
    hierarchy, 43, 104, 129, 216
    Metatron, 17, 48, 49n.62, 70,
    101n.200, 108, 109, 133, 232
    Michael, 44, 46, 50, 105-107,
    189, 206, 209
    'Orpani'el, 45, 74, 75n.122, 76,
    104, 189, 209
    Palmi'el, 104
    Pamali'el, 210

253